CW01583473

SAP PRESS e-books

Print or e-book, Kindle or iPad, workplace or airplane: Choose where and how to read your SAP PRESS books! You can now get all our titles as e-books, too:

- By download and online access
- For all popular devices
- And, of course, DRM-free

Convinced? Then go to www.sap-press.com and get your e-book today.

GDPR and SAP®

SAP PRESS

SAP PRESS is a joint initiative of SAP and Rheinwerk Publishing. The know-how offered by SAP specialists combined with the expertise of Rheinwerk Publishing offers the reader expert books in the field. SAP PRESS features first-hand information and expert advice, and provides useful skills for professional decision-making.

SAP PRESS offers a variety of books on technical and business-related topics for the SAP user. For further information, please visit our website: *www.sap-press.com*.

Volker Lehnert, Katharina Stelzner
Authorizations in SAP Software: Design and Configuration
2010, 684 pages, hardcover and e-book
www.sap-press.com/2316

Jonathan Haun
SAP HANA Security Guide
2017, 541 pages, hardcover and e-book
www.sap-press.com/4227

Joe Markgraf, Alessandro Banzer
SAP System Security Guide
2018, 574 pages, hardcover and e-book
www.sap-press.com/4307

Christian, Iyer, Sudhalkar
Implementing SAP Governance, Risk, and Compliance
2014, 712 pages, hardcover and e-book
www.sap-press.com/3373

Volker Lehnert, Iwona Luther, Björn Christoph, Carsten Pluder, Nicole Fernandes

GDPR and SAP®

Data Privacy with SAP® Business Suite and SAP S/4HANA®

Rheinwerk Publishing

Editor Meagan White
Acquisitions Editor Emily Nicholls
German Edition Editor Sven Clever
Translation Nicole Fernandes
Copyeditor Julie McNamee
Cover Design Graham Geary
Photo Credit Shutterstock.com/386619208/© Who is Danny
Layout Design Vera Brauner
Production Graham Geary
Typesetting SatzPro, Krefeld (Germany)
Printed and bound in the United States of America, on paper from sustainable sources

ISBN 978-1-4932-1712-0
© 2018 by Rheinwerk Publishing, Inc., Boston (MA)
1st edition 2018
1st German edition published 2018 by Rheinwerk Verlag, Bonn, Germany

Library of Congress Cataloging-in-Publication Data
Names: Lehnert, Volker, 1969- author. | Luther, Iwona, author. | Christoph, Bjorn, author. | Pluder, Carsten, author. | Fernandes, Nicole, author.
Title: GDPR and SAP : data privacy with SAP business suite and SAP S/4HANA / Volker Lehnert, Iwona Luther, Bjorn Christoph, Carsten Pluder, Nicole | Fernandes.
Other titles: Datenshutz mit SAP. English
Description: First edition. | Bonn : Rheinwerk Publishing, [2018] | Translation of Datenshutz mit SAP: SAP Business Suite und SAP S/4HANA. | Includes index.
Identifiers: LCCN 2018021596 (print) | LCCN 2018022695 (ebook) | ISBN 9781493217137 (ebook) | ISBN 9781493217120 (alk. paper)
Subjects: LCSH: Data protection. | Database security. | SAP HANA (Electronic resource)
Classification: LCC QA76.9.D314 (ebook) | LCC QA76.9.D314 L4413 2018 (print) | DDC 005.8--dc23
LC record available at https://lccn.loc.gov/2018021596

All rights reserved. Neither this publication nor any part of it may be copied or reproduced in any form or by any means or translated into another language, without the prior consent of Rheinwerk Publishing, 2 Heritage Drive, Suite 305, Quincy, MA 02171.

Rheinwerk Publishing makes no warranties or representations with respect to the content hereof and specifically disclaims any implied warranties of merchantability or fitness for any particular purpose. Rheinwerk Publishing assumes no responsibility for any errors that may appear in this publication.

"Rheinwerk Publishing" and the Rheinwerk Publishing logo are registered trademarks of Rheinwerk Verlag GmbH, Bonn, Germany. SAP PRESS is an imprint of Rheinwerk Verlag GmbH and Rheinwerk Publishing, Inc.

All of the screenshots and graphics reproduced in this book are subject to copyright © SAP SE, Dietmar-Hopp-Allee 16, 69190 Walldorf, Germany.

SAP, the SAP logo, ABAP, Ariba, ASAP, Concur, Concur ExpenseIt, Concur TripIt, Duet, SAP Adaptive Server Enterprise, SAP Advantage Database Server, SAP Afaria, SAP ArchiveLink, SAP Ariba, SAP Business ByDesign, SAP Business Explorer, SAP BusinessObjects, SAP BusinessObjects Explorer, SAP BusinessObjects Lumira, SAP BusinessObjects Roambi, SAP BusinessObjects Web Intelligence, SAP Business One, SAP Business Workflow, SAP Crystal Reports, SAP EarlyWatch, SAP Exchange Media (SAP XM), SAP Fieldglass, SAP Fiori, SAP Global Trade Services (SAP GTS), SAP GoingLive, SAP HANA, SAP HANA Vora, SAP Hybris, SAP Jam, SAP MaxAttention, SAP MaxDB, SAP NetWeaver, SAP PartnerEdge, SAPPHIRE NOW, SAP PowerBuilder, SAP PowerDesigner, SAP R/2, SAP R/3, SAP Replication Server, SAP S/4HANA, SAP SQL Anywhere, SAP Strategic Enterprise Management (SAP SEM), SAP SuccessFactors, The Best-Run Businesses Run SAP, TwoGo are registered or unregistered trademarks of SAP SE, Walldorf, Germany.

All other products mentioned in this book are registered or unregistered trademarks of their respective companies.

Contents at a Glance

Dear Reader,

It's not often I get the chance to edit a book that will teach me something I need to know for my day-to-day work. GDPR has been everywhere for the last several months, from news reports to emails about updated privacy policies, to training sessions at work. Even though we don't use SAP software to help us edit books, learning about the regulations and what they mean has helped me understand my part in ensuring compliance here at SAP PRESS.

This book will not only teach you the concepts and theories behind GDPR, it will show you how to implement them in your SAP system using existing SAP tools. With the help of their expert translator, Nicole Fernandes, the authors of this book—Volker Lehnert, Iwona Luther, Björn Christoph, and Carsten Pluder—have brought to bear their decades of experience with SAP, data privacy, security, and compliance to help you get compliant with GDPR.

What did you think about *GDPR and SAP: Data Privacy with SAP Business Suite and SAP S/4HANA*? Your comments and suggestions are the most useful tools to help us make our books the best they can be. Please feel free to contact me and share any praise or criticism you may have.

Thank you for purchasing a book from SAP PRESS!

Meagan White
Editor, SAP PRESS

meaganw@rheinwerk-publishing.com
www.sap-press.com
Rheinwerk Publishing · Boston, MA

Contents

Foreword

Data protection requirements are nothing new. The worldwide debate on data protection began in the 1960s with the US government's plans to set up a national data center in which the data of all US citizens should be registered. In 1970, Hesse introduced the world's first data protection law. This was followed in 1977 by the German Federal Data Protection Act (GFDPA), which focused on establishing the requirements for the introduction of data protection officers and the primacy of the protection of personal data. The European Data Protection Directive 1995/46/EC was passed in 1995.

In December 2015, the EU General Data Protection Regulation (GDPR) was passed, which harmonized European data protection law on a very large scale when it became enforceable on May 25, 2018. Companies that store or process the personal data of EU citizens must now comply with these guidelines. In the future, the maximum fine for data breaches may be up to EUR 20 million or up to 4% of the total worldwide annual turnover generated in the previous financial year, whichever is higher of the two.

Since SAP was founded in 1972, data protection and data security have remained a top priority, and our customers expect not only full compliance but also ongoing support with their own data protection projects and the adaptation of their IT infrastructure. In close dialogue with both our customers and our partners, it's our common goal to continuously develop security in every respect. As the backbone for the strategic and operative management of the entire company, the SAP ERP system is of decisive importance.

In recent years, this publication's author team has played a key role in the creation of the functionality necessary in SAP Business Suite and SAP S/4HANA to enable data protection-compliant operation. With this book, the team wants to provide detailed guidelines and instructions to help you get the most out of these interconnected data protection functions and features.

The avid expert will be aware that it's impossible to provide a single function that can simply "switch on" data protection. Data protection must be guaranteed continuously and completely at every single level of data processing. This not only has an effect on the organization of data and processes but also on the presentation of the line organization itself.

This book reduces the complexity to a necessary minimum but doesn't replace the legal commentary, the revision guide, or the documentation of technical details for basic operations, for example. However, it does offer a perspective that supports the reliable and data-protection-compliant combination of legal requirements, business necessities, and technical possibilities.

In the age of digitalization, data protection is becoming increasingly important. According to a representative survey of the digital association by Bitkom (2017) on the subject of smart homes, 84% say that high data protection standards, guaranteed by the manufacturer, are important to them, whereas 68% also ensure when purchasing that smart home data is only stored in Germany. In other words, looking to the future, data protection will remain essential across the board. I firmly believe digitization will only succeed if data is protected.

I hope you enjoy reading this book.

Bernd Leukert
Member of the Executive Board SAP SE
Products & Innovation

Preface

You are holding a book dedicated to data protection in SAP Business Suite and SAP S/4HANA. You are presumably doing so because on May 25, 2018, the European Union's General Data Protection Regulation (GDPR) entered into force and, with it, the threat of serious fines.

GDPR has been in force since May 25, 2016, and SAP has continued to refine their functions and features to meet the new requirements. However, most of the requirements—in our opinion—had already been established in the 1995 EU Data Protection Directive 95/46.

In the following, we'll introduce you to the objectives and the content of the book. Most readers of such technical books use them for reference purposes; we'll also provide you with a general theme, that is, a note on what you should be reading to get an overview.

Objective of the Book

This book is intended to help you ensure data-protection-compliant operations in your SAP landscape, which requires some thought about the application of the law. Under no circumstances should these deliberations replace legal advice or legal opinion. Essentially, our explanations serve the contextualization and the justification regarding which features can be used, how they can be used, and why. These also serve as the first two essential subobjectives of our book: an examination of the possible applications of law from a software perspective and an understanding of the features provided.

The next important subobjective is to suggest the best way to start such an implementation project.

In this respect, this book is a triad of assumptions about the legal facts, technical functions, and a procedural model. By making the legal assumptions transparent, you also have the opportunity to draw other conclusions and develop your own process model.

This triad is supplemented by two short chapters on additional software made available by SAP, namely SAP Master Data Governance (SAP MDG) and SAP Test Data Migration Services (SAP TDMS), which we consider as much simplified; SAP Information Lifecycle Management (SAP ILM), which is necessary for simplified blocking and deletion; and the SAP Governance, Risk, and Compliance (SAP GRC) suite, to which reference is made in several sections.

Composition of the Book

The book is composed of 12 chapters. For better orientation, we've briefly summarized what you can expect in each chapter, for whom the chapter in question is intended, and for whom reading it is an absolute must.

Chapter 1: Introduction to General Data Protection Regulation

In **Chapter 1**, we address the legal principles we believe should be taken into account when dealing with system operations. We recommend that you work through this chapter completely!

Although we inform you in this chapter about impending fines and the geographical scope of the legal regulations, we primarily deal with processes, data, and system operation in accordance with our objectives. We begin by clarifying the essential basics of processing. Among other things, we discuss what we believe should be fulfilled before personal data can be processed at all, as well as which data must be treated as particularly problematic, that is, data of a special category.

Subsequently, we compare the respective requirements with the technical implementation options and their logical limits.

Particular emphasis is given to Section 1.1.11, and Section 1.1.12 where we discuss the challenges of technical security as well as permanent documentation and continuous verification. In principle, the tasks of "security" and "proof of security" lead to an endless cycle of controls that must begin with a data protection impact assessment (DPIA) when new products are introduced or procedures are changed (as outlined in Section 1.1.13). The record of processing activities, which we deal with in Section 1.1.14, also belongs to the range of verification activities.

In the following Section 1.2, we discuss the requirements for mandatory technical implementation, such as proof of the intended purpose of processing (Section 1.2.1); the deletion of data, which always has been the traditional focus of the supervisory authorities in Germany (Section 1.2.3); and the right of access to information (Section 1.2.6).

In Section 1.3, we discuss requirements that don't necessarily have to be supported by a technical solution but which can be simplified significantly by a technical solution (examples provided in Section 1.3.1 and in Section 1.3.4).

Chapter 2: Personal Data in SAP Business Suite and SAP S/4HANA

In **Chapter 2**, we provide examples of different types of personal data, such as the customer master record, the central business partner, and related transactional data. In this chapter, we also discuss the relationships between master data and transactional data.

If you're familiar with SAP Business Suite and understand the relationship between master data and transactional data with regard to data protection, you can skip this chapter.

Chapter 3: Implementation Approach

In **Chapter 3**, we develop our proposal for the project procedure. We therefore recommend that all those who have to or would like to deal with the challenges of an introductory project read this chapter.

In Section, 3.1.1 of Chapter 3, we explain why, at least in a legacy system, the truth lies in the data; a top-down approach therefore generally doesn't make sense. We show why each existing project should begin with blocking and deletion, and how the project can then be carried out, step by step, through to the audit, verification, and documentation steps (explained in Section 3.1.10) to meet your verification obligations. Finally, in Section 3.2, we explain why our bottom-up approach also simplifies presentation when recording processing activities.

Chapter 4: Blocking and Deletion with SAP Information Lifecycle Management

Chapter 4 is intended for readers who also have to technically implement blocking and deletion functions. First, we introduce you to notions and contexts. Approaches to "classic archiving" aren't given, however, because although this is possible, it's not recommended for data-protection-related blocking and deletion. Section 4.2 then shows you the mandatory preparatory measures and settings that have to be made to implement simplified blocking and deletion based on SAP ILM. In Section 4.3, we look at the development of the business perspective of blocking and deleting. Remember that the data we're talking about must be viewed in a complex business context, which, in addition to the necessity of blocking and deleting, also requires business-related and legally compliant storage. We continue this consideration in Section 4.4 for deletion. In Section 4.5, we present the procedure that was originally intended for handling retention obligations associated with legal cases but is also suitable for implementing the "right to restrict processing" pursuant to Art. 18 GDPR. Finally, Section 4.6 describes the special features of blocking in SAP ERP Personnel Administration (PA) in SAP ERP Human Capital Management (SAP ERP HCM).

Chapter 5: Purpose-Based Processing

Chapter 5 is a challenging chapter that describes how you can ensure the purpose-related data separation in the system. After an introductory thought in Section 5.1, in which we develop the mandatory connection between a legal entity in the sense of the GDPR (data controller) and the purpose of processing, we describe in Section 5.2 and Section 5.3 how line and process organization in the system should be configured to verify purpose-related processing in the client domain. In Section 5.4, we finally unite the two dimensions of the line and the process.

If you receive an instructive overview of the subject matter or deal with authorizations or blocking and deletion in your professional practice, reading this chapter is a must, even if the subject matter is (at first) dealt with in a very abstract way.

Chapter 6: Data Controller Rule Framework

Chapter 6 thematically follows Chapter 5. In the previous chapter, we dealt with model considerations that can be derived systematically; we now make concrete considerations about the steps necessary for the negative business process of blocking and deleting (Section 6.1). Furthermore, we introduce the latest development of the Data Controller Rule Framework, which is based on the abstraction made in Chapter 5, and, from a business perspective, the framework simplifies the maintenance of rules in SAP ILM. (Patent applications for this solution are pending.)

Chapter 6 is therefore essential for simplifying blocking and deletion and is consequently compulsory reading for all those who have to deal with it.

Chapter 7: Authorization Concept

Chapter 7 focuses on the derivations from the separation of purposes for the authorization concept. Therefore, the chapter is only intended for the authorization concept and the audit of the authorization concept or for those who are looking for an introduction to this complex matter.

In Section 7.1, we first deal only in a very general way with the subject of authorizations, and then, in the following two sections, we apply our findings from Chapter 5 on the subject of "separation of purposes" to the authorization concept. Section 7.4 deals with the definition of authorization risks.

Chapter 8: Information Retrieval Framework

Chapter 8 is addressed to those who deal with information, advance information, and possible uses for reporting processing activities. In this chapter, we'll illustrate how the new Information Retrieval Framework can help you provide transparent information to affected data subjects (the patent applications are pending for this feature as well). After a general introduction, in which we also explain the connection between information and advance information, we'll deal with the actual setup in subsequent sections. Finally, we'll describe how the procedure of providing information is carried out.

Chapter 9: Read Access Logging

Chapter 9 is important for readers who want to introduce logging of read access to personal data as a special form of monitoring protection. To begin with, we present the area of tension in which read logging is inevitably located in order to then describe the technical setup in detail.

Chapter 10: SAP Master Data Governance

Chapter 10 is intended for all who are interested in permanent solutions for legally compliant cross-platform data quality. In this chapter, we describe how you can use the additional SAP MDG solution to ensure that certain data can be processed in a cross-platform, data-protection-compliant manner, on a permanent basis. While data correction is possible in the standard system, SAP MDG enables you to keep particularly important data permanently data-protection compliant.

Chapter 11: SAP Test Data Migration Server

In **Chapter 11**, we deal with software dedicated to a very simple problem: What should you do with the test data? The use of real data in test systems should—on a regular basis—have the deficiency of a missing reference to purpose or missing consent. Accordingly, we consider it problematic to simply use the real data as the starting material for the test data. SAP TDMS offers an effective solution.

If you're testing with the real data, this is a must read. In addition, if you use other methods of depersonalization, we recommend that you work through this chapter as well. This will tell you whether your preferred solution can be optimized.

Chapter 12: Accountability: Protection, Audits, Controls, and Documentation

As already mentioned, in our opinion, the GDPR will trigger an endless cycle of control and verification. Our responsible developers would have liked to inflate **Chapter 12** to several hundred pages to do justice to the matter, but the interested reader requires just a simple introduction. From the relevant legal basis of the GDPR, we're gradually developing in this chapter which controls are necessary. We begin with Section 12.1 (on control frames) and Section 12.2 (on fairness and transparency), which are still of an abstract-general nature. We then focus on specific GDPR audit areas, such as the intended purpose or integrity and confidentiality. Finally, in Section 12.10, we arrive at specific but still exemplary control actions.

If you're only interested in an overview, we recommend that you only read Sections 12.1 to 12.9. Section 12.10 is addressed to the technically experienced reader who wants to get a first impression of what needs to be done in terms of controls and verifications. We've deliberately kept this to a minimum because it's important that you get an idea of what needs to be done.

Appendix A: Relevant Transactions, Reports, and SAP Notes

Last but not least, **Appendix A** contains relevant transactions, reports, and SAP Notes.

Throughout the book, we've also provided several elements that will help you access useful information:

[+] **Tips**
Boxes with this symbol provide you with recommendations as to how you can simplify your work.

[»] **Notes**
Boxes marked with this symbol contain additional information or important contents that you should keep in mind.

[Ex] **Examples**
Boxes marked with this symbol provide practical scenarios and explain, in detail, how particular functions can be applied.

[!] **Warnings**
Boxes with this symbol contain details worth considering. Moreover, it warns you of common errors or problems that might occur.

Acknowledgments

When you start writing the acknowledgments, you finally realize that work is coming to an end. Writing a book is a true challenge, in the course of which, the authors repeatedly wondered what they had burdened themselves with.

"Burden" is then also a nice keyword: Mrs. Eva Tripp from Rheinwerk Verlag has been editor of our main author Volker Lehnert for many years. Initially, he burdened her with proposing this book to the publishing house, then she burdened us, together with Sven Clever (also from Rheinwerk Verlag), with hundreds of remarks from the editorial office.

We would also like to thank Nicole Fernandes who translated this book into English and became a coauthor while doing so.

Let's carry on with the burden: We would like to thank all colleagues in and outside of SAP, whom we spontaneously invited to work ("Could you quickly ... until tomorrow evening ..."). We would like to start with Walter Pichl (Erste Group IT International, Vienna). It was a pleasure for us to discuss data separation with you; we have adopted many suggestions! Dieter Goedel, Frank Buchholz, and Marie-Luise Wagener (SAP SE) helped us this time with comments, especially on the sections regarding necessary controls. Anna Otto, Andreas Oesterle, and Horst Liermann (SAP Deutschland SE & Co. KG) from our consulting department have critically examined almost every chapter; furthermore, in recent months, they have helped to develop the process model for implementation. Even though Anna isn't with us this time, we'd like to say thanks for the wonderful cooperation in data protection and writing books for more than 12 years!

We would also like to thank our contributors who spontaneously agreed to join us: Reiko Enghardt (SAP SE) wrote to us asking if he could contribute to the chapter on SAP MDG. Reiko, that was hopefully the beginning of a long collaboration at Rheinwerk Verlag! Colleagues Christian Geiseler (SAP SE) for SAP MDG and Dr. Boris Hoffarth (SAP Deutschland SE & Co. KG) for SAP TDMS didn't have to be asked twice. Tanja Rueckel and Thomas Freye (both SAP SE) had taken on the task of correcting the first drafts.

Of course, the issue of burdening must also be considered with regard to our families. Thank you for letting us steal your precious time! We thank

Volker's loved ones, Dr. Monika Dittrich and Sara Dittrich (who at the age of 10 is happy to finally be mentioned again in a book). We also thank the dear little and big Luthers of Iwona for the permission to say "yes" when they were one day asked to participate in writing this book—and then stood there and couldn't help but do so. Many thanks also to Sandra and Vanessa, Carsten's loved ones, for their patience and support in this excitingly different way of spending your free time. Of course, we would also like to thank Björn's loved ones, but Björn would especially like to do his (very proud) grandmother the favor of mentioning her by name in this book: Thank you, Eva Unger, for your encouragement to participate in such a project!

These acknowledgments were translated from German to English. There was no need to change them in the eight months since the German original published. However, translation is hard work, so it is time to thank Nicole Fernandes for the great work she has done!

Volker Lehnert, **Iwona Luther**, **Björn Christoph**, and **Carsten Pluder**

Chapter 1
Introduction to General Data Protection Regulation

The privacy policy is both new and not new. Although data protection was given considerably more weight with the entry into force of the EU Data Protection Basic Regulation on May 25, 2018, there are essentially no new requirements. Most of the requirements have already been in force since the 1995 EU Data Protection Directive 95/46.

The term *data protection* is misleading because protection is granted to those individuals to whom the data refer, and to protect those individuals, personal data should be particularly protected. Data protection doesn't mean that the data in question may no longer be processed, however. Data protection regulations represent an attempt to strike a balance between the interests of the *data subjects* and the legitimate interests of the *processing entities*. The guidelines on data protection and cross-border flows of personal data agreed upon by the Organisation for Economic Co-operation and Development (OECD) in 1980 (revised in 2013) have already provided this framework. They are designed to lay the foundations for international data exchange while protecting the rights of the data subject.

This introduction presents the legal requirements that demand technical solutions (from a factual point of view), can be simplified by technical solutions, or are essential in creating an overall context. Data protection law will only be addressed to the extent necessary to cover the subject matter.

1.1 What Does the GDPR Mean for you?

After well over 20 years of obligatory data protection regulations, the question arises as to why the European Union (EU) General Data Protection Regulation (GDPR) is triggering extensive activity in numerous companies.

Expensive reinforcement of fines

There are presumably two reasons for this activity: First, the substantial fines imposed, as some infringements can be fined up to 4% of the worldwide gross annual turnover. Second, requirements that should have been implemented throughout Europe since 1995 may not been implemented to their full extent. More precisely, European companies that comply with their national data protection laws should not face any major challenges in implementing the requirements of the GDPR.

The following outlines the concepts that will help you implement the GDPR in SAP Business Suite and SAP S/4HANA.

1.1.1 Conceptual and Factual Principles

The term *personal data* is defined in Art. 4 (1) of the GDPR as follows:

> *'[P]ersonal data' means any information relating to an identified or identifiable natural person ('data subject'); an identifiable natural person is one who can be identified, directly or indirectly, in particular by reference to an identifier such as a name, an identification number, location data, an online identifier or to one or more factors specific to the physical, physiological, genetic, mental, economic, cultural or social identity of that natural person.*

When is data personal?

This is a very extensive and wide-ranging definition of personal data. When can an individual be identified indirectly? It's useful to remember that only a few attributes are sufficient to identify a person. Following is a common example: In German companies, only a small proportion of management positions are held by women. If there is only one woman among many men at the management level, the attribute "female" is identifying. Basically, of course, the possibility of being identifiable increases with the number of stored attributes. The data protection wiki of the Federal Commissioner for Data Protection and Freedom of Information (BfDI in Germany), 2016, contains a far-reaching absolutization:

> *The law knows . . . no legal risk. The data controller therefore has no choice but to treat all data as personal data as a precautionary measure. (BfDI, 2016)*

The assessment to determine which data is considered personal varies considerably from one company to another in practice. These differences have a lot to do with the risk propensity of an organization, as well as with the specifics of separately regulated industries such as insurance. The decision as to which data you treat as personal data is first and foremost the responsibility of your company.

Per Art. 2 of the GDPR, very briefly speaking, the GDPR applies to the partially or completely automated processing of personal data, unless this is carried out exclusively for family or personal purposes.

[«]

Purpose of This Book

This work is a book written by legal laymen for interested parties, most of whom are also legal laymen. Taking this into consideration, we make numerous curtailments, provided that this helps to make the content easier to understand and is appropriate for the operation of SAP S/4HANA and SAP Business Suite. For example, criminal prosecution is not an area of application for SAP Business Suite or SAP S/4HANA so a discussion of GDPR's applicability to the topic does not seem worthwhile. However, criminal prosecution isn't an area of application for SAP Business Suite or SAP S/4HANA. Hence, a thematic discussion doesn't seem worthwhile at this point.

Far-reaching applicability

Per Art. 3 of the GDPR, the GDPR is applicable to any controller for the provision of goods or services in the European Economic Area or for monitoring the behavior of persons in this area.

Transposition into national law?

In contrast to the previous Data Protection Directive 95/46/EC, which had to be transposed into national law as an EU directive, the GDPR takes direct effect and doesn't need to be transposed into national law. However, GDPR does contain clauses authorizing supplementary national legislation on a case-by-case basis. Accordingly, the German Data Protection Adaptation and Implementation Act EU (DSAnpUG-EU) was issued in Germany on June 30, 2017. The content of the DSAnpUG-EU replaces the old German Federal Data Protection Act (GFDPA) with a new law, which we'll refer to as GFDPA-new for reasons of differentiation. This includes various supplementary and special national regulations. For this book, the protection of employee data privacy, amended in § 26 GFDPA-new, is particularly important.

GDPR's entry into force

When will the GDPR apply? The GDPR was issued on April 27, 2016, and entered into force on May 25, 2018. The standards and possible fines apply in their entirety from the effective date. As soon as the European Data

Protection Committee begins its work, further details and specifications are expected.

What does processing mean?

The term *processing* applies to almost every handling of personal data. The legal definition also includes mere storage. As we'll illustrate later, an objectively justifying fact is also necessary for the simple retention of personal data on a storage medium.

Figure 1.1 shows the legal definition of processing in Art. 4 (2) of the GDPR, along with the lifecycle of personal data.

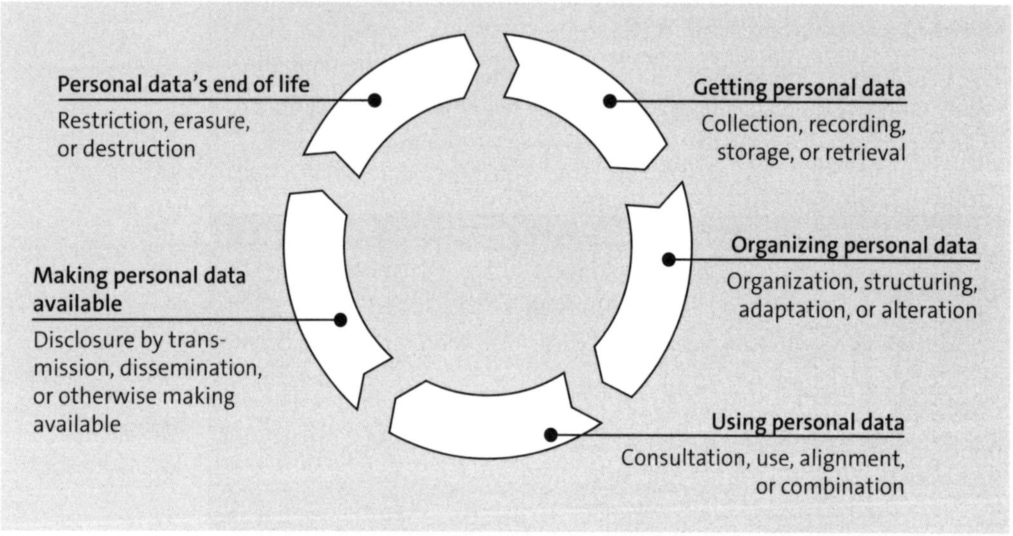

Figure 1.1 Processing Stages in the Lifecycle of Personal Data

Only one controller

Art. 4 (7) GDPR defines the data controller as an organizationally independent unit (*the natural or legal person, public authority, agency or other body*), which, alone or together with others, will determine the purposes of the processing. When operating SAP Business Suite or SAP S/4HANA, this unit is, in most cases, a single legal person.

It's important to understand that this is a single legally independent entity because the differentiation has both legal consequences and substantial technical implications. Therefore, two different groupings are feasible for the data controller:

- The purpose of the processing is determined by an organizationally independent legal entity.
- The purpose of the processing is determined by a relevant contract between several affiliated, organizationally independent legal entities (see *joint controllers* in Art. 26 GDPR).

All other requirements are ultimately based on the construction of the data controller as the most important norm addressee of the regulation because as *norm addressees, the data controllers are subject to the claims of the data subject or to the supervisory measures of the respective authorities* (Albrecht and Jotzo, 2017). The legal construction of the controller is the base line for the following legal definitions:

- Processing on behalf of the controller by a contractor (Art. 4 (8) GDPR)
- Disclosure of data to a recipient (Art. 4 (9) GDPR)
- Disclosure of data to a third party (Art. 4 (10) GDPR)
- Processing in a group of undertakings (Art. 4 (19) GDPR)

The relationship between the data controller and the purpose is described in more detail in Chapter 5.

Processor

The *processor* is the entity or person responsible for processing personal data. The processor is the second major norm addressee of the Regulation.

Recipient

The *recipient* is any entity or person to whom personal data is disclosed and who isn't an investigative authority with a legitimate mandate to investigate. Art. 4 (9) excludes inquiring public authorities as recipients. The assumption is that such an authority becomes a quite specific third party with a legitimate interest based on more specific legislation such as tax legislation. This has some consequences regarding the transparency requirements and other data subject rights.

Third party

A *third party* is every entity or person (other than the data subject, controller, processor) to whom personal data are disclosed.

Figure 1.2 illustrates the relationships when disclosing data. As described for the data controller, this person is at the center of attention as an organizational unit that determines the purpose.

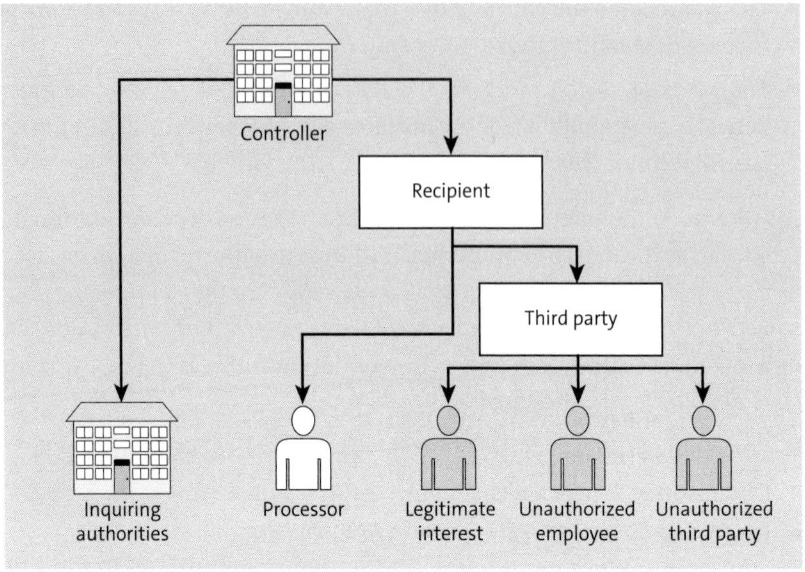

Figure 1.2 Recipient, Processor, Third Party

In this book, we only go deeper into processing on behalf of the controller in a few necessary sections. Processing on behalf of the controller is regulated in the GDPR as follows:

- A contract is required.
- The processor has numerous independent obligations.
- The processor may be subject to sanctions.

Ultimately, however, the processor on behalf of the controller will act on instructions from the data controller, who determines the purposes of processing.

1.1.2 An Essential Legal Consideration

The data protection law regulates general data protection rights and obligations, and it's restricted by numerous, more specific regulations.

[Ex]

The More Specific Law Takes Precedence

If you contact your HR department to prohibit them from continuing to provide tax authorities with your personal data (e.g., your income), the HR department will inform you that, in this case, tax law has precedence as the more specific right.

Standards, standards, and even more standards

Numerous other legal norms justify access rights of authorities (e.g., tax, Social Security) or third parties (e.g., auditors) and justify very different retention periods of various kinds. Some of these mentioned regulations are based on international standards such as International Financial Reporting Standards (IFRS). Others are subject to national legislation. For instance, in Germany, more than 1,900 standards need to be considered. Countless other legal standards define to whom the data is to be transmitted, who is allowed to view data, and how long data is to be retained.

[Ex]

Data Protection in Hospitals

To acquire a deeper understanding, think about a hospital that must comply with existing data protection regulations. However, it's also necessary to consult the standards of the social security codes for employees and patients (different in both cases), hospital-specific accounting regulations, general tax laws, commercial law regulations, legal-form-specific regulations where applicable, legal sources for pharmacies, legal sources of employment law, sources of workers codetermination law, and so on. If the hospital is a university clinic, the higher education law of the country, the civil service law of the country, and so on will also apply. In the United States, the Health Insurance Portability and Accountability Act (HIPAA) is applicable for health care in the given example.

1.1.3 Principles of Processing

The most essential basis for processing is legal. Personal data may only be processed if this is done in accordance with the law (Art. 5 (1)(a) GDPR).

Lawfulness

The processing is lawful in accordance with Art. 6 (1) if it has the following attributes:

- Based on consent
- Necessary for the fulfillment of a contract
- Necessary for the fulfillment of legal obligations
- Serves to protect vital interests
- Required for carrying out the tasks of public authority
- Serves to meet legitimate personal interests

Purpose limitation

A further elementary principle for the processing of personal data is the purpose limitation of processing. This implies that the purpose must be specified, explicit, and legitimate, and further processing must be compatible with the initial purpose (Art. 5 (1)(b) GDPR). We'll elaborate on the purpose limitation further in Section 1.2.1.

Purpose and data minimization

The purpose, however, doesn't permit the processing of arbitrary data. Only personal data that are adequate, relevant, and limited to what is necessary for the purpose may be processed (Art. 5 (1)(c) GDPR). An example from practice is the "ethnic identification" of tenants (Section 1.1.4). This is a requirement that has been imposed by individual property owners in the real estate sector. This requirement is illegal in many respects, including the fact that tenants may not be selected or classified according to ethnic criteria. See § 7 in conjunction with § 1 of the German General Equal Opportunities Act (AGG). Obviously, ethnic identity marking isn't necessary, appropriate, or significant. Section 1.3.2 deals with data minimization.

Accuracy of data

The accuracy of the data is explicitly required by Art. 5 (1)(d) GDPR. Data must be accurate and up to date; inaccurate data must be deleted or corrected. This requirement may appear odd because the processing of incorrect data is economically unreasonable. However, note that incorrect data can damage reputations or lead to unnecessary and burdensome consequences. On one hand, the accuracy of data must be ensured by means of correction options (Section 1.2.2), and, on the other hand, data management (Section 1.3.3) can have a supportive effect.

Storage limitations

Personal data may not be processed endlessly. Art. 5 (1)(c) GDPR stipulates that the personal reference of data may be retained only as long as necessary for the purpose of processing. Also (as shown in Figure 1.4) other principles such as Art. 5 (1)(b) relating to purpose limitation and Art. 5 (1)(e) relating to storage limitation indicate the need to delete personal data. This means that the data must be deleted following the retention requirements of the legitimate purposes of the data processing, as described in Section 1.1.8. Under certain conditions, pseudonyms are also permitted (Section 1.1.12).

Integrity and confidentiality

Art. 5 (1)(f) is concerned with the integrity and confidentiality of processing. It's necessary to ensure an adequate level of data security to ensure *appropriate security of the personal data, including protection against unauthorised or unlawful processing and against accidental loss, destruction or damage, using appropriate technical or organisational measures*; these measures are outlined in Section 1.2.4.

Accountabilities

Finally, Art. 5 (2) establishes accountability for compliance with the processing principles outlined previously. Proof of compliance may in some cases be subject to mandatory technical functions, which are described in more detail in Section 1.2.5. Moreover, the accountability, verification, and control obligations are described in more detail in Chapter 4, when we discuss SAP Information Lifecycle Management (SAP ILM). The record of processing activities according to Art. 30 GDPR and the impact assessment of data protection in accordance with Art. 35 GDPR are subject to a general compliance management system that can only be supported technically. We'll address compliance management in Section 1.3.6.

1.1.4 Special Categories of Personal Data

Art. 9 (1) prohibits the processing of special categories of personal data, unless exceptions in Art. 9 (2) apply. Prohibited data contains the following information:

- Racial and ethnic origin
- Political opinions
- Religious or philosophical beliefs
- Trade union membership

[«]

Racial Origin

The concept of *racial origin* has already caused confusion in the past. The EU therefore makes it clear in the recitals that *the use of the term "racial origin" in this Regulation does not imply an acceptance by the Union of theories which attempt to determine the existence of separate human races* (see recital 51 GDPR).

In addition, the following prohibited data included information for the unique identification of a person:

- Genetic data
- Biometric data

Finally, other prohibited data includes the following:

- Data concerning health
- Data on sexual life
- Data on sexual orientation

In Art. 9 (2) GDPR, the basic prohibition is broken through by exceptions. The following data of special categories are essential for SAP S/4HANA and SAP Business Suite in the personnel domain if a compliant purpose is given:

- **Religious beliefs**
  At least data relating to membership of a religious community that causes a tax liability are relevant.
- **Trade union membership**
  Some companies deduct the membership fee from the employee's income.
- **Data concerning health**
  Data on health are also relevant in some cases.

Special data categories in the employment relationship

The GDPR opens up the possibility of national regulations for the processing of personal data in employment relationships. The protection of employee data in Germany is regulated in § 26 GFDPA-new. To what extent the processing of trade union membership is still permissible may be worthy of discussion, but ultimately the decision lies with the user company.

Data concerning health are also collected in human resources. Further applications may also contain health data, such as the SAP Environment, Health, and Safety (EHS) Management solution. After all, industry solutions for the health-care sector, such as patient management, are designed to process such data.

Higher level of protection

The handling of special categories of data increases the level of protection that should be sought. Remember that Art. 5 (1)(f) demands an appropriate level of protection. Among other methods, this can be achieved using the authorization concept (Chapter 7) and the reading log (see Chapter 9 for Read Access Logging [RAL]).

1.1.5 Justifiable Facts for Processing

In Section 1.1.3, we cited justifications for processing personal data:

- Informed consenting
- Fulfilling a contract
- Fulfilling legal obligations
- Protecting vital interests
- Carrying out the tasks of public authority
- Defending one's own legitimate interests

Mostly organizational proof

As a rule, the justifiable facts generally require predominantly or exclusively, an organizational proof of the documentation, for example, in the records of processing activities in accordance with Art. 30 GDPR or within the scope of the transparency obligations of Arts. 12–15 GDPR. Contract and consent are also to be documented but can get proofed technically.

Contract

The initiation, existence, and execution of a contract can be proven at many points in SAP Business Suite and SAP S/4HANA. As part of the simplified blocking and deletion of personal data, numerous areas are validated against artifacts that show the existence of a contract.

Consent

Consent is a special case in that it only exists to justify data processing. While the other facts obviously serve the management of processes outside of data processing, consent under data protection law is, at least in numerous cases, concerned with data processing as a purpose in itself:

- Art. 4 (11) GDPR describes consent as an informed, freely given, specific, and unambiguous act of the data subject for certain cases.
- Art. 7 (1) GDPR establishes the obligation to provide proof that the data subject has consented to processing.
- Art. 7 (3) GDPR permits the data subject to revoke consent at any time.
- Art. 8 GDPR describes further conditions for the consent of a child.
- Art. 9 (2)(a) GDPR permits consent as a justifying factor for the processing of special categories of personal data.

Consent and deletion

Regarding Art. 6 (1)(a) GDPR, you should bear in mind that this describes the lawfulness of processing on the basis of a consent. Consequently, revocation of consent must lead to the deletion of data, unless other subparts of Art. 6 (1) permit further processing.

Consent in an employment relationship

Section 26 (2) GFDPA-new regulates the consent within the framework of an employment relationship. Section 26 (3) GFDPA-new also permits the processing of special categories of personal data on the based on a declaration of consent within the framework of an employment relationship and within narrow limits.

Generally speaking, consent in the context of an employment relationship is a difficult instrument. Art. 29 Data Protection Working Party (G29) explains:

> *Consent can only be valid if the data subject is able to exercise a real choice, and there is no risk of deception, intimidation, coercion or significant negative consequences if he/she does not consent. If the consequences of consenting undermine individuals' freedom of choice, consent would not be free. . . . where consent is required from a worker, and there is a real or potential relevant prejudice that arises from not consenting, the consent is not valid. (Data Protection Working Party, 2011)*

Consent more stringent

The GDPR makes the assessment of consent even more stringent in the recitals:

> *In order to ensure that consent is freely given, consent should not provide a valid legal ground for the processing of personal data in a specific case where there is a clear imbalance between the data subject and the controller, in particular where the controller is a public authority and it is therefore unlikely that consent was freely given in all the circumstances of that specific situation. (see Recital 43 GDPR)*

It should be emphasized here that there is always a clear imbalance in the employment relationship, which means that consent as an option would at least be called into question. Furthermore, in the context of labor law, executive prerogative must always be considered. In many cases, the employer can determine the use of a certain software or hardware while respecting the rights of codetermination of the employee representative committee.

The discussion about consent is thus essentially concerned with the question of when it can be assumed that the declaration of intent is sufficiently explicit and to what extent voluntary action can be assumed.

[«]

Further Reading

For more information on this topic, see also Frenzel (in Paal and Pauly, 2017), Art. 7 (18–21), and "Opinion 15/2011 on the definition of consent" (Art. 29 Data Protection Working Party, 2011). The most current EU opinion on consent is given in "Guidelines on Consent under Regulation 2016/679" (Art. 29 Data Protection Working Party, 2018).

Infinity of consent

Legally, consent doesn't have an expiration date. However, because the consent can only be granted for certain cases, and an event in the distant future is usually not to be regarded as definite, we assume that consent should be renewed on a regular basis, provided that the continued effect (e.g., by email advertising) isn't obvious to the data subject. Oberbeck (2017) explains:

> *The validity of declarations of consent has always been controversial. This is also not expressly regulated in the GDPR nor in the final draft of the E-Privacy Ordinance. However, the draft in Art. 9 of the E-Privacy Ordinance specifies concrete guidelines for revocation and indications relating thereto. In future, users will have to be informed of this revocation option at periodical intervals of six months.*

Clearly, consent is a suitable basis for processing, but it must also meet numerous conditions to be effective. Certainly, it can be used wherever there is a clearly voluntary relationship and where the data subject has an additional benefit, which can be achieved, for example, through discount systems. In Section 1.3.1, we'll look at the subject once again from a technical point of view.

1.1.6 Requirement of Transparency

Arts. 12–15 GDPR deal with the obligations for transparency in data processing. Figure 1.3 illustrates the transparency requirements and the associated articles. Because consent in accordance with Art. 7 GDPR is only possible in an informed context, the transparency of data processing is achieved right at the start of processing.

Record of processing activities According to Art. 30 GDPR, the records of processing activities (register of processing operations) allows both the data controller and the processor, as well as the supervisory authority, to obtain transparency concerning processing and contains partially comparable information such as those contained in Arts. 12–15 GDPR.

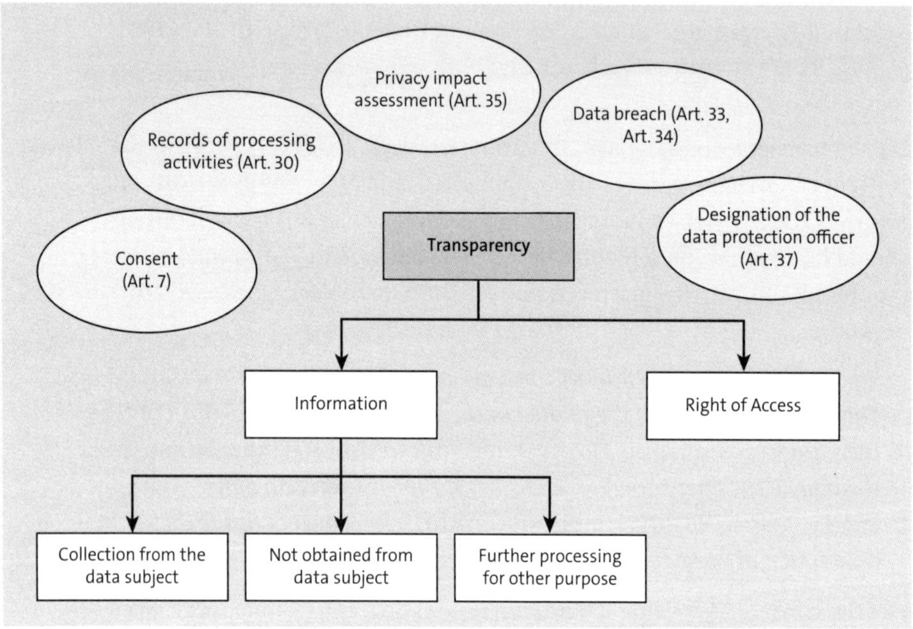

Figure 1.3 Transparency in Data Processing

Data breach The notification obligations set forth in Arts. 33 and 34 GDPR provide the data subject, on a case-by-case basis, with transparency as to whether or not a data controller or the processor has treated personal data correctly. Transparency will also be given to the supervisory authority.

Data protection impact assessment The data protection impact assessment is also a requirement for transparency in data processing. This is further described in Section 1.1.13.

Data protection officer The case-by-case appointment of a data protection officer as set out in Art. 37 GDPR or the mandatory appointment according to § 38 GFDPA-new (10 employees permanently involved in the automated processing of personal data), facilitate transparency for both the data subject and the supervisory authority. However, the transparency requirement is explicitly addressed in Arts. 12–15 GDPR.

Sufficient transparency

Art. 12 GDPR sets out the framework that the data controller must comply with to ensure that the data subject has sufficient transparency regarding the processing, protection, and exercising of his or her rights. Arts. 13 and 14 GDPR define the information to be provided in the case of data processing, which will be referred to as "advance information" to facilitate legibility. Art. 13 GDPR regulates the advance information if the data is collected directly from the data subject, and Art. 14 GDPR does the same if that the data isn't collected directly from the data subject.

Due to the good comparability of the information to be provided, we present extracts of these in Table 1.1.

Data Collection from the Data Subject	Data Collection *Not* from the Data Subject
Art. 13 (1)	**Art. 14 (1)**
(a) Data controller/controller's representative	(a) Data controller/controller's representative
(b) Data protection officer, if applicable (see the following Note box)	(b) Data protection officer
(c) Purpose and legal basis	(c) Purpose and legal basis
(d) Legitimate interest, if applicable	
	(d) Categories of data
(e) Recipients, if applicable	(e) Recipients, if applicable
(f) Transmission to third country/international organization The existence or absence of an adequacy decision by the Commission Guaranteed according to Art. 46 or Art. 47 or Art. 49 (1)(2) Entitlement to copy	(f) Transmission to third country/international organization The existence or absence of an adequacy decision by the Commission Guaranteed according to Art. 46 or Art. 47 or Art. 49 (1)(2) Entitlement to copy

Table 1.1 Comparison of Information to Be Provided in Extracts

Data Collection from the Data Subject	Data Collection *Not* from the Data Subject
Art. 13 (2)	**Art. 14 (2)**
(a) Retention periods or criteria for such retention periods	(a) Retention periods or criteria for such retention periods
	(b) Legitimate interest, if applicable
(b) Entitlement to information Entitlement to correction Restriction claim Erasure claim	(c) Entitlement to information Entitlement to correction Restriction claim Erasure claim
(c) Right to revoke consent	(d) Right to revoke consent
(d) Right of appeal to the supervisory authority	(e) Right of appeal to the supervisory authority
(e) To what extent the data is required for the contract or a legal basis is given and which consequences the nondelivery of the data would have	
	(f) Data origin
(f) If necessary, automated decision-making, including profiling	(g) If necessary, automated decision-making, including profiling
Art. 13 (3)	**Art. 14 (4)**
Notification of planned changes in purpose	Notification of planned changes in purpose

Table 1.1 Comparison of Information to Be Provided in Extracts (Cont.)

[»]

Appointment of a Data Protection Officer

According to GDPR, the appointment of a data protection officer isn't required in all cases (see Art. 37 GDPR). In Germany, however, Section 38 of the DSAnpUG-EU stipulates that those data controllers, who *employ at least ten people permanently in the automated processing of personal data* (Section 38 (1)(1)) and other matters enforce the appointment of a data protection officer.

Easily comprehensible and clear information

Art. 12 (1) GDPR requires that this information must be given *in a concise, transparent, intelligible and easily accessible form, using clear and plain language*. As correct and important as this requirement is, some may still wonder how all of the above information can possibly remain comprehensible to the data subject. The extent to which technical support can be provided for advance information is briefly explained in Chapter 8.

Information upon request

Art. 15 GDPR now specifies the right of access to information by the data subject, which must be made available upon request. Advance information has many requirements in common with the data subject's right of access, as shown in Table 1.2, which compares the requirements and the right of access. In addition to the information specified in Table 1.2, it's also necessary to provide full information on all related personal data undergoing processing.

Specifications according to Art. 15	In Art. 13	In Art. 14
Right of access	**Advance information**	
a) Purposes of processing	(1)(c)	(1)(c)
b) Categories of personal data		(1)(d)
c) Recipients or categories of recipients (also in third countries or with international organizations)	(1)(e) (1)(f)	(1)(e) (1)(f)
d) Retention periods	(2)(a)	(2)(a)
e) Correction, deletion, opposition, blocking	(2)(b)	(2)(c)
f) The existence of a right of appeal to a supervisory authority	(2)(d)	(2)(e)
g) Origin of the data		(2)(f)
h) Automated decision-making, including profiling	(2)(f)	(2)(g)

Table 1.2 Right of Access and Advance Information

Comparing right of access and advance information

The comparison should be sufficient to demonstrate that an organization that can provide legally compliant information to the data subject on request already meets the substantive requirements for the provision of advance information. Further notes concerning the right of access by the data subject can be found in Section 1.2.6, and more about advance information is available in Chapter 8.

1.1.7 Accuracy of Data

The accuracy of the data subject's personal data, as already described in Section 1.1.3, constitutes a basis for processing in accordance with Art. 5 (1)(d) GDPR. According to Art. 16 GDPR, the data subject also has the right to have the data corrected without delay and, if necessary, to have incomplete information supplemented by a declaration, if applicable, in relation to the purpose. On the correction of data, Section 1.1.7, and for the correctness of data, Section 1.3.3.

1.1.8 Right to Be Forgotten

Art. 17 GDPR establishes the right of the data subject to demand the deletion of his or her data. However, this right is to be viewed in a legal system: On one hand, the facts of the need for deletion are affected by various other stipulations in the GDPR; on the other hand, this right affects many other areas of law. Personal data needs to be deleted when the purpose has is no longer valid, but retention requirements of other legislation might necessitate that you retain such data.

Deletion according to GDPR

However, let's first turn to the GDPR-related approach. In Figure 1.4, we consider the several requirements for deletion, based on the temporary use of personal data. First, the storage limitation and, indirectly, the purpose limitation and the data minimization, can be derived directly from the principles of data processing according to Art. 5. Regarding all three principles, it should be noted that the necessity of personal data is decisive for the purpose defined in advance.

Purpose limitation of the data

The GDPR contains a prohibition with the right to conditional permission. It's therefore only permissible to process personal data if there is a justifying reason (as already presented in Section 1.1.3). This justifying reason is related to the previously defined purpose. When the purpose is no longer existent, the data may no longer be processed and must be removed or effectively depersonalized.

[«]

Depersonalization

Although undeniably a cumbersome word creation, topics related to depersonalization are discussed in more detail in Section 1.1.12.

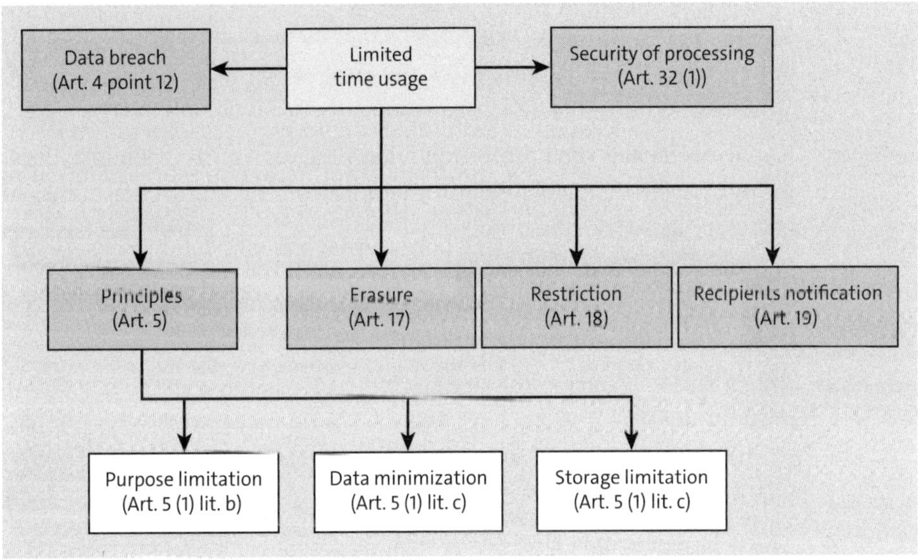

Figure 1.4 Deletion Pursuant to the GDPR

An overall picture of deletion

We assume that personal data in SAP Business Suite or in SAP S/4HANA will basically be processed for the following purposes:

- Fulfillment of a contract
- Based on consent
- Fulfillment of legal obligations

If the data is processed for these mentioned purposes and—as soon as this basis no longer applies—are submitted to a comprehensive, prompt, and rule-based blocking and deletion procedure, there can only be one processing operation that is permissible in accordance with Art. 17 GDPR. This topic is elaborated on in Chapter 4.

Deletion on request

Requesting that the data is deleted is of course still permissible; however, if the system has been configured correctly, there shouldn't be any data subject to individual deletion. Data that is only processed on the basis of consent should be deleted after consent has been withdrawn. This is very similar to deletion on request, especially if no further retention obligations apply. If you have technically implemented consent, it should also have been included in the block and delete logic.

Data breach

Temporary use will also reduce the risk of a personal data breach as defined in Art. 4 (12) GDPR. Data that are no longer there can also no longer be the subject of a protection breach. Nothing may be more annoying than having to pay fines for lost data that the company hasn't needed for a long time anyway.

Blocking on request

As one of the new data protection requirements, Art. 18 GDPR introduces the right to restriction of processing. Accordingly, in certain cases, it may be necessary to restrict the processing of retained data because this has been requested. This type of blocking is subject matter of the authorization concept, which is discussed in Section 1.2.4, and/or the overall blocking and deletion concept, which is covered in Chapter 4.

Informing recipients

Art. 19 GDPR regulates the organizational measure; each data recipient must be informed (unless it's impossible or requires disproportionate effort) of rectification, blocking on request, or deletion.

Obligation to block personal data

The old German Federal Data Protection Act (GFDPA) supplements the obligation to delete data with an explicit obligation to block personal data if, among other things, the data is only held due to other applicable legal, statutory, or contractual retention periods (§ 35 para. 3 No. 1 GFDPA-old). This kind of blocking therefore means the labeling of the stored personal data is blocked to restrict its further processing or use (§ 3 para. 4 No. 4 GFDPA-old). We assume that this obligation to block is based on—albeit implicitly—both the old EU legislation (Directive 95/46/EC of the European Parliament and of the Council of October 24, 1995, on the protection of individuals with regard to the processing of personal data and on the free movement of such data) and on the GDPR.

This obligation to block data can be derived from the GDPR definition of a personal data breach pursuant to Art. 4 (12), and from the requirement for appropriate technical and organizational measures pursuant to Art. 32 (1) in conjunction with Art. 32 (2), which makes the adequacy of the level of protection subject to, among other things, the prevention of unauthorized access. Furthermore, they are also subject to the principles of Art. 5 and, in particular, the principles of purpose limitation pursuant to Art. 5 (1)(b), data minimization pursuant to Art. 5 (1)(c), and the temporal storage limitation in accordance with Art. 5 (1)(e).

Blocking means blocking

We consider blocking to mean that, under no circumstances, may the data be used for aggregations, totals, quantity determination, and so on. Without a clear obligation, the data must appear as if it weren't there.

[!]

Delete or Block

Data must be deleted if it's not processed within the scope of the intended purpose. This doesn't hold true if other retention periods apply. In this case, data must be blocked due to the additional data protection requirements.

1.1.9 Data Portability

According to Art. 20 GDPR, data portability is the data subject's right to receive, on request, all data that has been provided by him or her based on a declaration of consent or on a contract. It must also be in a format that can be used by third parties. The data subject also has the right to pass this data on to another controller without being hindered.

Machine-readable delivery

This requirement is expected to be fulfilled formally by means of any information access report, which can be transferred to a machine-readable format, and with the corresponding adaptation of the output. It remains to be seen whether this requirement will become sufficiently detailed in industry standards or supervisory authority regulations to render it practical in business-to-consumer (B2C) systems. We have our doubts as to whether such a download of data from SAP Business Suite and SAP S/4HANA could easily be used in another installation without specifically carrying out tangible data migration. If data portability is to be fully understood, it involves hundreds to thousands of data fields. For this very reason, we're hoping for an introduction of norms or a standardization that would ensure the usability of this data.

1.1.10 Objection, Automated Individual Decision-Making, and Profiling

In certain cases, the data subject has the right to object to the processing of data (Art. 21 GDPR). Processing must also be avoided in cases that are regulated by law. However, with the exception of the right to object to direct advertising, this is likely to be an exceptional case in the immediate context of SAP Business Suite and SAP S/4HANA.

Automated decision-making

Automated decision-making, including profiling, pursuant to Art. 22 GDPR is much more important in our context. The data subject essentially has the right not to be subject to a decision based solely on automated processing that is detrimental to him or her (e.g., produces legal effects). The data subject is granted the right of intervention at the very minimum. However, this is not the case, for example, if this automated decision is necessary for the conclusion of a contract or is based on a legal provision. This legal regulation is clearly only concerned with providing the possibility of intervention (Art. 22 (3) GDPR); thus making it possible to take automated decisions, unlike previous directives which principally excluded the possibility of fully automated decision-making (see Art. 15 of Directive 95/46/EC of the European Parliament and of the Council of October 24, 1995 on the protection of individuals with regard to the processing of personal data and on the free movement of such data).

Profiling

Automated decision-making is often based on profiling. Art. 4 (4) GDPR explains that profiling is a procedure in which personal data is used for analysis or predicting the data subject's behavior. Although profiling is a permissible action, it's also subject to the transparency requirements of Arts. 13–15 GDPR, the data subject's right to object pursuant to Art. 21, and to the data protection impact assessment pursuant to Art. 35 GDPR.

Profiling and automated decision-making can still be regulated by the European Data Protection Committee.

1.1.11 Appropriateness of Measures, Documentation, and Proof

The requirements concerning the handling and security of data are supplemented by the requirements for verification and documentation. Art. 24 GDPR stipulates that, in the context of risk assessment, the controller must implement the *appropriate technical and organisational measures to ensure and be able to demonstrate that processing is carried out in accordance with this Regulation,* and that these measures will be reviewed and updated if necessary.

Data protection by design and by default

Art. 25 GDPR is titled "Data protection by design and by default." Processing must be structured in such a way to comply with the data-protection principles of the regulation; data minimization is cited as an example of this.

Default settings must be defined to ensure that only the necessary personal data is processed. This obligation is specified in more detail in Art. 25 (2) regarding the amount of personal data as well as *the extent of their processing, the period of their storage, and their accessibility*. In particular, the data may not be made accessible to any indefinite number of other natural persons. An approved certification mechanism must also be used to prove compliance with these requirements.

1.1.12 Security of Processing

Art. 32 (1) GDPR describes the following measures to ensure the security of processing:

- Pseudonymization and encryption
- Safeguarding the confidentiality, integrity, availability, and resilience of processing systems and services
- Backup/disaster recovery
- A process for regularly testing, assessing, and evaluating the effectiveness of technical and organizational measures for ensuring the security of processing

Pseudonymization and anonymization

The GDPR proposes the pseudonymization of data in several places. To discuss this further, we need to take a look at the legal definition of pseudonymization in Art. 4 (5) GDPR:

> *Pseudonymisation means the processing of personal data in such a manner that the personal data can no longer be attributed to a specific data subject without the use of additional information, provided that such additional information is kept separately and is subject to technical and organisational measures to ensure that the personal data are not attributed to an identified or identifiable natural person.*

This corresponds content-wise to the legal definition laid down in the older § 3 para. 6 BDSG concerning anonymization; the essential difference under GDPR is that it's legitimate to store factors used for identification separately. Both states are almost impossible to achieve with dependent data chains. This problem can also be seen in studies on k-anonymity and differential privacy.

[»]

K-Anonymity

K-anonymity is an approach developed by Samarati and Sweeney (Protecting Privacy when Disclosing Information: k-Anonymity and Its Enforcement through Generalization and Suppression, 1998), in which the directly identifying attributes are removed from a data mass with comparable data records, and the indirectly identifying attributes are selected in such a way that the group shows at least k data records that show the same indirectly identifying attributes.

[»]

Differential Privacy

Differential privacy is a concept in which data in a data set are changed in such a way that it's significantly more difficult to draw conclusions about the person. This is achieved by randomizing selected attributes so that all information for the selected attribute is highly likely to be retained; however, individual information will have been changed (Dwork, Differential privacy, 2006).

To identify a person, it's necessary to first identify which indirectly identifying attributes or which combination of attributes might be sufficient to do so. The attribute "female" isn't identifiable as such in the work environment. In most German companies, the combination of "low- to mid-level manager" and "female" is also not identifying. However, this combination could already be identifying in top-level management or in special company divisions, especially when additional meaningful attributes such as years of service and age are added. In such a case, the aim of anonymization wasn't achieved.

Depersonalization

To avoid any misunderstanding, we'll use the term *depersonalization* with the understanding that success can only be assessed when the data is complete. This would probably correspond to the scientific debate. However, we'll deliberately be using a different term.

Decisive for the success of depersonalization, as well as for the continued usability of the data, is the assessment to determine for which reports the data is significant. Attributes that aren't required for the desired reports shouldn't be retained at all. Because the processing of personal data in SAP Business Suite and SAP S/4HANA is conducted on the basis of permission cases, this particular subject is of secondary importance. The customer should take this into account when exporting data to the SAP Business Warehouse (SAP BW) system.

Encryption

Encrypting data is of paramount importance for the transfer of data. Furthermore, some industry standards, such as the credit card industry's Payment Card Industry (PCI) standard, demand encryption of certain data. In data processing, encryption comes at the cost of performance. For this reason, encryption should probably be limited to data that, resulting from the risk assessment, are relevantly sensitive. We were confronted with the demand for encryption of all data when working with a large insurance company in a system where all employees could see all data without restriction. In the end, it's the combination of different measures that always counts.

Confidentiality

Confidentiality of the systems must be ensured by pertinent measures. Traditionally, since 1976, these have always been described differently in German data protection laws as *technical and organizational measures* (TOMs). The TOMs are described in further detail in Section 1.2.4. In Section 1.2.1, among other things, we'll look at the scope of purpose-independent processing.

Integrity

When referring to the protection of systems against undetectable manipulation, Marit Hansen (2012) uses the term *integrity*. Accordingly, numerous measures must be taken to ensure and control the systems' integrity. The focus will most likely be on the following:

- Code protection and logging changes
- Protecting configuration and logging changes

- Protection of interfaces and logging usage
- Other technical measures to avoid the unintentional manipulation of personal data, such as access control, sharing control, and transfer control

In the context of this book, it's important that the security patches provided are installed promptly.

[»]

Security Patches

SAP is continuously working on closing security gaps that are detected by internal or external tests. The software repair measures made available in this way are called *patches* or *security patches*. Unfortunately, many customers wait a long time before installing the patches. If a patch wasn't installed, and subsequently data is misused, it will probably be considered a chargeable offense.

Availability

The term *availability*, which is specified more precisely in Art. 32 (1)(b, c), deals with standard availability control. Personal data must remain available. The aim is to protect data against accidental loss and destruction. In addition to backup procedures, these include disaster recovery and business continuity concepts. Lehnert and Dopfer-Hirth (2016) address this in "Data Protection Requirements and Their Support in HR Systems Demonstrated Using SAP ERP HCM":

> *Even if these concepts should be obvious as a business necessity and should not require any additional data protection reasons, experience shows that there are still a lot of issues with this in companies.*

Process for regular testing

Art. 32 (1)(d) GDPR stipulates that *a process for regularly testing, assessing and evaluating the effectiveness of technical and organisational measures for ensuring the security of the processing* should be regarded a comprehensive procedure. It's advisable at this point to think about the requirement of evidence as explained in Section 1.1.11.

Figure 1.5 shows the logical sequence of the continuous definition and control processes, which respectively lead to documentation and verification obligations.

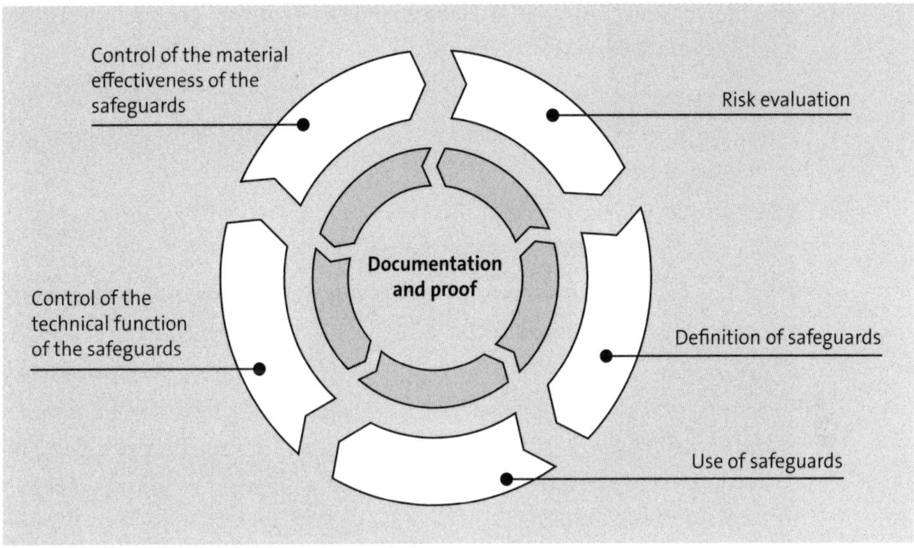

Figure 1.5 Control Circuit/Detection Circuit

We'll illustrate this using a simple example from the authorization concept: A system processes personal data belonging to special categories, which entails a high demand for data protection (evaluation). Access to this data must therefore be restricted in such a way that only those persons with an explicit purpose for which this data is intended can access it (definition). The authorizations are defined accordingly (use). A conclusive authorization analysis is used to determine whether this protective measure is effective (technical function control). Whether the protective measure is objectively effective is determined not only through logs but also through expert consultation (control of the objective function). Each step is documented and ideally linked to a software-supported control process. This is discussed further in Section 1.3.6.

1.1.13 Privacy Impact Assessment

The GDPR also includes the privacy impact assessment (PIA).

Specific duty to provide evidence

Although data protection experts are discussing whether or not there is a comparability with the BDSG's ex ante control, it's of course significant that the data protection impact assessment deals with the specific obligation to provide evidence. Art. 35 (7) GDPR stipulates that the impact assessment must include at least the following:

- *(a) a systematic description of the envisaged processing operations and the purposes of the processing, including, where applicable, the legitimate interest pursued by the controller;*
- *(b) an assessment of the necessity and proportionality of the processing operations in relation to the purposes;*
- *(c) an assessment of the risks to the rights and freedoms of data subjects referred to in paragraph 1; and*
- *(d) the measures envisaged to address the risks, including safeguards, security measures and mechanisms to ensure the protection of personal data and to demonstrate compliance with this Regulation taking into account the rights and legitimate interests of data subjects and other persons concerned.*

Risk assessment

In other words, PIA is a purpose-oriented risk assessment based on the processing steps and the identification of the measures envisaged to minimize risks.

PIA is to be carried out in accordance with Art. 35 (3) GDPR, in cases where processing involves special risks, in particular, when the following conditions are met:

- *(a) a systematic and extensive evaluation of personal aspects relating to natural persons which is based on automated processing, including profiling, and on which decisions are based that produce legal effects concerning the natural person or similarly significantly affect the natural person;*
- *(b) processing on a large scale of special categories of data referred to in Article 9(1), or of personal data relating to criminal convictions and offences referred to in Article 10; or*
- *(c) a systematic monitoring of a publicly accessible area on a large scale.*

1.1.14 Records of processing activities

Art. 30 GDPR renders it obligatory for the controller (Art. 30 (1)) and the processor (Art. 30 (2)) to keep a record of processing activities; this must be submitted to the supervisory authority on request (Art. 30 (4)). Art. 30 (5) GDPR specifies possible exemptions from the obligation to keep such records.

Take a look at the information required for processing activities in Table 1.3, and you'll quickly discover that, in turn, it at least partly concerns data that was already discussed as part of the transparency obligations in Section 1.1.6.

Specifications of Art. 30	Art. 13	Art. 14	Art. 15
Controller's name and contact details	(1)(a)	(1)(a)	
Where applicable, the name and contact details of the data protection officer	(1)(b)	(1)(b)	
Purposes of processing	(1)(c)	(1)(c)	(1)(a)
Categories of personal data		(1)(d)	(1)(b)
Recipients or categories of recipients (including those in third countries or international organizations)	(1)(e)	(1)(e)	(1)(c)
Transfers to a third country or international organization and, where applicable, documentation of suitable safeguards	(1)(f)	(1)(f)	
Retention periods	(2)(a	(2)(a)	(1)(d)
A general description of the technical and organizational measures			

Table 1.3 Record/Information/Preliminary Information

The addition of the general description of technical and organizational measures is new. In Section 1.3.5, we'll take a more detailed look at the technical support necessary for such records.

1.2 Which Requirements Require Technical Support?

While some GDPR requirements obviously need organizational support—for example, the possible appointment of a data protection officer—and some tasks may benefit from technical support (Section 1.3), there are some requirements that call for technical solutions or at least technical possibilities. We'll focus on these issues in the following sections.

1.2.1 Purpose Limitation of Processing

The term *purpose* isn't legally defined; the controller must therefore specify the purposes of processing. From a business point of view, the purpose should be conceived and defined as an end-to-end process, for example, the processing of a sales contract.

[»]

Discussion of Processing Purposes

The expert debate also specifically focuses on the question of how to meaningfully define purposes. Naturally, as we're not lawyers, we're not involved in this expert debate. Our organizational and technical point of view is based on the idea of being guided by the business process.

If the concept of purpose is understood in such a way that each individual factual purpose is differentiated, micro-purposes will be created. These can't be represented in blocking and deletion or the authorization concept, nor can they be represented in transparency obligations. They would also fail to provide the data subject with sufficient transparency. Kramer (2016) writes the following:

> *The GDPR's compatibility check (Art. 6 (4)) requires a precise determination of whether the original purpose of data processing is still being pursued or whether a new secondary purpose that has to be checked for compatibility exists. For example, an original purpose is pursued if, in a sales contract, sales contract data is passed on to a debt collection company for collection purposes because the data subject has failed to pay.*

It makes sense to define purposes in such a detailed way that transactions, to which various other legal norms apply, are also shown as having different purposes. In Section 1.1.2, we outlined that countless other legal sources also have an influence on data protection.

[Ex]

Differentiating between Purposes in Sales

Imagine a company offering two products: peppermint oil and cough syrup. For peppermint oil, the only applicable sources are likely to be the standard commercial and food laws; for cough syrup, the pharmaceutical industry's much stricter legislation has to be applied (cf. Lehnert & Pluder, 2016).

Purposes and other legal grounds

It's important to structure the different purposes of processing in line with other applicable legal sources and in such a way to allow for the sufficiently differentiated processing of the data. For example, if your business model entails trading in both peppermint oil and cough syrup, and if only one purpose has been defined, all data may be stored for the same length of time, which means at least partially longer than necessary, which would be illegal.

It's also important that you think about the connection between the purpose and the responsible body. Every purpose always belongs to the controller. The legally independent German company A is a different controller from the legally independent German company B. Even when dealing with the same business transactions and, therefore, comparable purposes, such as the sale of peppermint oil, there are still different purposes: "Sale of peppermint oil Company A" and "Sale of peppermint oil Company B".

Therefore, it's necessary to outline the relationship to the controller on the one hand and the relationship to the business process on the other. In organizational terms, the relationship to the controller is line-based, the relationship to the process is process-oriented. The combination of line- and process-organizational characteristics maps the purpose of processing.

Essential structure

To map the purposes appropriately, a software program has to make it possible to structure the data in this way. For further information on how to do this in SAP Business Suite and SAP S/4HANA, see Chapter 5.

1.2.2 Data Accuracy: Rectification

As mentioned in Section 1.1.3, personal data must be accurate and up to date. This requirement implies that it must be possible to rectify incorrect personal data. This is generally also possible in SAP Business Suite and SAP S/4HANA.

As a general rule, documents that require proof may not be changed retrospectively. In this case, you can correct the entries by canceling and then reposting.

Incorrect data in business letters

In addition, note that any further data that may have to be retained—for example, in business letters pursuant to the German Commercial Code (HGB)—can only be changed or deleted in our general, lay opinion when the primary obligation to retain data ends.

This means that accuracy of data can be achieved by correcting it manually. This alone isn't enough, however. It's important to make sure that the data is correct and up to date. This can't be achieved by a simple technical solution alone but is subject to organizational measures that can be technically supported. We'll comment further on this in Section 1.3.3.

1.2.3 Data Deletion and Data Blocking

The subjects of data deletion and data blocking are dealt with in more technical detail in Chapter 4. The following section generically explains business consequences and dependencies.

As explained in Section 1.1.8, we assume that data must be blocked that is no longer used for the initial purpose but that still must be retained.

Negative business process

Blocking and deleting personal data can be regarded as a negative business process, which means that the data in its process-related dependency must be blocked and subsequently deleted. Figure 1.6 shows a simplified process.

A customer order and a sales offer are created together. Following this, the accepted sales order is processed, delivery takes place, and ultimately the payment is processed. The assumed negative business process is intended to remove data that was, at some point, once generated in the business process from the system.

Without presupposing or interfering with the customer's assessment, we can still show that it's very likely that data relating to the customer will be generated directly or indirectly at each stage of the process. Accordingly, it would therefore be necessary to delete personal data at each of the process steps described. For the purpose of a clear example, we also assume that we're dealing with one purpose and that uniform retention periods are applicable.

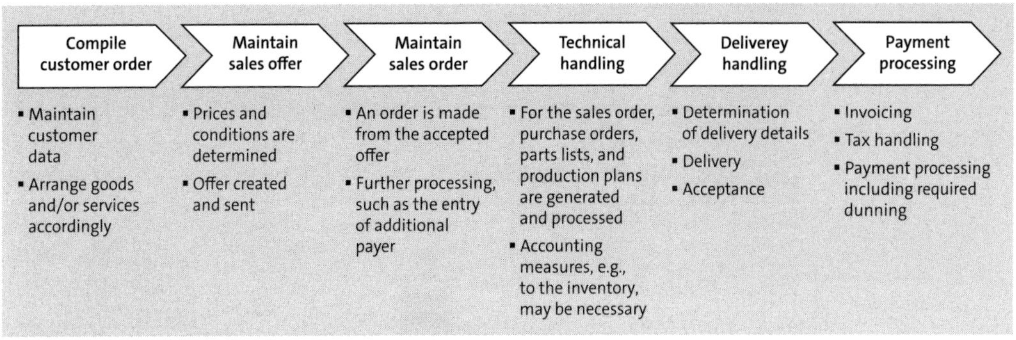

Figure 1.6 A Simplified Process of Data Deleting/Blocking

Integrated perspective

The schematized diagram in Figure 1.7 clearly shows that for partial steps of the process, several different assumptions concerning retention can be made. Our assumptions only represent a small number of the possible assumptions; the assessment must be made for each purpose, process, and retention obligation. The screen assumes that posting documents (e.g., purchase orders or withdrawals) are created in certain steps of the business process. In this case, it's possible to check whether the customers' master record should also be retained for use as an evidence. This is irrelevant, however, if we're solely concerned with the area of business retention obligations. Because customer data and payment processing documents have to be verifiable, the master data can only be deleted after these documents have been deleted. Business letters are different because they can be deleted after expiry of the corresponding retention period.

This schematized view is to be complemented by the question of which further retention periods are applicable. We still remain undecided as to whether there is a conclusive list of all retention periods solely for the Federal Republic of Germany. In the DSAG Working Group on Data Protection (Deutschsprachige SAP Anwendergruppe), attorney Antonio Reschke pointed out on several occasions that more than 1,900 retention regulations were applicable. Naturally, these are based on significantly fewer legal sources.

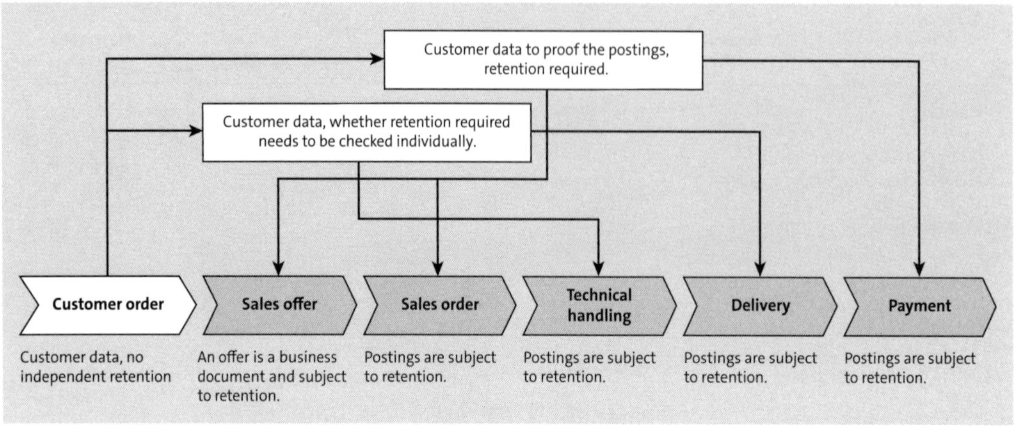

Figure 1.7 Retention Obligation and Dependencies

A legislative nightmare

To understand this nightmare of differing requirements, you should bear in mind that data protection law is, in its essence, a subsidiary right that regulates general circumstances insofar as this isn't regulated by more specific legal provisions. (How this works out in countries outside the European Union is a separate topic that needs to be discussed with experts of legislation in the respective country.) In practical terms, after a purchase has been completed, payment has been received, and all legally required reporting is complete, the data has to be deleted. The more specialized provisions of commercial or tax law do apply here, however: data must be retained accordingly. So much for the simple case! If you deal with goods that are subject to other, more specialized norms, a 30-year storage period may be necessary. If you can prove radiation exposure of your employees in the system, the retention regulations of the German Radiation Protection Ordinance would apply. In this case, this information would have to be retained until employee reaches the age of 75, or at least 30 years after employment is terminated and at the latest until the age of 100 (§ 42 para. 1 Radiation Protection Ordinance – *StrlSchV*). If claims for damages can be filed within the scope of Section 823 of the German Civil Code (*Bürgerliches Gesetzbuch*, BGB), this provision will give you grounds for blocked retention. Project experience shows that simply determining the applicable periods can take up to 12 months.

An administrative nightmare

If you're familiar with the complex system landscapes of SAP S/4HANA or SAP Business Suite, you're probably worried that it won't just be a legislative nightmare. Data blocking or deletion has to be performed in the system landscape consistently. Consistent means both that deletion is carried out in a legally and commercially consistent manner and that it's also technically consistent. From a business and legal point of view, you also have to ensure that all the necessary correlations concerning retention data are available. If, in compliance with the German Radiation Protection Ordinance or X-ray Ordinance, you only store information about the radiation exposure of your employee Timothy Miller, with personnel number 12061975, in connection with the personnel number, but you delete all identifying attributes such as name, Social Security number, and so on in your HR system, you can no longer prove that it was Mr. Miller who was exposed to a certain type of radiation. Technically consistent means that all applications that use that information are unlikely to be able to handle situations where this information is not present.

The nightmare transcends system boundaries

Figure 1.6 and Figure 1.7 illustrate a system-neutral handling of transactions. The previously mentioned problem of consistency can, of course, also be found in system landscapes in which various different software solutions are used for processing. If you complete the steps "Edit offer" and "Edit order" outside of SAP Business Suite, you need to take this into account not only in your concept but also during technical processing.

What's gone is gone!

One of the most interesting moments during such a project is probably the day when the data was blocked or deleted—at that point, specialist departments will realize that "gone" really does mean gone.

[!]

Pay Careful Attention to the Consequences!

Blocking and deleting means exactly that: *deleting* is the irretrievable destruction of information, and *blocking* is the reversible process of removing information that allows only specially authorized persons, such as the tax inspector, to access it. This has a direct impact on all reports that use this data. The data also no longer appears in these reports. Therefore, if you want to perform historical analyses, you must ensure that the data is made available, without personal reference, using SAP BW aggregate and comparable measures.

1.2.4 Technical and Organizational Measures

GDPR only names a few concrete examples of protective measures such as pseudonymization. Further protective measures are presented in §64 of the GFDPA, but in some cases with overlapping and very general descriptions. Most of the technical measures are also relevant to proof of compliance with other legislations, so if you have experience in auditing, you'll be familiar with most of them.

In Figure 1.8, you can see the TOMs of the GFDPA and the exemplary TOMs of the GDPR in conjunction with the technical measures.

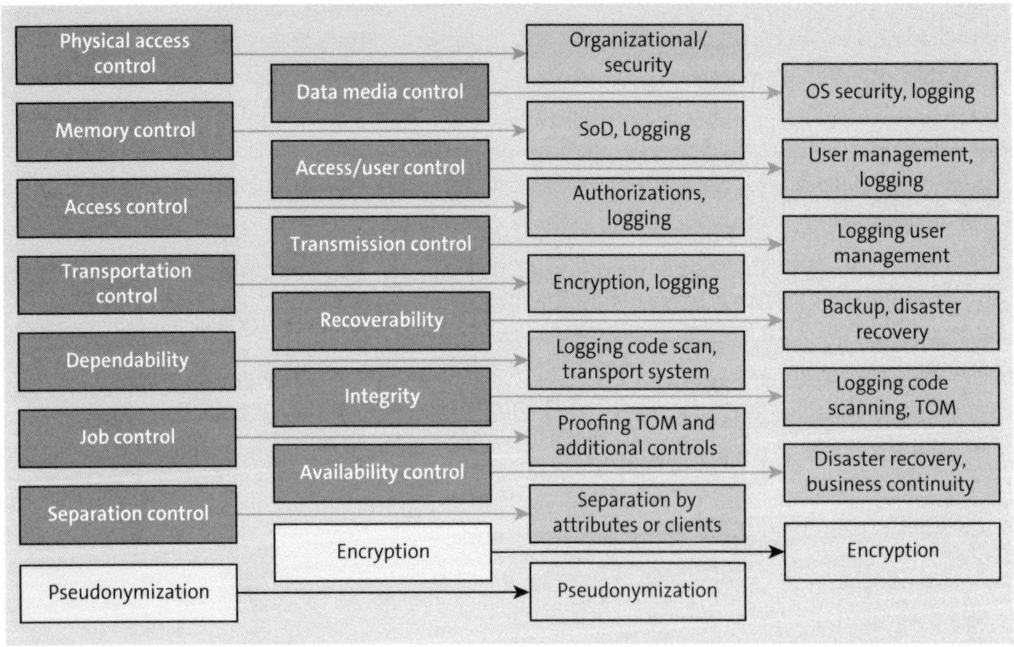

Figure 1.8 German and European TOMs

We'll now take a closer look at the following TOMs of the GFDPA:

- Physical access control
- Data media control
- Memory control
- User control
- Data access control

- Transmission control
- Transportation control
- Recoverability
- Dependability
- Data integrity
- Order control
- Availability control
- Separability

In the following, we'll briefly outline the definitions that will apply in the future. This is because the necessary TOMs have been specified in more detail. However, please be aware that this list may also not be exhaustive.

Physical access control

Unauthorized persons must be denied physical access to the data processing systems. Measures are required to physically prevent access to the zones in which data is processed. In our opinion, these protective measures should include a mandatory printer policy. Access restriction is problematic with mobile devices (e.g., laptops and smartphones). Accordingly, far reaching measures are necessary, depending on the sensitivity of the data, and mobile devices must be protected by conventional measures such as password protection, encryption, and so on. In addition, there is a problem concerning physical interfaces. In our experience, it's quite an exception that USB ports or DVD writers are disabled.

Data media control

Data media control stipulates that data media may not be read, copied, modified, or deleted without authorization. This demand reflects the fact that personal data is not only processed in systems but also stored on data media as part of the processing. It's irrelevant whether the data storage media are connected to a system or whether personal data has been transferred to a USB stick. Data storage media can be encrypted using state-of-the-art technology. They may also be subject to user control and data access control.

[«]

Data Media Control for Whole Systems

In 2016, we were again involved in a debate on whether we could copy an entire system onto an external data storage medium and then transfer it to another organization for the purpose of maintenance/technical fault

> analysis. Without addressing the numerous other related pitfalls associated with data protection law, we don't believe that this approach is feasible without encrypting the data on the data storage medium in such a way that only authorized persons can access the data. In the daily handling of data, however, the case of the nonencrypted USB stick that gets lost somewhere along the way is likely to be a much more frequent occurrence.

Memory control

The purpose of the memory control is to prevent unauthorized persons from submitting, reading, or deleting personal data. This can be achieved by, among other options, separating the database, program, and operating system in such a way that the data can only be viewed and edited by the users of the program in question. This requirement plays a significant role in the processing of an order (i.e., the cloud).

User control

The access to processing systems being used must be restricted to authorized persons. In addition to the allocation of passwords and the use of chip cards, log data of password usage (see Gola, Klug, Körffer, and Schomerus, 2015) § 9 marginal number 23 and other measures concerning password usage are explicitly taken into account (see DSAG Working Group on Data Protection; Carlberg et al., 2014, p. 67). *Single Sign-On (SSO)* is essentially a convenient feature. However, authentication using a (Kerberos) certificate is much more secure than simply using a user name and password with all its drawbacks! We therefore recommend authentication via certificates. For SAP NetWeaver, this means using SSO. If SSO is used, operating system functions such as screen savers must be used with password protection. Because the exchange of user data is one of the biggest problems regarding physical and data access control, we strongly recommend that you check whether a user ID (used in conjunction with the terminal for home workers) of a person on leave is being used. Access control also systematically includes the control of remote function call (RFC) users and a comprehensive RFC policy.

Data access control

Persons authorized formally (organizationally) to use an automated processing system must only have access to the personal data covered by their access authorization and must only access the data for which they are responsible. This involves, among other things, the business authorization concept, that is, the respective implementation of the technical possibilities of the authorization concept. The major challenge here is to provide authorizations in accordance with the minimum or need-to-know principle that are sufficiently restrictive in terms of function and organization. Although problem awareness and a transparent solution with associated and/or structural authorizations are in place in SAP ERP Human Capital Management (SAP ERP HCM), the protection of a lot of data, such as customer and vendor master data, is dependent on the relevant and detailed assignment of attributes. (For further information, see *Authorizations in SAP Software* by Lehnert and Stelzner [SAP PRESS, 2010, *www.sap-press.com/2316*], where you'll also find out more about the difference between the business authorization concept and the technical authorization concept.) For further information about data access control, see Chapter 7.

Data access control: RAL

The read in log should be considered a part of data access control. *Read Access Logging (RAL)* enables the logging of employee read access activities. In the past, the German Federal Financial Supervisory Authorities (Guidance Protocol, 2009) have demanded the logging of reading access for personal data, among other things, as a result of a ruling of the European Court of Human Rights (ECHR judgment of July 17, 2008, I. against Finland [individual complaint No. 20511/03]).

One practical example also illustrates this necessity: At a Hamburg savings bank, it was discovered that accounts held by so-called celebrities were accessed more frequently than could be explained by the purpose of processing. After several investigations, it was discovered that staff members, mostly trainees, had been looking at the accounts simply out of personal interest or pure curiosity. This turned out to be a problem because the employees needed access rights in the event that the celebrity wished to withdraw money at the counter. So how can the misuse of appropriate access rights be prevented? The answer is by logging sensitive data access. The aforementioned logging work aid makes this obligatory, provided that it's also analyzed. Because access logs clearly represent a form of behavioral control—they are supposed to check whether there has been any unauthorized access or attempted access—they are subject to the codetermination rights of the works council in Germany pursuant to Section 87 (1) No. 6 BetrVG (German Works Constitution Act) as well as codetermination principles in other European countries.

Transmission control

Within the framework of transmission control, all possible data communication facilities (technical: interfaces) and all actual communication paths must be documented. To meet this very demanding requirement, SAP Business Suite can be used to transfer data in many ways:

- **Intermediate Document (IDoc)**
  An *IDoc* is a standard format used for electronic data exchange between systems in the SAP Business Suite as well as for sending data to non-SAP systems. IDocs are distributed using Application Link Enabling (ALE) middleware in SAP NetWeaver.
- **Remote Function Call (RFC)**
  In SAP Business Suite, an *RFC* is a standard method for using function modules in a different ABAP system or for opening program elements beyond the scope of ABAP.

[»]

ABAP

ABAP is SAP's own programming language, in which large parts of SAP Business Suite and SAP S/4HANA are written.

- **SAP Landscape Transformation Replication Server**
  The *SAP Landscape Transformation Replication Server* is an SAP system that enables you to replicate data from one or more source systems to one or more target systems. The source systems can be either SAP systems or non-SAP systems.
- **OData services**
  OData services are based on the Open Data Protocol (OData) and are mainly used in SAP S/4HANA.
- **SAP Enterprise Services**
  SAP Enterprise Services are service functions within the framework of Enterprise Service Architecture (ESA) that can allow access to data from different systems.
- **Email**
  A simple email function that can be used to send generated lists from the system is available in SAP Business Workplace.
- **Download**
  A download is the tiresome means for the user to download data from

various places in the system. This option can be disabled. In our opinion, it should also be eliminated in a productive system because downloading the data permanently prevents it from being checked regarding whether it's still being processed for the intended purpose.

- **Fax**
  A simple fax function that can be used to send generated lists from the system is also available in SAP Business Workplace.
- **File-based interfaces**
  File-based interfaces allow data to be downloaded or uploaded in the form of a file with predefined structures. These are supported by different technologies.

Note that these are technical interfaces in a technical system; this system may contain several various procedures with differing purposes. Therefore, you need both a complete inventory of all *possible* routes of communication and a complete inventory of all routes of communication *used*; the latter must be verified in relation to the respective procedures/purposes. In doing so, you must ensure that authorizations for the paths of communication are also restricted in such a way that there is no possibility of use in the scope of another procedure or purpose. The most frequently used automated path of communication is RFC, which enables transfer between different systems. Many clients still lack clarity as to which RFC connections are set up in their productive applications. Furthermore, they are often not adequately restricted. How this can be achieved is described in more detail in Chapter 18 of *Authorizations in SAP Software* (Lehnert and Stelzner, 2010).

Transportation control

The transportation control complements other TOMs by explicitly demanding that unauthorized persons aren't able to access the data during transport or transfer. This can be achieved by means of encryption, secure connections, or checksums.

Recoverability

The paragraph with the clause on data recoverability (§ 64 (3) 9 GFDPA) also provides an explication of obvious requirements. Accordingly, in the event of a malfunction, the systems that were used must be restored. Some traditional measures are mirroring, disaster recovery, backup, and business continuity concepts (see also our comments regarding availability in Section 1.1.12).

Dependability The requirement of dependability included, on the one hand, the *guarantee that all system functions are available and, on the other hand, that any malfunctions are reported* (§ 64 (3) 10 GFDPA). While the first part of this requirement may seem a little strange—no one will question the accuracy of the idea that it's always good when the functions work—the second part, from a software point of view, is highly relevant: suitable functions must be set up to detect and report faulty system behavior and thus achieve the objective of the first part, namely the functioning of the system.

Data integrity For information on data integrity, refer to the comments regarding integrity in Section 1.1.12.

Order control The party responsible must ensure that the contractor meets all requirements.

Availability control Personal data must be protected against accidental destruction or loss. The accidental destruction of data must be prevented at various levels; first, this must also be ensured by means of the business authorization concept. Both the business authorization concept and its technical implementation must ensure that authorizations for any form of mass processing are assigned restrictively; authorizations for operating system commands or access to the file system must also be included. Here, the measures mentioned previously regarding transmission control and physical access control must also be implemented. This should also include measures for the recovery and availability of data. DSAG mentions, among other things, a regular data backup (DSAG Working Group on Data Protection, 2009, p. 69). We would also like to mention the archiving concept; see our comments regarding availability in Section 1.1.12.

Separability The relation between purpose based processing and separability was discussed in Section 1.2.1. The requirement of § 64 para. 3 no. 14 of GFDPA generally continues to hold that data collected for separate purposes must also be processed separately.

1.2.5 Accountability and Auditability

Figure 1.5 in Section 1.1.12 showed you the control circuit (verification circuit). Now we'll discuss the basic control measures that have to be available in the system. We work on the assumption that, in a system audit, fundamental audit procedures are comparable; that is, a business system audit doesn't raise fundamentally different questions than a data protection audit. Both audits must prove that processes can only be performed the way they are defined in organizational terms. Both have to be aware of the risk that code alterations, parameter adjustments, and configuration changes will change or even intentionally damage the process.

Audit: system integrity

The legally compliant processing of personal data is only possible if the system in which the processing takes place is secure. The following, among others, must therefore be verifiable:

- All relevant security patches have been installed for standard software such as SAP Business Suite.
- The only changes that reach the productive system are those that take place within the framework of the processes defined in the organizational structure.
- Program and configuration changes are verifiably logged.
- System parameters that determine system behavior are in accordance with the organizational specifications.
- Changes made to system parameters must be traceable back to the person who made the changes.
- Possible technical interactions with the operating system or database must be defined, and changes to this specification must be verifiable.

Audit: system communication

We've mentioned the security of transfer on several occasions, including in Section 1.1.12 and Section 1.2.4. We've shown that there are numerous routes for data transmission. We've also already discussed the problem that, in many cases, certain systems are often used for several processing purposes. Accordingly, it's necessary to establish a comprehensive and accurate overview of the communication interfaces and to check whether the interfaces can be used only for the related purposes. This also includes checking which privileges can be used for access. In the previously mentioned area of RFC communication, there is often an absolutely inadequate granting of authorizations with almost universal privileges.

Audit: logging

As already explained, changes to personal data have to be documented in a verifiable manner. In Section 1.2.4, we briefly addressed the necessity of keeping reading logs. The BDSG-new additionally stipulates that there must be a reporting system for malfunctions and logging of communications. This obviously leads to numerous requirements for logging:

- Reading log
- Logging of changes made to personal data
- Logging of configuration changes
- Logging of system transports
- Logging of transmissions
- Logging of system events

Based on the audit requirements, it has to be possible to check whether these logs exist, whether they are switched on, and how long the data will be available; the logs themselves have to be accessible.

Audit: authorization system

The verification of authorizations takes on an important role in the data protection guidelines of DSAG (Carlberg et al., 2014), which is reasonable. As already illustrated, authorizations are to be granted based on a strict minimum principle. An audit should examine whether adequate definitions of risk exist and how the risks are to be dealt with.

Audit: blocking and deletion

It's also imperative to check whether data is blocked and deleted. If you're using the SAP concept of simplified blocking and deletion of personal data, the following should be checked:

- Are blocking identifiers set in the master data?
- Is the data archived?
- Is personal data processed beyond the intended purpose of the system?
- Are authorizations to access blocked data sufficiently restricted?
- Have time periods been defined for specific purposes, also taking into account the responsible party?

[»]

Other Methods Are Available

If you use a different blocking and deletion procedure, you need to carry out the relevant checks.

Audit: verification of personal data

In the next section, we'll explain the technical requirements needed to disclose personal data. This possibility is of course also the subject of an audit. The availability of information provides easier access to information such as which personal data in the system network can be processed for which purpose. This verification is not only necessary to satisfy the right to information but also to prove the accuracy of the list of processing activities in accordance with Art. 30 GDPR and to support the requirements of the data protection impact assessment.

Chapter 12 is dedicated to the topic of auditing.

1.2.6 Right of Access

In Section 1.1.6, we discussed the right of access to information in the context of transparency. Art. 15 GDPR requires the following information:

- The data itself
- Information on the processing purpose
- The categories of personal data
- The recipients or categories of recipients and recipients in third countries or international organizations
- Information on retention periods
- Right of rectification, deletion, objection, and blocking
- The existence of a right to appeal to a supervisory authority
- The origin of the data
- Possible automated decision-making, including profiling and information on the type of profiling

This list makes it clear that the disclosure of data itself is the only information that requires a mandatory technical solution; other requirements—such as the right to appeal—are purely organizational in nature, and some requirements should be supported technically.

Information about the data

The simple listing of data isn't enough to provide information. Information that contains Infotype 9040, attribute 42, for example, is completely incomprehensible to the data subject. Recital 39 of the GDPR clearly states that all the data subject's information must be *easy to understand, and that clear and plain language be used*. Art. 12 GDPR also stipulates that all of the data subject's information must be written in a *concise, transparent, intelligible and easily accessible form, using clear and plain language*. Accordingly, the purely technical information has to be translated. Infotype Z4949, attribute 42, might then be translated as special properties and comprehensive knowledge in the example.

Information about the purpose of processing

Information concerning the intended purposes of use isn't necessarily available immediately in the system, but they can be systematically modeled retroactively when the data is processed, as shown in Chapter 5 and Chapter 6. If you use this modeling option correctly, the processing purpose can also be provided technically.

Information on categories of personal data

The GDPR itself only lists personal data in special categories. Because the literature we're familiar with doesn't go into more detail as to the formation of a category, we assume that it's a matter of grouping comparable data into categories in terms of their significance for processing. It might make sense, for example, to form the category "Name information" from the name "Dr. Sarah C. Miller, née Maier-Smith." The option to create and store such categories in the system is desirable, but category formation basically remains an organizational measure.

Information about recipients

The information about recipients is technically more complex. Although partially active interfaces for the transmission of data are provided in the system, from the system's point of view, the recipient is just another system. Downloads, in particular, aren't controllable. Even in the most favorable case, organizational measures must be implemented to meet the request for information.

Information on retention periods

To enter information on retention periods (*envisaged periods* in legal wording), these must be defined in the system for a specific purpose. As described in Chapter 4 and Chapter 6, you specify these deadlines in the system as soon as you're using the SAP approach for simplified blocking and deletion of personal data. SAP also provides functions that centrally provide these periods for specific purposes. If you follow this model, specific periods can be added to the information. If you're pursuing other solutions for blocking and deleting, you'll have to add organizational measures to the periods.

Information that must be organizational

Information on the rights to rectification, deletion, objection, blocking, and the existence of a right of appeal with a supervisory authority is of an organizational nature only. This generally also applies to the origin of the data.

Automated decision-making and profiling

Automated decision-making and profiling represent a technical and organizational challenge. As a rule, the system can't judge whether a decision has been made completely automatically. Although you can provide information about the use of profiles, you have to intervene organizationally because this way of profiling should only be described logically.

Cross-system information?

Information should be available in SAP Business Suite across all applications. SAP also enables you to do this using the information retrieval framework. In Chapter 8, we explain how to connect the systems accordingly. When it comes to data protection, however, it's increasingly clear that SAP Business Suite isn't the only system being used. For this reason, the information retrieval framework provides interfaces that allow information to be supplemented by data from other systems.

Kinds of information actually provided

The information retrieval framework allows you to generate a model of personal data that will be delivered with a sample. You'll have to adapt this model yourself, however. In Section 1.1.1, we already pointed out that you have to evaluate company data to determine which of the data is personal. This also applies in exactly the same way when it comes to the right to information. You also need to assess the extent to which certain technically feasible information interferes with the rights of third parties. In our opinion, the right to information ends precisely at the point where the rights of third parties are infringed. For example, it's probably inappropriate to report the information as to which employee issued a release.

Table 1.4 shows which information can be provided via the information retrieval framework (possible = technically possible; organizational only = not technically supported).

Information According to Art. 15	Information Retrieval Framework
All personal data	Inclusive
Processing purposes	Possible
Categories of personal data	Possible
Recipient or categories of recipients, recipients in third countries and international organizations	RFC interface only
Retention periods	Possible
Rectification, deletion, objection, blocking	Organizational only
Existence of a right of appeal with a supervisory authority	Organizational only

Table 1.4 Scope of the Information Retrieval Framework

Information According to Art. 15	Information Retrieval Framework
The source of the data	Organizational only
Automated decision-making, including profiling	Organizational only

Table 1.4 Scope of the Information Retrieval Framework (Cont.)

1.3 Which Requirements Can Be Technically Supported?

In this section, we'll discuss which functions aren't technically mandatory but can be usefully supported.

1.3.1 Consent

Obtaining consent for processing data is first and foremost an organizational measure. As the basis for processing, however, it has a significant impact on the processing of personal data.

If processing is based on consent, any preliminary information, pursuant to Art. 13 (2)(c) and Art. 14 (2)(d) GDPR, should include a reference informing the data subject of his or her right to withdraw consent.

Furthermore, in many cases, the withdrawal of consent will result in the fact that there is no longer any basis for processing and that the data must be deleted accordingly. In terms of simplified blocking and deletion, this means consent as the basis for processing would have to be verified during the assessment for the expiry of the intended purpose. This logic should also be implemented for transactional data.

1.3.2 Data Minimization

In any event, the most secure kind of personal data is personal data that isn't recorded. In other words, you should avoid storing data simply on the grounds of suspicion. The only data that may be recorded at all is the data that is actually needed for use.

Minimize, remove, delete

Simplified blocking and deletion of personal data has a number of positive effects on data minimization:

- Data that is no longer required to fulfill its intended purpose will be deleted or removed from the system for further storage in accordance with the applicable retention obligations.
- Previous projects are also characterized by a vast amount of faulty data that could have been disposed of.
- This type of blocking and deletion project involves the need to determine the purposes of processing and any retention periods that may apply. This often leads to the conclusion that a purpose can't be assigned: if you don't need it, get rid of it!

Central master data management

Centralized master data management is an integral part of data minimization in SAP Business Suite. This ensures that personal master data doesn't have to be created redundantly and kept synchronously more than once. In Section 1.3.3, we refer briefly to SAP Master Data Governance (SAP MDG), to which we've dedicated Chapter 10.

Minimization via transparency

When the list of processing activities is drawn up (Section 1.3.5), lots of unnecessary data likely will come to light, especially if an inductive route is adopted, that is, when determining from the data. In our proposed procedure for a project (see Chapter 3), we use a step-by-step procedure, starting with the blocking and deletion concept. This approach quickly provides a transparent overview of the relevant data, which is then categorized into a list of processing activities. Let's say you're processing your employees' union membership. When blocking and deleting, you may find that this data is of no use for payroll purposes. This data is included in the information provided, which raises the question as to its purpose. It finally becomes evident that it's data of a specific category, as defined in Art. 9 GDPR, in the list of processing activities. If you haven't yet found a legitimate reason for processing this information, you should keep it out of the record in such a way that you delete it in the original data.

Minimization via organizational instruction

Data minimization isn't just a question of technology. It can also be achieved by means of clear organizational instructions. When using your computer, you'll usually find lots of files and emails containing personal data that you could have deleted a long time ago. This should also be specified in organizational directives. If you often work with data from SAP Business Suite, it's highly likely that you have several Microsoft Excel lists with data that was generated by download. If your organization defines specific expiration dates, for example, downloads need to be updated or deleted after one month or fully processed emails should be deleted after three years, they will be of considerable benefit to the goal of data minimization.

1.3.3 Data Accuracy: Data Management

This requirement can be supported using SAP Master Data Governance (SAP MDG) as a tool. SAP MDG, delivered as SAP ERP business functions, was developed specifically for the creation, maintenance, deletion, and distribution of master data. It also prevents unwanted system redundancies (duplicates) and ensures a consistent synchronization of master data beyond system boundaries. As a core component of SAP MDG, SAP Business Workflow helps to create and manage master data processes. We'll go into more detail on this subject in Chapter 10.

1.3.4 Advance Information

Table 1.1 in Section 1.1.6, compares information and advance information (information about the data subject) with each other, and how the obligation to provide information can be fulfilled is illustrated in Section 1.2.6.

Table 1.5 shows which information can be provided. The advance information is by its nature an organizational measure because it mainly describes future-oriented objectives. Nevertheless, we still assume that providing advance information can be supported. To this end, phenotypic information is generalized and depersonalized, making it possible to obtain advance information using the information in Table 1.5.

Information Pursuant to Arts. 13 and 14	International Retrieval Framework
Processing purposes	Possible
Categories of personal data	Possible
Recipient or categories of recipients, recipients in third countries and international organizations	RFC interfaces only
Retention periods	Possible

Table 1.5 International Retrieval Framework Support for Advance Information

1.3.5 Records of Processing Activities

The record of processing activities includes, as already explained in Section 1.1.14, data that is also relevant in the context of information or advance information. Data fields, categories of data, processing purposes, RFC interfaces, and retention periods can all be transferred from the information retrieval framework to the record of processing activities. The transfer of data fields isn't a special GDPR requirement, but with regard to the records, it does have the advantage of maintaining the connection between "personal data field" and "category of personal data," thus making it possible to verify completeness. If the directory is kept in a system in which additional verification and control options are provided, the transfer of data fields also has the function of documenting the security measures down to the field level and, if necessary, of being able to carry out technical audits.

In addition to SAP Business Suite, SAP offers products from the SAP Governance, Risk, and Compliance (SAP GRC) portfolio that can also be used to create and maintain a list of processing activities as well as the necessary controls.

Procedure: deductive and inductive

There are basically two possible ways of creating such records/directories. At first glance, a deductive approach may seem to be the obvious choice when considering the question of processing purposes for personal data. Deductive means that from an abstract, general perspective of the processes, the purposes, data categories, and communication channels are concluded. We understand that this approach doesn't seem to make sense for existing systems. The method of choice for the completely new introduction of a process would naturally be the deductive method.

The other approach, the inductive method, initially appears to be highly complex, but will prove to be more sustainable, faster, and ultimately cheaper—at least in system landscapes where large amounts of data are processed in SAP Business Suite or SAP S/4HANA—because the existing systems already process personal data. Accordingly, it's important to get as accurate an image as possible and, based on this, to make sure that the verification of processing is added to the directory. With the help of the information retrieval framework, we find this easy to illustrate (see Chapter 8). After it has been set up, the international retrieval framework can provide all personal data relating to an individual. Based on several case examples, you can categorize the data manually. We've also proposed that such categorization should also be made possible in international retrieval framework directly.

1.3.6 Accountability: Compliance Management

As already mentioned on several occasions and illustrated in Figure 1.5, it's not only essential that both the necessary and appropriate measures are taken to safeguard the data subjects' rights and to establish appropriate technical and organizational measures, but you should also be able to provide evidence of these in the future. In addition, you must be able to check them periodically in terms of their effectiveness and suitability, and you must also be able to demonstrate the verification of this review.

Figure 1.9 offers an overview of the necessary measures and supporting features or products. You can use the selectable products without incurring additional license fees. Without these products, for example, the International Retrieval Framework, an operation that is compliant with data-protection regulations would not be possible. Figure 1.9 illustrates the technical and organizational measures in exactly the same way; they serve as core measures and are surrounded by features and products that help implement these measures.

The data subjects' rights and the technical and organizational measures are surrounded by boxes with numbers. The boxes labeled with ❶ represent the solutions for implementing the data subjects' rights:

- **SAP ILM**
  This approach is the cornerstone for the simplified blocking and deletion of personal data and will be dealt with in later chapters (Chapter 4 and Chapter 6).
- **SAP MDG**
  SAP MDG is the solution to help keep data accurate and up to date (see Chapter 10).
- **Information retrieval framework**
  The information retrieval framework was dealt with in Section 1.2.6.
- **Data Controller Rule Framework**
  The Data Controller Rule Framework is used to generate blocking and deletion rules, supplies the international retrieval framework, and is a place to document the attributes for processing purposes (see Chapter 6).

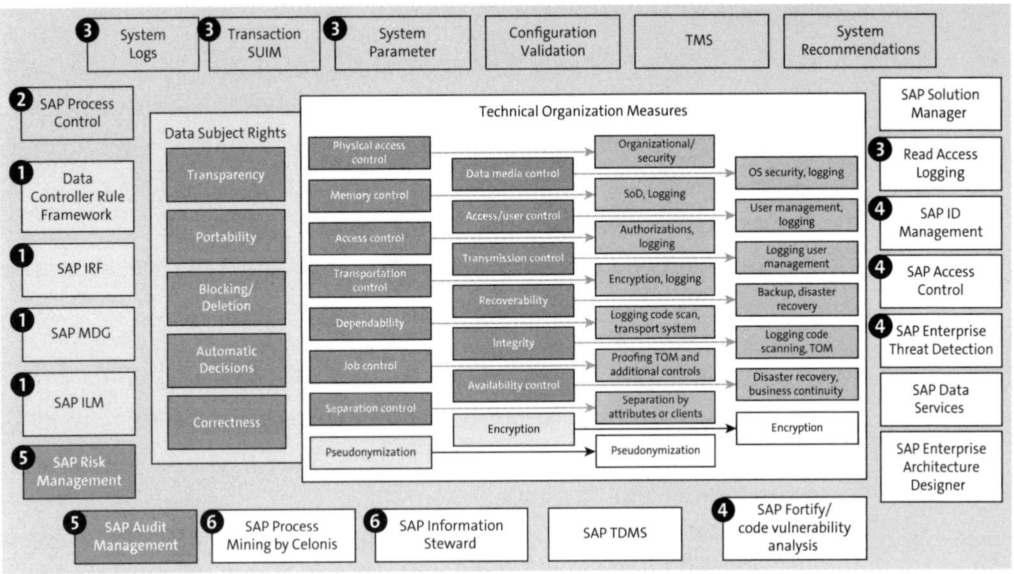

Figure 1.9 Necessary Measures and Supporting SAP Solutions

- **SAP Process Control**
  The solution SAP Process Control ❷ is not only used to fulfill basic documentation and verification obligations but also to automate control activities, that is, system monitoring.

The boxes labeled with a ❸ show the solutions and features that are necessary or supportive in connection with the previously mentioned TOMs. Some of them are outlined briefly here:

- **System logs**
  System logs are an essential part of demonstrating the integrity and security of data processing.
- **User information system**
  The user information system (Transaction SUIM) is where extensive analyses of users and authorizations can be conducted. If you have specific definitions of risk (Chapter 7), you can identify those users with authorizations that give rise to privacy concerns.
- **System parameters**
  System parameters are parameters that you can set and check, for example, to use password rules or tables for logging.

- **RAL**
  RAL enables reading access to be logged and is further described in Chapter 9.

The boxes labeled ❹ offer additional supporting functionality, although only a few of them are specified:

- **SAP Access Control**
  User control with SAP Access Control is much more convenient than with the user information system.
- **SAP Identity Management**
  SAP Identity Management (SAP ID Management) assists in the assignment of users and authorizations throughout the whole system infrastructure and therefore simplifies memory control, for example.
- **SAP Enterprise Threat Detection**
  SAP Enterprise Threat Detection is a solution that enables you to detect external threats in the system infrastructure or to identify potentially problematic employee usage.
- **The SAP Fortify software by Micro Focus/SAP NetWeaver Application Server, add-on for code vulnerability analysis**
  SAP Fortify and the code vulnerability analysis add-on provide a solution that enables you to test your customer-specific code for vulnerabilities. The code delivered by SAP is subject to code scanning by default. These tools add to SAP's efforts toward providing secure code by scanning your own code.

The following comprehensive compliance solutions are also available ❺ as listed in Figure 1.9:

- **SAP Audit Management**
  SAP Audit Management helps you plan, execute, and document audits. This can, of course, also be used in data protection.
- **SAP Risk Management**
  The SAP Risk Management solution can be used both as a central risk management solution for data protection and also as a data protection impact assessment system in accordance with Art. 35 GDPR.

Finally, the following solutions ❻ should also be mentioned:

- **SAP Process Mining by Celonis**
  Based on SAP HANA, SAP Process Mining by Celonis allows the visualization of actual processes across the whole system environment. Non-SAP solutions can also be analyzed.
- **SAP Information Steward**
  SAP Information Steward allows you to analyze data in a complex system infrastructure, even with non-SAP solutions. Data profile and metadata management tools are available that allow you, for example, to find personal data in addition to the ABAP-based information retrieval framework.

[«]

Further Information about Controls and Verification

The subject of controls and verification is dealt with in greater detail in Chapter 12.

1.4 Summary

This chapter provided an overview of data protection requirements and initial information on how to find a suitable solution. As already pointed out at the beginning, this book isn't intended to be the umpteenth (legal) commentary on data protection, but instead to provide you with instructions for the SAP Business Suite and SAP S/4HANA.

We—the authors of this book—have been working together since 2012 to implement data protection features in SAP Business Suite and SAP S/4HANA. In writing this first chapter, we've once again become aware that data protection has to be a coherent concept, starting with process planning together with the associated safeguards and transparency obligations, in order to ensure that data is adequately protected throughout its entire lifecycle until it's finally deleted. The GDPR also significantly reinforces monitoring and verification obligations.

The following chapters will focus on raising awareness and developing a project approach. We'll then go into more detail about several functions that could only be touched on in this first chapter.

Chapter 2
Personal Data in SAP Business Suite and SAP S/4HANA

The widely held opinion that nobody processes personal data outside SAP ERP Human Capital Management is deceptive because personal data is actually processed in many areas of SAP Business Suite and in SAP S/4HANA.

Many, if not most, of the data records in the SAP Business Suite have a direct connection to a person or can be related to a person on a case-by-case basis (see Chapter 1, Section 1.1.1). Master data, such as the central business partner, customer, vendor, and employee, includes, as a rule, identifying characteristics (e.g., names, addresses, and telephone numbers). However, a link to a person may also emerge from a design of master data if the number of individuals related to the master data record is very small. Examples of this include the material that can only be used by one employee or the cost center to which only one person is allocated.

In this chapter, we'll first briefly discuss the difference between master data and transactional data; subsequently, we'll show you how to obtain an overview of the components that are actually used. Finally, we'll provide tangible examples for areas where personal data is processed or can occur.

2.1 SAP Business Suite and SAP S/4HANA Data

SAP Business Suite and SAP S/4HANA combine numerous applications on a common technological basis. The central component in the SAP Business Suite is SAP ERP, which provides functions for the following:

- External financial accounting: SAP ERP Financials (FI)
- Internal financial accounting: SAP ERP Controlling (CO)

- Materials management: SAP ERP Materials Management (MM)
- Sales management: SAP ERP Sales and Distribution (SD)
- Planning and controlling of production: SAP ERP Production Planning (PP)
- Human resources management: SAP ERP Human Capital Management (SAP ERP HCM)

Besides the central component, there are SAP solutions for extensions (called *satellites*), such as SAP Customer Relationship Management (SAP CRM) and SAP Supply Chain Management (SAP SCM). Furthermore, there are industry-specific solutions in conjunction with the SAP Business Suite, such as SAP Policy Management (FS-PM) for SAP for Insurance or SAP Patient Management for hospitals. Even though SAP has checked all solutions within this range and adjusted them to be more data protection-oriented, the sheer number of applications (more than 120) prohibits a detailed description. For this reason, we'll only be focusing on a few examples. Let's start with a general look at the master and transactional data.

Master data relates to the component that uses the respective master data record or provides it for different manners of use. For example, a description of a cost center is logically related to the CO component in SAP ERP. In general, *master data* consists of information that is permanently stored in the system and integrated into business operations. It's created in relation to the organizational levels and based on a sort and control characteristic such as the *material type*, the type of cost center, or the account group.

Interaction of master data and transaction data

Figure 2.1 shows that the master data for **Material**, **Vendor**, **G/L Account**, and **Cost Center** are combined in one purchasing document—in this case, a purchase order. Here, the cost center represents an account assignment object. Master data provides, among other things, the following data:

- **Control keys**
  Control keys are attributes that determine the behavior of the system, for example, when used in the creation of a sales document.
- **Reference data**
  Reference data consists of data records (e.g., quantities or prices) that are suggested when used in a process such as the creation of a sales document.

- **Binding data**
  Binding data (e.g., quantities or prices) is unchangeably applied when used in a process such as the creation of a sales document.

Avoiding redundancy

Master data ensures uniqueness and avoids redundancy. For instance, material doesn't have to be created repeatedly: the pencil will always be the pencil.

When creating a purchase order, reference is made to a variety of master data records that complete many fields of the purchase order with defaults or unchangeable values. Further time-related/case-related data is added manually. After all the data has been entered, the purchase order is created. The system generates a document that includes the master data and case-related data such as date, quantity, and price. Further documents are generated in other modules, and they stay assigned to the respective business transaction. The documents generated this way document transactional data.

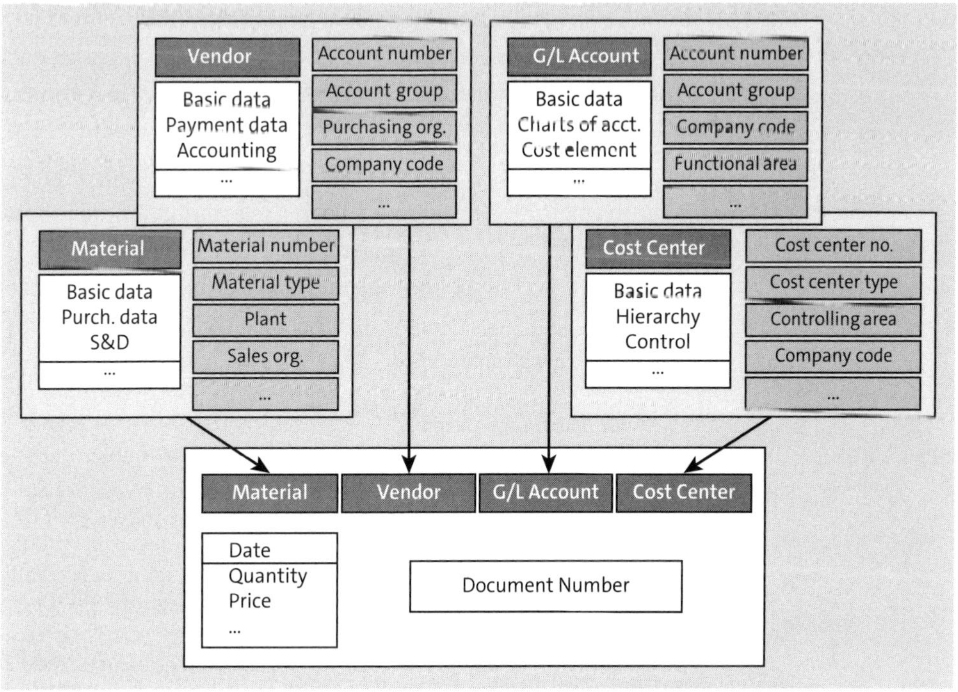

Figure 2.1 Master Data and Transactional Data

Reusability Simply put, master data is permanently stored, reusable data, which often remains unchanged across a variety of applications. Transactional data, however, is created in a process and stored in documents. Figure 2.1 shows the master data **Material**, **Vendor**, **G/L Account**, and **Cost Center**, which are transferred to a document that has a document number.

2.2 Personal Data in SAP ERP

SAP ERP was developed from SAP R/3, which in turn was developed on the basis of SAP R/2. Numerous data protection functions, for example, in authorizations, have been improved over the past decades. SAP S/4HANA continues with these improvements. In the following section, we'll explain central master data.

2.2.1 Business Partner

The *SAP business partner* is a natural person, legal entity, or a group of natural persons or legal entities. The business partner is a central master data record in SAP Business Suite and SAP S/4HANA; it can also be centrally recorded and administered for various business transactions within SAP Business Suite.

One partner, several roles This makes sense wherever a business partner is relevant in different business roles, for example, as an ordering party and as the recipient of goods. For integration in other SAP solutions, predefined interfaces and procedures are available.

Under data protection law, the relevant business partners are those who constitute individual natural or legal persons.

Business partner model The *business partner model* is of particular interest if it's possible that the same person is involved in a variety of roles:

- The customer who is also a vendor.
- The employee who is also a customer.
- The employee who is a customer as well as a vendor.

In this case, the business partner can be assigned different business roles. With regard to the requirement for transparency and for data minimization, this model provides several advantages. After all, the data related to one individual stays interconnected with this individual through the higher ranking abstraction of the business partner with different roles in SAP Business Suite. In addition, redundancy is also kept to a minimum.

[«]

Business Partner

The business partner is mandatory in several SAP Business Suite components and in SAP S/4HANA. In SAP ERP FI, the business partner *can* be used, although it's not compulsory in order to create a debtor or creditor.

2.2.2 Direct Personal Data Records in SAP ERP Financials

Direct personal data is initially included in customers (debtors) and vendors (creditors). Both of these types of data are master data. It's often difficult to distinguish between natural persons and legal entities because one natural person may be "hidden" behind numerous legal entities.

[Ex]

One-Person Limited Company

Common examples are small limited companies in the consulting industry, of which the owner is not only the managing director but also the only employee. A statement regarding the creditworthiness of a one-person limited company is of course also a statement about the natural person.

[!]

SAP Business Suite versus SAP S/4HANA

Please note that creditors and debtors can be created manually in SAP Business Suite. In SAP S/4HANA however, they are created and changed via the central business partner.

Let's first take a look at the *vendor*. You record this centrally through Transaction XK01 (Create Vendor [Centrally]). Restricted creation is possible through Transaction FK01 (Create Vendor [Accounting]) or Transaction MK01 (Create Vendor [Purchasing]). **Vendor**

Figure 2.2 shows several of the input masks in Transaction XK01; Table 2.1 reveals the possible content.

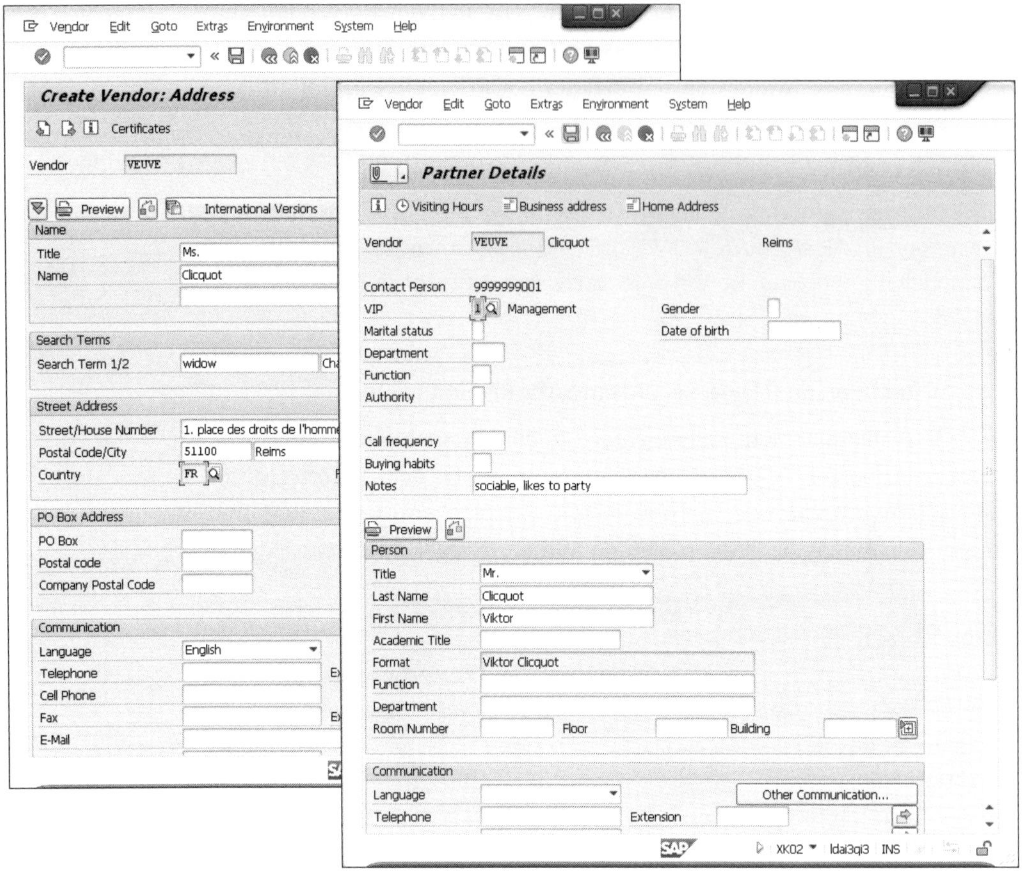

Figure 2.2 Input Masks (Selection) When Creating a Vendor

Input Mask	Specifications Concerning the Creditor
Initial screen	Company code, purchasing organization, and account group
Address	Title, name, search term, street address, and communication
Control	Corresponding debtor, authorization (group), tax information, and reference data
Payment transactions	Bank details and payment recipient

Table 2.1 Data for Vendor

Input Mask	Specifications Concerning the Creditor
Contact persons	First name, last name, telephone, department, function, visiting hours, and partner details, including private address, comments, and buying habits
Accounting info	Account management, interest, withholding tax, and reference data; among others, minority indicator and certification data (pure attributes required by US law)
Payment transactions	Payment data and automated payment transactions
Correspondence	Dunning data, correspondence, and so on, free-text field account notes
Purchasing data	Conditions, sales data (seller), and control data
Partner functions	Customer, goods recipient, goods vendor, invoice recipient, and invoicing party
Additions: text and documents	Free text

Table 2.1 Data for Vendor (Cont.)

Vendor master tables

The data is saved in the following different tables:

- Table LFA1 Vendor Master (General Section)
- Table KNVK Customer Master Contact Partner
- Table LFB1 Vendor Master (Company Code)
- Table LFB5 Vendor Master (Dunning Data)
- Table LFBK Vendor Master (Bank Details)
- Table LFC1 Vendor Master (Transaction Figures)
- Table LFLR Vendor Master Record: Supply Regions
- Table LFM1 Vendor Master Record Purchasing Organization
- Table LFM2 Vendor Master Record: Purchasing Data

As you've seen in Table 2.1, the individual person is described using a variety of data. Accordingly, a detailed picture depends on the use of the input options.

Sensitive information

Parts of this information may—provided the creditor/vendor is a natural person—also be sensitive in terms of data protection. The minority indicator, which is a mandatory characteristic in the United States used to certify the support of minorities, is an example of this type of sensitive information. Further sensitive information might be stored in the available free-text fields (due to ignorance or improper entry). The entry highlighted by a frame in Figure 2.3 is quite common: in many companies, "sociable" is used as a synonym for an alcoholic. Such specifications will turn a free-text field into a data record of a special category pursuant to Art. 9 (1) General Data Protection Regulation (GDPR).

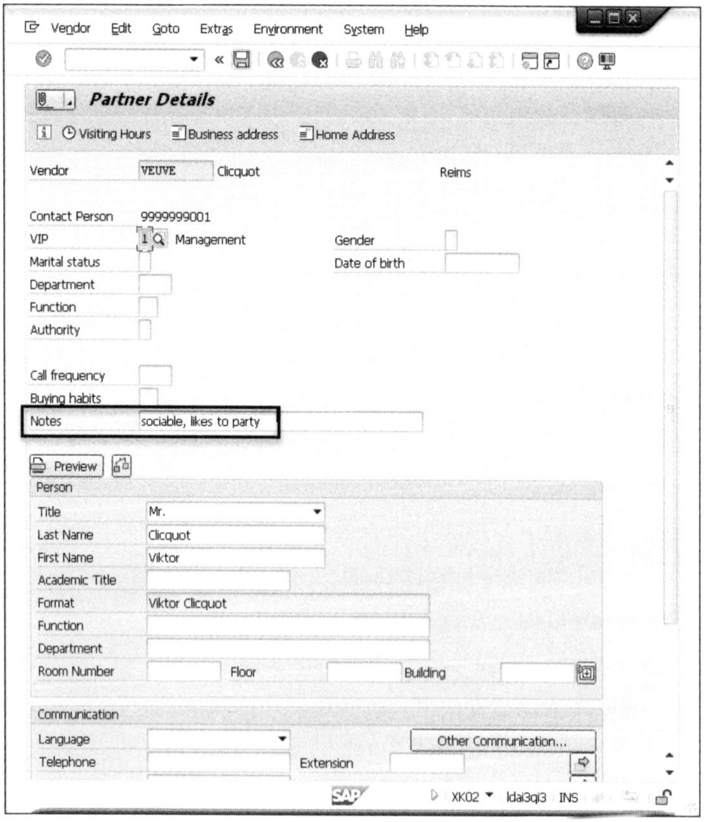

Figure 2.3 Partner Details: Natural Person

In addition to the direct information about the person behind the vendor, further personal information of possible contact persons can be recorded. It's also possible to make judgements, for example, in the **Buying habits** field and **Notes** free-text field, as shown in Figure 2.3.

Minority indicator

The minority indicator is used to qualify a person as a member of a minority. It can be checked through the following path: **SAP Customizing Implementation Guide • Financial Accounting (New) • Accounts Receivable and Accounts Payable • Vendor Accounts • Master Data • Preparations for Creating Vendor Master Data • Define Minority Indicators**.

[!]

No Minority Indicator in EEA Countries!

The minority indicator is a particularity of US law and should under no circumstances be used by companies located in European Economic Area (EEA) countries.

It's possible to restrict access to creditors through authorization groups in such a way that only those clerks who are actually linked to this business process are granted access. The authorization group as a blocking concept is explained in Chapter 4, which will include the introduction of an essential attribute for blocking data.

Customer

Internal *customers*, that is, employees, are also often customers. Customer data regularly includes more information about lifestyle than vendor data. Consequently, access to internal debtors should imperatively be restricted by allocating them to an internal account group. Figure 2.4 shows how to carry out this allocation during the creation process.

On the other hand, protection through an authorization group may also be required (see Figure 2.5). However, this doesn't only hold true for internal customers because it also often makes sense to limit access to customers via authorization groups. The authorization group is an essential attribute for blocking data within the framework of the authorization concept.

The account group and authorization group protective measures use authorization objects in the role assigned to a user.

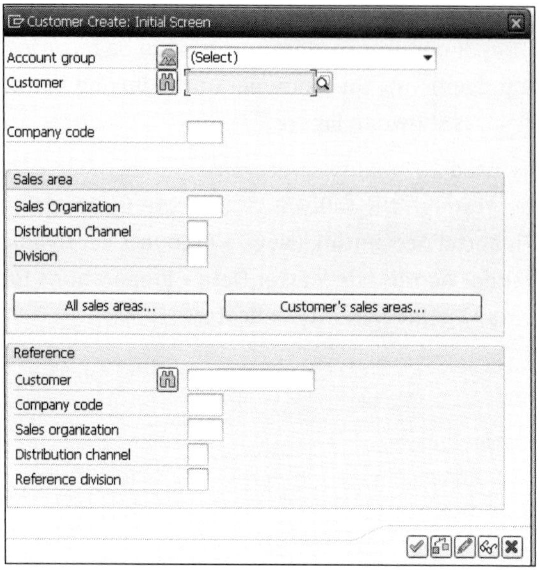

Figure 2.4 Account Group Customer

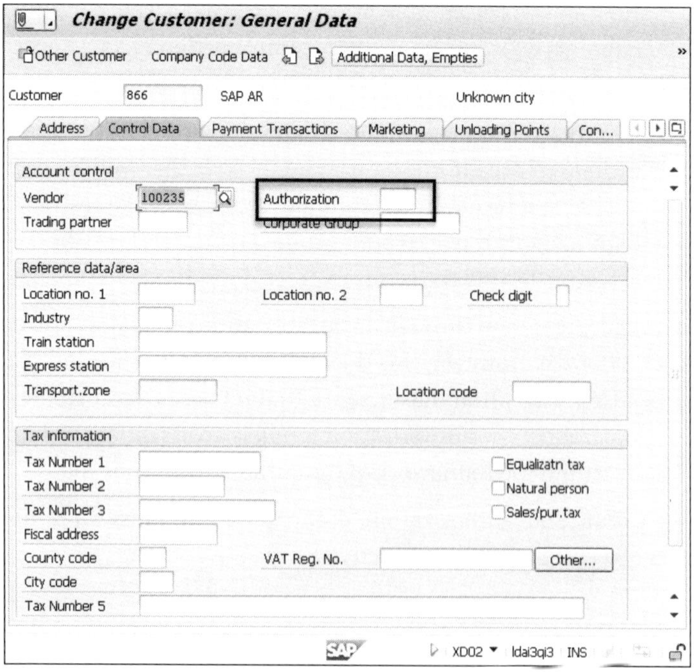

Figure 2.5 Authorization Group Customer

[«]

2

Imperative and Optional Access Restriction

Assigning a customer or a vendor to an account group is compulsory. In standard situations, the assignment to an authorization group is optional. However, this setting can be changed in Customizing.

Both options are frequently used for employees' accounts, but you can also protect other random data this way.

The authorization group is an essential attribute for blocking data within the framework of the authorization concept (see Chapter 4 and Chapter 7).

2.2.3 Further Personal Data Records in SAP ERP Financials

Further data incurring in FI can also be considered personal data on a case-by-case basis. Figure 2.6 shows a report that edits a customer's payment behavior.

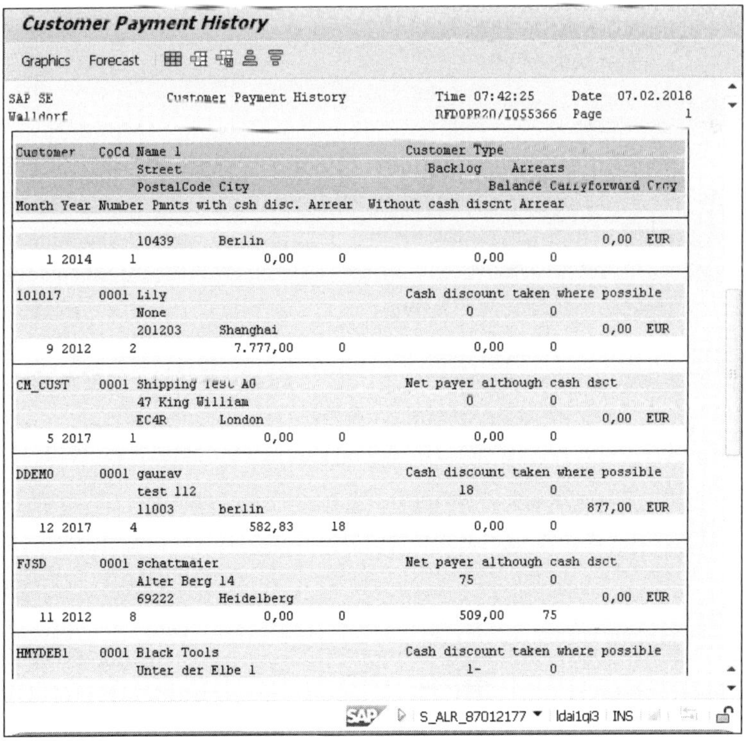

Customer Payment History

Graphics Forecast

SAP SE Customer Payment History Time 07:42:25 Date 07.02.2018
Walldorf RFDOPR20/I055366 Page 1

Customer CoCd Name 1 Customer Type
Street Backlog Arrears
PostalCode City Balance Carryforward Crcy
Month Year Number Pmnts with csh disc. Arrear Without cash discnt Arrear

10439 Berlin 0,00 EUR
1 2014 1 0,00 0 0,00 0

101017 0001 Lily Cash discount taken where possible
None 0 0
201203 Shanghai 0,00 EUR
9 2012 2 7.777,00 0 0,00 0

CM_CUST 0001 Shipping Test AG Net payer although cash dsct
47 King William 0 0
EC4R London 0,00 EUR
5 2017 1 0,00 0 0,00 0

DDEMO 0001 gaurav Cash discount taken where possible
test 112 18 0
11003 berlin 877,00 EUR
12 2017 4 582,83 18 0,00 0

FJSD 0001 schattmaier Net payer although cash dsct
Alter Berg 14 75 0
69222 Heidelberg 0,00 EUR
11 2012 8 0,00 0 509,00 75

HMYDEB1 0001 Black Tools Cash discount taken where possible
Unter der Elbe 1 1- 0

S_ALR_87012177 ldai1qi3 INS

Figure 2.6 Personal Data Record in FI: Customer Payment Behavior

The information displayed is undisputedly personal; it emerges from the combination of master data (customer) and transactional data (documents and invoices).

Reports

Figure 2.6 shows a report in FI, based on Transaction S_ALR_87012177 (Customer – Payment History). Even though there are legal grounds for this report, you should bear in mind that the report contains personal data, which could, in practical terms, lead to misuse.

It's important to note that even transactions of this type contain information considered relevant to data protection, which in turn leads to a corresponding demand for protection.

2.2.4 Employee Data in SAP ERP Financials

Besides the user data (see Section 2.2.5), employees are also often registered as internal customers or vendors. In this case, it's also highly advisable that appropriate protection is in place. This can be established by means of a specific account group and, where necessary, an additional authorization group.

2.2.5 User Data

Document header data

User data related to the person entering data and the person changing data must be added to all of the FI documents. Figure 2.7 shows an example of the entry **Entered by**, which is the recorder's user ID, in a document header. In every company, a number of individuals are involved in further processing, routine or event-driven inspection according to technical supervision or budget responsibility, or other steps of a procedure. These procedures necessitate the identification of the entering user, and accordingly many users will need to be able to view the document header data.

If you're using the concept of simplified blocking and deletion of personal data on the basis of SAP Information Lifecycle Management (SAP ILM), as outlined Chapter 4, the change documents are archived, that is, blocked, together with the transactional data and master data.

We consider this protection measure appropriate because the recording of the data and changes made to it must be as verifiable as the data itself. If the data (or the data stored in the archives) is deleted after expiration of retention regulations, the same will apply for the corresponding change documents.

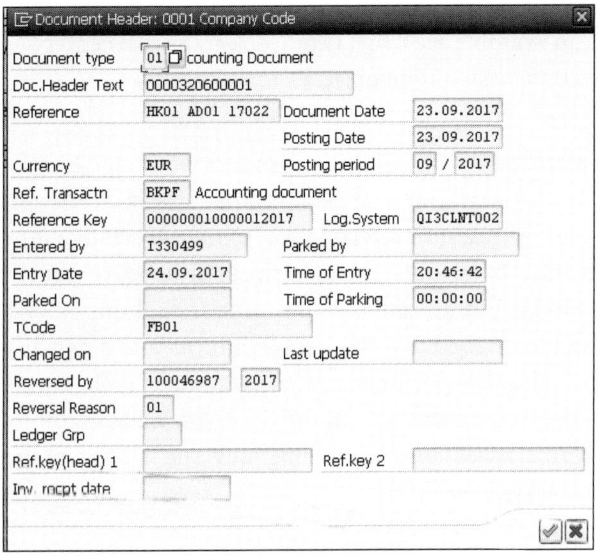

Figure 2.7 Entering User in Document Header

> **Note**
>
> The explanations in this section can be also applied to the CO component as well as SAP ERP HCM.

2.2.6 Direct Personal Data Records in SAP ERP Controlling

There should be little immediately direct personal data in CO. This can be justified both from a business perspective and because the protection of employees' personal data is, at this point, of particular importance. In all cases, the immediate personal data consists of the processing user and the controller, whereby both can be defined in relation to a cost center or a profit center.

Function of CO

As a function of internal accounting, CO initially doesn't follow any regulations relevant to accounting. The company is free to decide on how to organize its own controlling processes. CO provides both account assignment objects and allocation characteristics. It's mostly used to offset costs and services (management accounting) in a preferably cause-related manner so that planning, pricing, and monitoring purposes can be pursued, allowing you to see whether objectives have been achieved.

Account assignment objects

To provide you with an example, we'll first take a look at the cost center and the internal order account assignment objects:

- **Cost center**
  A *cost center* is a permanently stored location of cost incurrence/service provision. It's quite common for cost centers to be based on the line organization of the company; that is, one cost center generally corresponds to one organizational unit. From a business perspective, usually more than one individual is assigned to an organizational unit. If only one individual can be assigned to a cost center, it turns into a personal data record of an immediate personal nature. Even worse is that every single posting in this cost center will, in turn, automatically become a personal data record. Consequently, assigning only one individual to a cost center should be avoided entirely.
- **Internal orders**
  Internal orders are temporary cost collectors; the classic example is a trade fair order. Those internal orders are—commonly—handled in a similar way to projects and allow for a supplementary and thus more exact reporting in relation to the cost centers. However, creating internal orders on the basis of personal data should also be avoided wherever possible.

2.2.7 Indirect Personal Data Records in SAP ERP Controlling

Indirect personal data records may be related to an individual due to the information they contain. This is of great importance, first and foremost, in reporting.

Controlling reports

A variety of information that may include the reference to a person is processed in a typical *controlling report*. The reporting Transaction S_ALR_87013611 (Cost Centers – Actual/Plan/Variance) identifies the incurred and planned charges and credits of a cost center in conjunction with the actual costs (primary costs) and plan costs (secondary costs). Figure 2.8 shows the part of the report that identifies the costs, including the secondary costs (e.g., for services received).

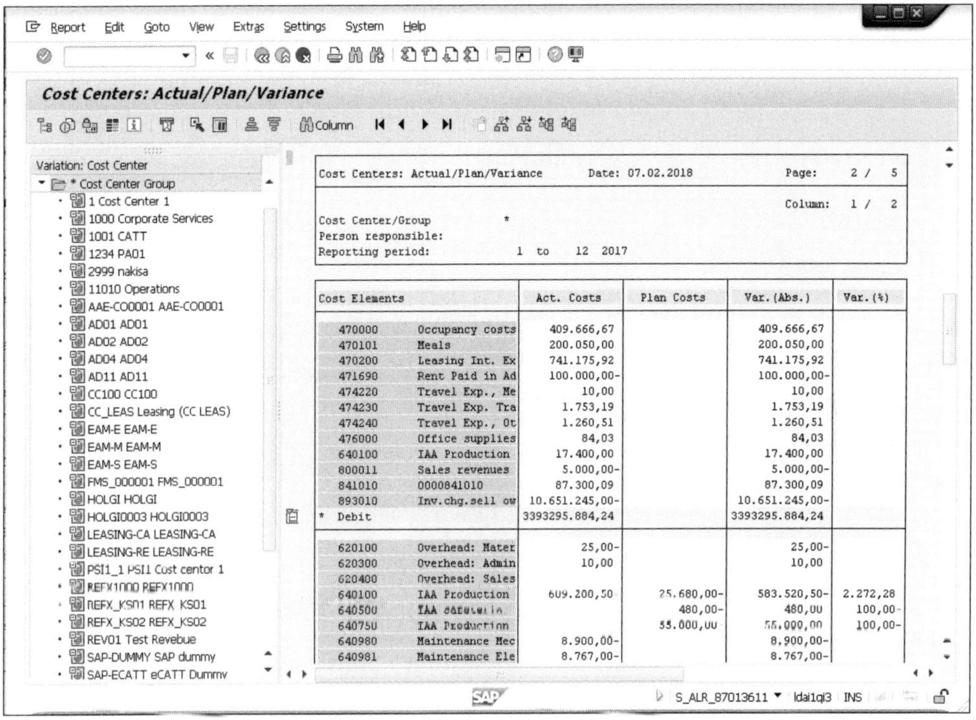

Figure 2.8 Report Cost Centers: Actual/Plan/Variance

Statistical key figures and activity types are shown, among other things, to provide a better explanation. With the cost center, the statistical key figure, activity type, primary costs, and secondary costs, there are already five types of data that may be a personal data record in conjunction with others (e.g., cost center and service type). Activity types and statistical key figures are included in the same report in Figure 2.9. In our example, these are the hours of repair.

[Ex]

Indirectly Obtained Data Record

Imagine, for example, a cost center in SAP ERP Plant Maintenance (PM) with the activity types "Project Lead hours," Engineering hours," and so on. If only one engineer has been assigned to the cost center, and if only this engineer is permitted to post services within it, the identification of activities (e.g., 10 hours) or the identification of a plan deviation is then a direct personal data record that needs to be protected accordingly.

Cost Centers: Actual/Plan/Variance   Date: 07.02.2018   Page: 5 / 5

Column: 1 / 2

Cost Center/Group *
Person responsible:
Reporting period: 1 to 12 2017

Activity Types	Act. Acty	Plan Acty	Var.(Abs.)
EAMTM EAMTM		100.000 H	100.000- H
EAMTS EAMTS		1 H	1- H
LAAD01 LAAD01	282,00 KG	240,00 KG	42,00 KG
LAAD02 LAAD02		120,00 KG	120,00- KG
LAAD07 LAAD07			
LAAD21 LAAD21	100,00 KG		100,00 KG
MAINTL Maintenance Electric	79,7 HR		79,7 HR
MAINTM MAINTM	89,0 HR		89,0 HR
PCK001 (Packing)			
REFX Production hours		30.000,0 HR	30.000,0- HR
TM-IH1 TM-IH1	1,0 HR	1.200,0 HR	1.199,0- HR

Figure 2.9 Report—Cost Center: Actual/Plan/Variance: Activity Types

Accordingly, you need to consider that cost centers and other account assignment objects are assigned to many individuals. This means that conclusions about individuals are inhibited via activity types or statistical key figures. In any case, without the use of additional available data, it isn't possible to draw a conclusion.

Salary specifications

In Germany, it's customary to identify *salaries* in the cost center as average rates per pay scale group rather than actual costs, provided they are recorded in different pay scale group-specific accounts. This means that it isn't the salary (which usually has individual shares) but the average salary of a group with the same qualification that is reported. As a result, as far as the actual amount of salary is concerned, the personal reference will be lost.

While there is a solution for salaries, this is rather difficult for *activity types* (e.g., engineering activities). In the sense of a cause-related assignment, the information is significant as to whether an engineering activity or a project management has been performed.

Possibility of person-related conclusion?

It must therefore be checked whether the activity types performed by a cost center allow conclusions to be drawn about an individual person. If this is the case, the assignment of authorizations for access to this cost center should be restrictive.

2.2.8 Reporting Tools in SAP ERP Controlling and Customer-Specific Reporting

Report Painter/ Report Writer

In addition to many standard reports, CO also offers extensive possibilities for your self-defined reporting. You can easily create your own reports using the *Report Painter* and the *Report Writer*. Report Painter and Report Writer reports are protected by the standard authorization concept.

Easy but critical

However, because their creation is so easy, new reports can be created that may be considered questionable under data protection law. To ensure that this remains data-protection compliant, you should ensure that all reports and analyses based on your data protection concept are created exclusively in the development system and—only then—transported to the production systems. This is necessary because, among other things, the possible access to data and therefore each executed transaction or report must be defined in advance. A free combination of data in a report created by a user in a productive system can't meet this stipulation.

In addition to the options provided by reporting tools, many companies use customer-specific reports to enable evaluations. In terms of data protection, note that customer-specific reports must be subject to at least comparable protection by authorizations.

2.2.9 Direct Personal Data in SAP ERP Sales and Distribution

In the preceding sections, you've already familiarized yourself with direct personal data in SD. This involves both the business partner with all the related contact persons, if any, and the debtor.

Contact person

To sensibly take care of a customer, contact persons, in addition to the customer himself (often a legal person), are usually recorded for the customer. In some cases, as you can see in Figure 2.10, qualifying characteristics are also collected for contact persons. Therefore, personal data is formally processed to a not inconsiderable extent.

Different personal information relating to the contact person (natural person) can be stored. Depending on the permitted attribution, these can also be delicate or—in the legal sense—sensitive in character. The screen marked ❶ in Figure 2.10 allows you to enter a private address and contact details. In addition, you can enter comments in a free-text field ❷. Under **Additional Data** ❸, attributes can be maintained, depending on the definitions in Customizing. The example in Figure 2.10 concerns the issue of trade unions and similar interests, if the attributes are maintained accordingly.

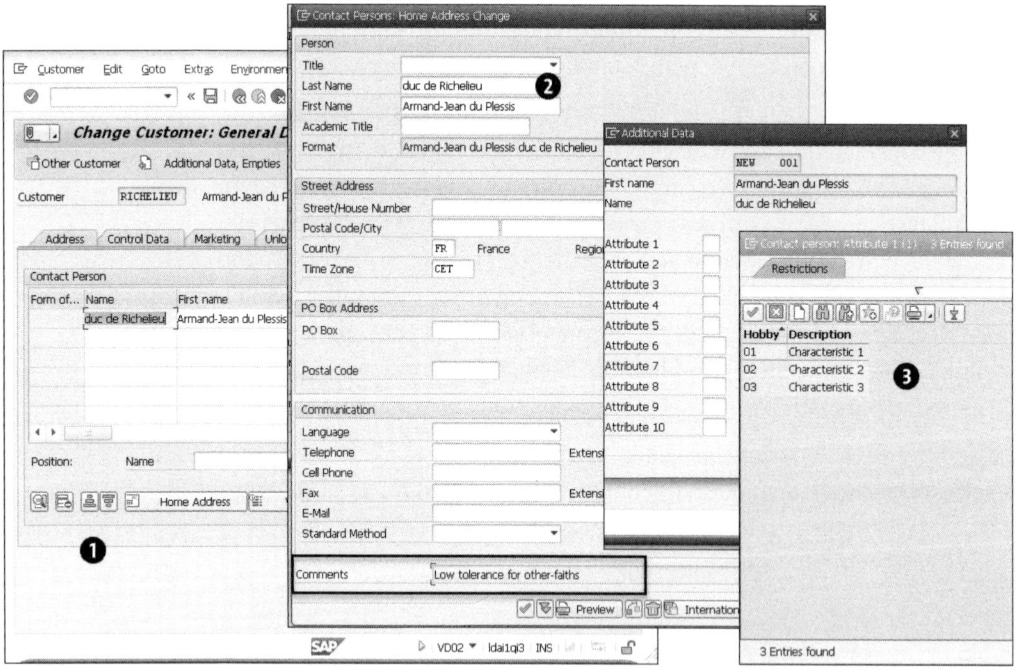

Figure 2.10 Contact Person's Data in Conjunction with Customer

Independent of contact person the maintenance

The main difference to the creditor is likely to exist in relation to the end consumer, at least in cases where the debtor is a natural person and consumer. In some exceptional cases, it may even be required to record sensitive data.

Health care customers, medical aid manufacturers who receive customized manufactured remedies, and severely disabled people who need a special car are all cases that may justify the collection of sensitive data. In these cases, you must first check how much data is required for contract processing accounting. Furthermore, this data must be protected separately, which is possible via configuration.

2.3 Personal Data in SAP ERP HCM

The processing of personal data in HR systems is sufficiently obvious. In this section, we'll provide transparency on the data types and structures, as well as explain the infotype concept.

2.3.1 Types of Personal Data

SAP ERP HCM processes data from individuals who may have different relationships with the company:

- Employees
- Applicants
- External employees or external service providers
- Users of the SAP ERP HCM application

At this point, let's consider the terms used in connection with SAP ERP HCM, which we'll also use repeatedly in the following sections.

Infotypes

Master data for human resources is stored in *information types*, also referred to as *infotypes*. Infotypes can consequently contain personal and organizational data and represent a bundling of similar data fields according to HR criteria. An infotype is always identified by a unique four-character key. For example, you can find personal data in Infotype 0002, basic pay in Infotype 0008, and absences in Infotype 2001. Infotype 0002 (Personal Data), for example, consists of the **Name**, **First name**, and **Date of birth** fields.

Infotype namespaces

The four-character keys of the infotypes are divided into different namespaces:

- 0000–0999 and 3200–3999: Master data
- 1000–1999: Planning
- 2000–2999: Time management
- 4000–4999: Applicants
- 9000–9999: Reserved for customer-specific infotypes

Country specifics

In addition to the generally valid infotypes, such as Infotype 0002 (Personal Data), there are country-specific legal requirements that are also mapped using infotypes.

[Ex]

Information Relevant to Social Insurance

Examples of the various infotypes used for entering information relevant to social insurance per country include Infotype 0013 for Germany, Infotype 0044 for Austria, and Infotype 0036 for Switzerland.

For each infotype defined in SAP ERP HCM, there is a corresponding infotype table in which the infotype data and technical entries, such as keys, are stored. The data stored for Infotype 0002 (Personal Data) can be found in table PA0002.

Storage in tables

SAP ERP HCM master data is usually stored in tables PA*; in addition, tables PCL* (SAP ERP HCM cluster tables) and tables HRP* (staff planning, e-recruiting) are also relevant. Data related to the older staff recruitment are located in tables PB*. With the newer releases of SAP ERP HCM, these boundaries can no longer be clearly defined.

[»]

Note

For a detailed overview of the HR tables, see the ABAP Dictionary (Transaction SE12).

Infotypes are maintained depending on the SAP ERP HCM component to which they will be assigned. HR master data is maintained using Transaction PA30 (Maintain HR Master Data). See the example shown in Figure 2.11.

Time constraint

In principle, time-dependent storage is available for all infotypes, making it easier to evaluate historical data. SAP ERP Personnel Administration (PA) distinguishes between different classes of *time constraint*, depending on whether one or more data records can exist at the same time.

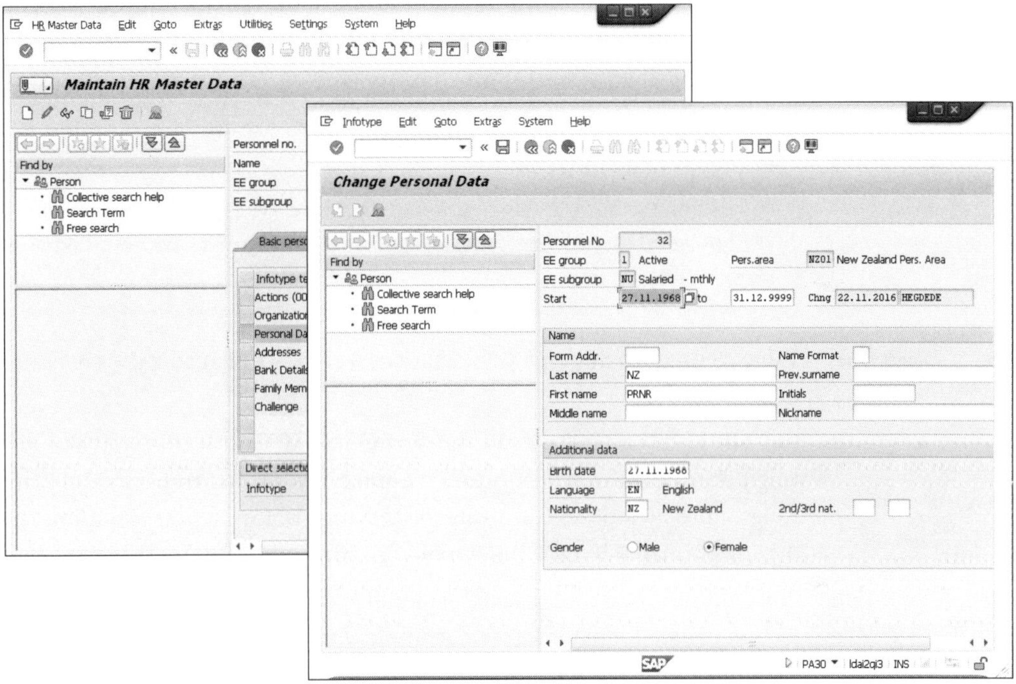

Figure 2.11 Maintaining Infotype 0002 with Transaction PA30

Free-Text Fields

Within the infotypes, user-defined text fields are allowed that enable uncontrolled entry of information and thus also personal data. From a data protection perspective, this option must be assessed as critical and regulated. If free-text fields are used, the entry should be limited in time and, for example, organizationally limited to the purpose-related or factual information.

2.3.2 Info Subtypes

In SAP ERP HCM, infotypes are subdivided into even smaller units called *info subtypes* or *subtypes*. Subtypes are mainly intended to enable the implementation of various control characteristics within an infotype. Control characteristics are, for example, the time constraint described previously as well as the control of authorization access. An infotype can therefore be divided into different subtypes.

[Ex]

Infotypes and Subtypes

For example, the following subtypes (absence types) exist for Infotype 2001 (Absences): Absence, Illness, Desc. Illness, and or Sick without Certificate.

Object types

Table T591A (Info Subtype Characteristics) shows which subtypes exist for an infotype.

SAP ERP HCM Organizational Management (OM) in SAP ERP HCM also distinguishes between *object types*. The infotypes related to personnel planning and development are categorized into object types, including the organizational unit (O), employment (C), position (S), and person (P).

Plan variant and planning status

The *plan variant* is also used in personnel planning to define a specific collection of data for planning. For example, you can use planning to calculate the effects of a planned increase in personnel. You can map several plan variants with different data separately. The relevant objects also have one of the following *planning statuses*: **Active**, **Planned**, **Requested**, **Approved**, or **Rejected**. If you're dealing with future-related personnel planning, these plans must be particularly protected.

Overview of the stored data

Report RPDINFO1 provides you with an overview of the infotype structures available in SAP ERP HCM, as well as the infotypes for which data records exist (see Figure 2.12).

The evaluation clearly displays the relevant information for the existing infotypes. The system displays statistics on the infotypes obtained (the values in the **Infotypes Determined** column); all infotypes are displayed separately with their subtypes and the corresponding number of data records for employee data and applicant data. The underlying table and its table authorization group are displayed as additional information.

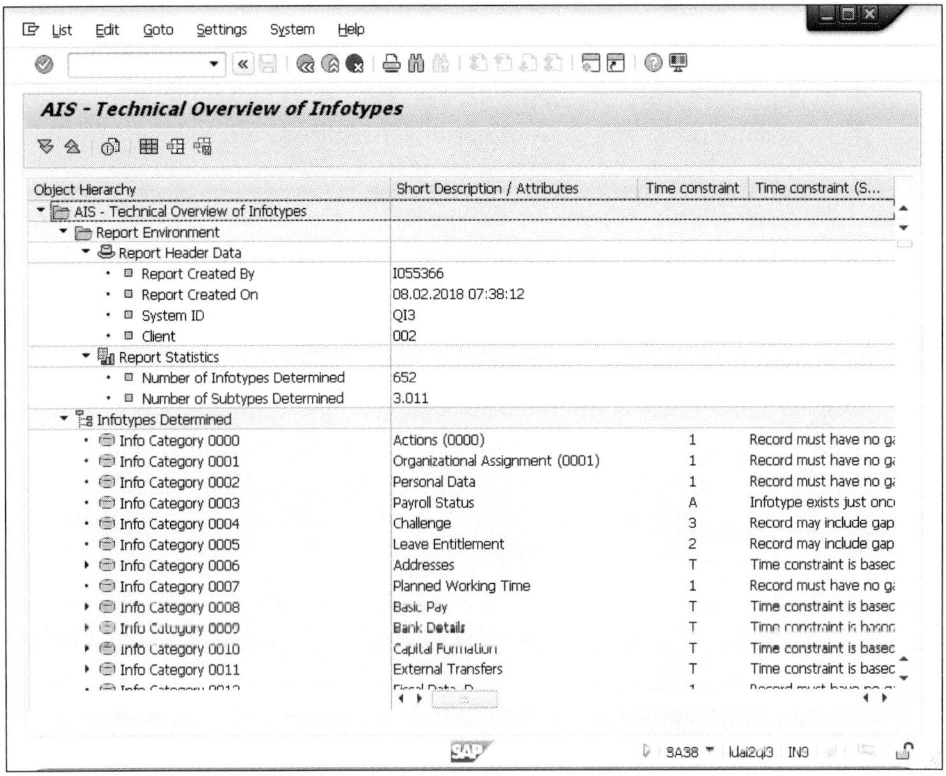

Figure 2.12 Sample Evaluation of Report RPDINF01

> **Report RPDINF01: Technical Overview of Infotypes**
>
> Report RPDINF01 displays the personal data that is actually available in a specific client at a certain point in time in SAP ERP HCM. This is carried out by displaying the infotypes used, their subtypes, and the number of data records stored for each info record. You can't view the personal data itself with this report.

2.4 Personal Data in SAP CRM

Our assumption is that the data processing of customers will become particularly important when the GDPR comes into force. Accordingly, in the following section, we'll discuss personal data in SAP CRM.

2.4.1 Business Partners as Master Data

All persons and organizations involved in business processes in SAP CRM are mapped as business partners. Business partners are therefore persons, organizations, or groups of persons in which a company has a business interest (see the SAP online help and the glossary here).

Role of business partner

Because business partners can appear in different roles (e.g., , as an organization, ordering party, contact person, or employee), these exact roles are also mapped as *business partner roles* in SAP CRM. The business partner role thus defines which rights and obligations a business partner has in a business transaction in the SAP system.

Type of business partner

Business partners are stored in different *business partner types*, which specify whether the business partner is mapped as a person, organization, or group in the SAP system. Business partners can generally occur as follows:

- **Account**
  An account corresponds to a company, person, or group with whom you have a business relationship. Accounts include, for example, vendors, prospects, ordering parties, ship-to parties, consumers, or sales partners as channel partners.
- **Contact person**
  Contact persons are people in companies with whom you maintain business relationships. The contact person is usually assigned to the company via a business partner relationship.
- **Employees**
  The business partner in the business partner role of the employee corresponds to the employee in your company who fosters or initiates business relationships with customers, vendors, or ordering parties. However, in the case of a shared service center, the employee can also be treated as processor and requester.

These business partner roles, which are available in SAP CRM as in SAP ERP, can be enhanced either as an individual industry solution or with customer-specific requirements. Business partners in SAP CRM include further information in addition to the business partner role.

Business partner relationships

Business partner relationships define the type of relationship between two business partners. Relationships may be assigned properties, such as a company address. Figure 2.13 shows different types of business partners and the possible relationships between them. This means, for example, that an employee in the company is maintained as the employee responsible for a particular customer. As a result of this relationship, the employee responsible is also maintained in all business transactions related to the customer.

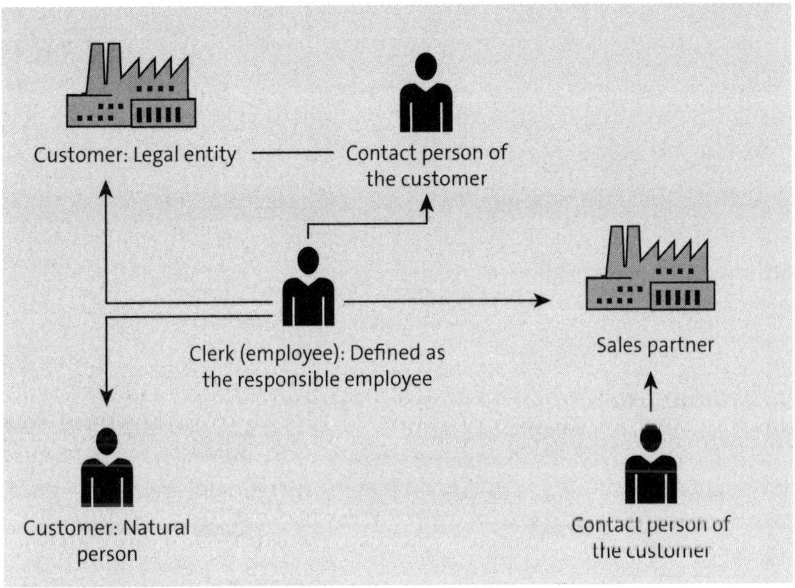

Figure 2.13 Types of Business Partners and Their Relationships

Attributes for classification or marketing

Business partners in SAP CRM can also be assigned *classification* or *marketing attributes*. These are freely definable criteria for categorizing a business partner. The categorization can be used for segmentation or, in certain marketing activities, for target group definition of business partners in marketing.

Contact details

You can maintain addresses for different address types for each business partner. For example, you can distinguish between the invoicing address and the delivery address. You can also maintain general data for each business partner, such as the types of communication you may use to contact the business partner.

Archiving

To determine whether a business partner is no longer valid for business transactions, you can flag it for archiving. This business partner can subsequently be archived and deleted from the database.

You can maintain sales area data for a business partner to determine the sales area for which its business transactions are to be created. These include information on the sales organization, division, and distribution channel.

Another functionality for the business partner is the *information sheet*. All information on the business partner is displayed in a summarized form on the information sheet. This may be general information on the business partner, business transactions, or information from connected systems. The business partner can download the information sheet in a PDF so that it can also be made available offline.

History of changes

All changes that affect the business partner are logged in change history. To restrict access to business partners using authorizations, you can create authorization groups in Customizing and subsequently assign them to the business partner.

2.4.2 Transactional Data of Business Partners

Mapping business processes

Transactional data maps business transactions in SAP CRM. These refer to certain master data, such as customers, prospects, and products. In SAP CRM, transactional data may be, for example, activities, customer and service orders, leads, sales opportunities, or invoicing documents. This data can be clearly assigned to a customer. We'll now show you the typical information that is stored in the respective business transactions.

Transactional data contains, for example, information about a product that is the subject of the business transaction, including product details and the price of the product. This information is relevant for carrying out the subsequent processes in SAP ERP, such as invoicing or shipping the product.

Furthermore, all parties involved—the customer, the contact person at the customer, the employee responsible for the process, and possibly other employees working on the process—are assigned to the respective business transaction.

A document can be assigned to a sales organization and contain additional information in the form of notes or attachments.

2.4.3 Data Exchange with Other SAP Systems

Data can be exchanged with different backend systems in a variety of business areas in SAP CRM. Typical cases are the exchange with SAP ERP and SAP Business Warehouse (SAP BW).

SAP ERP

Business partner data and documents are usually replicated in SAP ERP as soon as a potential customer (prospective customer) has become a customer with an associated sales offer and customer order. SAP ERP is usually the preferred system for customer data because payment processing also takes place there. The maintenance authority for the customer is then also in SAP ERP. When business partner data is replicated, business partner fields, such as **Business Partner Role**, **Name**, **Address Details**, and **Business Partner Relationship**, are also transferred.

The data from SAP CRM can also be transferred to SAP BW. In SAP BW, reports can be created using SAP CRM data to check, for example, which products are sold the most or what the anticipated sales pipeline for the next quarter looks like.

Business Planning and Simulation

The planning tool Business Planning and Simulation (BPS) can be used to execute planning with such data. BPS is part of SAP BW and can be fully integrated with SAP CRM. It will be prompted automatically on the user interface of the SAP CRM Web Client when you start key figure planning in SAP CRM, although it does run in a different system.

2.4.4 Report Options for Business Partners in Marketing

To conduct personalized marketing activities for business partners, as much information as possible must be collected from customers.

Marketing attributes

Business partners can be filtered according to certain criteria and divided into target groups. These criteria are, for example, the age of the customer, occupation, income, and hobbies. They are defined using *marketing attributes* that can be freely defined by the marketing manager. These marketing attributes and their values are then ready to be assigned to the business partner. Marketing attributes are structured so that all attributes are collected in one attribute group. This attribute group contains various attributes to which values are then assigned in the business partner. This group can now be assigned various attributes, such as **Hobby**, **Salary group**, and so on. The values can also be determined in advance.

Target groups The user then selects, directly from the customer, the marketing attribute **Hobby** and can also add default values from a list. These values can be used to create target groups for customer-specific marketing activities. This marketing activity is, for example, the sending of product recommendations to special customer groups that have been identified via the target groups.

2.5 SAP Business Suite Technical Integration Example

Business partner search The aforementioned integration of numerous applications in SAP Business Suite results in highly configurable integration scenarios. An abstract understanding of these is crucial because numerous processes in such a system landscape run across several instances that are only technically connected via interfaces. These integration scenarios can also only be depicted as examples.

Master data, such as that of business partners, is used in all business areas. The business partners are linked to all business transactions and can be filtered using marketing attributes for target group selection in the marketing environment. These marketing attributes in combination with the target group selection can be used, for example, to find out which customers should be sent newsletters based on their hobbies. The customer's hobby could be stored in the marketing attribute. This attribute value (e.g., soccer, sailing) is assigned to the customer. Using the target group selection, all business partners who are enthusiastic about the same hobby can now be filtered and sent personalized newsletters.

By default, SAP CRM runs in conjunction with several SAP applications, such as SAP ERP or SAP BW. This means that business partners and their documents from SAP CRM can be replicated via SAP CRM middleware, for example, in SAP ERP.

SAP CRM middleware With *SAP CRM middleware*, it's possible to replicate, distribute, and synchronize data from and to several applications. Business partners, objects for pricing, sales and service orders, and billing documents can be exchanged via middleware. This data exchange can also be performed with non-SAP systems. The order is then replicated in the SAP ERP system in which delivery and payment processing takes place. A prerequisite for payment processing is that not only the order but also the business partner is replicated between the SAP CRM system and SAP ERP. The protection of data must therefore also be considered and guaranteed beyond system boundaries.

2.6 Summary

In SAP Business Suite and SAP S/4HANA, personal data can be verified in numerous locations. From a data protection law perspective, the interaction of master data and transactional data must be considered particularly carefully. In this chapter, we've given you an exemplary overview to help you address such issues for other applications.

Chapter 3
Implementation Approach

With the challenges and consequences of the GDPR in mind, many customers may wonder whether the legislature is serious about the newly introduced regulations. After all, the effort and expense involved in turning systems that aren't in compliance with data protection regulations into systems that do comply with data protection regulations is huge—and this applies to most systems.

The implementation of the requirements described in Chapter 1 is an extensive project. In Chapter 1, Section 1.2.3, we describe blocking and deleting as a negative business process.

In this chapter, we work on the assumption that most customers need to implement data protection compliance into their systems from scratch. If this is the case, you're at the very beginning of a project that will take over a year and require thousands of working days. In this chapter, we'll provide you with a detailed explanation of how to do this.

The chapter provides an introduction to our implementation approach, which should make it easier for you to carry out your project in consecutive steps. It also enables you to benefit from the preceding steps at all subsequent stages.

3.1 Project Implementation Steps

In this section, we'll briefly guide you through the steps we recommend when implementing the project.

The measures to ensure that your SAP system complies with data protection requirements, as outlined in Figure 3.1, depend on the risks and the processing purpose that has been set up for the information in the system.

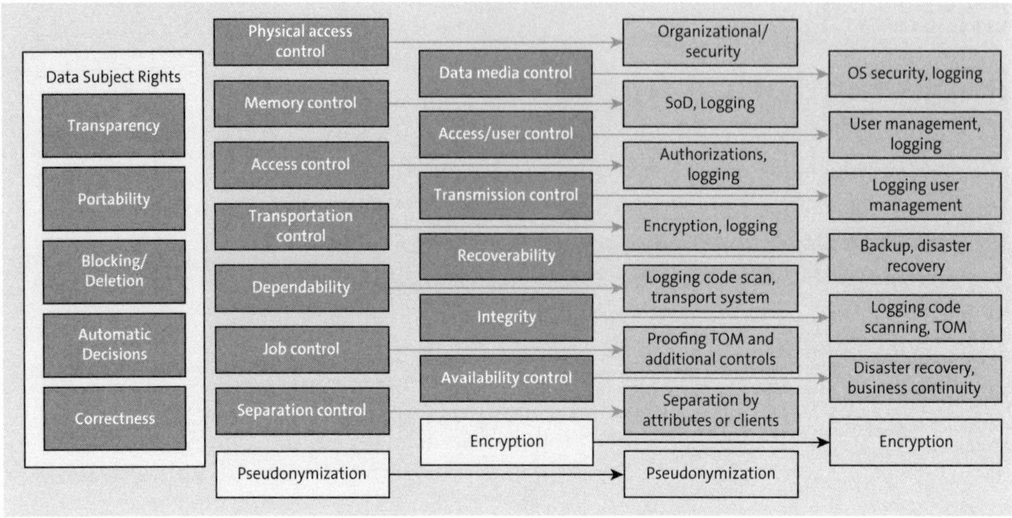

Figure 3.1 Essential Technical and Organizational Measures

The legally established approach prior to the introduction of any such procedure begins with an evaluation of whether or not a data protection impact assessment (DPIA) is really necessary. Impact assessments typically provide an explanation of the processing purpose and operations (see Chapter 1, Section 1.1.13). Furthermore, the data will be evaluated in relation to the processing purpose, and appropriate safeguards will be determined.

Deductive approach

This deductive approach is also the only sensible way to ensure greenfield implementation whereby you'll be creating a brand-new procedure (as if on a fresh greenfield).

Inductive approach

However, the most pressing question for our installed base customers is how data protection compliance can be achieved in an existing business environment. The inductive approach, which is essential for this, is illustrated in Figure 3.2. Note the following points:

- The numbers describe the sequence of measures we recommend.
- Any processing of personal data is based on its intended processing purpose. The arrows indicate this dependency.
- Technical security is always the foundation of every kind of data protection policy. Without technical safety, the other measures would be completely pointless.

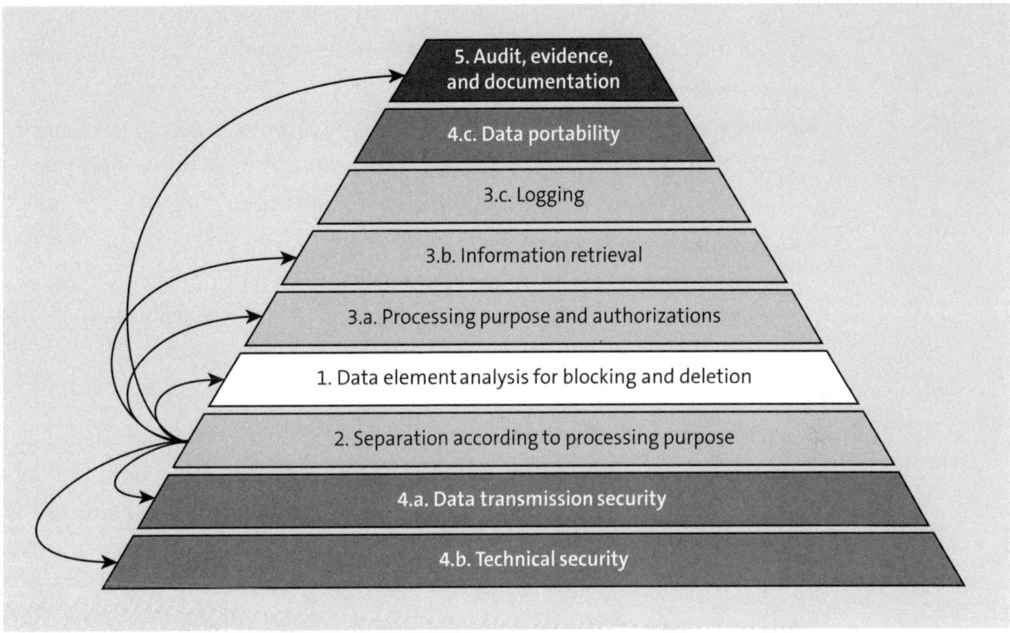

Figure 3.2 The Inductive Approach

The approach adopted in the project is based on the assumption that the purpose of processing is the core element for most measures. We therefore describe the processing purpose briefly in Figure 3.2:

- **Purpose of processing**
  All of the personal data you store in your company must be linked to a specific purpose of processing (see Chapter 1, Section 1.2.1). The purpose is indicated by data attributes; that is, the data is always clearly identifiable. As a reminder, we're assuming that a purpose is usually connected to a specific controller. This person is normally a separate legal entity. This also applies if the legal entity is defined within a corporate group. Furthermore, we assume that different business processes should be considered as having different purposes at the latest after they have been identified by different legal sources with different retention periods.
- **Purpose and time limits**
  The purpose of the processing has a direct effect on the blocking and deletion of data. If the purpose, as outlined previously, has been chosen

according to type in relation to the applicable retention rules, it's possible to define retention periods for the data under one specific purpose.

- **Purpose and authorizations**
  Because access to personal data may only take place within the scope of the defined purpose, the authorization concept must also reflect this by means of authorizations separated by their related purposes.
- **Purpose and information**
  Both the advance information pursuant to Arts. 13 and 14 GDPR and the right of access to information pursuant to Art. 15 GDPR contain the necessity to state the purposes of processing.
- **Purpose and transfer**
  The purpose limitation also of course applies to the transfer of data. Such transfers must be secured in a way which ensures that only the data intended for that purpose can be transmitted or retrieved. In other words, even the system interfaces have to be configured for specific purposes.
- **Purpose and security**
  The connection between the purposes, risks, and protective measures is described in numerous places in the GDPR, for example, during the DPIA in accordance with Art. 35 GDPR or in the measures for the security of processing pursuant to Art. 32 GDPR. Because this is also a matter of providing evidence that the measures have been taken, the link between the purpose and the measures must be clear.
- **Purpose and proof**
  Along with the DPIA or the obligation to provide evidence in accordance with Art. 32 GDPR, a record of processing activities (RoPA) also requires purpose-related evidence. In this respect, the purposes must also be documented.

3.1.1 What Is the Inductive Approach?

With ever-increasing surprise, we acknowledge that many companies now have relevant but unfortunately top-heavy data protection projects. This is because these projects only reach those responsible for processes and the operation of the SAP software slowly and bit by bit. It becomes obvious that a deductive approach is often chosen in the projects: They look at an abstract level to see what procedures exist and for what purpose they are used.

The truth lies in the data

Our approach, however, is exactly the opposite: the truth lies in the data. We therefore assume that stocktaking in the system at the level of real data is objectively necessary! Furthermore, this approach allows us to reach our goal much faster and to record the actual data situation much more accurately. The inductive approach therefore starts from the current status to determine which purposes are actually pursued in data processing.

What has to go?

Taking inventory of data that is initially unrelated to a purpose isn't exactly what we recommend as a starting point. Instead, start by blocking and deleting personal data. The existing systems are generally mature systems in which an increasing amount of data has been processed for an ever-greater variety of purposes. The projects in which these systems were introduced modeled the necessary data across all business processes. In this context, a blocking and deletion project is a negative business process. One of the main differences to the modeling of a positive business process is that the business process data already exists and therefore no longer needs to be ascertained. However, the data must also be made deletable. Because most personal data needs to be deleted, it's possible and advisable to start with this reverse transaction.

In doing so, you'll quickly find out which personal data should no longer be available. Of course, the question arises as to which of the data collected in this way is in fact personal: this is something you'll ultimately have to decide for yourself. Complete implementation of simplified blocking and deletion and of the information retrieval framework will provide you with a complete overview of all relevant data. You can use this as a basis for determining which data is personal.

3.1.2 Blocking and Deleting Personal Data as Your Starting Point

In our experience, *blocking* and *deletion* is of paramount importance. At least in Germany, blocking and deleting is the main focus of the supervisory authorities' audits and complaints. Bear in mind that personal data which is no longer used for purposes based on data protection law and is otherwise no longer subject to a retention obligation has absolutely no legal basis for processing. Therefore, this data has to be removed from the system. Concerning data protection, the importance of deletion constitutes the legal justification for starting with this step.

Technical transparency

There are also numerous technical reasons for starting with this step, which will provide you with technical transparency: You have an overview of the personal data stored across all system boundaries, interfaces, and organizational structures.

More specifically, this process begins with the determination of which data should be deleted in SAP Business Suite or SAP S/4HANA, such as master data, transactional data, payment data, and communication data. Figure 3.3 illustrates how these types of data are related to each other.

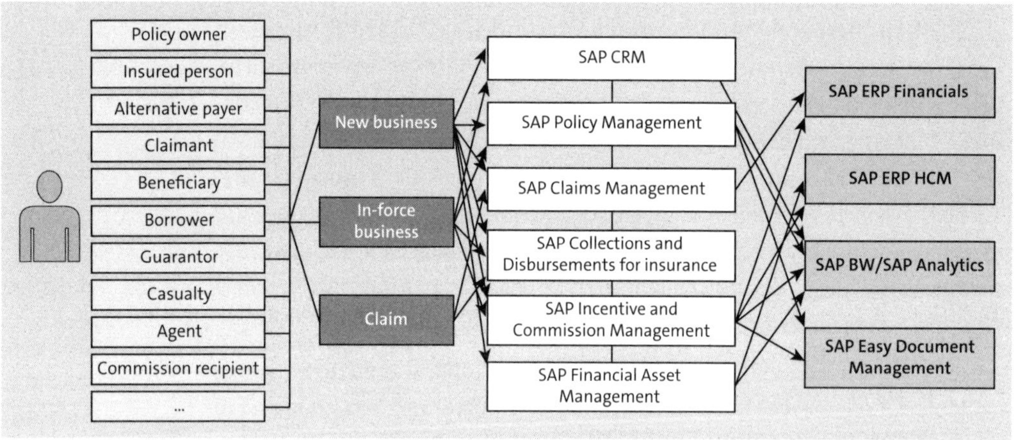

Figure 3.3 Dependency on Data Based on the Example of the Insurance Solution Scopes

[Ex]

Data Dependency in the Insurance Industry

In the depicted solutions framework (which in this diagram is based on processing within SAP Business Suite), an insurance benefit payment is due, for example, in connection with an insurance policy held in SAP Policy Management (FS-PM). This is then processed in SAP Claims Management and results in a payment via SAP Collections and Disbursements for Insurance and, of course, postings in SAP ERP Financials (FI). Important personal master data is stored in the business partner. When blocking and deleting data, dependent documents must be taken into account in such a way that the data remains consistent.

Consistency beyond system boundaries?

If the entire process is carried out in SAP Business Suite, the dependent data that you haven't yet taken into account will become apparent when testing the solution. If dependencies are mandatory, the blocking and/or deletion of the data will be technically impossible. The next step is therefore to analyze which data still needs to be deleted.

Procedures that go beyond the system boundaries of SAP Business Suite are much more difficult. If, for example, you're using a business partner management system that isn't part of SAP Business Suite, blocking or deleting data can lead to inconsistent data in SAP Business Suite. If you process data in a financial services policy management system that isn't part of SAP Business Suite, this may cause inconsistencies because blocking or deletion is performed in SAP Business Suite. Both of these effects can only be prevented by analyses and appropriate tests.

In this analysis, you can also determine whether your data is kept for a specific purpose.

[Ex]

Different Retention Periods in the Insurance Industry

Let's continue in the generally understandable context of insurance: You can imagine that the retention periods of a travel cancellation insurance policy are considerably shorter than those for liability insurance because the business itself is considerably shorter than for liability insurance (in some cases, retention periods of up to 30 years). If both types of insurance have the same data attributes (controller/legal entity, order types, contract types, etc.), you can no longer differentiate the data automatically. This means that if blocking and deletion are automatically processed, you would probably only be able to delete the data after 30 years. This would probably be illegal with regard to the travel cancellation insurance data. In this step, you'll determine whether you really want to keep your data for a specific purpose or (and this is the rule in our experience) whether you need to change the master data and organizational structures.

Cleanse data

Experience has shown that initial technical tests will certainly allow you to identify large amounts of out-of-date and inconsistent personal data. This is the result of erroneous transfers, program crashes that weren't investigated immediately, unenforced claims, and old data migration projects.

In summary, this step provides you with the level of transparency in terms of data and the relationships between data and data structures that you need for subsequent steps. It's likely, however, that you won't be able to delete any data after this step because you still have to clean up the data structures.

3.1.3 Separation Based on Purpose

In the vast majority of your systems, you'll probably have to restructure master data in a purpose-specific manner and redefine the organizational structures of the software.

Organizational structures

By organizational structures, we mean the characteristics that are used in SAP Business Suite applications for organizational classification. As shown in the much-simplified Figure 3.4, these classification characteristics are linked to the company code in a way that has to be defined.

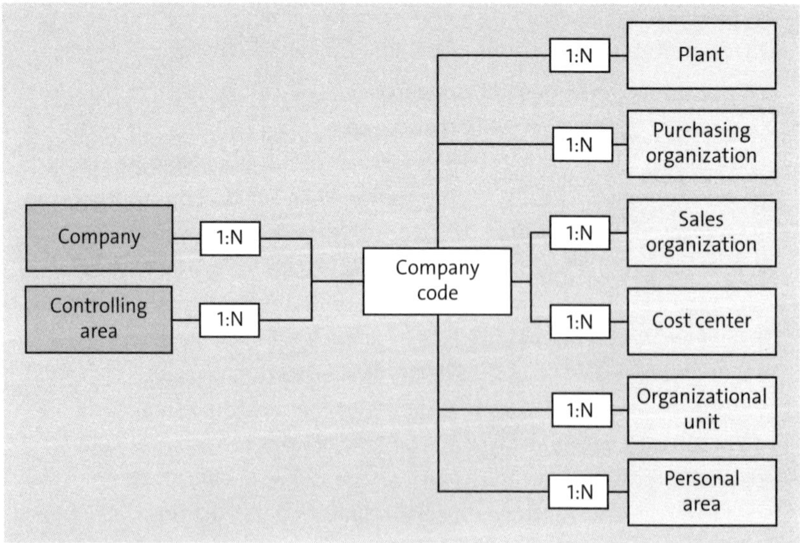

Figure 3.4 Simplified Organizational Structure

Company code = controller

The company code represents an independent accounting unit. As a rule, the company code is the legal entity responsible and therefore the *controller*. In other words, you should arrange the organizational structure in such a way that there is a clear reference to the company code, so that each subsequent unit is assigned uniquely to this company code. The same principle should apply even if the applications are only loosely coupled on a case-by-case basis. In the following, we'll refer to these characteristics, for example, company code or purchasing organization, as *line organizational attributes* (LOAs).

All data storage is based on these characteristics. This means if you've created a different structure, it's possible that some personal data might be stored that can't be clearly assigned to a controller or to a specific purpose, resulting in no verifiable legal basis for the processing of such personal data.

Further differentiation in the process

As already illustrated in the example of travel cancellation insurance and liability insurance, other attributes such as contract type or order type are still needed because they provide further details of the respective purpose in the relevant organization. These attributes are referred to below as *process organizational attributes* (POAs).

[!]

Line Organizational Attributes (LOAs)

In each application, your LOAs must be designed in such a way that the connection to the controller can be proven at all times. Within the controller, you can differentiate between the various purposes using other POAs.

Both POAs and LOAs are needed in a wide range of data protection activities, such as blocking and deletion, and in the authorization concept.

Necessity to cleanse

If—as mentioned earlier—these structures have to be adapted, the number of resources needed for the project could increase considerably; this doesn't change the basic principle, however, that legally compliant data processing can only be achieved in this way. If you're now moving on to the correction of POAs and LOAs, this is the right time to start giving data accuracy more substantial thought. The best way of ensuring the accuracy of data is through governance processes. IT tools, such as SAP Master Data Governance (SAP MDG), can be used both to correct the current status and to ensure data accuracy in the future. In other words, if you have to correct data anyway to get it in line with the purposes, it makes sense to do so systematically and, in doing so, to also take the other aspect, namely data accuracy, into account. Both of these tasks can be carried out with the help of IT tools.

Setting up the Data Controller Rule Framework

If you've reached a high level of transparency in terms of data and structures, and you use SAP Information Lifecycle Management (SAP ILM), it's now time to set up the *Data Controller Rule Framework*. This combines the LOAs and POAs with SAP ILM objects in such a way that the retention rules only have to be defined for the purpose, while the technical rules are then derived.

As an intermediate result, please note the following: In addition to transparency and the general deletability of data, you can actually delete data after it has been cleansed. You've set up the Data Retention Rule Framework and are now able to generate retention rules. Finally, you'll be able to implement the other measures.

The next step is to differentiate authorizations according to their purpose.

3.1.4 Separating the Purpose and Authorizations

At this point, you only need to have a general look at our proposed procedure to introduce you to the basic requirement of authorization differentiation.

Organizational differentiation

The authorization concept in SAP Business Suite allows you to differentiate authorizations precisely by specifying exactly what is possible with a certain number of authorizations. In the previous section, we explained how to approach organizational differentiation within the scope of the intended purpose. You'll need suitably formulated LOAs and POAs.

[Ex]

Organizational Differentiation in the Insurance Industry

If we stay with the example of insurance companies, a clerk responsible for processing travel cancellation insurance, for example, must be able to access the documents related to this purpose under LOAs and POAs. Conversely, if the case handler isn't authorized to process liability insurance, he may not access documents related to the purpose of liability insurance under LOAs and POAs. In *Authorizations in SAP Software* by Lehnert and Stelzner (SAP PRESS, 2010, *www.sap-press.com/2316*), the entire third chapter is devoted to organizational differentiation.

Differentiation of activities

The other differentiation requirement is permitted activities: Should the clerk responsible be able to process personal data or not? Activities, LOAs, and POAs together very accurately define for which purpose the case handler is connected to which organization, that is, which activities a clerk may carry out.

SOX alone was yesterday

Working on the authorization concept is an unpopular task in many organizations, but it also has to be done on a regular basis. Until now, however, it has mainly been done from a business-related point of view. *SOX compliance* is the best-known buzzword in this area: In accordance with the US Sarbanes-Oxley Act of 2002 (SOX for short), authorization concepts were checked for conflicts concerning the separation of functions. To this end, thousands of these types of conflicts have been defined as a genuine technical risk, and authorizations often had to be corrected accordingly. In terms of data protection, we'll now have to take the strict principle of minimization much more seriously. In addition, the clerk should only be able to read and access personal data that is within the scope of the intended purpose and his explicit area of responsibility, and only then when it's absolutely necessary. We don't consider this to be feasible without a powerful analysis tool such as that provided in *SAP Access Control*.

Define risks

This means that you have to define the risks in terms of activities, LOAs, and POAs; use these risk definitions to check their roles and users; and cleanse them accordingly. To carry out the analysis, you can store the cleansed data in SAP Access Control or—less conveniently—in the user information system.

Technical users

We'll address the issue of secure data transmission in Chapter 12. The safe transfer of data, however, depends on whether the technical users have relevant and restricted authorizations in the interfaces. The authorization concept is described in further detail in Chapter 7.

3.1.5 Informing the Data Subject

Depending on the resources available for the project, you may be able to perform further partial steps simultaneously. One partial step is to establish the means of providing information.

As we explain in Chapter 8, there is also a close technical connection between the information retrieval framework and SAP ILM.

Therefore, if during the first step, you already introduced the concept of simplified blocking and deleting of personal data based on SAP ILM, a large amount of what you can now use is already available.

Leverage what is already familiar

As we'll explain, the information retrieval framework "reads" the connections between the SAP ILM objects (this is where the data is archived) and the data fields themselves. This is then used to generate a model that is available for further processing and completion. It's essential that you actually process the data yourself because in your procedure, the SAP system can't decide which data is actually personal. It would be extremely helpful for maintenance if you're already using SAP ILM structures when blocking and deleting, and you're already familiar with the structures and fields.

Purposes and periods from SAP ILM

If you've also set up the Data Controller Rule Framework, this will provide you with the option of transferring purposes to your information model. You can also copy the periods defined in SAP ILM for the respective purpose.

After you've set up a model of the disclosure of information in accordance with Art. 15 GDPR, you can use it to help with categorization to support the provision of advance information pursuant to Arts. 13 and 14 GDPR. You can also use the categorized model to provide data to the RoPA.

3.1.6 Logging

Logging can also be set up parallel to other tasks in the project. Setting up includes checking the usual logs for suitability, as well as configuring and activating the reading log—Read Access Logging (RAL).

Technical logs

A large number of technical logs in SAP Business Suite record all technical occurrences; here you should check whether these have been set up effectively and are active (for further information, read Chapter 9):

- **Table logging**
  With regard to the *logging of modifications to verify configuration changes*, it's important to check whether table logging is active. This is essential to ensure the integrity of the configuration.
- **Change logging: Master and transactional data**
  Check for *change logging*, in particular to see whether these also cover customer enhancements. All changes to personal data are included in the change logging.

- **Read logging**
  Read logging is a procedure used to ensure that access is only granted by employees when it's in line with the purpose and tasks of the employees. The basic principles of read logging were previously addressed in Chapter 1, Section 1.2.4; however, in Chapter 12, we'll take a more detailed look at read logging use and configuration.

SAP delivers sample configurations for RAL that are based on the special categories of data specified in Art. 9 (1) GDPR and which can additionally log any access to bank details. You'll have to determine which data is worth logging and also define the method for evaluating these access logs. It makes sense to combine it with SAP Process Control or SAP Enterprise Threat Detection. After evaluation, the log records, which don't reveal any facts that are contrary to data protection regulations, should be deleted because they both represent behavioral control and can be used as proof of any highly critical data in log form. The deletion of this data is technically possible. In addition to the reasons stated in data protection law for deletion, this is also technically advisable because considerable amounts of data are generated by logging. When defining your SAP Enterprise Threat Detection, also be aware of access channels such as the remote function call (RFC).

3.1.7 Data Transmission Security

As part of the blocking and deletion step, you'll have already identified some of the interfaces that are or can be used for data transfer.

Directory of interfaces

To ensure security in data transmission, it's first necessary to create a directory of all possible and all utilized interfaces. The next step is to check the purpose for which these interfaces are used.

If transparency has been achieved for the interfaces and their purposes, data access/transmission will have to be restricted in accordance with the purpose. This must be done in such a way that data can only be transferred to the extent justified by the purpose of processing in that particular processing step.

UCON

In one customer's case, we also found systems with more than 300 RFC connections that had been set up but not documented, the purposes of which were mostly unclear and which were assigned the authorization `SAP_ALL` for technical users; with this authorization you can carry out all activities in SAP Business Suite. Such systems aren't only "a hacker's darling": After you get in, anything is possible! They are also compelling evidence that the operation in compliance with data protection regulations isn't desired. In the field of RFC security, SAP has made it much easier for you to come to grips with RFC security by means of the Unified Connectivity solution (UCON). In an administration framework, the UCON concept combines the connectivity components of the ABAP server (RFC, HTTP services in the Internet Communication Framework [ICF]) in an administration framework to simplify configuration and thus improve the security of all communication channels.

Encryption of data transmissions

To ensure security during data transmission, it's essential that data sent to recipients outside of the secured internal system network is encrypted. For details on how this can be achieved, see "M 5.125 Protection of Communication with SAP Systems" in the IT Basic Protection Catalogue of the Federal Office for Information Security (BSI) (2013).

3.1.8 Technical Security

The subject of technical security for system operations is very extensive. The secure operation of systems is also subject to various types of audits; this book is intended to provide you with a general overview.

In our procedural model, we already addressed the following technical security issues:

- Authorization concept
- Logging
- Data transmission security

In Chapter 1, Section 1.1.12, we broadened the field a little further and cited the following principles:

- Code protection and change logging
- Protecting configuration and logging changes
- Protecting interfaces and logging usage
- Other technical measures to avoid the unintentional manipulation of personal data, such as physical access control, data access control, transfer control, and so on

All these points should be considered and solved with our procedure model. For further information see the SAP Security Guides at *https://help.sap.com*, as well as "M 2.341 Planning and Use of SAP" in the BSI's Basic Protection Catalogue (German Federal Office for Information Security, 2013).

The technical security of SAP systems not only is a fundamental prerequisite for data-protection-compliant operations but also for legally compliant operations as a whole, for example, with regard to the principles concerning the orderly management and storage of books, records, and documents in electronic form, and data access (GoBD, published by the German Federal Finance Ministry). In this book, we mainly focus on the specifics of data protection. We therefore address some aspects but don't explain every possible measure.

Based on the assumption that system security will also have to be demonstrated for other reasons, data protection for topics not explicitly dealt with here will seek to provide a general overview of the measures and their effectiveness. The measures should be well documented.

3.1.9 Data Portability

We already addressed the issue of data portability in Chapter 1, Section 1.1.9, where we also expressed our doubts as to whether this can be achieved in a useful way. From a technical point of view, the step described in Section 3.1.5 is a preparatory step for data portability. During that step, you configured the information report, which you can either use directly for transferring the data to a machine-readable format or create a template based on it that allows you to provide a smaller amount of data.

3.1.10 Audit, Verification, and Documentation

Obligation to provide proof

The last step in our procedural model concerns the *obligation to provide proof*. This should not, however, be interpreted in a schematic way; you should consider the necessity of submitting evidence at all stages and then document it accordingly. For this purpose, there are numerous points at which—in the scope of the presented solution—you can generate facts naturally for further documentation:

1. **The initial transparency of the first step**
   Right from the very first step, you'll obtain transparency concerning the personal data that is processed. You'll also gain insight into processing purposes, the retention periods to be applied, and the interfaces involved in your procedure. You therefore have a sound basis for both listing procedural activities and verifying measures and controls. By using SAP ILM, you can also provide evidence of the actual blocking and deletion of personal data.

   If, as we propose, you implement simplified blocking and deletion based on SAP ILM and also use the Data Controller Rule Framework as specified, you'll have a model presentation of the LOAs and POAs that characterize the processing purposes and of the periods to be created for verification obligations. Alternatively, you can finally achieve this by cleansing the organizational structures and master data during the next step.

2. **Verification procedure for accuracy**
   If, during this second stage, you implement a procedure—such as SAP MDG—to ensure that the data is correct, this procedure also enables you to prove how your company's data is being kept accurate and up to date.

3. **Proof of authorization risks**
   The risk-based cleansing of the authorization concept proposed in the third step not only yields an authorization concept that complies with data protection requirements but also serves as proof that you're using an authorization concept that monitors explicit data protection risks. If you're using the most up-to-date tools, such as SAP Access Control in SAP GRC, they not only manage user authorizations on a risk basis but also carry out regular checks on the necessity of certain authorizations for a particular user.

4. **Proof and other data basis**
   Working on the step for providing information will lead to a number of verifications, first of all proof of the mere possibility of providing information in accordance with Art. 15 GDPR. Using the categorization options, you can also provide documentation for the possibility of advance information pursuant to Arts. 13 and 14 GDPR. Furthermore, by using the categorization of data, you can also create the best possible real database for the RoPA. We'll take a closer look at this in a moment.

5. **Proof of read logging**
   The introduction of a read logging system doesn't initially provide much further information and thus serves primarily as proof that a read log has been introduced as a protective measure. Depending on which data you log, dealing with the read log can be understood to be part of the risk assessment, which would then also have to be documented.
6. **Verification of interfaces**
   If carried out as proposed, the step dedicated to the security of transmission provides a complete overview of interfaces (transmission channels), their use, and the purposes of use.
7. **Proof of technical measures**
   If you've checked, supplemented on a case-by-case basis, and documented the measures set up as proposed, you'll have acquired a detailed description of the systems' security measures, which in this current stage cover part of the documentation required.
8. **Proof of data portability**
   The final stage of data portability provides no other form of proof besides the proof that data portability is possible.

In Chapter 1, Section 1.1.14, we outlined the requirement of recording processing activities, and in Chapter 1, Section 1.1.13, we carried out a privacy impact assessment (PIA). In Chapter 1, Section 1.1.12, we introduced the control circuit (proof circuit), and, finally, in Figure 1.5 in Chapter 1, Section 1.3.6, we placed the burden of proof in an overall context. Note that the following will lead to the control and proof circuit described earlier:

- PIA
- RoPA
- Various evidentiary obligations
- Proof of continuous monitoring of adequacy

We can take a closer look at this in Figure 3.5.

The light gray (e-book: light blue) elements represent information that you've already determined during the course of the proposed procedure. You can now use them.

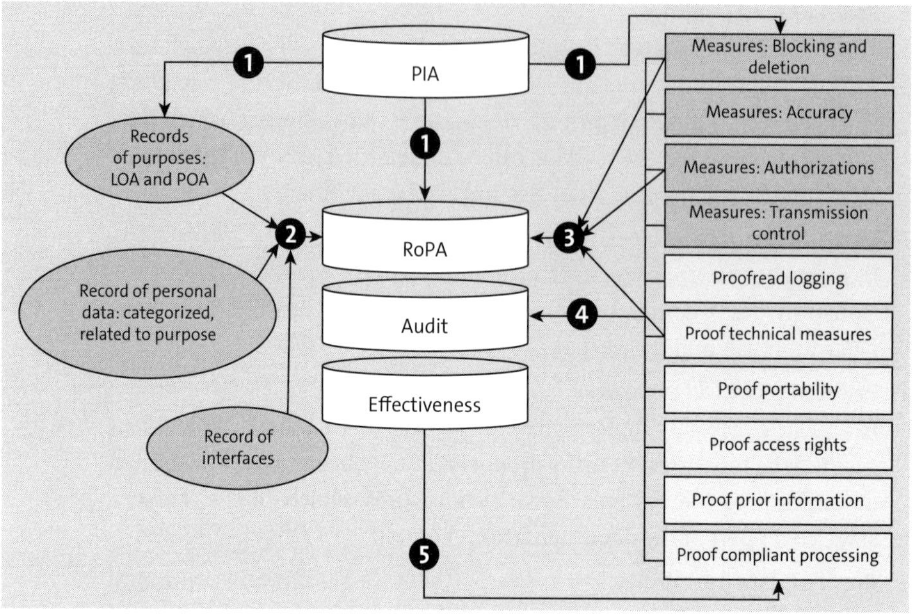

Figure 3.5 Audit, Proof, Documentation

Privacy impact assessment (PIA)

However, we'll start systematically with the PIA, which, in certain cases (see Chapter 1, Section 1.1.13), should be conducted before you implement a procedure for processing personal data. A PIA may also be required for procedural changes. If you're running a PIA, it will also contain data, purposes, and measures that need to be appropriately adopted (Figure 3.5 ❶). Our proposed procedure, however, is based on the assumption that we're using an existing system; accordingly, we don't start with a PIA, but with the information and proof in the blue boxes that were previously recorded in our procedure.

Record of processing activities (RoPA)

Figure 3.5 ❷ shows that the Data Controller Rule Framework has already recorded the purposes relating to LOAs and POAs, recorded and categorized personal data in SAP information retrieval framework, and recorded the interfaces involved in the project stage of transmission security. This information may serve as qualified and wide-ranging basic information for the *record of processing activities* (RoPA). This also applies to certain proof and measures connected with the RoPA (Figure 3.5 ❸).

In turn, Figure 3.5 ❹ makes it clear that all proof and measures have to be subject to regular *audit activities*. In addition to the full formal audits, it's essential to monitor certain aspects more frequently or even continuously (e.g., the granting of authorizations).

Audit

Finally, the GDPR also stipulates that a process for regularly testing, assessing, and evaluating the effectiveness of technical and organizational measures for ensuring the security of the processing (Art. 32 (1)(d) GDPR) must be implemented (Figure 3.5 ❺).

Procedure for regular monitoring

It's significantly more efficient to use a product such as SAP GRC suite for overall mapping to prevent the data from being stored redundantly more than once and to ensure that the cross-system connections of information is preserved.

A case for SAP GRC suite

[«]

Outcome of Our Procedural Model

If you've been following all the steps of our procedural model, you'll find that you have an extensive package of data protection measures:

- Transparency
- Data-protection-compliant data storage
- Deletability of personal data
- Data-protection-compliant authorization concept
- Report that supports the provision of information
- Advance information support
- RoPA support
- RAL
- Transparency and security of data transmission
- Transparency of security measures and amendments on a case-by-case basis
- Data portability report
- Concise verification management

3.2 Record of Processing Activities Approaches

Our approach involves filling in the RoPA in passing with real data and categories based on it, the applicable retention periods, and the purposes of processing. When it comes to the data in SAP Business Suite or SAP S/4HANA, filling in the record is as complete and correct as the underlying project. This seems to be the most logical approach—at least as far as SAP legacy systems are concerned. However, we would also like to compare the two approaches.

3.2.1 Inductive versus Deductive Approach

There are basically two possible ways of creating such a record. At first glance, it appears that a deductive approach to the question of the purposes for which personal data is processed seems obvious. Our approach illustrates that this method isn't sensible for legacy systems. Of course, the *deductive approach* is the method of choice for completely new process implementations.

Inductive method: only apparently more effort

The other way of proceeding, the *inductive approach*, may initially seem very complex; it's based on the fact that the legacy systems already process personal data. Accordingly, the aim is to get as accurate an idea as possible and, based on this, to add proof of processing to the record. Table 3.1 compares the two approaches schematically.

Inductive Approach	Deductive Approach
What personal data is processed? (necessary step for deletion and transparency)	Definition of purposes and legal provisions
When does this data have to be blocked and deleted? (necessary step for deletion and transparency)	When does the personal data have to be blocked and deleted?
Are there any dependencies on other data/data records in the system group? (necessary step for deletion and transparency)	Possible detailing of the purpose due to different retention regulations

Table 3.1 Inductive versus Deductive Project Approach

Inductive Approach	Deductive Approach
Can the data relating to the retention regulations be separated according to "type," that is, assigned separating attributes? (necessary step for deletion and transparency)	Possible impact assessment pursuant to Art. 35 GDPR
Determination of the purposes while observing the retention regulations	Detailed information on data categories in specific data fields
Definition of a concept of deletion	Detailed description of recipient categories and identification of all system interfaces
Written documentation of the purposes and legal provisions	Definition of a concept of deletion
Definition of a concept for information and access to information on collected personal data (Arts. 13, 14, 15 GDPR)	Definition of a concept for information and access to information on collected personal data (Arts. 13, 14, 15 GDPR)
Categorization, among other things, with regard to Arts. 32 and 35 GDPR	Definition of suitable security measures pursuant to Art. 32 in conjunction with Art. 5 GDPR
Data categorization; categorization of recipients, including all system connections; and identification of retention rules	Comparison of the data fields
Possible impact assessment pursuant to Art. 35 GDPR	Implementation of a deletion concept, including dealing with incorrect organizational structures and incorrect master data structures as well as cross-system processes; structuring of data in accordance with the purposes
Definition of suitable security measures in accordance with Art. 32 in conjunction with Art. 5 GDPR	Dealing with the mismatch between defined purposes and data retrieved

Table 3.1 Inductive versus Deductive Project Approach (Cont.)

Inductive Approach	Deductive Approach
Demonstrate effectiveness, completeness, adequacy, and implementation of the measures	Implementation of a concept for the provision of information
Comparison of the data fields	Demonstrate effectiveness, completeness, adequacy, and implementation of the measures

Table 3.1 Inductive versus Deductive Project Approach (Cont.)

3.2.2 Where the Two Approaches Meet

During normal operation, a combination of both methods is generally used. Our preferred approach quickly reaches its limits when other systems are involved. It's worth considering whether SAP Business Suite and SAP S/4HANA are central to your system group. If this is the case, you should always discuss our model. If your central processes are located in different software, and if this software can provide you with the necessary support, it may also be worth considering an inductive approach.

In any case, there needs to be a comparison of the deductively determined purposes and inductively determined data because the task of relating the data to data categories and purposes still needs to be done.

The task of identifying reservation and retention periods, which should also always be suited not to counteract the necessary analyses, also still has to be carried out.

3.3 Summary

We're convinced that an effective implementation in the system should be based on the data that is actually processed. This chapter provides a description of what this process may look like. SAP Consulting also adopts this approach (at the time of publication). This approach is in fact the result of a combination of consulting experience and the knowledge of SAP's data protection capabilities.

Chapter 4
Blocking and Deletion with SAP Information Lifecycle Management

Most clients didn't pay much attention to the deletion of data in the past. The fact that you're holding this book on data protection in your hands implies, however, that this procedure will be given more weight and higher priority in the future.

Experience has shown that part of the first substantial step toward achieving data protection compliance is a comprehensive *blocking and deletion concept*. Besides the practical experience that has been gained so far, there are also objective reasons for this. When developing this concept, cross-system dependencies become evident, and incorrect master data structures become obvious. The implementation of a blocking and deletion concept will lead to extensive and mandatory transparency of data and interfaces; we've outlined this accordingly in our procedure model (see Chapter 3). In this chapter, we'll show you how to proceed when blocking and deleting, as well as why *SAP Information Lifecycle Management (SAP ILM)* plays such a key role.

4.1 Introduction to SAP ILM

Simplified blocking and deletion

Simplified blocking and deletion of personal data is a subfunctionality within the *Information Retention Manager (IRM) scenario* in SAP ILM. The concept is referred to as simplified blocking and deletion because using SAP ILM does indeed provide considerable simplification. Blocking and deletion is still possible, however, by using classical data archiving.

[»]

Legal Aspects

The legal aspects concerning blocking and deletion based on data protection, deletion upon demand, and restrictions of processing are addressed in Chapter 1, Section 1.1.8.

Let's begin by describing some fundamentals of SAP ILM.

4.1.1 Fundamentals of SAP Information Lifecycle Management

Categories of a rule framework

First of all, let's take a look at the basic principles behind SAP ILM. With SAP ILM, your SAP default version will be enhanced by the functionality to manage the Lifecycle of your data—whether archived or not—on the basis of *rules*. The focus lies on two types of rules:

- **Retention rules**
  With regard to the *retention rules*, the question is how long you can or must retain the data related to a business object within the universe.
- **Residence rules**
  With regard to the *residence rules*, the question is how long you want to keep the business-object-related data on the database before you archive it.

You can now see, after the mention of the term data archiving, that SAP ILM uses classic data archiving. To ensure this, some SAP ILM-specific enhancements have been added.

Main functionalities

Following are the main SAP ILM functionalities:

- **Lifecycle management**
  This is about the *management* of your data's *lifecycle* with the help of the previously mentioned rules. These rules are designed to map legal regulations and to apply them to the respective data (both archived data and data contained in the database).
- **Legal Case Management**
  Legal Case Management is about blocking data that is relevant to legal cases. The related functionalities serve to protect such data from destruction by a final deletion, even if the retention period has expired.

- **Data destruction**
  This is about *data destruction* with regard to the previously mentioned legal regulations and blocking data related to legal cases.
- **Secure data storage**
  This functionality ensures *secure storage of data*, which you've archived, within the SAP ILM Store. This store is an SAP ILM-certified WebDAV server. This type of store provides you with a guarantee that the data is stored unchangeably and that you can observe the retention periods.

We'll now look at the two application cases in SAP ILM as displayed in Figure 4.1:

- **Retention Management (RM)** RM and RW
  You'll usually select the RM in your productive system to apply the main functionalities described previously to your productive data (whether archived or not).

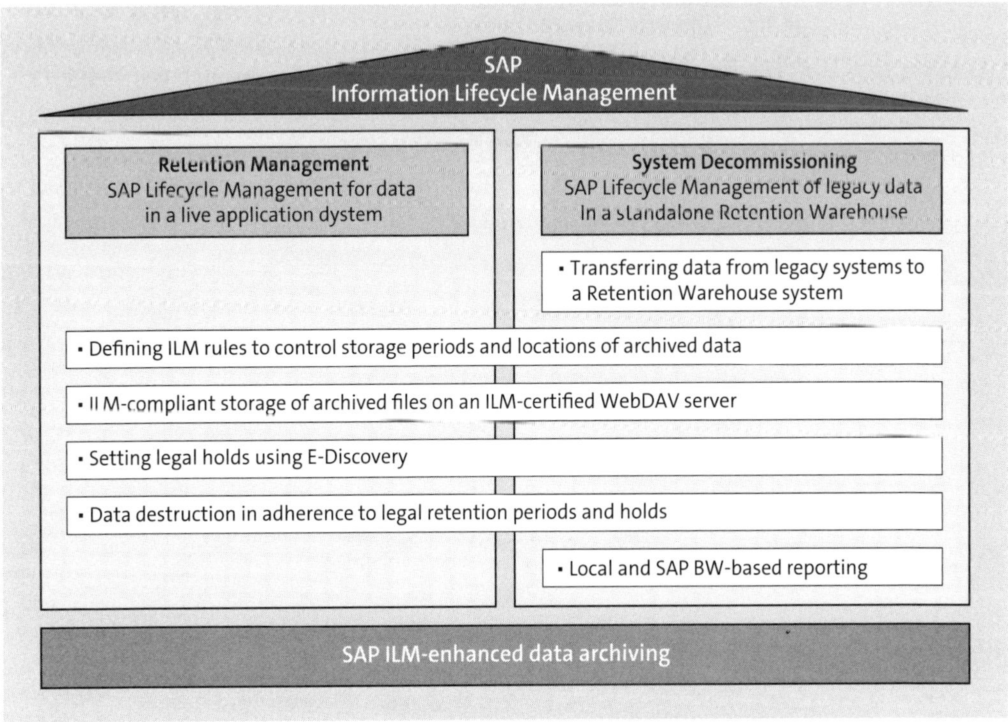

Figure 4.1 The SAP ILM Temple

- **Retention Warehouse (RW)**
  On the other hand, you'll apply the RW within an SAP system that has been specially installed for this purpose. The goal, in this case, is to shut down data from old systems (legacy systems). The newly set up RW system serves as a shared residence for all data you still want to retain. At this point, SAP ILM provides you with functionalities to extract this data from the legacy system and store it as archive files within the RW system, to analyze it, and of course to destroy it at the end of its lifecycle.

You'll have to choose one of these two options for each system.

[»]

Further Information

For further general information on SAP ILM, see *https://help.sap.com* or the SAP Training Course BIT665.

4.1.2 Lifecycle Management

IRM in SAP ILM enhances the SAP default version insofar as it enables you to manage the *lifecycle* of your productive data, which you save in the database or in the Archive Development Kit (ADK) archive, on the basis of rules. We'll refer to these rules as *IRM rules*. SAP ILM uses the SAP ILM-specific, enhanced functions of ADK data archiving.

SAP ILM-based archiving

SAP ILM-based data archiving focuses on bulk data subject to retention that you might like to export to the archive mainly for performance reasons. In this case, the primary purpose is the retention period, for instance, according to the tax code (see Figure 4.2).

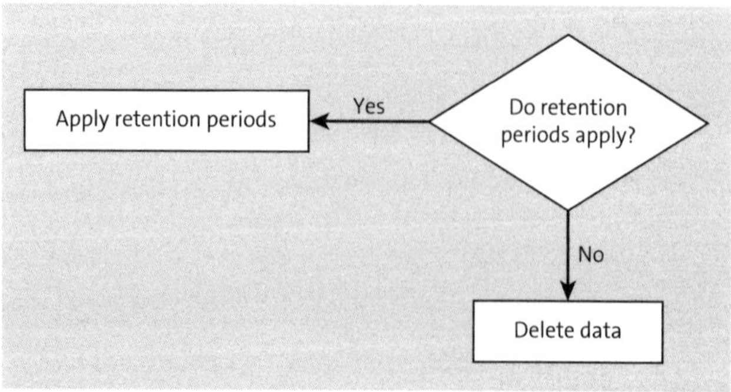

Figure 4.2 SAP ILM Logic without the Data Protection Perspective

Data protection perspective

The data protection perspective, on the other hand, deals with processing personal data within the scope of the intended purpose. This is referred to several times in the book; the purpose is discussed, among others, in Chapter 1, Section 1.1.3, and also in Chapter 5.

If the primary or initial purpose of processing no longer exists, retention may only be carried out due to other mandatory conditions, such as legal retention periods. In the discourse, these are also often referred to as *other purposes*.

In Figure 4.3, you can see the sequence of possible steps in the checking procedure, resulting from the data protection perspective.

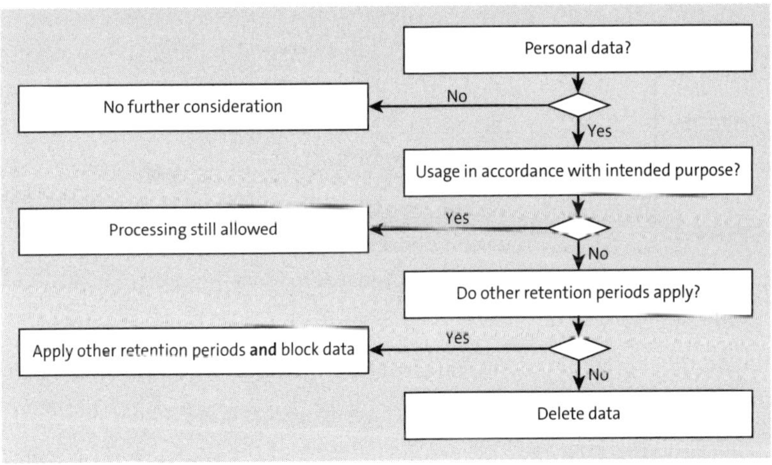

Figure 4.3 SAP ILM Logic with the Data Protection Perspective

Lifecycle

This results in the pattern for the lifecycle of personal data as displayed in Figure 4.4.

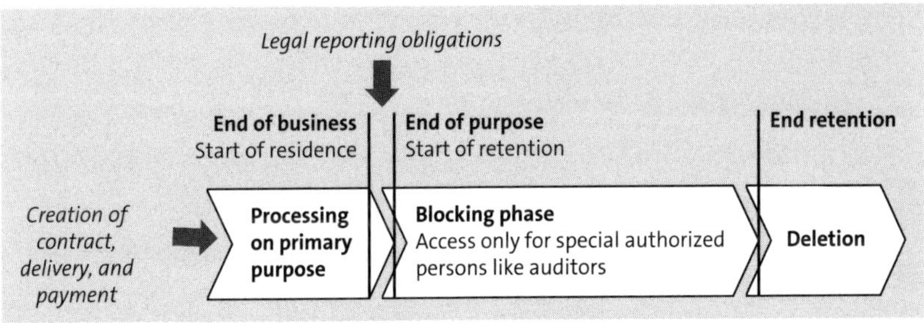

Figure 4.4 Pattern for the Lifecycle of Personal Data

The following rules need to be observed:

- Personal data for which a processing purpose no longer exists must generally be *deleted*.
- An exception to deletion applies if other retention periods are to be applied; in this case, the data must be *blocked*.

Processing pursuant to purpose

With regard to our example, this means we're dealing with processing pursuant to the intended purpose. For instance, consider a simple sales transaction: the customer orders goods, a contract is concluded, payment is made, and so on. All personal data necessary for this transaction must be requisite for the intended purpose. We're also assuming that legally binding reporting obligations must be added to the purpose of the actual business transaction. Pursuant to the International Financial Reporting Standards (IFRS), it's mandatory to make comparisons related to the comparative period (the previous year). This is only possible when the data from the comparative period can actually be processed.

Blocking stage

The subsequent *blocking phase* means that other legal, contractual, or statutory retention periods must be observed after the intended purpose has expired. In this case, the data shouldn't be deleted but instead must be blocked.

Blocking must effectively inhibit every type of processing that isn't based on legal, contractual, or statutory obligations.

Deletion stage

We subsequently enter the phase of a *deletion* of the personal data. When there are no longer any further legal, contractual, or statutory retention periods, the personal data must be deleted. SAP ILM simplifies this requirement considerably.

In this context, destruction means that the data can no longer be restored.

[»]

EoB and EoP

Two definitions that may come out during reading are as follows:

- End of business (EoB)
  End of business is the start of the residence period.
- End of purpose (EoP)
  End of purpose is the end of the residence period.

To conclude, we'll now compile the concepts and their related definitions in the manner they are used within the context of this book:

- **Defining the purpose of processing beforehand**
  When personal data is processed in SAP Business Suite, the purposes of processing should have been previously defined.
- **Intended purpose, reporting obligations, legal grounds**
  Purpose isn't a specifically defined legal term; it needs to be interpreted by the processing entity. Some additional considerations are as follows:
  - Reporting obligations that arise pursuant to law or in a legally equal manner from the original legal transaction may be regarded as an intended purpose on a case-by-case basis.
  - Further legal grounds, such as IFRS, may be applicable.
- **Residence rules and retention obligations**
  Residence rules (residence periods) and retention obligations may be derived from the intended purpose and the type of data.
- **Varying purposes**
  This implies that different business transactions have different intended purposes: Trading peppermint oil would accordingly have an intended purpose which differs from that when trading with cough syrup. In the first case, a 10-year retention period might be deemed necessary, whereas in the second case, a 30-year retention period may be considered necessary.
- **Residence rules (residence periods)**
  Residence rules (residence periods) are periods within which the data may be processed pursuant to the intended purpose.
- **Retention periods**
  Retention periods are periods of time within which the data must be retained because of purposes differing from the original purpose. In this case, the data has to be blocked.
- **Obligation to delete**
  The obligation to delete corresponds to the obligation to block. It makes sense to determine and store the periods for both facts at the same time.

You should only store data in the system for which there is a legal, contractual, or other legally compliant basis for processing.

4.1.3 Overview of Solutions

In Figure 4.5, you can see at which two central points the SAP ILM periods are used:

- When defining the residence time (residence periods)
- When defining the retention periods

Blocking via an archive file

This applies to both your master data and your transactional data.

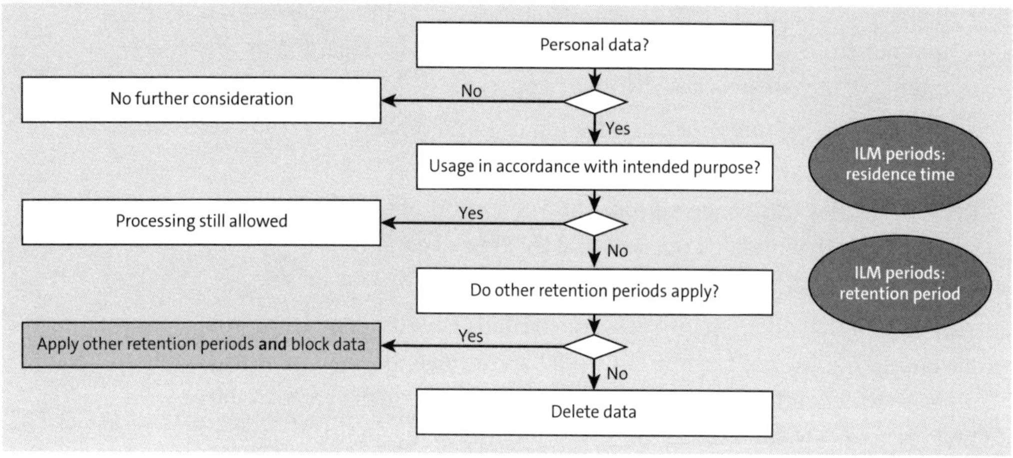

Figure 4.5 Blocking and Deletion from a Data Privacy Perspective: Technical Consideration (Training Course BIT665, 2017)

This takes us to the diagram displayed in Figure 4.6, which we'll now discuss in more detail. Irrespective of the master data based blocking, a business object can be blocked by means of an archive file ❶.

The residence periods and the retention periods for the respective SAP ILM objects are stored in SAP ILM as outlined previously. When a business object (e.g., a customer order) has to be archived, the system will check whether the following requirements are fulfilled *cumulatively*:

- The object has been closed (reason: data in the archive file can no longer be modified).
- The residence (residence periods) has expired—provided you've already defined this.

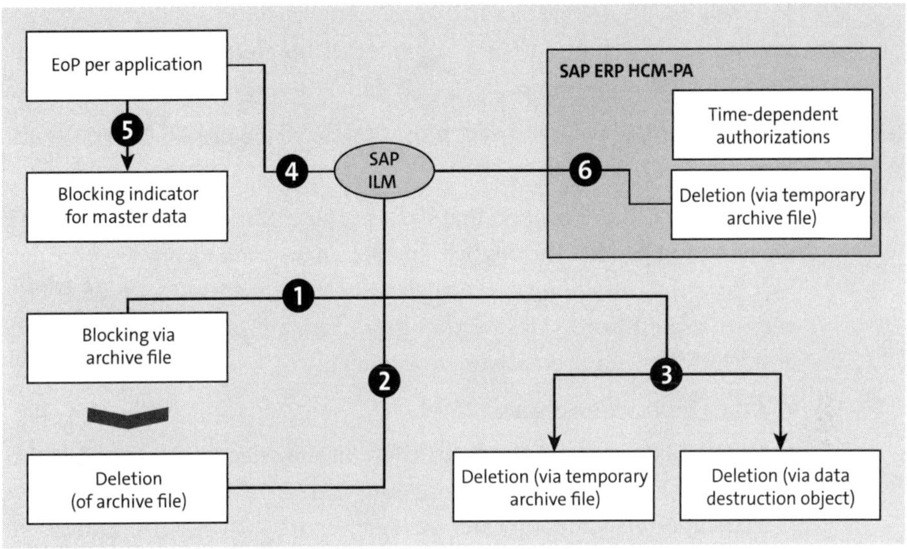

Figure 4.6 Blocking and Deletion with SAP ILM Methods

After passing the *archivability checks*, the customer order will be written into an archive file. This archive file is protected by authorizations, so that access to the customer order is effectively blocked.

You have the following options when transferring the data to an archive file:

- The retention period can be determined by SAP ILM, provided you've defined corresponding retention periods and all field values can be determined.
- The retention period can't yet be determined by SAP ILM if you've defined corresponding retention periods, but not all of the required field values can be determined. This may be the case with complex business transactions, for example, in the insurance sector or within the human resources field.

[Ex]

Beginning of the Retention Period

The retention period begins when the employee leaves the company. This date hasn't yet been reached.

At this point, it's irrelevant whether the archived data has been allocated at the end of the retention period or whether the date remains open to be determined at a later time.

Deletion of blocked data

At some point, the blocked data must be deleted (Figure 4.6 ❷). This is also controlled with SAP ILM.

Deletion without blocking stage

It's important to understand that if the purpose of the data processing and the retention periods are identical and both have expired, blocking the data isn't necessary, although you can delete the data directly (Figure 4.6 ❸). The periods related to this destruction procedure are of course obtained via IRM. The following alternatives are available:

- A data destruction object.
- The SAP ILM action **Data destruction** on the selection image of an SAP ILM-enabled archiving write program. This SAP ILM action is referred to as **Deletion via temporary archive file** in Figure 4.6. The writing phase will generate an archive file that will be deleted automatically at the end of the destruction phase by the ADK. The file isn't stored, and the Archive Information System (AS) indices won't be updated.

Blocking based on master data

After you've taken care of the residence periods and retention periods in SAP IRM, a master data blocking will proceed as follows: Every registered application is run, and their *end-of-purpose-checks* (Figure 4.6 ❹), given the following requirements, are performed:

- There is no other application that requires the data you want to block.
- The periods determined by SAP ILM for the residence periods you initially defined have expired.

Block indicator

When *both* prerequisites are fulfilled, a block indicator will be added to the master data relating to customer, vendor, and/or central business partner (Figure 4.6 ❺).

The transactional data related to this master data record subsequently can't be displayed regularly or only partly. They can no longer be modified, and it's no longer possible to create new business transactions.

The display of data is protected via authorizations, which means access is still possible for authorized persons (e.g., a tax auditor or a financial auditor).

Situation in SAP ERP HCM PA

In SAP ERP HCM Personnel Administration (PA), the data isn't blocked in the previously outlined manner. The data here is only deleted via SAP ILM (Figure 4.6 ❻). For further information, refer to Section 4.6.

4.2 Preparatory Steps

In this section, we'll explain the preparatory steps you need to take for the simplified blocking and deletion of personal data with SAP ILM.

4.2.1 Blocking Master Data in Transaction SPRO

Preparatory steps for central business partner

Let's now discuss the preparatory steps you should take in Transaction SPRO (Customizing – Edit Project) when blocking master data, such as customers and vendors, within a business transaction. As an example, we'll use the previously mentioned master data: vendor and customer.

The initial path is **Cross-Application Components • Data Protection**.

[«]

> **Preparatory Steps for the Central Business Partner**
>
> When necessary, similar preparations must also be made for the central business partner. Figure 4.7 shows you the corresponding position in Transaction SPRO • **Customizing • Edit Project**.

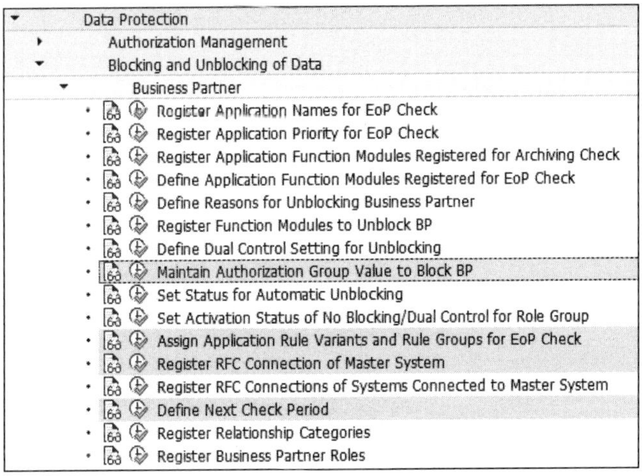

Figure 4.7 Customizing for Your Central Business Partner

Business functions

In the first step, we need to activate the required business functions:

- **BUPA_ILM_BF**
  SAP ILM-based deletion of business partner data.
- **ERP_CVP_ILM_1**
  SAP ILM-based deletion of customer and vendor master data.
- **ILM_BLOCKING**
  SAP ILM blocking functionality (reversible).
- **FICAX_BUPA_BLOCKING**
  An example for an industry-specific business function.

Depending on the industry solution you run, you might require additional industry-specific business functions. Figure 4.8 shows how these can be activated.

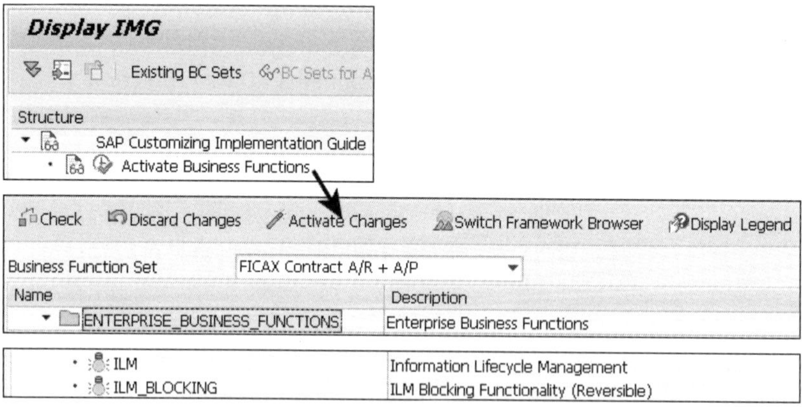

Figure 4.8 Business Functions to Activate

Next check date period

The next step (see Figure 4.9) is to define the *check date period*.

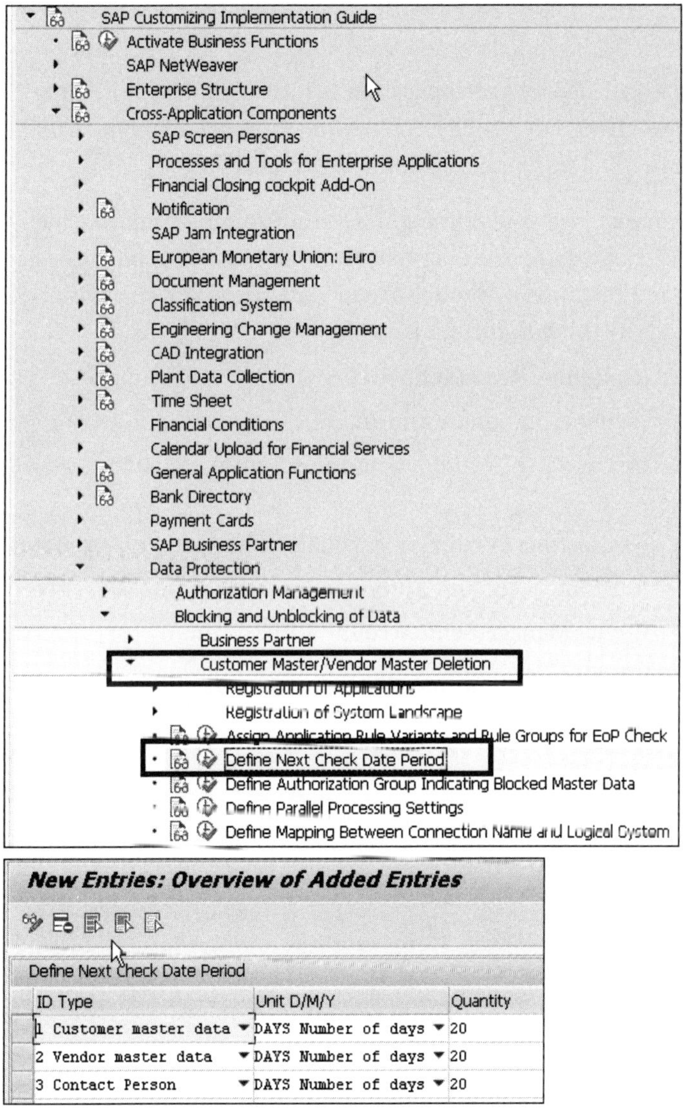

Figure 4.9 Defining the Next Check Date Period for Master Data

This is the period of time between two checks on the basis of the end of the intended purpose. The value that you specify here will only be considered if one of the following requirements is met:

- If the application doesn't specify such a date when checking on the basis of the end of the intended purpose related to a customer or vendor
- If the date specified by the application is too far in the future, that is, when a next check date period existed with a later point in time than the one you specified within this Customizing activity

Indication of blocked master data

The next step involves you defining the authorization group to which a user, by means of a corresponding role, must be allocated, so that he can display blocked customer or vendor master data. The following authorization objects verify this authorization group:

- F_KNA1_BED (Customer: Account Authorization)
- F_LFA1_BEK (Vendor: Account Authorization)
- F_BKPF_BED (Accounting Document: Account Authorization for Customers)
- F_BKPF_BEK (Accounting Document: Account Authorization for Vendors)
- V_KNA1_BRG (Customer: Account Authorization for Sales Areas)
- F_KNKK_BED (Credit Management: Account Authorization)

Figure 4.10 and Figure 4.11 show the related Customizing activity.

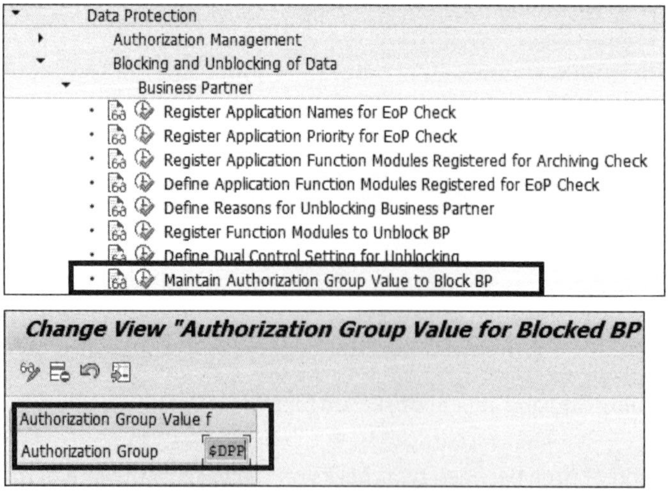

Figure 4.10 Definition of the Authorization Group to Indicate Blocked Master Data: Business Partner

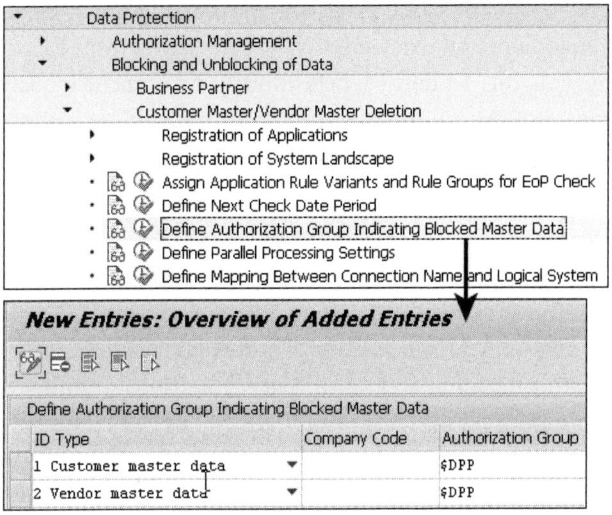

Figure 4.11 Definition of the Authorization Group to Indicate Blocked Master Data: Customers and Vendors

RFC connections

During the next step (see Figure 4.12), you can register the master system's (logical system) ID, where the data for the end of the intended purpose will be consolidated. The interim results will be read from the connected systems and submitted to the master system.

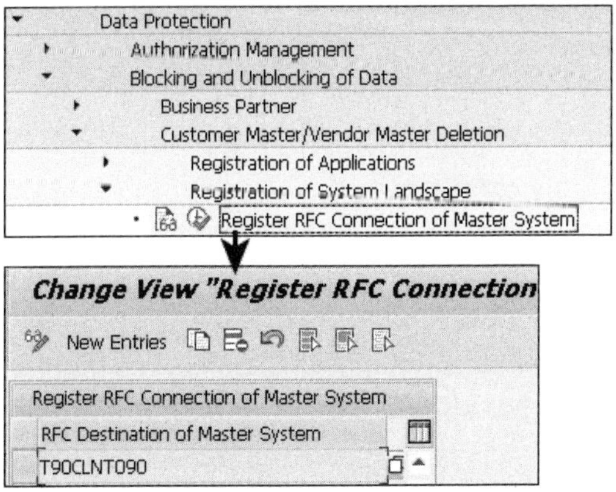

Figure 4.12 Registration of the Master System's RFC Connection

You can only make one entry in this table; a customer or vendor block can only have one system as its master system.

Distribution of blocks

The check conducted prior to blocking a business partner and the distribution of blocks is carried out in all connected systems, starting from a leading master system. This can be done synchronously or asynchronously (with corresponding RFC function modules or Enterprise Services), as well as via Application Link Enabling (ALE).The latter can be used in particular for the distribution of blocking information related to blocked customer or vendor master data.

Further details about configuration options for setting up the system landscape can be found on *https://help.sap.com/* by following the menu path, **Data Protection • Configuring Data Protection Features • Defining Customizing Settings • System Landscape and Other System Settings**. Figure 4.13 shows you part of this.

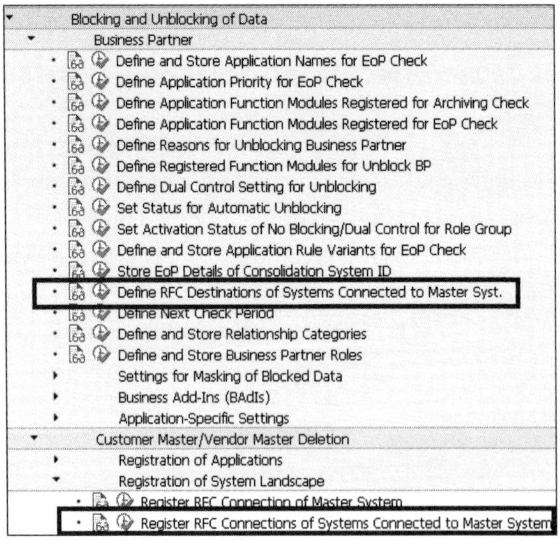

Figure 4.13 Distribution of Business Partner Blocks

Preparations provided by SAP

Figure 4.14 shows the *application names* for applications that use customers and vendors, and which SAP has already entered as such in Customizing.

Figure 4.14 Preparations Made by SAP

The application name is used to carry out the check of the end of the intended purpose for customers and vendors, within the specified applications. It also serves as a condition field when creating the rules (Transaction IRMPOL – ILM Policies) for residence and retention periods for customers, vendors, or contact persons.

Within the Customizing delivered, SAP thus provides predefined application names and application classes for default applications. Changes made to the SAP namespace are modifications.

Customer namespace

You can add further application names and application classes for your applications within the customer namespace, which requires a check of the end of the intended purpose with customers and vendors.

4.2.2 Blocking Transactional Data in Transaction SPRO

Preparatory steps for transactional data

To block transactional data, you need to activate the business function `ILM_BLOCKING` (SAP ILM: blocking functionality) within Transaction SPRO (Customizing – Edit Project). This preparatory step was already addressed in Figure 4.8. Although this only has to be carried out once, it's a prerequisite for blocking both transactional and master data.

4.2.3 Blocking Master Data in SAP Information Lifecycle Management

Residence time (residence periods)

Let's now take a closer look at the period highlighted in Figure 4.15. This is the period of the residence time (residence periods). We'll now explain how to define the residence rules for master data.

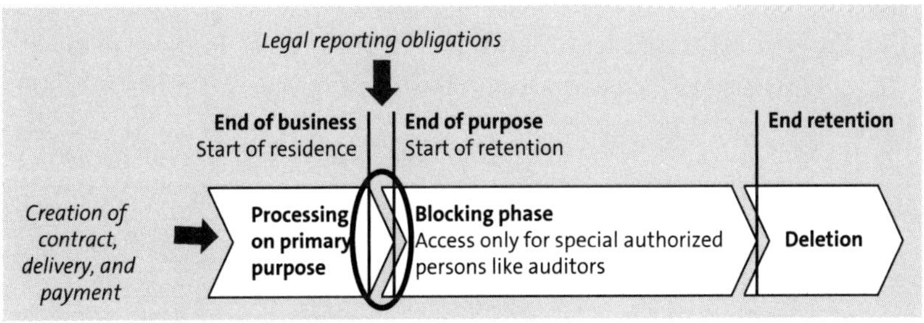

Figure 4.15 Defining Residence Rules for Master Data: Lifecycle of Personal Data (Training BIT665, 2017)

Assigning SAP ILM objects to the audit area BUPA_DP

First, in Transaction ILMARA (Audit Area Processing), you need to assign the relevant SAP ILM objects to the audit area **BUPA_DP** (see Figure 4.16).

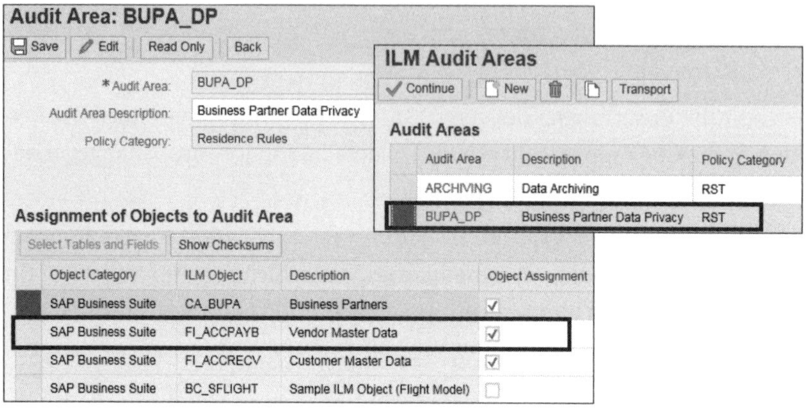

Figure 4.16 Assigning SAP ILM Objects to the BUPA_DP Audit Area

The possible SAP ILM objects are as follows:

- CA_BUPA
- FI_ACCRECV
- FI_ACCPAYB
- FI_ACCKNVK

Further information can be found in the SAP documentation under *https://help.sap.com/* by following the menu path, **Data Protection • Configuring Data Protection Features • Configuring IRMPOL • Residence Rules**.

Unique feature of audit area BUPA_DP

It's important that you use the precise audit area BUPA_DP and no other audit area. This audit area will be used specifically during the EoP check and the residence period checks it contains. We'll discuss these in more detail at a later stage. However, consider the following example for a better understanding.

[Ex]

EoP Check

The following happens during an EoP check:

- All related applications are queried as to whether they have any further use for the data you want to block.

- The system checks whether the periods related to the residence times, which you defined, have expired. For example, if you don't want a customer to be blocked until *n* days have passed since his last modification, you need to define this period of *n* days as the residence rule in audit area BUPA_DP (as explained earlier).

In this context, the time reference offered, **Start of Retention Period** (see Figure 4.17), then always refers to the date of creation or the last modification of the master data to be blocked. This is true for customers, vendors, and the central business partner.

Residence rules for master data

During the second step, you need to define the residence rules for master data in Transaction IRMPOL (ILM Policies).

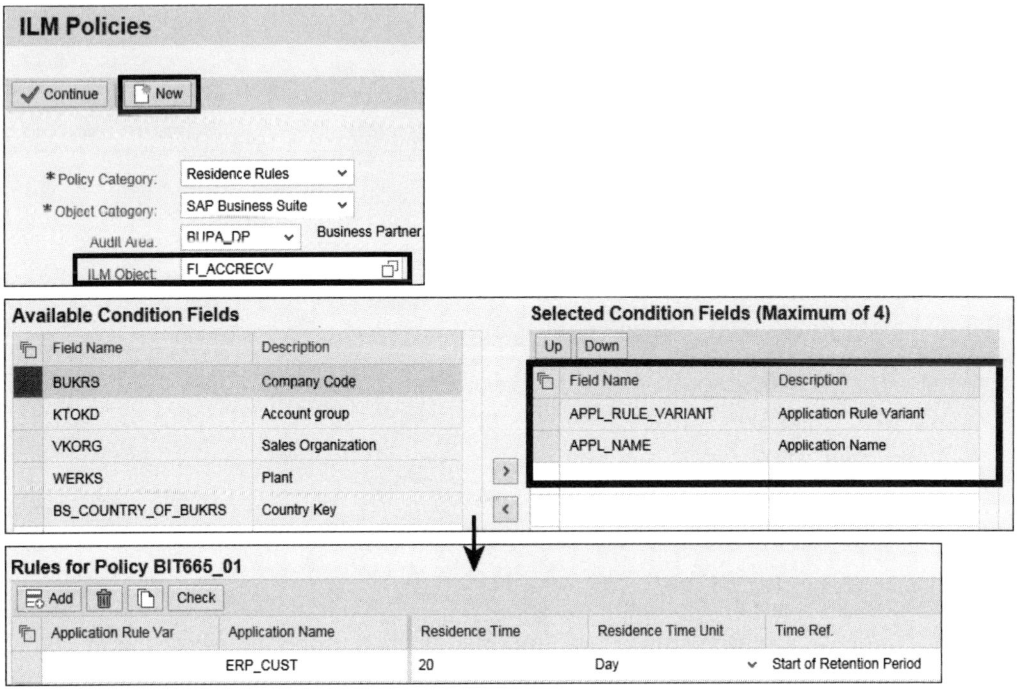

Figure 4.17 Defining Residence Rules for Master Data (SAP ILM Policies 1/5)

Figure 4.17 shows you how to create such a policy and which fields you should choose when doing so.

[»]

Meanings

A few notes on terms are as follows:

- The time reference **Start of Retention Period** refers to the EoB.
- EoB is the beginning of the residence period.
- EoP is the end of the residence period.
- The **Application RuleVar** (application rule variant [ARV]) column will be explained in more detail later in this chapter.

Note that the **Application Name** highlighted in Figure 4.18 is identical to the application name of the SAP Reference Implementation Guide (IMG) Customizing outlined earlier in Figure 4.14.

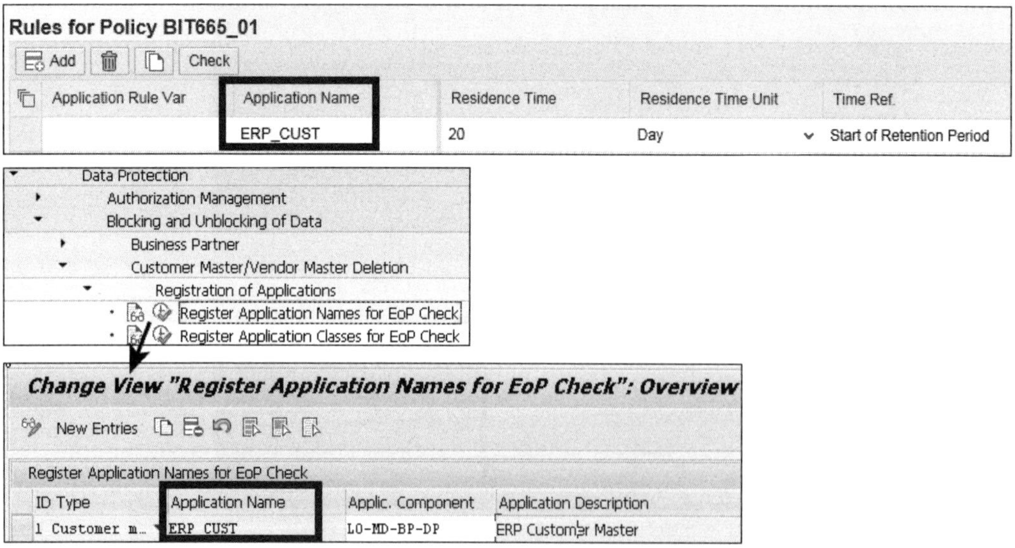

Figure 4.18 Defining Residence Rules for Master Data (SAP ILM Policies 2/5)

A master data record (e.g., customer) can only be blocked after you've defined a suitable IRM rule for the residence period. The minimum specification of such a rule is shown in Figure 4.18.

Minimum specification for the residence period

In this example, a customer can only be blocked when both of the following requirements have been met:

- All of the applications registered in Customizing confirm that there is no open business with the customer.
- The entered residence period has expired since the last modification to the customer master data.

A more complex rule

A more complex rule could look like the one shown in Figure 4.19.

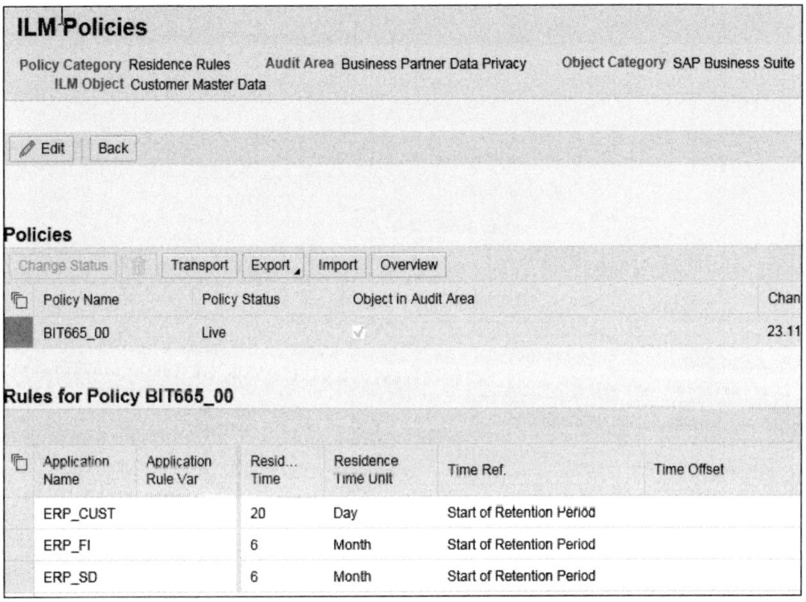

Figure 4.19 Defining Residence Rules for Master Data (SAP ILM Policies 3/5)

In this example, a customer can only be blocked when the following three requirements have been met:

- All of the applications registered in Customizing confirm that there is no open business with the customer.
- The entered residence period has expired since the last modification to the customer master data.
- Six months have passed since the clearing of the last related SAP ERP Financials (FI) or SAP ERP Sales and Distribution (SD) accounting document.

If the residence period for the transactional data (e.g., FI or SD) is dependent on the organization units (e.g., company code), you may use the ARVs. We'll take a closer look at these in Section 4.2.6.

Figure 4.20 shows you further SAP ILM objects that are available for use, such as the vendors and business partners.

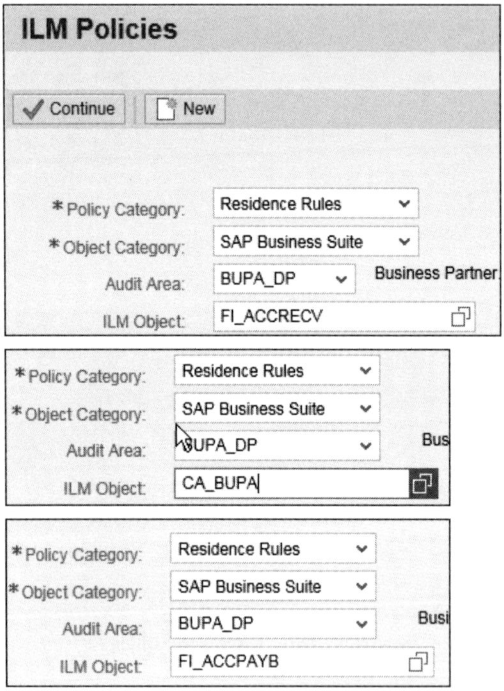

Figure 4.20 Further SAP ILM Objects Available: Vendors and Business Partners

Moreover, Figure 4.21 shows you how the possible rules would look and, in particular, which application names you need to use for each one.

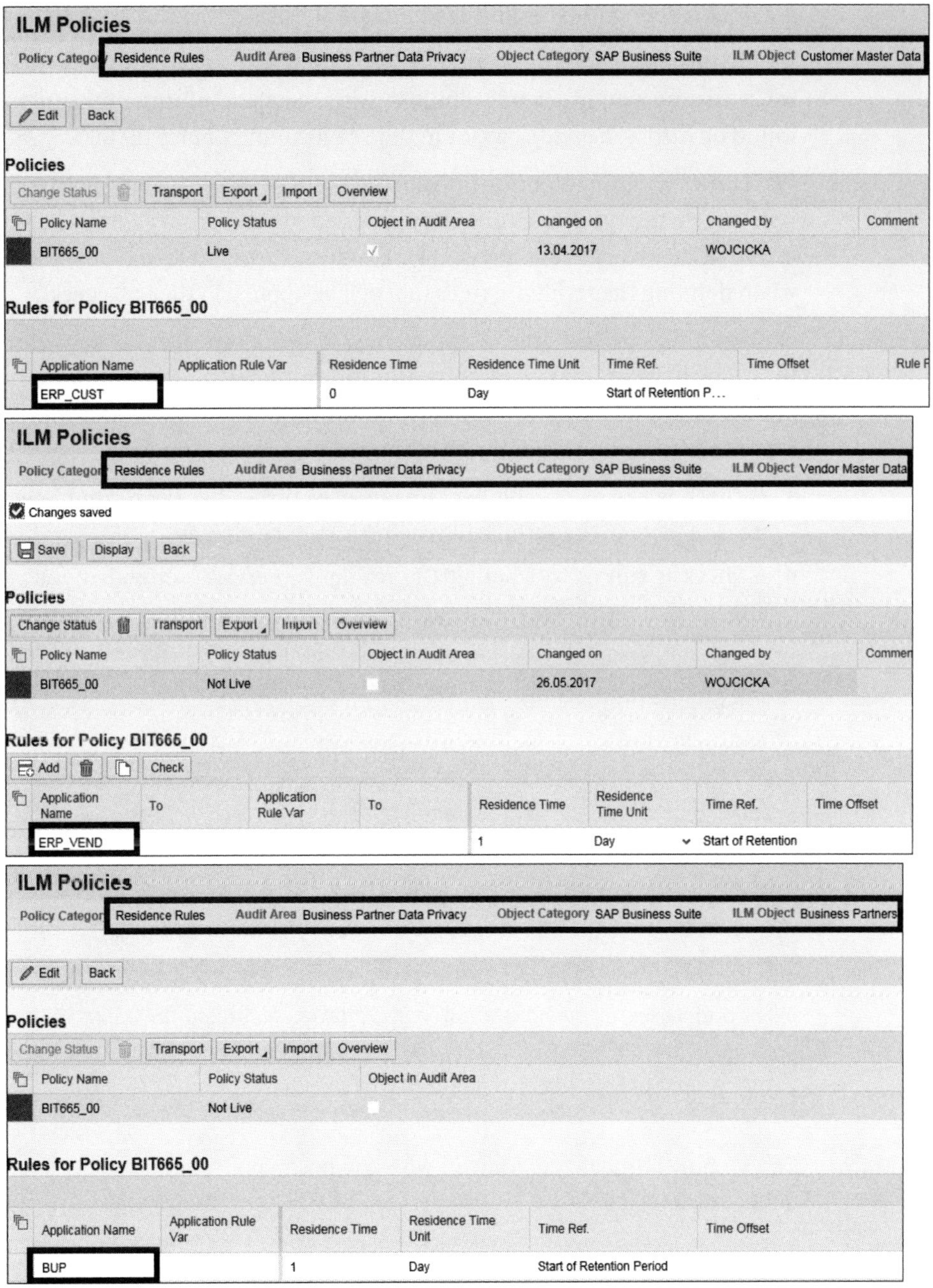

Figure 4.21 Defining Residence Rules for Master Data: Overview

4.2.4 Archiving Master and Transactional Data

Archiving master and transactional data is a separate field of expertise that we'll assume you're already familiar with. Further information can be found on *https://help.sap.com* or in the SAP Training Course BIT660.

Residence rules with the EoP check

We'll now focus our attention on a special point of interest where both topics overlap: the residence rules. As explained in relation to Figure 4.15, it's essential that you use audit area BUPA_DP—no other audit area is possible—when defining the residence rules that will be applied in the EoP check.

Residence rules and archiving

However, the original area of application of residence rules is the period until which the data may be archived. In connection with Figure 4.6, we outlined that if a business object (e.g., a customer order) is to be archived, it first needs to be checked for both of the following requirements:

- A check is run as to whether the business object has been completed. (reason: data in the archive file can no longer be changed.)
- A check is run as to whether the residence periods—provided you've already defined these—have expired.

[»]

The Application Decides

The application decides which of the following two possible methods will be applied to enable maintenance of the residence rules (residence periods)—that will be considered within the checks for archivability—for your archiving object:

- Archiving objects developed before SAP ILM provide application-specific transactions for this.
- New archiving objects allow using the ARCHIVING audit area.

For both cases, all previously stated information regarding the application range of the BUPA_DP audit area, and accordingly to the residence rules in the context of EoP checks, is still applicable.

Two application areas of residence rules

You've now familiarized yourself with the both application areas for residence rules:

- With checks for the archivability of data
- With EoP checks

We'll now return to the preparatory steps for archiving master and transactional data, as well as the points where these affect SAP ILM. Should an archiving object offer the maintenance of residence rules (residence periods) with SAP ILM, your task is to create suitable, productive IRM rules in the ARCHIVING audit area. Accordingly, these steps are just a generalization of the activities illustrated in Figure 4.16 and Figure 4.17:

- You assign the relevant SAP ILM objects to the ARCHIVING audit area.
- You create suitable, productive IRM rules.

4.2.5 Destruction of Master and Transactional Data

The final deletion—that is, the destruction of master and transactional data—is a separate field of expertise with which we assume you're already familiar. Further information can be found on *https://help.sap.com* or in the SAP Training Course BIT665.

Defining retention rules

In short, if you want to permanently delete—that is, destroy—your data on the basis of IRM rules, you need to execute the following steps:

- Decide how many audit areas you want to use and which names these should have.
- For each audit area, define suitable, productive retention rules for the relevant SAP ILM objects.
- Install a certified SAP ILM storage for the archive files, which should be entered in the **ILM Storage** column of your policy, provided you want to archive the data before destruction.

We'll now proceed to the main subject of our book and the special knowledge you need about SAP ILM in connection with the simplified blocking and deletion of personal data.

Retention rules: Authorization group column

In this context, you need to pay attention to the **Authorization Group** column of your retention rules and its meaning when blocking data. In discussing Figure 4.6, we promised to explain in more detail how an archive file is protected by authorizations so that access to the data it contains is effectively blocked. Let's illustrate this using the example of a delivery (see Figure 4.22).

As soon as you activate the business function ILM_BLOCKING, Transaction IRMPOL (ILM Policies) also provides the new **Authorization Group** column. In the example used in Figure 4.22, you can see the value **FIAU**.

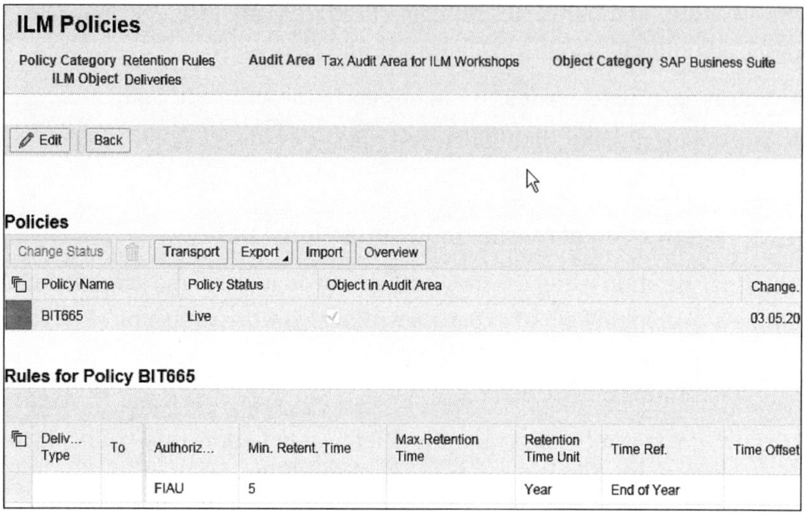

Figure 4.22 Column Authorization Group in Retention Rules

Authorization object S_ARCHIVE

In addition to the S_ARCHIVE authorization object, a user must have rights for the authorization group specified in this column if he wants to access archived data.

Additional authorizations

As soon as you've archived the data, it's protected by additional authorizations, so that access to that data is effectively blocked.

The check is performed for an archive file if a suitable, productive retention rule for the corresponding SAP ILM object exists.

Applicability

A few notes on this check are as follows:

- This check is independent of the archive file's creation date.
- The check is even effective for archive files without a calculated retention period because the check can be run directly on the basis of the data from the data object of the archive file.
- Further information can be found in SAP Note 2167473.

Authorization object S_IRM_BLOC

Figure 4.23 shows authorization object `S_IRM_BLOC`, which allows you to set up the authorizations for the archived data in more detail by using the following:

- Audit area
- SAP ILM object
- Assigned authorization group

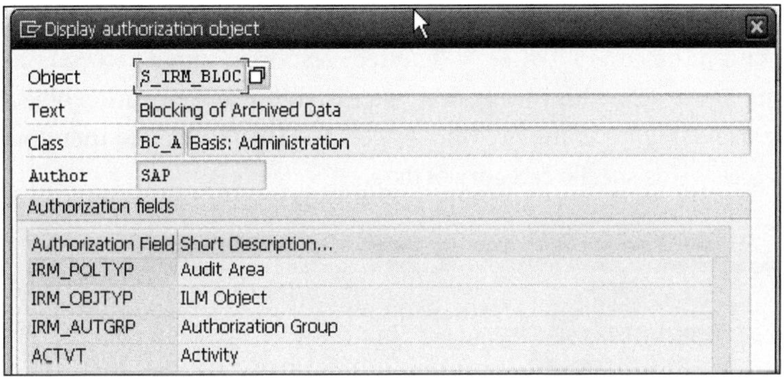

Figure 4.23 Authorization Object S_IRM_BLOC: Block Display of Archived Data

The logic behind this is based on the audit areas in SAP ILM; you can store authorization groups in their rules as described earlier. If the data is already in the archive, the system then determines the corresponding audit area and the retention periods stored there for the requested, archived data. It also checks in the user master data of the user requesting the data regarding whether the stored authorization group has been assigned.

You can only use the blocking discussed here by means of archive files if you've configured the required settings in SAP ILM. See the following:

- SAP Note 2169333 (Blocking of Already Archived Data)
- SAP Note 2167473 (User-Specific Blocking of the Display of Archived, Personal Data)

We'll close this subject with some important information about special cases.

Retention period expired

A special case is the constellation in which the user is authorized to view blocked data, but the data's retention period has expired. The system will treat this case as if the user doesn't have access rights to the data. The requested data won't be displayed because it should have been destroyed already.

Retention period expired and legal case

However, there is an exception. You might anticipate a case in which access to such data is mandatory; namely when the requested information is contained within a legal case. For this reason, you're provided with a special authorization object—`S_IRM_BL_M` (expired resources grant access)—as shown in Figure 4.24. This means that you assign the authorization object to those users in your company who process the legal cases and therefore need to access this special category of data.

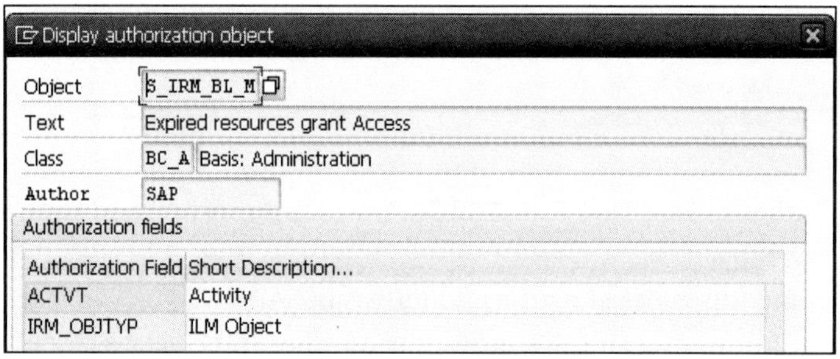

Figure 4.24 Authorization Object S_IRM_BL_M

4.2.6 Blocking and Deleting Master Data: Application Rule Variants

Let's now focus our attention on the previously mentioned application rule variants (ARV). What do they represent and when should you use them? You'll recall that the ARV (refer back to Figure 4.17) is a possible column when creating policies in Transaction IRMPOL (ILM Policies).

The area of application

The ARV is only offered for master data, for example, ILM object `FI_ACCRECV` (customer master data). ARVs aren't necessary for the retention or residence rules of application data (e.g., FI documents); therefore, this column isn't available for selection (see Figure 4.25).

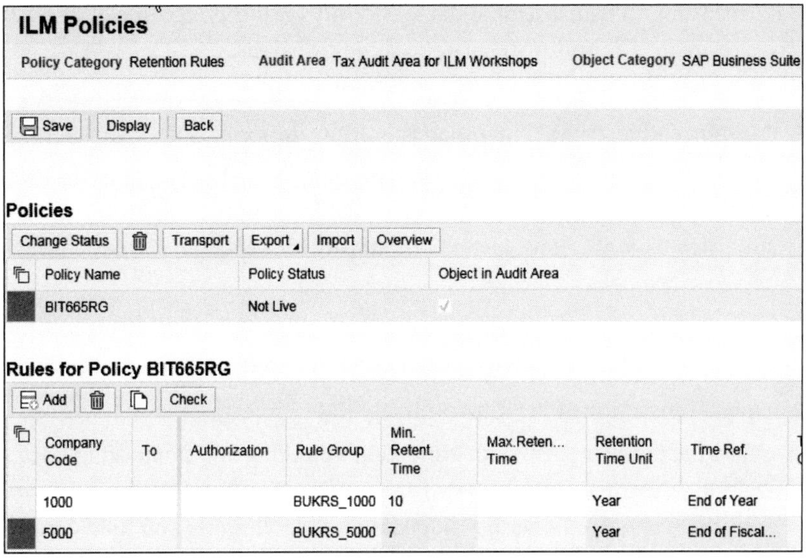

Figure 4.25 Retention Rules for Transactional Data

Application scenarios

What areas of application are there for the ARVs when dealing with master data? In the main case A, which is applicable for master data and the retention rules thereof, the focus is on creating a connection between the retention period of master data and the retention period of all transactional data from a master data record.

Although it may seem like the obvious way to go, retention periods for master data aren't determined by inheritance. This means that the longest retention period of the corresponding application documents won't be determined automatically by the system and won't be used as the retention period for the corresponding master data.

Double maintenance of retention periods

As a result, you'll have to define the retention period of master data by means of an IRM rule. For you, this means double maintenance. We'll shortly go into more detail to explain how the concept of the ARV can actually simplify the double maintenance.

Residence rules depending on organizational units

But first, let's look at a second possible area of application (Case B), which lies with the residence rules for master data. First, it's important that you check whether this provides you with any added value. This is the case if you want to define residence rules that are dependent on the organizational unit for master data (e.g., company codes), which include a master data record with transactional data. The ARVs are therefore used in such cases to create a connection between these two areas.

[Ex]

Residence Rules That Depend on the Organizational Unit

One example could be a case where you only want the customer to be blocked when all corresponding FI and SD documents have been closed and when 6 months have passed in company code 1000 and 14 days have passed in company code 5000.

Let's now take a look at how you can define the ARVs:

1. Open Transaction SPRO (Customizing – Edit Project).
2. Select the familiar path, **Data Protection • Blocking and Unblocking Data • Deleting Customer Master Data/Vendor Master Data Deletion,** and subsequently choose the **Assign Application Rule Variants and Rule Groups for EoP Check** activity.
3. When you get to the next screen (see Figure 4.26), enter the following:
   - In the **ID Type** ❶ and **Appl Name** ❷ columns, enter the applications that uses the respective type of customer master data.
   - In the **Application R** column ❹, enter the corresponding rule groups. This can be defined in Transaction IRM_CUST_CSS (IRM Customer-Specific Settings).
   - In the **Rule Group** column ❸, assign a name for the ARV that you're defining.
   - Finally, in the **Application Rule Variant Description** column ❺, enter a suitable description for your ARV.

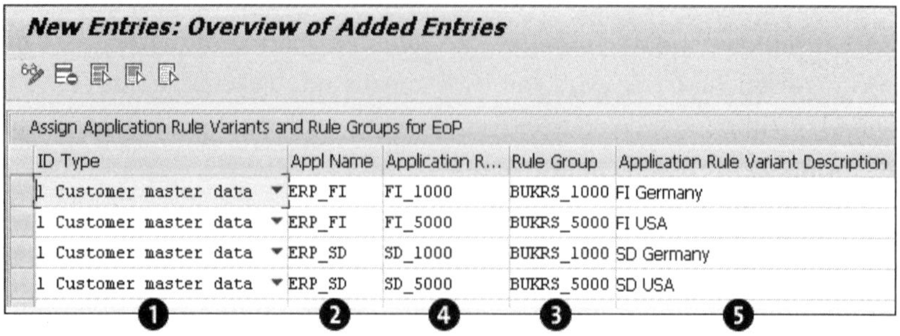

New Entries: Overview of Added Entries

Assign Application Rule Variants and Rule Groups for EoP

ID Type	Appl Name	Application R...	Rule Group	Application Rule Variant Description
1 Customer master data	ERP_FI	FI_1000	BUKRS_1000	FI Germany
1 Customer master data	ERP_FI	FI_5000	BUKRS_5000	FI USA
1 Customer master data	ERP_SD	SD_1000	BUKRS_1000	SD Germany
1 Customer master data	ERP_SD	SD_5000	BUKRS_5000	SD USA
❶	❷	❹	❸	❺

Figure 4.26 Transaction SPRO (Customizing – Edit Project)

> **Where is the Assignment Stored?**
>
> In the EoP check coding, you'll find that, for example, FI_ACCRECV is included in **ID Type Customer master data.**

The ARV created this way is now a combination of the customer master data type (ID type), the name of the application, and a rule group. You could now use it in Transaction IRMPOL (ILM Rules). Therefore, we'll now take a look at the two possible use cases you may choose from (A and B).

Case A: Retention Period for Master Data

Case A (see Figure 4.27), one of the main areas of use, is about the retention period for master data and the previously mentioned double maintenance.

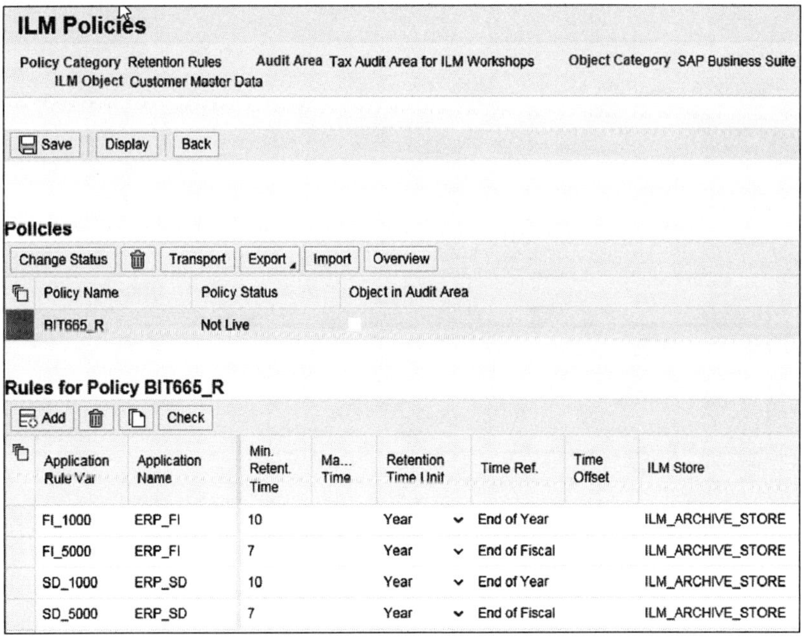

Figure 4.27 Case A: Double Maintenance of Retention Period for Master Data (1/2)

Simplified double maintenance of the retention period

You can use the ARV to make double maintenance easier; the gray columns of the rule group, to which you assigned the ARV when you defined it, will be filled automatically. This means you don't have to enter them again manually, which in turn means fewer mistakes and a reduction of the time and effort necessary for double maintenance.

[»]

Using ARVs for the Application Name of Master Data

You can't use the ARVs for the application name of the master data (e.g., ERP_CUST), as illustrated in Figure 4.28 by the horizontal line (bottom left). If you've entered a value here, you'll see that a corresponding error message will appear.

If you have a case where you want the retention period of the master data to be based on the retention period of the corresponding transactional data and it has been *n* years since the date was last changed (10 years in our example), you should leave the **Application Rule Var** column blank.

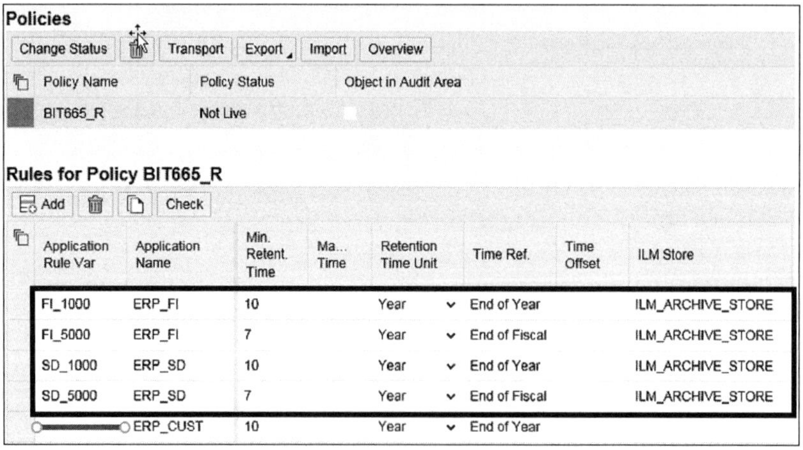

Figure 4.28 Case A: Double Maintenance for Retention Period of Master Data (2/2)

At this point, it's important to note that the use of ARVs makes a lot of sense when dealing with cases such as the previously illustrated Case A—the retention period definition for master data depending on the corresponding application names and transactional data (e.g., ERP_FI). At the beginning, we referred to this as double maintenance.

Case B: Residence Period after the Clearing of Transactional Data

Residence time of transactional data

Let's now move on to a second possibility, Case B, which is illustrated in Figure 4.29 and was also touched on briefly within the scope of Figure 4.19. The ARVs are available for use here if the residence time of your transactional data (e.g., FI or SD) is dependent on the organizational units (e.g., company codes).

The specified 6 months or 14 days in the residence rule of the BUPA_DP audit area mean that to block a master data record (e.g., customer), the following criteria must be fulfilled for transactional data:

- All FI and SD documents in company code 1000 (5000) are closed, *and* it has been 6 months (14 days) since then.
- If there are no FI–SD documents for the customer in the corresponding company code, the rule should be ignored.
- A day has passed since the last change was made or, if no change has been made, since the creation date of the master data record.

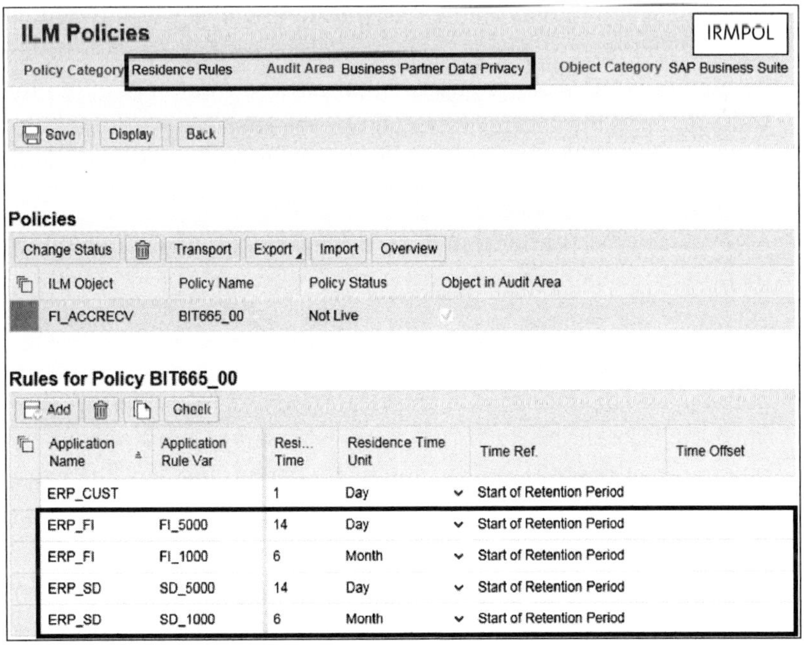

Figure 4.29 Case B: Residence Time after the Clearing of Corresponding Transactional Data That Are Dependent on the Organizational Units

Regarding the first point on the list, in case you were wondering how the system knows that company code 1000 or 5000 has to be taken into consideration, we'll now go into that in a little more detail. The following steps are taken for all registered application names (see Figure 4.29); we'll take a look at them using the example application name ERP_FI and the FI documents:

1. The implementation of the application class for the application name ERP_FI specifies that all FI documents, concerning the customer to be blocked, will be checked. The checks will only continue after they have all been completed. Otherwise, it's already clear that the master data can't be blocked.
2. If the master data record could be blocked, the next step determines which retention and residence periods are valid for this application name. You already entered these as one of the preparatory steps for the master data SAP ILM object (e.g., FI_ACCRECV) in Transaction IRMPOL (ILM Policies) for the application name (e.g., ERP_FI).
3. For this application name, it will now be determined which condition fields of the corresponding SAP ILM objects are relevant for further checks. For SAP ILM object FI_DOCUMNT, these would be, for example, the company code, the document type, and the posting key.
4. This information determines the retention rules that you specified in Transaction IRMPOL (ILM Policies) for the values of the condition fields. At the same time, the rule groups used are also determined. You can see them in the column with the same name in Figure 4.25.
5. The ARVs you defined in the IMG will be determined for these rule groups (see Figure 4.26).
6. At this point, the system has all the data it needs to determine the retention periods for the master data. It's now necessary to check whether the residence periods you entered for BUPA_DP audit area and the corresponding master data SAP ILM object have expired (in our example, 6 months or 14 days), as follows:
   - If this isn't the case, the EoP for this application name hasn't been reached, and it's not yet possible to block the master data record.
   - The future date calculated for the end of the residence periods will be saved and will be used to calculate the date of the next EoP check.

- At this point, as explained in connection with Figure 4.9 shown earlier, the maximum number of days determined until the next check will also be taken into account. If necessary, it will override a date determined by the application that is too far in the future.
- If the residence periods have expired, however, the master data can be blocked.
- For the combination of the ARV and the application name, the result of the EoP check that will be saved is the end of the transaction as the start of the retention period.

No variants of application rules

Still focusing on the previously explained usage case B, we conclude that, conversely, you don't need any ARVs if one of the following applies:

- The residence periods don't depend on your organizational units.
- You don't want to define any application-specific residence periods. The fact that the corresponding application documents have been completed and the residence period defined in the master data record itself (application name ERP_CUST) has expired is sufficient for you.

Only in conjunction with the master data

We initially said that ARVs are only offered for master data. They aren't required for retention or residence rules of application data, and this column therefore won't be available for selection.

Finally, let's take a further possibility for where you could enter an ARV, which would make very little sense in practice, however (see Figure 4.30).

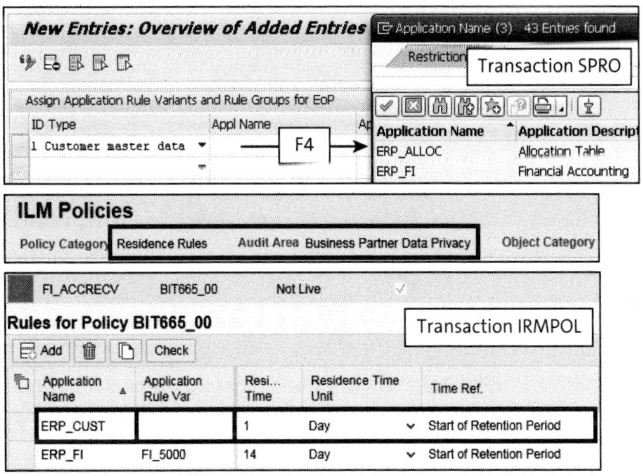

Figure 4.30 Residence Time from the Last Change to the Master Data Record

A value of **1 Day** in the residence rule means that the following criteria must be met cumulatively to block a master data record (e.g., customer):

- The end of business must have taken place.
- It must have been at least one day since the last change to the customer master data.

No variants of application rules

The key message here is that the EoP checks related to master data (e.g., application name ERP_CUST) don't use ARVs. Therefore, the corresponding application names (e.g., ERP_CUST) aren't available for selection when you create an ARV, as shown in the field help [F4].

For that reason, leave this column of the policy blank. Alternatively, when defining a policy, don't select this column at all if the policy is only intended for retention periods related to master data; that is, you don't plan to enter application names such as ERP_FI.

4.3 Blocking from a Business Perspective

We're now going to look at how you can block master data and subsequently, how you can block transactional data. In doing so, we'll also show you what access options you still have to such data.

4.3.1 Blocking Master Data in the Business Process

To show you how to block master data, we'll use one customer master data record.

Case 1: Customer Can't Be Blocked: No Business; Residence Period Not Expired

Let's start with an easy example in which we'll create a customer in Transaction XD01 (Create Customer – Central) and then try to block the customer.

Take a look at the residence periods you defined in Transaction RMPOL (ILM Policies), as shown in Figure 4.31. In this particular context, the specified start of retention period always means the date on which the master data record was created or last changed. This applies to customers, vendors, and the central business partner.

Because we've only just created the customer master data, the required residence period hasn't yet expired. So let's check to see whether it really isn't possible to block the customer.

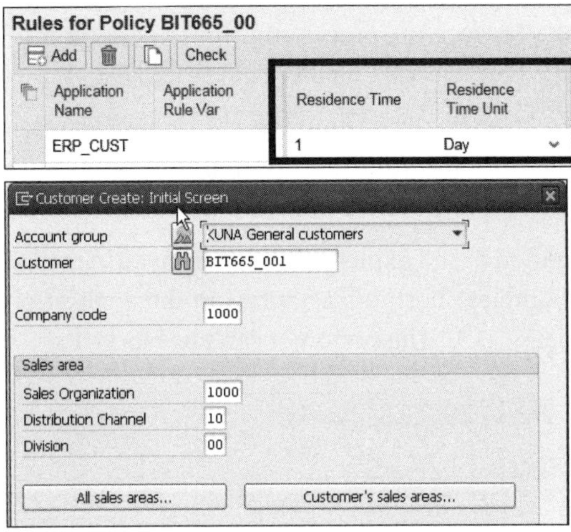

Figure 4.31 Case 1 Customer Can't Be Blocked: No Business with the Customer; Residence Period Not Expired (1/3)

Blocking customer and vendor master data

Figure 4.32 shows Transaction CVP_PRE_EOP (Block Customer and Vendor Master Data), which is used to block a customer or vendor.

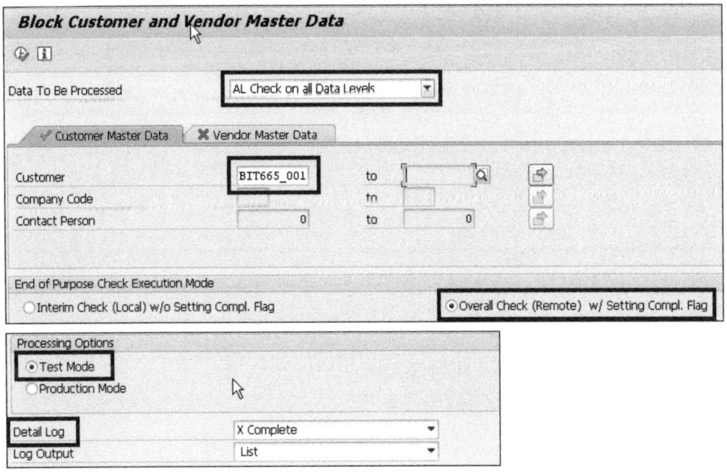

Figure 4.32 Case 1 Customer Can't Be Blocked: No Business with the Customer; Residence Period Not Expired (2/3)

Enter the data to be processed, and specify which customers you want to block. When doing so, your specifications in **End of Purpose Check Execution Mode** are also important. When starting the transaction in your leading master system, select **Overall Check**. We recommend that you first start the transaction in test mode. To trace the processing steps of the transaction, we also recommend that you select **X Complete** in the detail log.

Result of the EoP check

Figure 4.33 shows the log displayed by the transaction after it has been executed. You'll find that two partner records are displayed because a check was run on both general and company code levels.

As expected, the residence period hasn't expired. This is displayed in the log box that reports on the incomplete business activities in the application you're already familiar with: ERP_CUST. The customer can't be blocked.

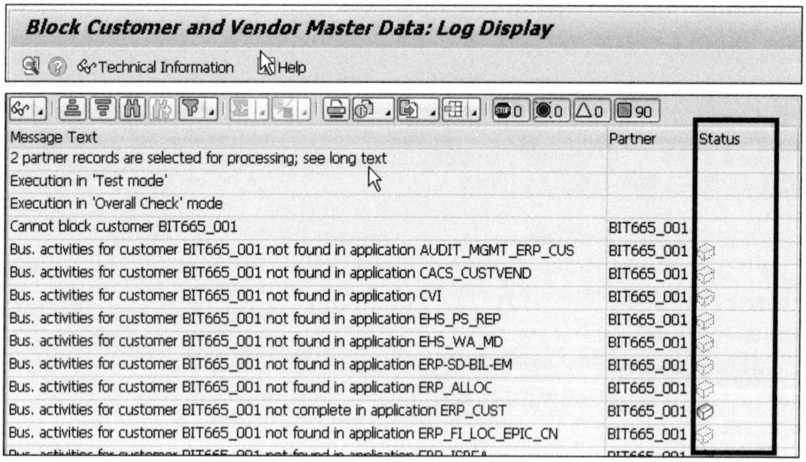

Message Text	Partner	Status
2 partner records are selected for processing; see long text		
Execution in 'Test mode'		
Execution in 'Overall Check' mode		
Cannot block customer BIT665_001	BIT665_001	
Bus. activities for customer BIT665_001 not found in application AUDIT_MGMT_ERP_CUS	BIT665_001	
Bus. activities for customer BIT665_001 not found in application CACS_CUSTVEND	BIT665_001	
Bus. activities for customer BIT665_001 not found in application CVI	BIT665_001	
Bus. activities for customer BIT665_001 not found in application EHS_PS_REP	BIT665_001	
Bus. activities for customer BIT665_001 not found in application EHS_WA_MD	BIT665_001	
Bus. activities for customer BIT665_001 not found in application ERP-SD-BIL-EM	BIT665_001	
Bus. activities for customer BIT665_001 not found in application ERP_ALLOC	BIT665_001	
Bus. activities for customer BIT665_001 not complete in application ERP_CUST	BIT665_001	
Bus. activities for customer BIT665_001 not found in application ERP_FI_LOC_EPIC_CN	BIT665_001	

Figure 4.33 Case 1 Customer Can't Be Blocked: No Business with the Customer; Residence Period Not Expired (3/3)

[»]

The Cubes as a Status

The cubes displayed in the **Status** column in Figure 4.33 allow you to quickly find the results of the check. This representation can have the following values:

- Shaded = no business with the customer
- Half-shaded = business transacted but not yet concluded
- Completely filled in/shaded = business transacted and concluded

Case 2: Customer Can Be Blocked: No Business; Residence Period Expired

The next step in our example is to wait for the duration of the residence period, which for test purposes is set to one day, and then execute Transaction CVP_PRE_EOP (Block Customer and Vendor Master Data) again on the following day. The log in Figure 4.34 shows the test results correctly for this particular case. The residence period for this customer has expired. Furthermore, there are no further (incomplete) transactions with this customer. The customer can be blocked.

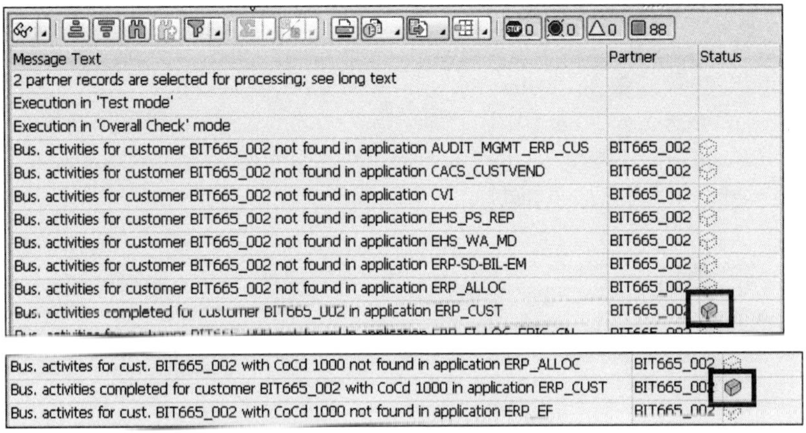

Message Text	Partner	Status
2 partner records are selected for processing; see long text		
Execution in 'Test mode'		
Execution in 'Overall Check' mode		
Bus. activities for customer BIT665_002 not found in application AUDIT_MGMT_ERP_CUS	BIT665_002	
Bus. activities for customer BIT665_002 not found in application CACS_CUSTVEND	BIT665_002	
Bus. activities for customer BIT665_002 not found in application CVI	BIT665_002	
Bus. activities for customer BIT665_002 not found in application EHS_PS_REP	BIT665_002	
Bus. activities for customer BIT665_002 not found in application EHS_WA_MD	BIT665_002	
Bus. activities for customer BIT665_002 not found in application ERP-SD-BIL-EM	BIT665_002	
Bus. activities for customer BIT665_002 not found in application ERP_ALLOC	BIT665_002	
Bus. activities completed for customer BIT665_002 in application ERP_CUST	BIT665_002	

Bus. activites for cust. BIT665_002 with CoCd 1000 not found in application ERP_ALLOC	BIT665_002	
Bus. activities completed for customer BIT665_002 with CoCd 1000 in application ERP_CUST	BIT665_002	
Bus. activites for cust. BIT665_002 with CoCd 1000 not found in application ERP_EF	BIT665_002	

Figure 4.34 Case 2 Customer Can Be Blocked: No Business with the Customer; Residence Period Expired

Case 3: Customer Can't Be Blocked: No Open Business

Building on our example, we'll now post a document in Transaction FB01 (Post Document) for this customer, and in the next step, we'll clear it with Transaction F-28 (Post Incoming Payments).

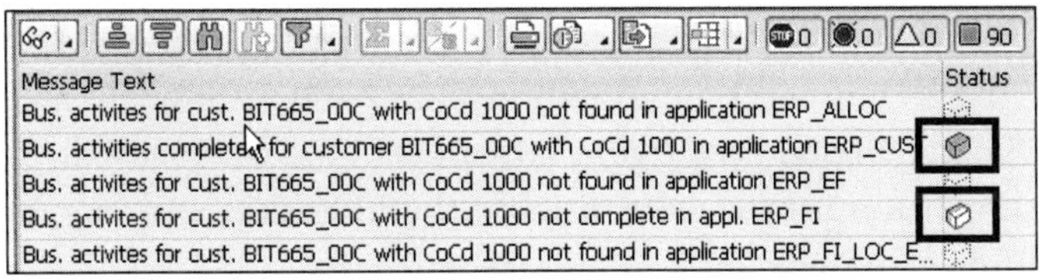

Message Text	Status
Bus. activites for cust. BIT665_00C with CoCd 1000 not found in application ERP_ALLOC	
Bus. activities completed for customer BIT665_00C with CoCd 1000 in application ERP_CUS	
Bus. activites for cust. BIT665_00C with CoCd 1000 not found in application ERP_EF	
Bus. activites for cust. BIT665_00C with CoCd 1000 not complete in appl. ERP_FI	
Bus. activites for cust. BIT665_00C with CoCd 1000 not found in application ERP_FI_LOC_E...	

Figure 4.35 Case 3 Customer Can't Be Blocked: Incomplete Business with the Customer; Residence Period Expired

Prior to clearing the document, Transaction CVP_PRE_EOP (Block Customer and Vendor Master Data) won't allow the customer to be blocked. This is shown in Figure 4.35 using the example customer BUCH_S3. In this case, the residence period has expired.

Case 4: Customer Can Be Blocked: Business Transaction Completed; Residence Period Expired

After all business activities for the customer have been concluded, it's possible to block the customer. Figure 4.36 shows the corresponding log.

> **Independent of Archiving**
>
> It's irrelevant whether parts of the corresponding documents have been archived or not because the archived data belongs to a business activity that has been fully completed.

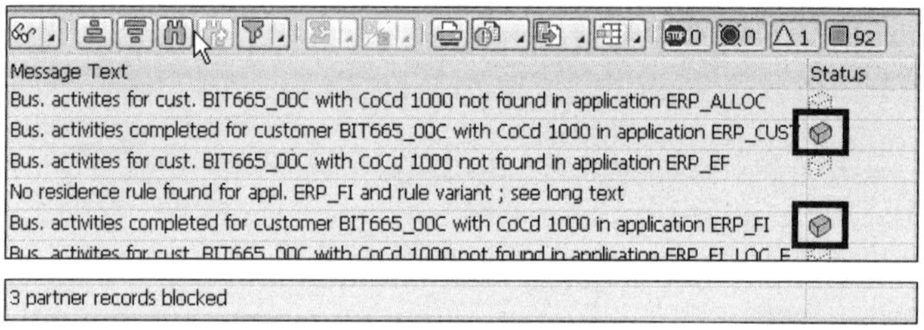

Figure 4.36 Case 4 Customer Can Be Blocked: Completed Business Transaction; Residence Period Expired

4.3.2 Display of Blocked Master Data in the Business Process

Blocked master data

Let's now take a look at our example to see the display of master data for a blocked customer. We'll demonstrate with the help of two users:

- One of the users has a check authorization and should therefore be able to see the blocked master data. Figure 4.11, earlier in this chapter, showed you in which Customizing activity to define the authorization group for flagging blocked master data.
- The second user doesn't have this special authorization; he shouldn't be able to see the blocked master data.

Case 1: Display Blocked Customer with Check Authorization

Figure 4.37 illustrates that a user with check authorization (authorization group for flagging blocked master data) is able to view the master data of a blocked customer in Transaction XD03 (Display Document). The system first sends a warning that the customer is flagged for deletion (blocked), and then, after confirming this information, the data will be displayed.

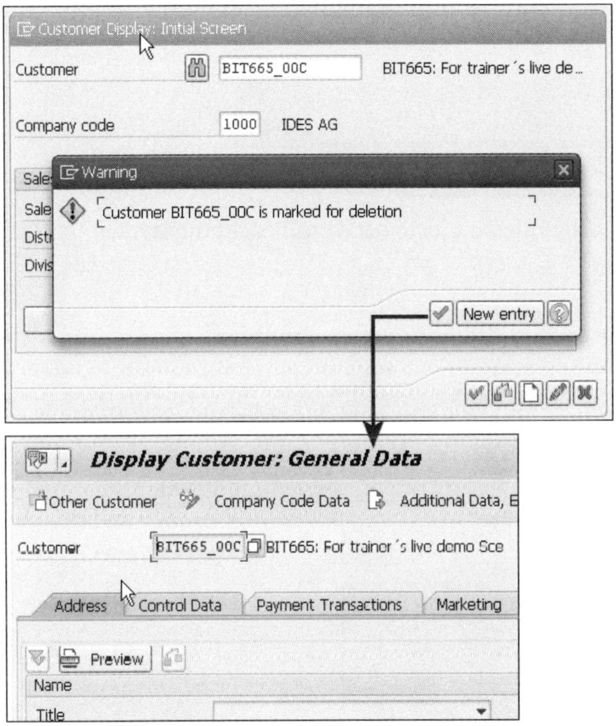

Figure 4.37 Case 1 Display Blocked Customer with Check Authorization: Transaction XD03

Case 2: Change Blocked Customer Master Data with Check Authorization

Figure 4.38 shows in case A (left) that a user with check authorization can't change the master data of a blocked customer in Transaction XD02 (Change Customer [Centrally]). The system sends an error message explaining this issue. In principle, it isn't possible to make changes to blocked data.

Case B (see right side of Figure 4.38) shows that the reviewer may not have any authorization at all for the transaction to change master data.

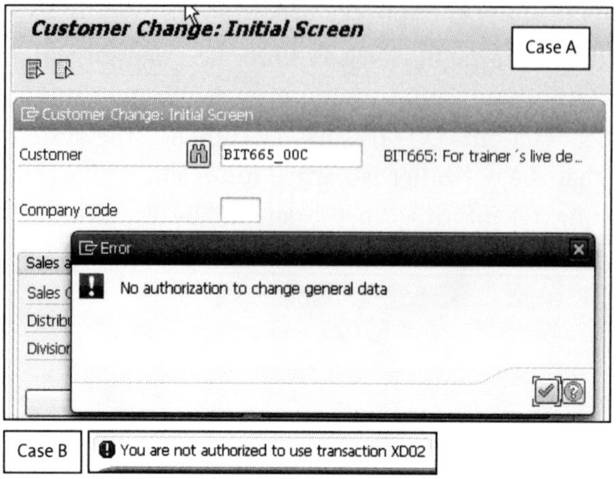

Figure 4.38 Case 2 Change Blocked Customer with Check Authorization: Transaction XD02

Case 3: Display and Change Blocked Customer without Check Authorization

No check authorization Figure 4.39 and Figure 4.40 show that a user without check authorization can't view or change the master data of a blocked customer.

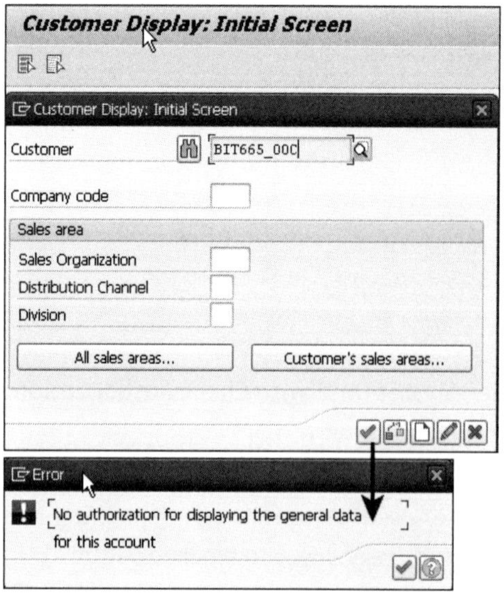

Figure 4.39 Case 3 Display Customer with User without Check Authorization Before/After Blocking: Transaction XD03

Neither Transaction XD03 (Display Customer [Centrally]) nor Transaction XD02 (Change Customer [Centrally]) allow processing.

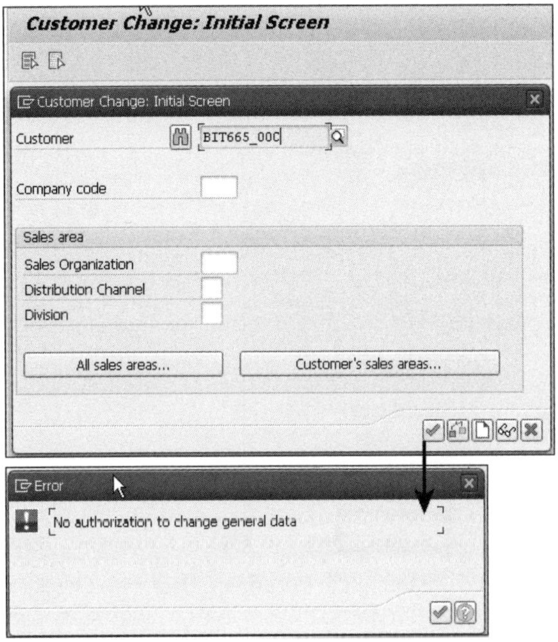

Figure 4.40 Case 3 Change Customer with User without Check Authorization Before/After Blocking: Transaction XD02

Case 4: Display Blocked Customer's SAP ERP Financials Document

In the following case, Figure 4.41 illustrates how Transaction FB03 (Display Document) allows a user with check authorization (authorization group for flagging blocked master data) to see all items of a document (not archived), especially item 1, which is related to the blocked customer.

In comparison, Figure 4.42 shows that a user without check authorization isn't shown the document item for the blocked customer. Transaction FB03 (Display Document) sends a notification explaining the issue.

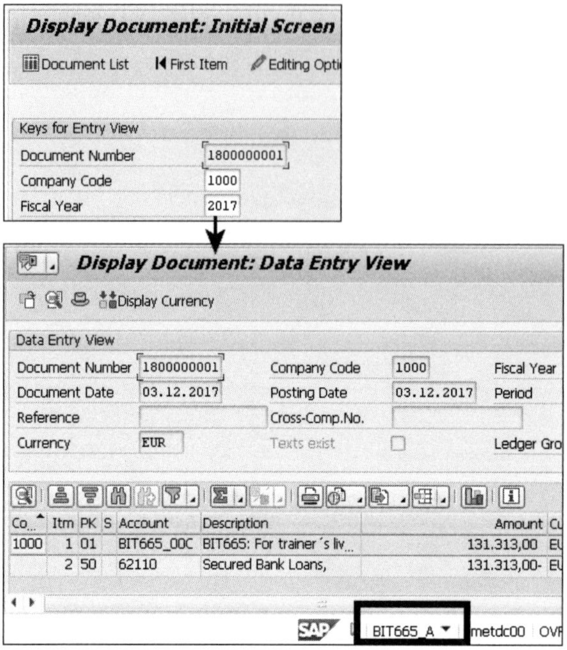

Figure 4.41 Case 4 Display Blocked Customer's FI Document: User with Check Authorization

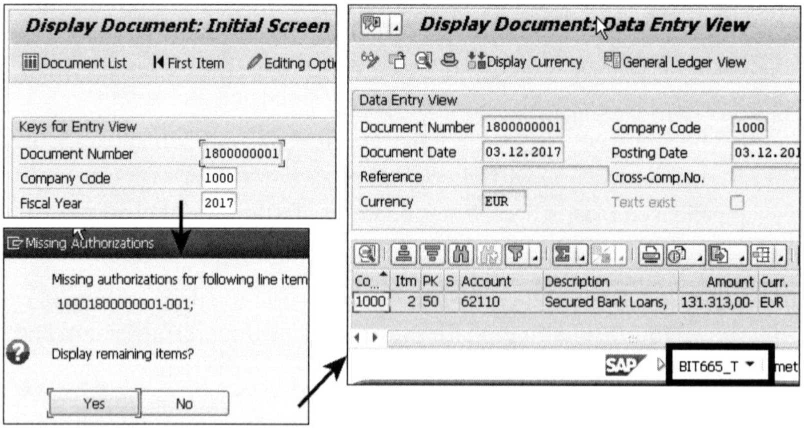

Figure 4.42 Case 4 Display Blocked Customer's FI Document: User without Check Authorization

Case 5: Customer Line Item List: User without Check Authorization

Transaction FBL5N

In Case 5, you'll see that the customer line item list in Transaction FBL5N (Customer Line Items), as shown in Figure 4.43, doesn't show a user without check authorization any items if he enters a blocked customer as the customer account.

If the same user also tries to obtain a list of all existing customers using field help (F4) for the **Customer account** field, no blocked customers will be displayed (see Figure 4.44).

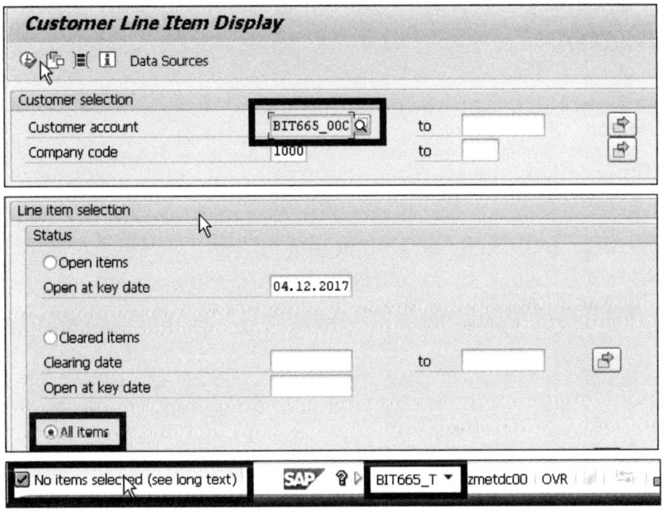

Figure 4.43 Case 5 Customer Line Item List (Transaction FBL5N): User without Check Authorization (1/2)

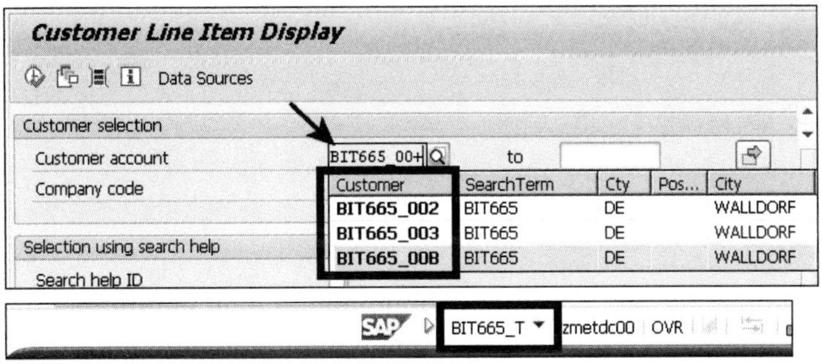

Figure 4.44 Case 5 Customer Line Item List (Transaction FBL5N): User without Check Authorization (2/2)

4.3.3 Unblocking Master Data in the Business Process

Rarely, but nevertheless of interest, you may also need the functionality for the reverse process—unblocking a master data record. Let's look at an example using a blocked customer, as follows:

Unblock request

1. **Create an unblock request.**
   Your first step is to open Transaction BUP_REQ_UNBLK (Business Partner Unblock Requests). As shown in Figure 4.45, choose the required **Object Type** (in our example, it's **Customer**). Some possible alternatives are as follows:
   - **Business Partner**
   - **Vendor**
   - **Contact Person**

   In the **Customer** field, specify the customers you want to unblock. Finally, you have to specify the reason for your request. To complete your actions, click on the **Request Unblocking** button.

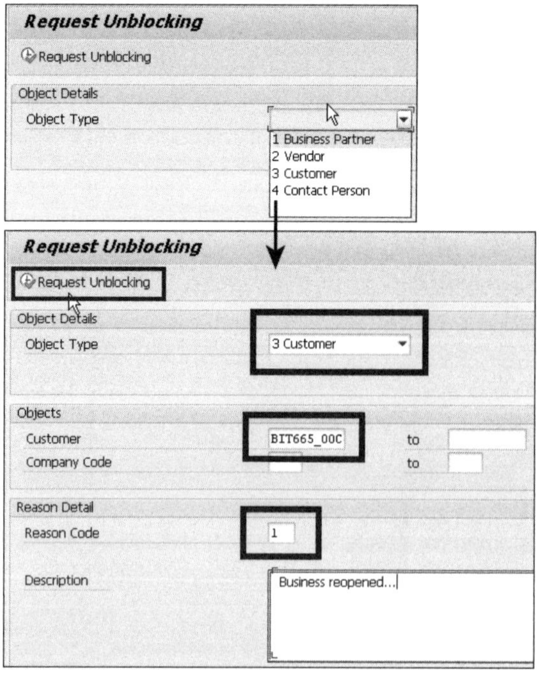

Figure 4.45 Opening Transaction BUP_REQ_UNBLK (Business Partner Unblock Request)

Transaction BUP_REQ_UNBLK (Business Partner Unblock Request) now creates an unblocking request for you.

2. **Approve unblocking.**
In the next step, an employee can approve the unblock request and carry out the unblocking process. This is done in one of the following two transactions:
   - Transaction CVP_UNBLOCK_MD (Unblock Customer and Vendor Master Data) for customers and vendors, as shown in Figure 4.46 and Figure 4.47.

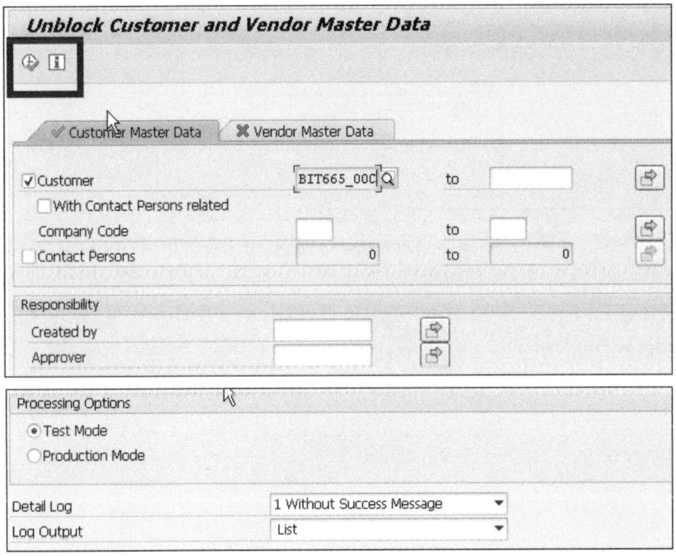

Figure 4.46 Transaction CVP_UNBLOCK_MD (Unblock Customer and Vendor Master Data) (1/2)

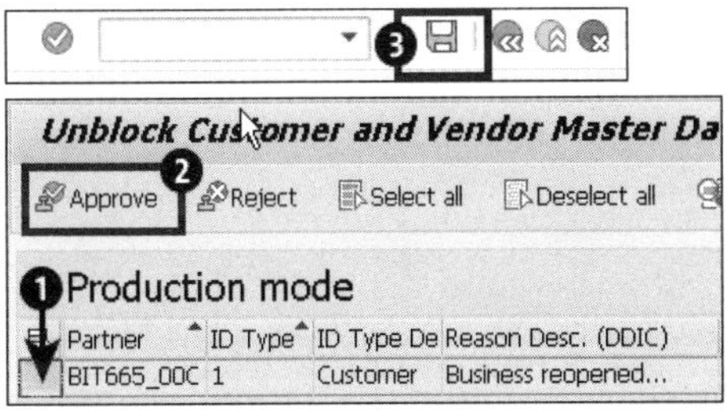

Figure 4.47 Transaction CVP_UNBLOCK_MD (Unblock Customer and Vendor Master Data) (2/2)

- Transcription BUP_REQ_UNBLK (Business Partner Unblock Request) for the central business partner, as shown in Figure 4.48.

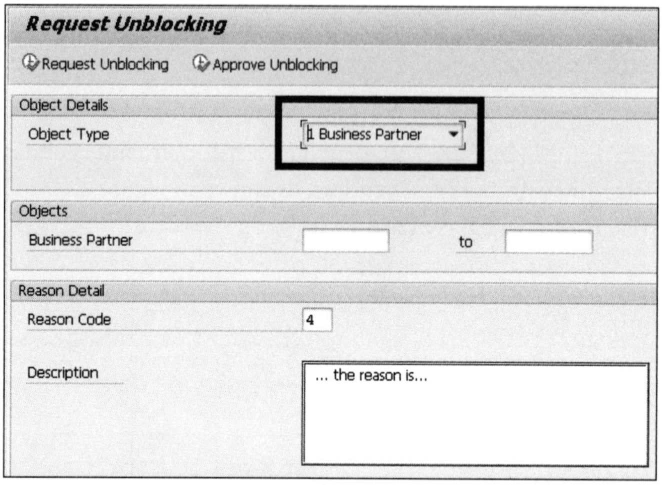

Figure 4.48 Transaction BUP_REQ_UNBLK (Business Partner Unblock Request)

Customizing for the Reason Code field

Finally, let's now take a look at the **Reason Detail** area for unblocking that you enter in the field of the same name, as explained in the previously addressed transactions (see Figure 4.49).

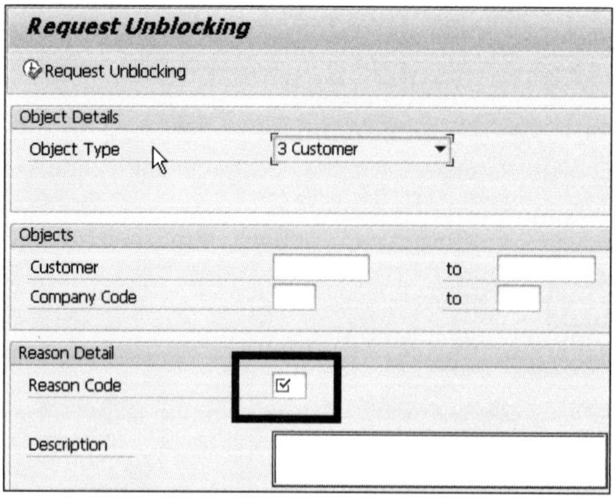

Figure 4.49 Transaction BUP_REQ_UNBLK (Business Partner Unblock Request): Customizing for the Reason Code Field (1/2)

You now have the freedom to predefine the values that may be entered in this field. The Customizing transaction shown in Figure 4.50 is available for this purpose.

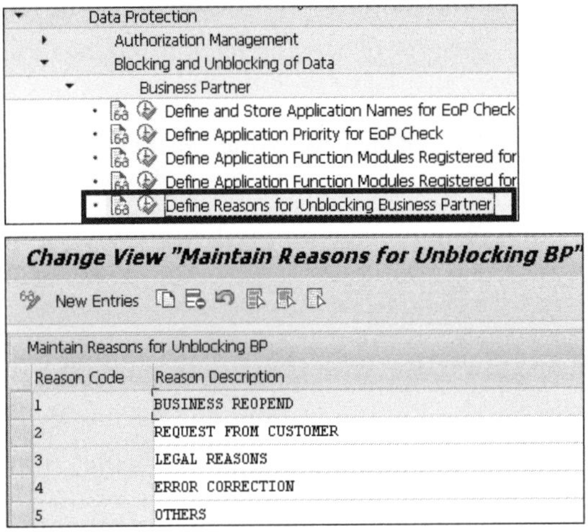

Figure 4.50 Transaction BUP_REQ_UNBLK (Business Partner Unblock Request): Customizing for the Reason Code Field (2/2)

> **The Reason Code**
>
> The defined input help for this field [F4] is available when unblocking not only business partners but also customers or vendors.

4.3.4 Blocking Transactional Data in the Business Process

To block transactional data in the business process, carry out the following steps in the same way as described earlier for blocking transactional data in the business process:

SAP ILM-based archiving of data

1. Archive data. Archiving data is an independent knowledge field that is essential for the simplified blocking and deletion of personal data with SAP ILM. Further information can be found, for example, under *https://help.sap.com* or in SAP Training Course BIT660.

SAP Training Course BIT660

2. Define and use the authorization group.
3. Enter the **Authorization Group** column in your retention rules, and use it accordingly in the authorization profiles of your users.

4.3.5 Display of Blocked Transactional Data in the Business Process

First, note that a particular type of transactional data display, which was archived due to blocking, is partly application specific. The checks explained previously to determine whether a user is authorized to see the data always follow the same logic. The type of user interaction and the messages sent may vary, however.

We'll demonstrate how to display blocked data in the business process using examples of SD deliveries and FI documents.

SD delivery policy Let's first take a look at the underlying policy for SD deliveries (refer to Figure 4.22).

SAP ERP Sales and Distribution Case 1: User with Check Authorization

Our first case involves a user with check authorizations and the display of deliveries (Transaction VL03N – Display Outbound Delivery) that have been archived due to blocking.

If you open Transaction VL03N (Display Outbound Delivery) in this configuration, the system displays the data and informs you that it has been read from the archive (see Figure 4.51).

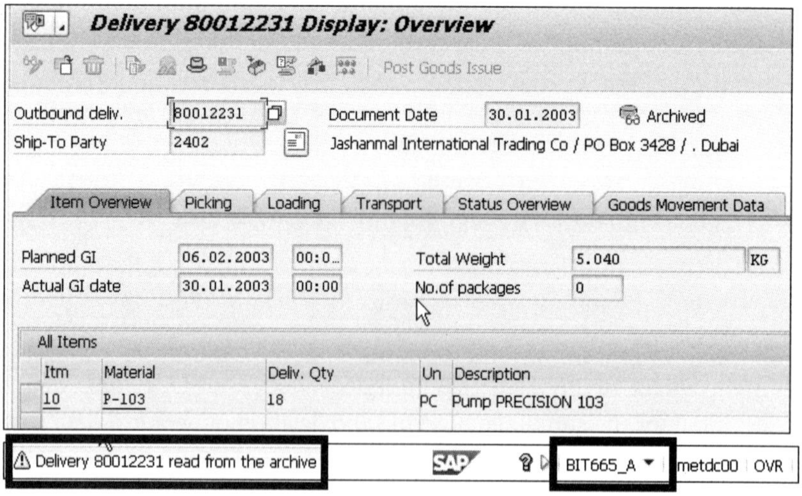

Figure 4.51 Case 1 Transaction VL03N (Display Outbound Delivery): User with Check Authorization

SAP ERP Sales and Distribution Case 2: User without Check Authorization

In Case 2, we take a look at the display of deliveries archived due to blocking (Transaction VL03N – Display Outbound Delivery) for a user without check authorizations (see Figure 4.52).

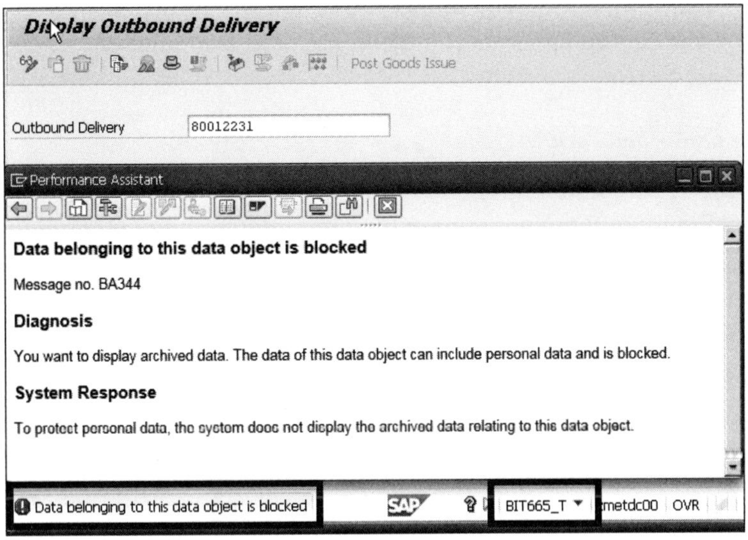

Figure 4.52 Case 2 Transaction VL03N (Display Outbound Delivery): User without Check Authorization

If you open Transaction VL03N using this constellation, the system won't show the data and will also explain the reasons.

Moving on to comparable cases for FI documents, let's take a look at the underlying policy as shown in Figure 4.53.

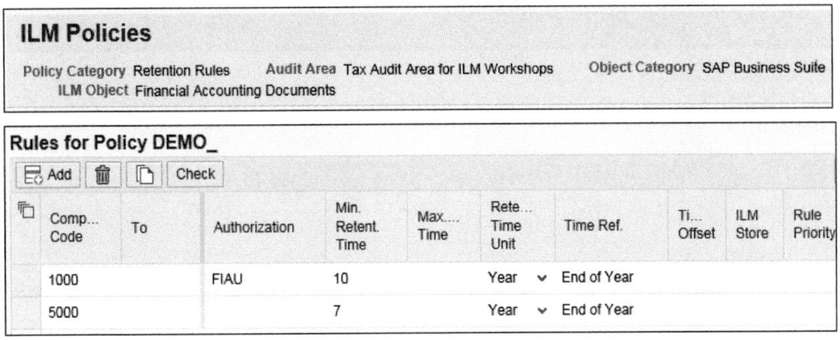

Figure 4.53 Transaction IRMPOL (ILM Policies): Retention Rules for FI Documents

SAP ERP Financials Case 1: User with Check Authorization

Case 1 addresses displaying FI documents (Transaction FB03 – Display Document) that have been archived due to blocking to a user with check authorizations.

Transaction FB03

If you open Transaction FB03 in this particular constellation, the system displays the data and informs you that it has been read from the archive (see Figure 4.54).

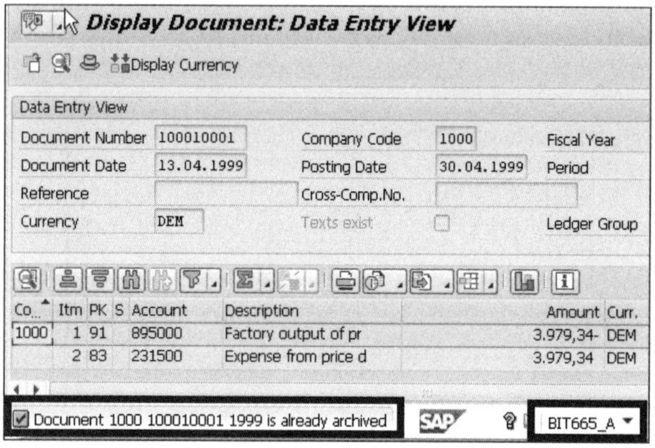

Figure 4.54 Case 1 Transaction FB03 (Display Document): User with Check Authorization

SAP ERP Financials Case 2: User without Check Authorization

In Case 2, we'll take a look at the displaying of FI documents (see Transaction FB03 – Display Document) that have been archived due to locks for a user without check authorizations (see Figure 4.55).

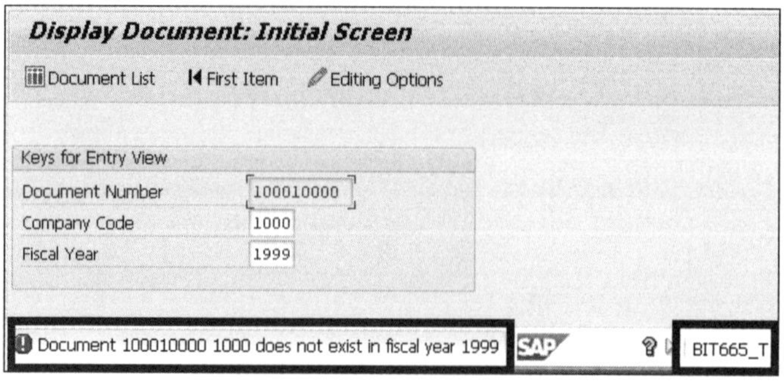

Figure 4.55 Case 2 Transaction FB03: User without Check Authorization

If you open Transaction FB03 in this constellation, the system won't display the data and will inform you of the reasons.

4.4 Deletion from a Business Perspective

Finally, let's take a look at how you can delete master or transactional data, that is, destroy it. In particular, we'll show what options are available and how to handle the corresponding transactions. This is the final phase in the lifecycle of personal data (see Figure 4.56).

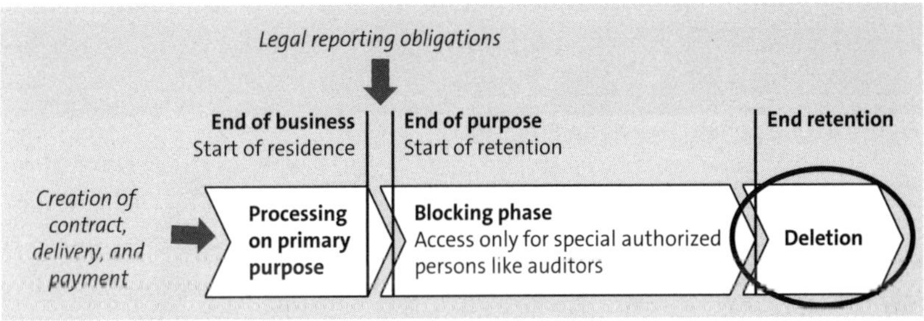

Figure 4.56 Pattern Lifecycle of Personal Data: Deletion

4.4.1 Data Destruction from the Database

First of all, we'll look at the two ways of destroying data in the database, that is, nonarchived data:

- SAP ILM **Data Destruction** action of the archiving object (Transaction SARA – Archive Administration)
- Data destruction object (Transaction ILM_DESTRUCTION – Data Destruction)

[«]

> **Archiving Object or Data Destruction Object**
>
> Each application decides which way to offer. An archiving object is generally offered if the corresponding data is archived before deletion, whereas a data destruction object is offered if archiving isn't necessary.

SAP ILM Data Destruction action

An archiving object that is assigned to an audit area via the corresponding SAP ILM object offers the three SAP ILM **Actions** in the **Write** program (see

Figure 4.57). You can use the SAP ILM action **Data Destruction** to delete data that you don't plan to archive before destruction (Figure 4.58).

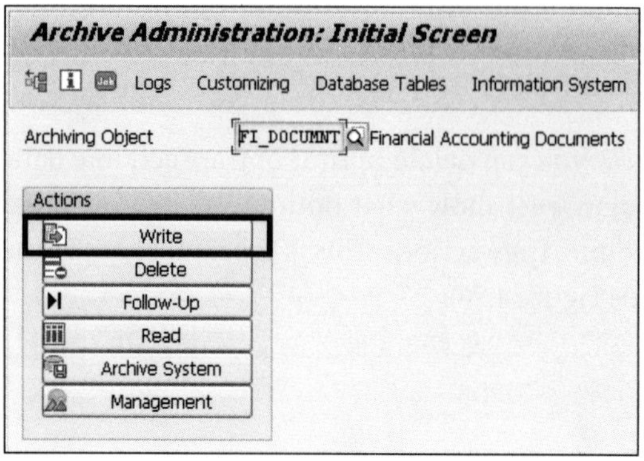

Figure 4.57 Opening the Write Program

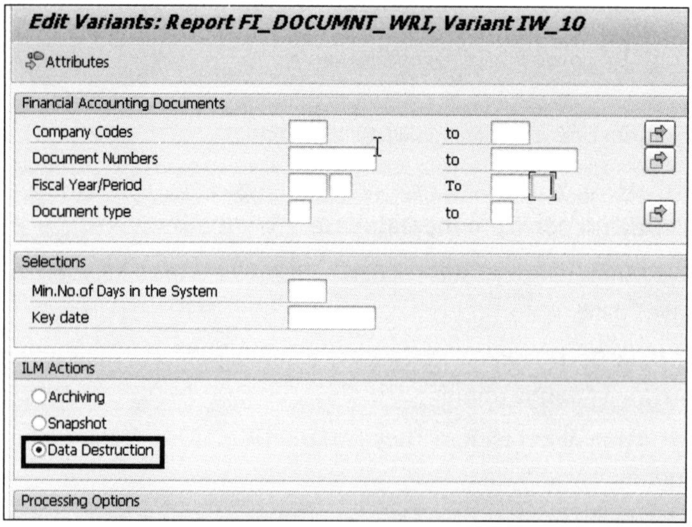

Figure 4.58 Data Destruction of the Archiving Object in Transaction SARA (Archive Administration)

Data destruction object

The second and relatively new way to destroy data is offered by a data destruction object. The corresponding transaction is Transaction ILM_ DESTRUCTION (Data Destruction), and in the **Type of Data to Be Destroyed** area of the screen, **Data from the Database** should be chosen (Figure 4.59).

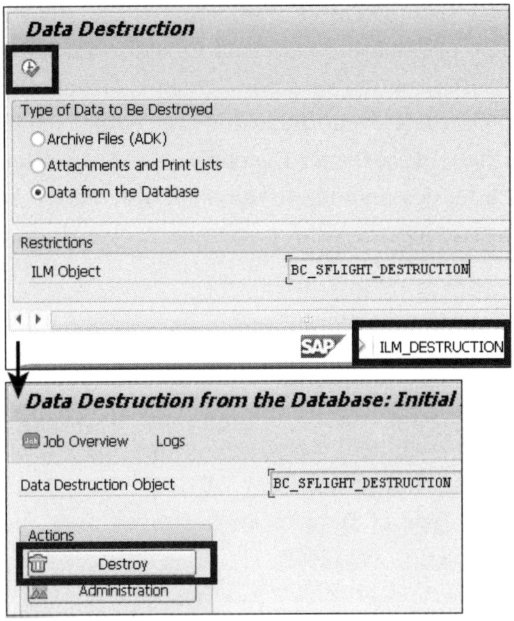

Figure 4.59 Data Destruction Object: Transaction ILM_DESTRUCTION (Data Destruction)

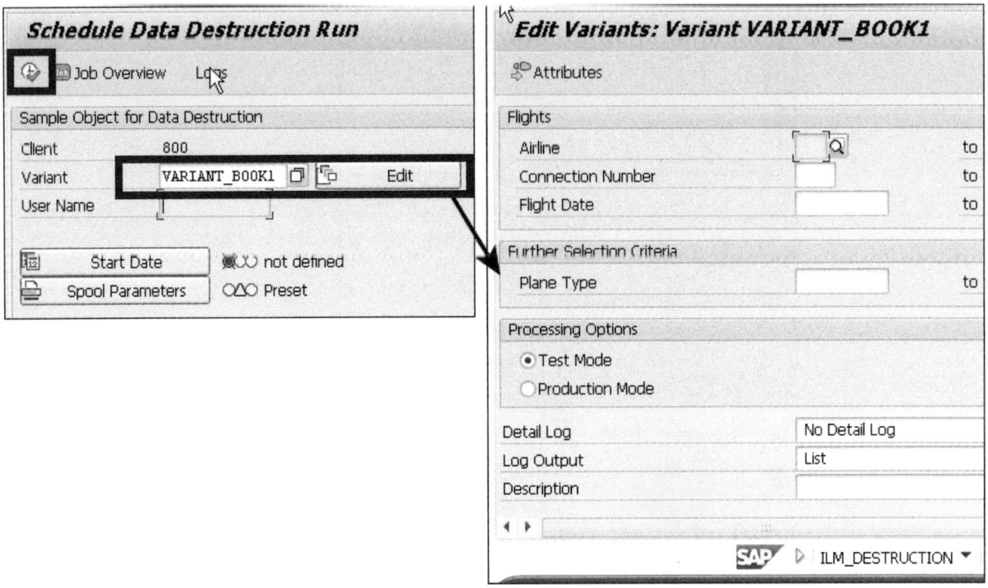

Figure 4.60 Schedule Data Destruction Run

The screens in Figure 4.60 are reminiscent of Transaction SARA (archive administration). However, you only have to perform one action: click the **Destroy** button. In the **Data Destruction** selection screen that appears, define which data you want to be destroyed. Processing is scheduled in the background, as is archiving. You can use the **Job Overview** button to display the corresponding background processes and the **Administration** button to display which destruction runs, and with which selections, you've already carried out.

4.4.2 Destruction of Archived Data

Destruction of archived data

Let's now take a look at how you can destroy data stored in the archive files after the retention periods have expired. Figure 4.61 shows that, when doing so, you should also use Transaction ILM_DESTRUCTION (Data Destruction). However, in the **Type of Data to Be Destroyed** area, the options available for selection are now as follows:

- **Archive Files (ADK)**
- **Attachments and Print Lists**
- **Data from the Database**

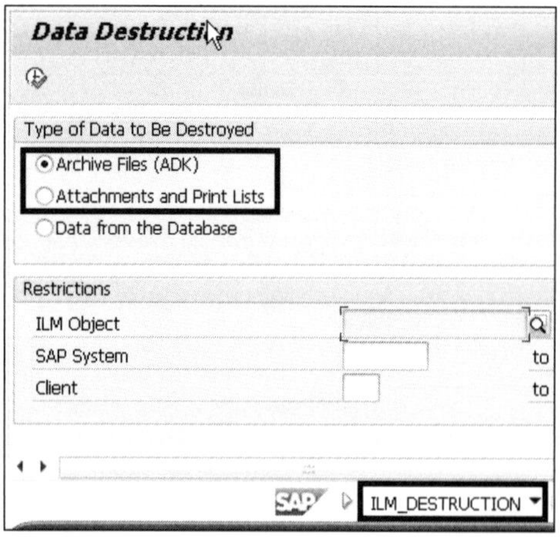

Figure 4.61 Data Destruction for Archived Files: Overview

After selecting the type and clicking the **Execute** (F8) button, you'll receive a list of all archive files that you've stored in a certified SAP ILM Store and for which the retention period has expired (see Figure 4.62).

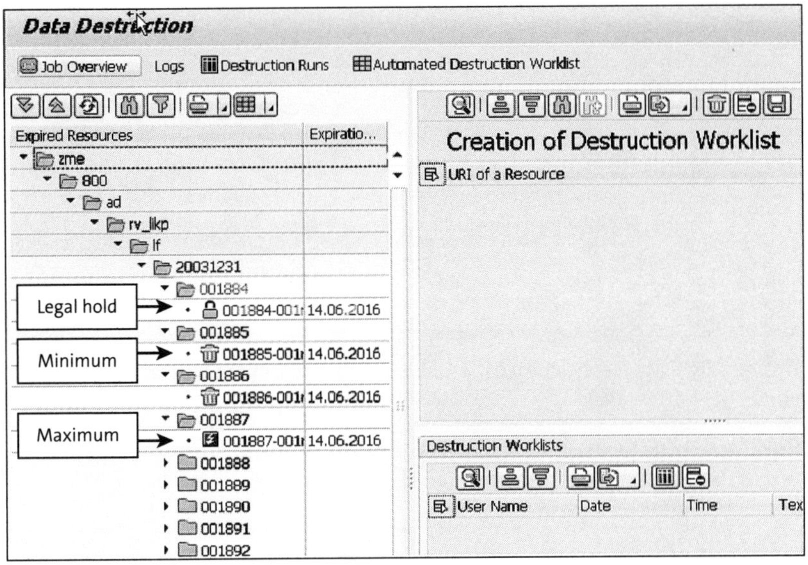

Figure 4.62 List of Relevant Archived Files

Archive files that you've created but not yet stored won't be displayed. Therefore, these files can't be destroyed. Archive files for which the retention period hasn't yet elapsed are also not displayed.

The three different icons mean the following:

Three icons

- **(Trash can)**
  This shows whether the minimum retention period has already expired so you can destroy the data.
- **(Flash)**
  This indicates whether the maximum retention period has already expired, meaning you must destroy the data.
- **(Lock)**
  This symbolizes that parts of the data in the archive file are blocked in a legal case and therefore can't be destroyed.

Destruction worklist

Figure 4.63 shows, in the step, how to move the desired archive files (resources) to a destruction worklist (on the right side) using the drag and drop feature. You can then save the worklist and give it a description.

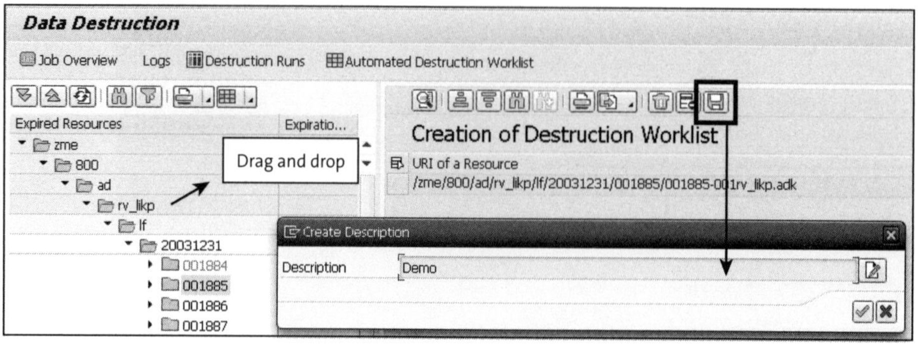

Figure 4.63 Data Destruction for Archived Files: Creation of Destruction Worklist

Destruction job In the final step, schedule a background job for the destruction worklist by using the **Schedule** button (see Figure 4.64).

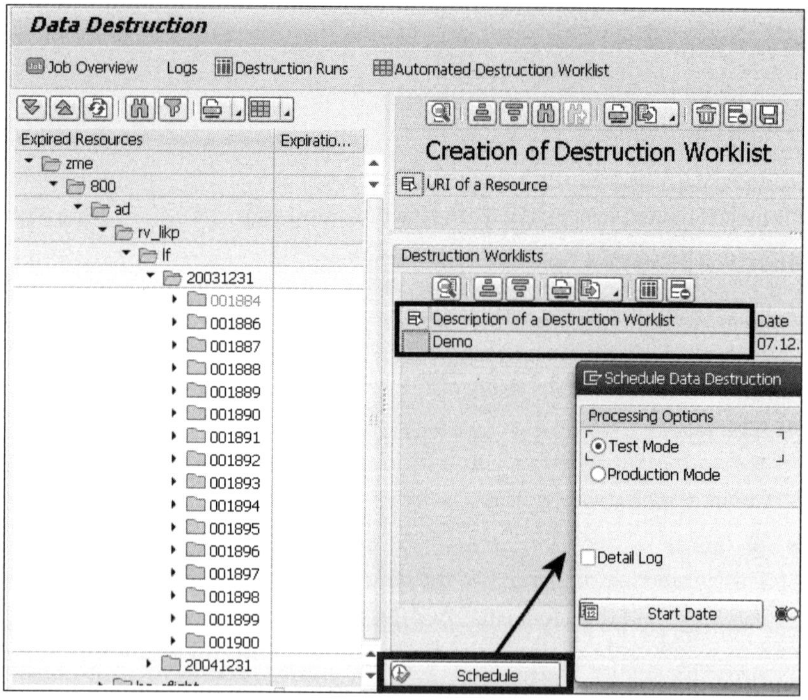

Figure 4.64 Data Destruction for Archived Data: Scheduling a Destruction Job

Dual control principle

You may also choose to apply the principle of dual control and assign the rights for this step to a different person than the one assigned the rights for creating the destruction worklist.

Further information can be found in the SAP_BC_ILM_DESTROY role and in the two authorization objects you can view in Transaction PFCG (Maintenance of Roles), as shown in Figure 4.65:

- **Authorization Object S_ARCD_OBJ: Execute Data Destruction Run for Data in the Database**
- **Authorization Object S_ARCD_RES: Add Destruction Worklist to Resources**

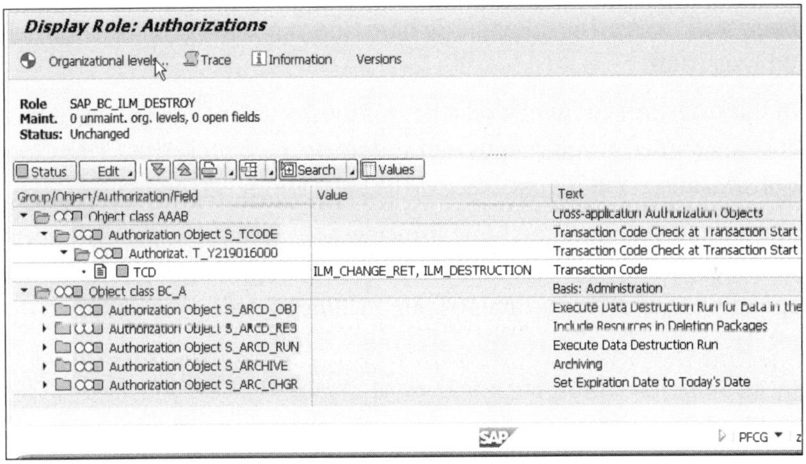

Figure 4.65 Transaction PFCG Role SAP_BC_ILM_DESTROY and Its Authorization Objects

4.5 Legal Case Management

We'll now provide you with a brief overview of one of the main SAP ILM functions mentioned above, Legal Case Management. We'll then move on to explain the role of the Extract Data Objects with Legal Hold (RSARC_EXTRACT_LEGAL_HOLDS) report.

Legal Case Management in short

Legal Case Management can be used to set and manage the blocking of data affected by a legal case. You can reach it in Transaction ILM_LHM (Legal Hold Management). Note that this transaction from SAP NetWeaver 7.31

will replace existing Transaction SCASE (Case Management), which was formerly used for this purpose.

If you want to add a particular document to a legal case to block it, you can add the document manually. To do this, select the **Add Objects** button, and enter the object key in the Business Object Repository (BOR) format (BOR object type and key).

E-discovery functionality

If, on the other hand, you want to add a particular document (e.g., a customer order) to a legal case, but this time, you want to include it together with all other dependent documents (e.g., material document, individual customer billing document, corresponding FI and CO documents, etc.), the e-discovery function, which you call up using the button of the same name, helps you do so. This function is based on the Document Relationship Browser (DRB).

In this case, the system first searches for the document you entered (e.g., a customer order). If you've activated and set up the appropriate AS information structures, this is done both on the database and in the archive.

The second step uses the same principle to search for dependent documents (e.g., material document, customer billing document, and corresponding FI and CO documents). All documents found are added to the legal case.

Propagation of legal holds on archive files

In an important third step, you must ensure that—if you have added archived documents in the legal case—the propagation of legal holds will also be applied to the corresponding archive file.

This action isn't performed automatically when saving the case, but you can trigger it with report ARC_LHM_PROPAGATE_LEGAL_HOLD (Apply Legal Holds to Archive Files). As you might rightly point out, the archiving of an affected document can take place any time after the document has been included in a legal case. For this reason, we recommend that you schedule the report as a periodic job in the background.

Further general information about Legal Case Management can be found under *https://help.sap.com* or in SAP Training Course BIT665.

Extraction of data objects with legal holds

To reach the second goal of this section, we want to point out that the data blocked in a legal case can't be subject to permanent destruction, which is the destruction discussed earlier. In this context, report RSARC_EXTRACT_

LEGAL_HOLDS (Extract Data Objects with Legal Hold) may be of interest to you (Figure 4.66).

If you have archive files with legal hold blocks that, according to the data retention time, could be deleted, the report extracts these data objects of the archive file to a new archive file that is subject to legal holds. The legal hold information is of course also taken over completely. The legal hold block is removed from the source file, so that you can execute final deletion with it, as described previously.

You can also schedule the report in the background for several archive files or archiving objects.

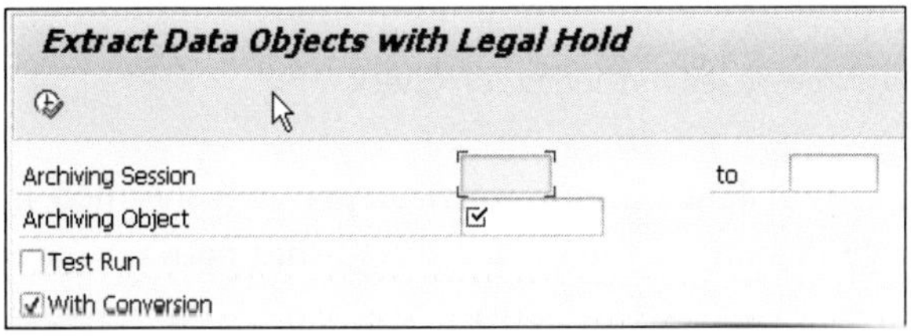

Figure 4.66 Report RSARC_EXTRACT_LEGAL_HOLDS

4.6 Time-Based Blocking of Personal Data in Personnel Management

We've now addressed the concept of simplified blocking and deletion of personal data in general. SAP ILM is also used to delete data in Personnel Administration (PA) in SAP ERP Human Capital Management (SAP ERP HCM).

Special case PA

Due to the different business perspective in PA in SAP ERP HCM, the concept differs fundamentally from other blocking concepts in SAP Business Suite. This is easy to understand because almost all PA data in SAP ERP HCM includes personal data, and the applicable legal sources impose a number of sometimes-conflicting conditions.

Time-based authorization check

The time-based authorization check enables you to restrict access to specific data-related periods in the past. The general rules for read and write access apply analogously. The concept of the time-based authorization check enables you to define the authorization for specific user groups individually. Figure 4.67 shows the effect of the time-based authorization check.

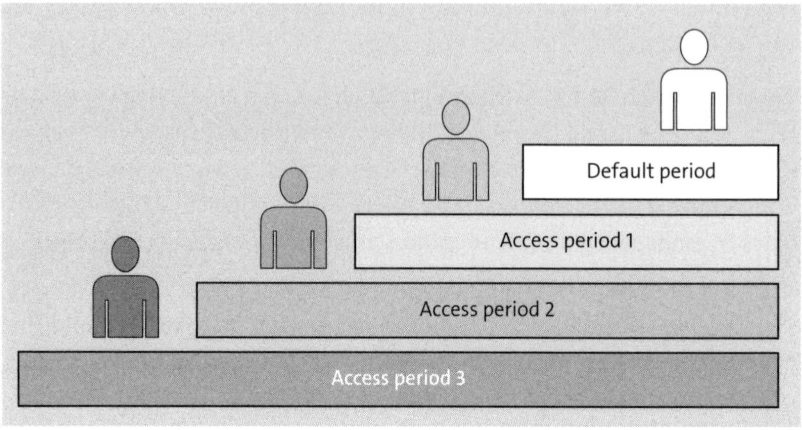

Figure 4.67 Effect of the Time-Based Authorization Check

You'll notice that, for certain data, the authorization period is specified. In SAP ERP HCM, the organization of the data distinguishes between infotypes and subtypes.

[»]

Infotype (Information Type) and Subtype

Infotypes are personal data, organizational data, and "other" data. The primary personal data is stored in Infotype 0002. Infotypes can be stored for specified periods of time. There are several hundred infotypes in the standard system, many of which are country-specific.

Subtypes are further subdivisions of the infotype.

First of all, you set up a default authorization period for an infotype or, more precisely, for a combination of infotype and subtype. This is then the minimum retroactive access authorization for all requests. If you've selected a default authorization period of 90 days, each user who is authorized to access this data can access a specific date retrospectively for 90 days. In Figure 4.67, this would be all users 1 – 4.

Authorization object P_DURATION

The only users who will have extended backdate access are those in roles who have been assigned authorization object P_DURATION (Authorization Time Periods for HR Master Data) with a time period ID and corresponding values for the infotype/subtype. In the diagram, for example, personnel administrator 2 has been assigned the period authorization for a period of

12 months, and data protection officer 4 has been assigned a period of 360 months.

Activation of the time-based check

To use the time-dependent authorization check, which allows you to define default authorization periods and specify the corresponding authorizations, you'll have to implement the Business Add-In (BAdI) `HRPADAUTH_TIME` (Time Logic in the PA Authorization Check).

For further information on this process, see SAP documentation under the menu path, **Personnel Management • Tools • Data Protection • Blocking • Time-Based • Blocking of Data • BAdI: Setting Up Customer-Specific Checks for Authorization Periods**.

4.7 Summary

In this chapter, we've shown you how the world of blocking and deletion is getting better. You now know the importance of clearly defining retention rules, how to block data, how to record it in the event of a litigation, and how to delete data after the retention period expires.

Chapter 5
Purpose-Based Processing

The question regarding the purpose of processing is almost philosophical. However you define the purposes—from a technical point of view—it's important that you're able to assign the personal data to these purposes.

5

This chapter deals with the representation of the purpose. The underlying assumptions are software-agnostic: the processing of personal data has to be based on a legitimate purpose. Proof of this purpose and the necessary technical and organizational measures require the data to be attributed by means of a specific purpose attribute or line organizational attributes (LOAs) and process organizational attributes (POAs). Because the main purpose of processing in SAP ERP systems is to process contracts and/or legal obligations, the use of LOAs and POAs is the method of choice; this is the only way to keep the purpose of processing personal data in the business process transparent.

At the end of this chapter, you should have a clear picture of how to display the purpose with LOAs and POAs and how to set them up.

[«]

> **Note**
> Basic knowledge of customizing the appropriate SAP applications will be helpful for a better understanding of this chapter. For more information, refer to the comprehensive and application-specific literature at SAP PRESS (*www.sap-press.com*).

5.1 Controller and Purpose

The purpose by law

Remember, the purpose must be defined prior to processing. The purpose doesn't, however, replace the justifying reasons (Art. 5 (1)(b) GDPR). The only personal data that may be processed is the personal data necessary to reach the purpose (Art. 5 (1)(c) GDPR). In relation to the purposes of processing, the personal data must be kept correct and up to date (Art. 5 (1)(d) GDPR). Finally, personal data may only be processed for as long as is justified by its purpose (see Chapter 1, Section 1.2.1).

Firstly, the question must be answered as to who defines the purpose of the processing. Art. 4 (7) GDPR answers this question. Accordingly, the data controller defines the purpose alone or together with other controllers.

[»]

Joint Responsibility

The joint responsibility of several controllers isn't discussed in this book as it's subject to many other conditions.

The controller is "the natural or legal person, public authority, agency or other body" (Art. 4 (7) GDPR). In our context, the controller is usually a legal person, that is, a legal entity. As a general rule, the controller of the processing of personal data isn't the "group of undertakings" (Art. 4 (19) GDPR) but a single legally independent unit (which reports independently in SAP ERP Financials [FI]).

Mandatory assignment of the controller

Pötters and Böhm (2017) explain this clearly (Art. 4 (marg. 28)):

> *There has to be a legal entity to which the processing of personal data can be assigned. The concept of "controller" is thus inseparably linked to the concept of "processing." This regulation stipulates that there should be a "controller" for each "processing." Consequently, "processing" that cannot be assigned to a "controller" is not possible.*

One purpose – one controller

This means that each piece of personal data should always be attributable to a controller and a purpose. Furthermore, we assume that a purpose is generally attributable to one individual controller.

How can different purposes be illustrated? Figure 5.1 shows some general possibilities:

1. **Unit of purpose and system**
   In literature, this is described as system separation.
2. **Client separation in one system**
   This means that personal data is kept completely and logically separate in one and the same technical system. This is possible in SAP Business Suite or in SAP S/4HANA using client-specific tables and settings.

❸ **Different purposes processed in one client**
This can be done in SAP Business Suite or in SAP S/4HANA by means of the relevant data attribution.

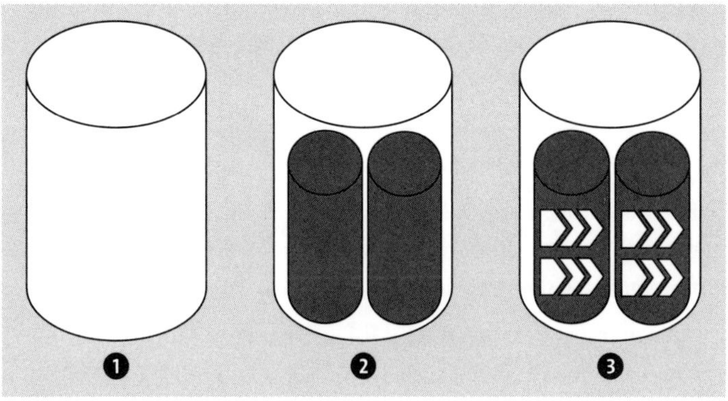

Figure 5.1 Separation by Purpose

The need for separation in German literature

How to separate processing was a long-standing subject of debate under the old German Federal Data Protection Act (GFPDA). Although the literature we've consulted comes up with comparable measures to ensure the separation of purpose limitations, preferences are set differently:

- Spatial separation or system separation
- Separation in the system through clients
- Separation in the client using the authorization concept
- Separation of functions

The principle of the separation of functions is always part of the technical and organizational measures, which in this case means between maintenance and use of the system.

[«]

System Separation Isn't Widespread Practice

We haven't met very many customers who have actually performed a system separation. We only know of one customer where the system separation was carried out to such an extent that the data could only be transferred by tape. The vast majority of system-separating customers allowed remote function call (RFC) communication; moreover, administration of the various systems was often performed by the same person.

> Our customer base includes customers with more than 100 productive SAP ERP clients. In most of these cases, the maintenance and control effort was considerable. In fact, effective controls in such a complex system landscape can be expensive and difficult. A physical system separation would again drive the costs up significantly and further increase the complexity.

[!]

> **Complexity Leads to Nontransparency**
>
> System or client separation not only leads to significantly higher maintenance costs but can also considerably complicate control options—at least from a corporate group's point of view.
>
> The SAP systems allow you to separate data according to purpose for end users in business processes (using organizational attributes). You can do this using standard means without client separation.

We can only answer the question as to how far the separation must go by assessing the general conditions:

- What is the legal basis of the processing? Are there compelling reasons for or against processing in the intended form?
- How sensitive is the processed data?
- Does processing take place in the same legal entity, or does it involve contractual data processing or processing by third parties in safe third countries or processing by third parties in unsafe third countries?
- In the case of a client separation/system separation, does the gain in formal security outweigh the loss of control due to increasing complexity?
- How can the general level of protection be assessed?
- How much time and effort is appropriate?

The following section discusses line-organizational separation options in the SAP Business Suite.

5.2 Organizational Structures (Line Organization)

In Section 5.1, we associated the controller with the independent accounting unit. The software described in this book is designed to handle the main business processes in a company or in an administration; it covers goods and services that are provided or procured. All of these, together with the fixed assets, have to be shown in the accounts with regard to the independent accounting department, which, as a rule, is identical to the controller. The company code is therefore of paramount importance, so we'll begin by discussing company codes.

5.2.1 Key Organizational Structures

Figure 5.2 shows a simplified overview of the organizational attributes of various applications, as described in the following.

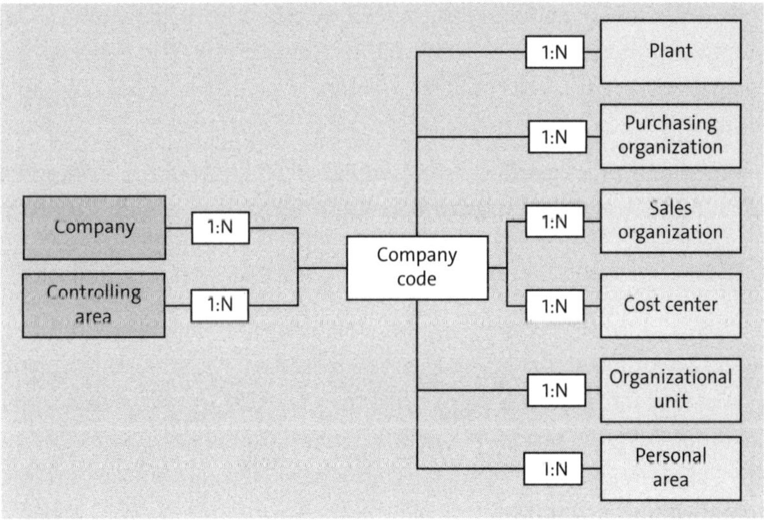

Figure 5.2 Simplified Organizational Structure

Client

The most general organizational subdivision of an SAP Business Suite or an SAP S/4HANA installation is the client. The client is the basic organizational level of the SAP System. The business settings in the system are client-specific. Business data is held on a client-specific basis.

Company code

A *company code* is the central organizational unit in accounting that structures the company from an accounting point of view. It represents the smallest independent accounting unit; all of the system's accounting information is related to it.

Companies Additionally, it's possible to set up *companies* that can subdivide the company in accordance with trade legislation. The establishment of companies is optional and is of particular relevance in consolidation. In the SAP System, the consolidation functions of FI are performed on the basis of companies. A company can comprise one or more company codes.

Controlling area Within a group of undertakings, the *controlling area* is the organizational unit for which comprehensive and, if necessary, cross-company cost accounting is carried out. Accordingly, a controlling area can include one or more company codes.

Cost center hierarchy There is a *cost center hierarchy* in each controlling area. This is the structural view of Cost Center Accounting (CCA). Their structure often corresponds to the organizational structure of a company. A cost center is an account assignment object. Specifically, in the authorization concept, the cost center hierarchy can be used frequently to restrict access rights for specific purposes.

Purchasing organization The *purchasing organization* is the company-code-related organizational level of SAP ERP Materials Management (MM), which is responsible for handling purchasing. A company code can include several purchasing organizations.

Plant The *plant* is certainly the most important organizational level in logistics. Various logistical master data, such as the material, is created for the plant. Plants can be set up for those parts of the logistical structure that differ from other parts in terms of organizational structure. Any number of plants can be assigned to a company code. The relation of plant to purchasing organization is random.

Sales organization Sales and distribution is divided into *sales organization, distribution channel,* and *division* organizational levels. The sales organization is the basic organizational level of sales and legally defines the organizational unit. Each business transaction is processed within a sales organization. Organizational units defined in this way conclude contracts with third parties. A sales organization is assigned to exactly one company code. However, several sales organizations can be assigned to one company code.

Personnel area

In SAP ERP Human Capital Management (SAP ERP HCM), the assumption is made that the client is "in itself a commercially, organizationally and data-technically closed unit within an SAP ERP system." In the client, the personnel areas of SAP ERP HCM must be set up with reference to the company codes. The personnel area is an organizational unit that represents a separate area of personnel administration. The personnel area is only used in Personnel Administration (PA) in SAP ERP HCM. Personnel areas are divided into personnel subareas. Personnel-related regulations are defined at the level of the personnel areas and personnel subareas. The regulations can be of a legal, collective, or company-internal nature. Only one company code is assigned to a personnel area. This company code contains the values relevant to FI that affect the personnel area.

The company's organizational structure can be displayed in *Organizational Management* (OM) in SAP ERP HCM.

Structure of OM

Starting with one *root organizational unit*, all organizational units are displayed from the top to the bottom. Positions are regularly assigned to the organizational units, and persons are assigned to the position. The position can be described by a job; the organizational units are assigned to the company code.

The description of a position by a job enables you to define comparable positions by bundling attributes in an organizational unit. In addition to storing the job, numerous significant technical, contract law, and personnel administration attributes can be stored. The technical attributes may include authorizations.

OM in the system landscape

The integration of OM with SAP Customer Relationship Management (SAP CRM), SAP Supplier Relationship Management (SAP SRM), and SAP Solution Manager is particularly noteworthy in the context of *business partner management*. This integration enables the position of the members of the organization to be presented in the same way as the members of business partners, customers, and suppliers.

Integration in SAP Business Warehouse (SAP BW) allows you to structure and authorizations according to the assignments in OM.

Simplified organizational structure

The organizational structure shown in Figure 5.2 and described in this section is significantly simplified in that the second-order organizational elements (e.g., the distribution channel) and the division aren't displayed nor are possible higher-level structure characteristics (e.g., the operating concern) or industry-specific structure characteristics (bank area). Instead of 27, we limit ourselves to 9 relations. The allocations shown in Figure 5.3, in part, can be found in the SAP Reference Implementation Guide (IMG) as follows: **SAP Customizing Implementation Guide • Enterprise structure • Assignment**.

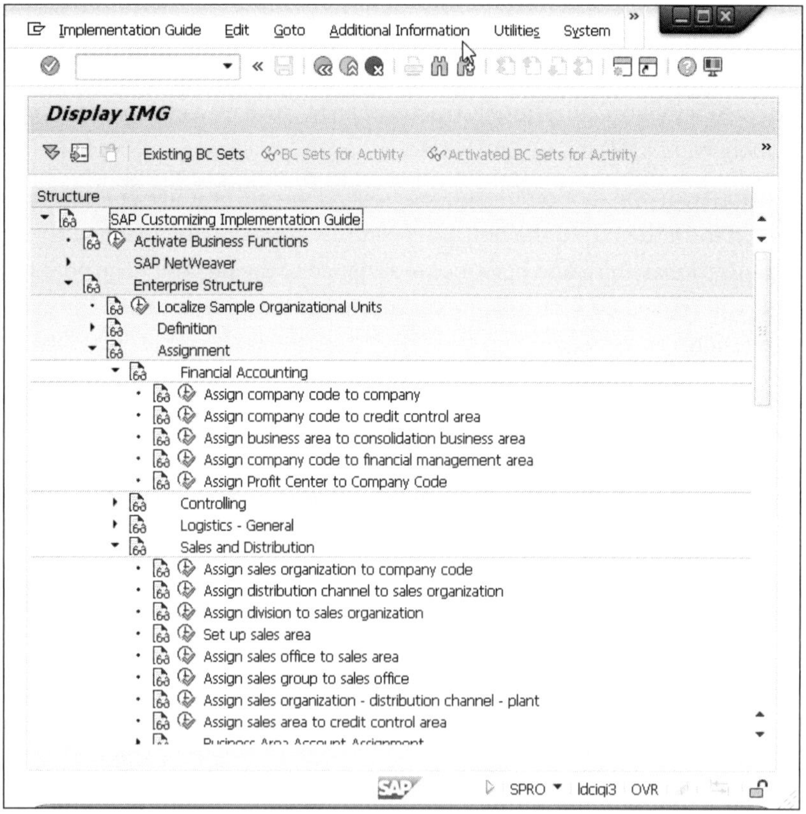

Figure 5.3 Maintaining Assignments

Figure 5.4 shows a schematic diagram of how companies within a company group can be represented. For the company as a legally independent unit or for the legal controller, we've explained that this structure must be reflected in the system in such a way that all line organizational attributes (LOAs) are clearly related to the company code. If the higher-level display, for example, in internal accounting, is at the operating concern level (Profitability Analysis [CO-PA]), this should be assigned above the company codes. The operating concern would then also be the LOA representative of the group of undertakings.

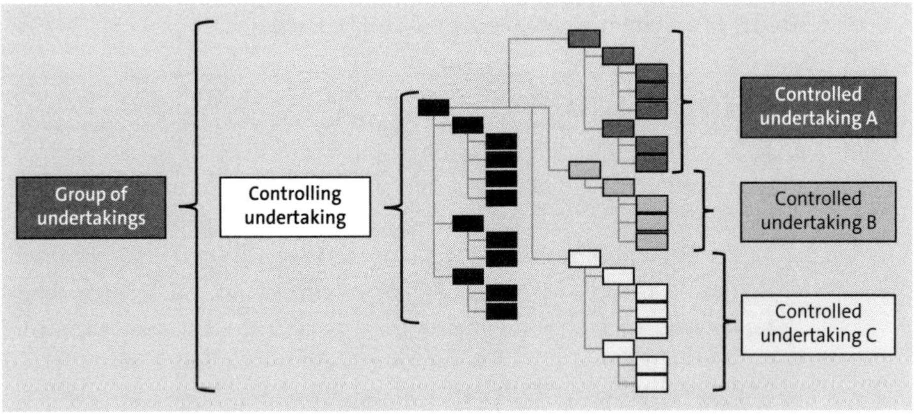

Figure 5.4 Presentation of Undertakings in a Group

5.2.2 Alternate Structure Arrangements

We believe that the organizational structures described are very well suited to the processing of data in relation to the respective data controller. These LOAs are taken into account in the authorization concept, in simplified blocking and deletion, and in purpose-related access rights. Together with other measures (e.g., separation of functions, restriction of authorizations for generic table access, or depersonalization of data for test systems) we consider the data to be sufficiently separated.

Separation of clients

If you consider these options insufficient for separating purposes with regard to the controller, the only solution left is the *separation of clients* for each controller on the basis of purposes. According to SAP, a client is a self-contained commercial, organizational, and technical unit within an SAP system with separate master records.

Clean structures are a prerequisite

If you don't want to run a separate client for each controller, the only option (in our opinion—this isn't legal advice) is to use the structures listed previously in such a way that they are always clearly assigned to the company code. We're well aware that for some customers, these structures have been set up differently. However, we don't see any alternative to a clearing-up project. In Section 5.1, we explained that one separation per system, one separation per client in the system, and one separation per purpose/controller in a client in one system may be discussed.

[+]

Controller Not Clear?

As described earlier, any such stringent and consistent LOA is assumed to be in compliance with data protection laws. It can't be ruled out that such conformity can also be achieved with considerable economic effort and with a different configuration or procedure. We do, however, assume that this would involve a great deal of effort in terms of installation, documentation, and control. Furthermore, there is also the risk that such an approach may be considered contrary to current technical standards and thus a violation of Art. 32 GDPR.

Therefore, note that if the LOAs haven't been set up in such a way that all lower-level LOAs always relate uniquely to one company code, data processing by several controllers in one client is presumably not data protection compliant.

The most important identification of the purpose is possible with the controller. The following section outlines how this can be supported by POAs.

5.3 Process Organizational Structures

Chapter 2 has already dealt with transactional data and master data. These generally display configurable characteristics that are used to control the business processes.

Business process

First of all, it certainly makes sense to take a look at what is meant by a *business process*. This is defined in *Authorizations in SAP Software* (Lehnert and Stelzner, SAP PRESS, 2010, *www.sap-press.com/2316*) as follows:

A business process is a targeted, temporally-logical, self-contained sequence of tasks that can be executed by several organizational units or organizations. In the configuration context, you can consider the process view as a sequence-oriented view across the organizational structure.

In general, personal data processing must be assigned to purposes in all applications of SAP Business Suite and in SAP S/4HANA using the relevant attributes. This can only be explained in an exemplary manner in this book. To this end, in the following sections, we'll take a look at the simplest possible business process—the sale of goods (see Figure 5.5).

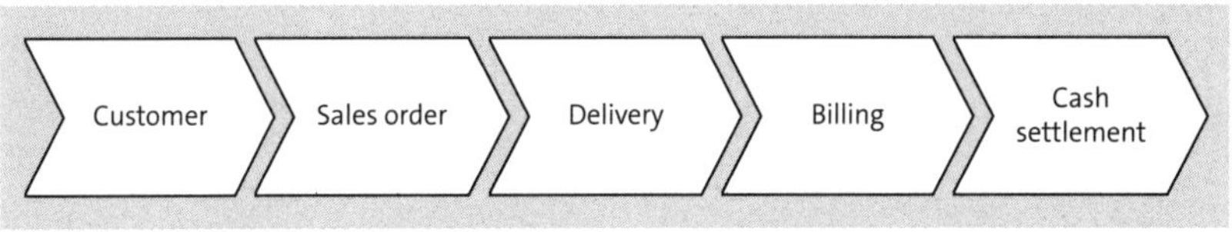

Figure 5.5 Simplified Business Process in SAP ERP Sales and Distribution (SD)

[«]

Purpose-Specific Customer System

In principle, you could also create customers for a specific purpose. This, however, very quickly reaches its logical limits, as numerous business relationships can be geared to quite different purposes. It's standard practice to at least use more general distinctions, such as marking employees as internal customers.

5.3.1 Account Groups

The type of customer and the information on the customer can be defined in Customizing using the following path: **SAP Customizing Implementation Guide • Financial Accounting (NEW) • Accounts Receivable and Accounts Payable • Customer Accounts • Master Data • Preparations for Creating Customer Master Data • Define Account Group with Screen Layout (Customers)**.

Checking/defining fields

If you follow the path specified in Customizing, the initial screen is as shown in Figure 5.6.

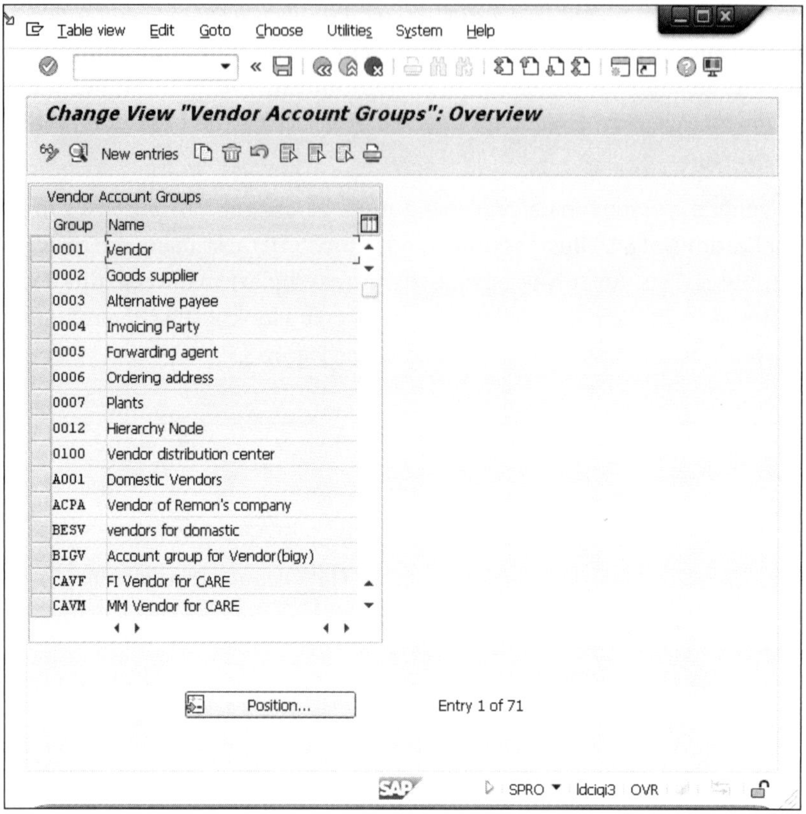

Figure 5.6 Account Group: Accounts Receivable

The screens in Figure 5.7 show how you can check or, in the case of a new account group, define the account group. By displaying or maintaining the field statuses, you can check or specify which data should be displayed, which should be suppressed, which can be maintained as an optional entry, and which is a required entry.

[!]

Data Minimization in the Customer

Note the previously mentioned principle of data minimization in accordance with Art. 5 GDPR. You may only enter the data that you really need for the purposes of processing. This also applies to the data of the contact person.

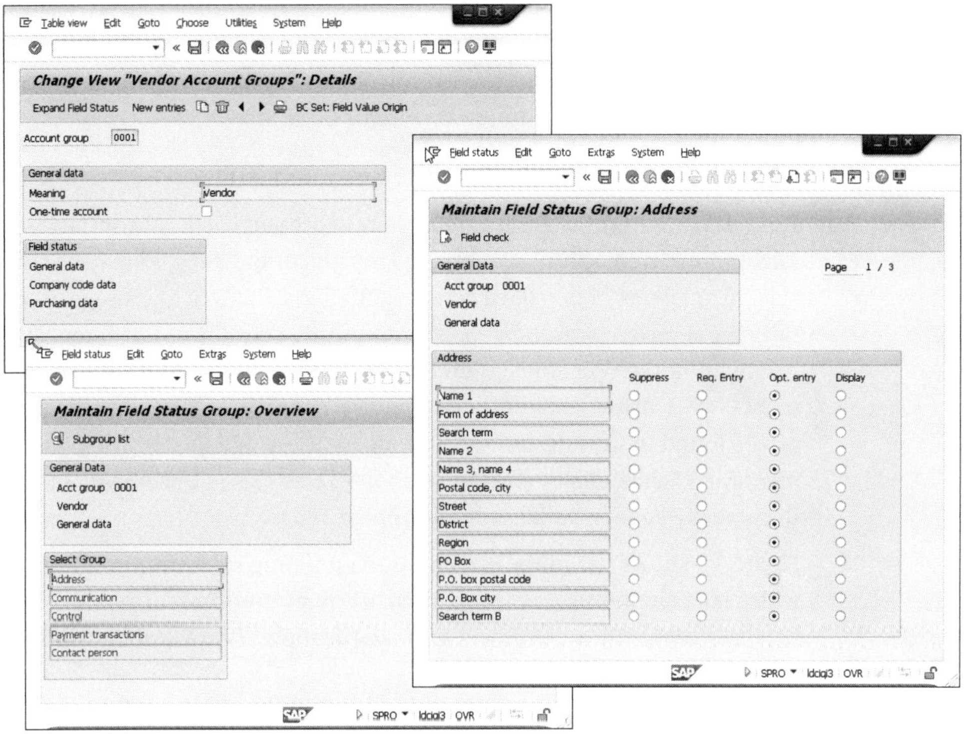

Figure 5.7 Settings for Customer Display/Maintenance

Contact persons

You can store contact persons in the vendor master record, in the customer master record, or in connection with a vendor business partner.

This is naturally particularly useful for customers, suppliers, and business partners who aren't natural persons. The attributes that are stored there are fully configurable, so it would make sense to check very carefully which attributes conform to the purpose of processing. In the center screenshot in Figure 5.7, you can see, among other things, the selection buttons for the contact person.

[+]

Using the Account Group

The **Account Group** field is a condition field for blocking and deleting. In authorizations, the **Account Group** field is subject to an authorization check (more on authorizations in Chapter 7). Whether it actually makes sense to assign customers to a purpose using the account group remains to be seen. In any case, it's advisable to define this grouping characteristic for blocking and deleting as well as for authorizations.

5.3.2 Business Objects in SAP ERP Sales and Distribution

Reflections on the sales order

The sales order is created or generated to represent the legal contract of a sale in the system. Until a contract is concluded, a *sales order* may be considered an object of precontractual negotiations. Content and usage of the sales order are controlled by the sales document type. This is offered both in the authorization concept and in SAP Information Lifecycle Management (SAP ILM) as a differentiation characteristic. The sales document type can be found in the IMG in the following location: **SAP Customizing Implementation Guide • Sales and Distribution • Sales • Sales Documents • Sales Document Header • Define Sales Document Types**.

Figure 5.8 shows the initial screen for maintaining sales document types, which is a complex process. It's particularly relevant from a data protection perspective that the sales order type is an adequate differentiation criterion in terms of purpose.

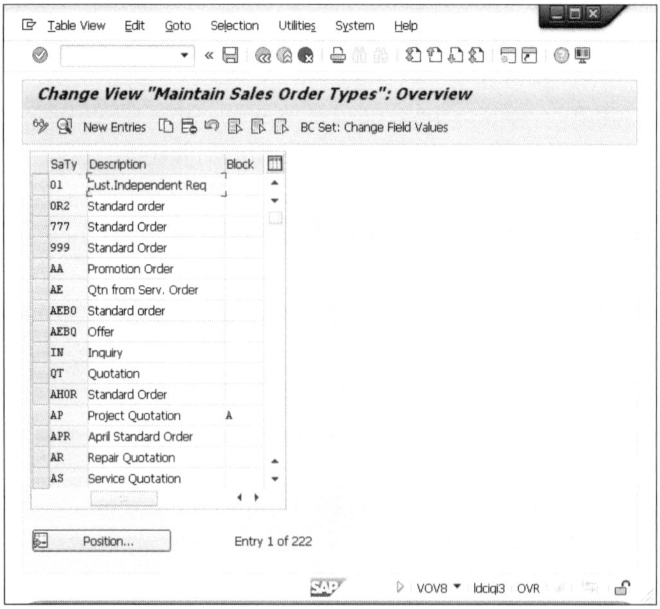

Figure 5.8 Maintaining Sales Order Types

Sales order—personal?

Personal data is usually maintained in the sales order to the extent that it may relate to a natural person—the data subject. The contents of such an order itself are of a procedural nature. In our opinion, a customer's order is personal data. The sales order—Transaction VA03 (Display Sales Order) as shown in Figure 5.9—contains the information that the sold-to party **TEST_CUST** is also the ship-to party, and the goods are **TEST_MAT** with the **Description** "test matr". The relevance in terms of the personal data becomes more vivid if, instead of the product **TEST_MAT**, you consider a product the purchase of which is usually perceived as more delicate. But no matter whether the goods are **Fifty Shades of Grey** or **TEST_MAT**, we assume that it's a clear reference to individuals.

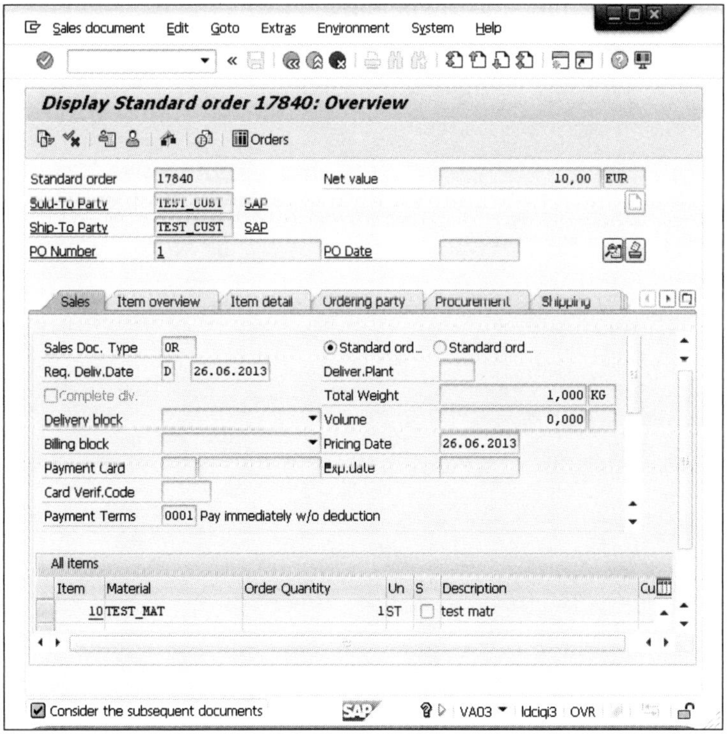

Figure 5.9 Sales Order

Thoughts on delivery

Delivery is usually made in relation to the aforementioned order; systematically, it's an action in the performance of the contract. The delivery is controlled by the delivery type. This is one of the possible selection criteria in archiving. You can find the delivery type in the IMG under the following path: **SAP Customizing Implementation Guide • Logistics Execution • Shipping • Deliveries • Define Delivery Types**.

The screen for this looks very similar to the sales document type screen. Delivery can be displayed using Transaction VL03N (Display Outbound Delivery), and, from a data protection perspective, it contains very few details other than those shown in Figure 5.10. The ship-to party may, however, deviate from the orderer.

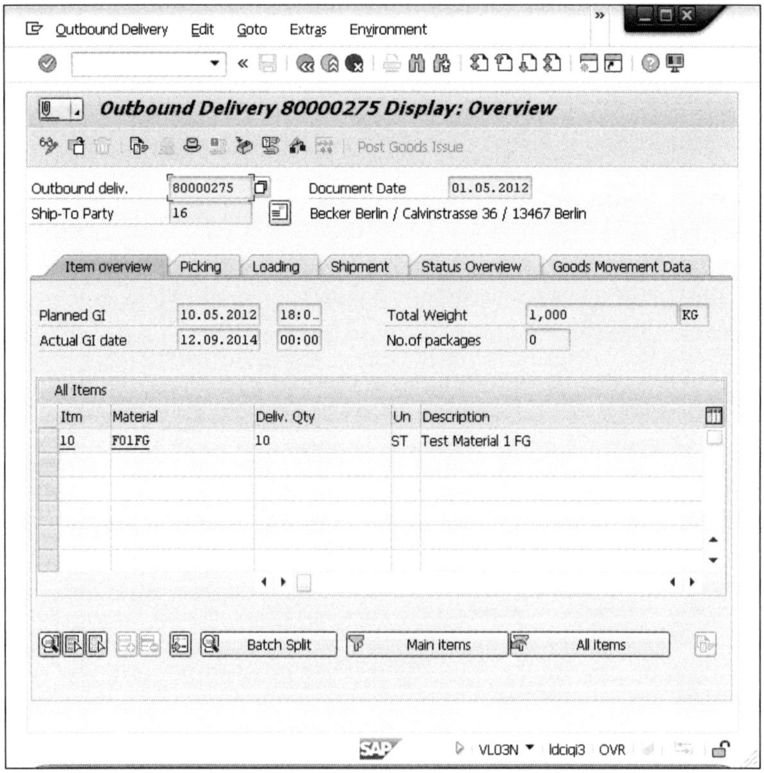

Figure 5.10 Display Outbound Delivery

Comments on the billing document

The *billing document* constitutes billing and is therefore a further step in contract processing. The billing document is predefined by the billing document type. For further information on the sales document type, see the IMG under **SAP Customizing Implementation Guide • Sales and Distribution • Billing • Billing Document • Define Billing Document Type**. In this case, too, it doesn't make sense to always show comparable types of Customizing. The *billing document type* is a differentiating feature in archiving. The billing document can be viewed with Transaction VF03 (Display Billing Document); the corresponding screen is shown in Figure 5.11.

The payer may be a person other than the ship-to party, the ordering party, or the bill-to party. When the billing document is created, the business transaction ends, and further processing is performed in accounting. The billing document type is a differentiating feature in archiving.

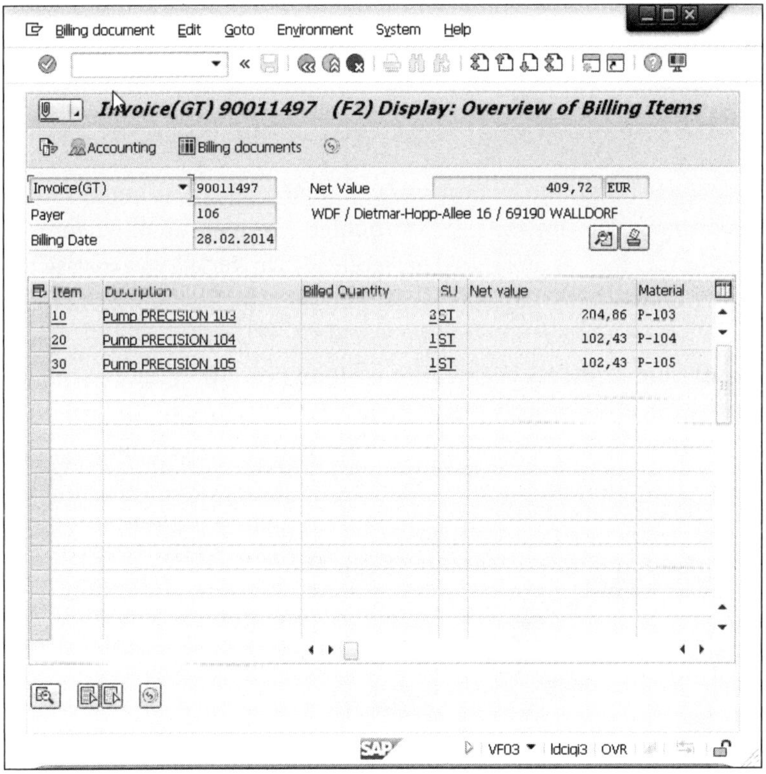

Figure 5.11 Display Billing Document

5.3.3 Purpose Attributes in Sales Order Processing

Attributing customer master records solely on the basis of their purpose is difficult because they may be used multiple times. This assumption can certainly be generalized for personal master data; reference to purpose and data minimization as legal requirements collide. We're assuming, however, that centrally held master data is indeed data protection compliant. The purpose-related attribution in SD can, however, be reached where necessary using the characteristics specified. In our presentations, we always try to make it clear that you should attribute data in such a way that different transactions with potentially different retention periods also have different attributes and are therefore distinguishable. The trade with peppermint tea has different storage needs than the trade with cough syrup. Accordingly, the data must be distinguishable; otherwise, you won't be able to block and delete it properly.

5.4 How Organizational Structures Define Purpose

We've looked at both the line organization and the process organization. We'll now try to describe these two attributes, which ensure the reference to purpose, together, as illustrated in Figure 5.12. On the left you can see the model of a corporate group, as described earlier in Figure 5.4. On the right, you'll see the simplified business process in SD, as shown earlier in Figure 5.5. This business process begins with customer care ❶. If necessary, customer care can cover aspects that are consistent throughout the corporate group; portions of the customer can also be used throughout the corporate group.

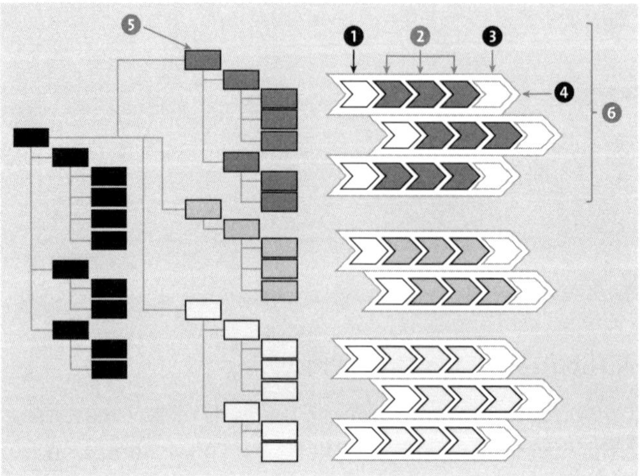

Figure 5.12 The Purpose in the Lines and Process Organization

Figure 5.12 presents the sales order, delivery, and billing document ❷; the processing in accounting ❸; and, finally, the entire process flow ❹, as well as the controller for the processing ❺. Together, the process flow ❹ and controller ❺ represent the purpose of the processing. Because a company always uses more purposes than just the data protection purpose for processing, the combination of ❺ and ❻ results in the set of purposes of a controller.

Complexity of Cross-Company Code Postings

Cross-company code postings can occur in a number of scenarios. In this case, the assumptions presented must be expanded accordingly. The legal definition of the controller must be clarified. This also includes, among other things, whether they may be jointly responsible for processing as defined in Art. 26 (1) GDPR. Technically, this requirement would have to be solved for these explicit cases through the use of unique POAs.

5.5 Summary

Data collected for different purposes must be processed separately. However, it's still useful to store master data centrally because it follows the requirement of data minimization, provided that the references to the purposes can be displayed at any time. The purpose is usually related to a controller. The LOA is therefore necessary to display it. This alone isn't sufficient, however, as a controller will generally have more than one purpose in data processing. To differentiate these, in addition to the LOAs, you'll also need the POAs, which are described by way of example in SD.

Chapter 6
Data Controller Rule Framework

The end of processing isn't a tangible point of time in the system, and it takes knowledge of the business processes used and their completion to delete personal data correctly.

6

In this chapter, we'll look into the question of when and under what conditions the blocking and deletion of personal data should begin. As previously explained in Chapter 4, this can be seen as a negative business process. However, the order of blocking and deleting isn't necessarily the simple reversal of the process. In addition, further steps that aren't always part of the normal business process are required—for each application—to mark the end of processing.

The knowledge and identification of the end of processing also characterize the start of the blocking and deletion procedure. This should be done promptly and in accordance with rules. With *Retention Management* (RM) in SAP Information Lifecycle Management (SAP ILM), this can be technically configured and carried out individually for each application.

The deletion functionality of the application ensures that this is done completely and consistently for the purpose of the application. Until now, however, a connection to the purposes of processing in the system has been missing or could only be described logically. The *Data Controller Rule Framework* is a new function that enables you to assign the applications involved and create retention rules for the respective SAP ILM objects with reference to the data controller and for the purpose of processing.

Business Example As previously described in Chapter 5, Section 5.3, using the example of the business process for the sale of goods, various additional data is required for the creation of the sales document, is necessary for the delivery and billing document, or is generated in the system during the process.

We've already dealt with the allocation of data using process organizational attributes (POAs) based on the purpose of processing and line organizational attributes (LOAs) related to the data controller. However, you can only allocate this data if you have a complete overview of the data that has been generated. Using the model procedure described in Chapter 3, can provide you with this important overview. You'll have to clarify the retention periods for this data. We assume that data for the same purpose in one data controller will have the same retention period. Consequently, in terms of scope and periods of time, the abstraction of the data into purposes of use and data controllers provides the deletion process with the necessary structure.

The sequence of deletion

This doesn't necessarily have to correspond to the *sequence of deletion*. Each application must ensure that data consistency is maintained; accordingly, referencing data must be deleted first in most cases. The network graphic in Transaction SARA (Archive Administration), as shown in the example in Figure 6.1, provides an insight into archiving objects; however, additional checks can also be performed. Because most of these are designed as nonexistence checks, further prerequisite steps are necessary in the deletion sequence.

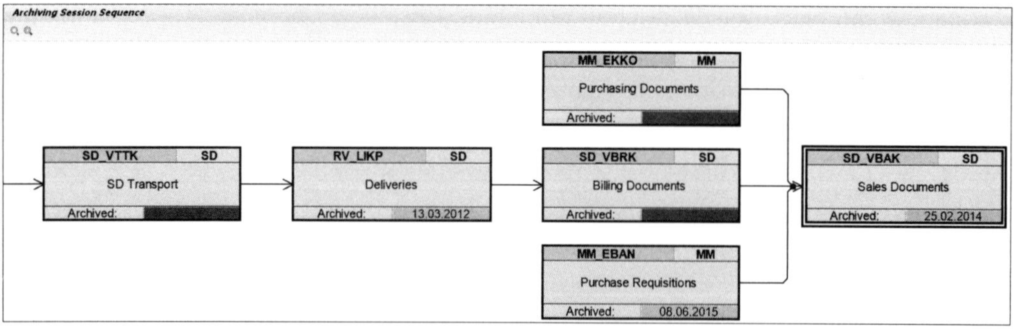

Figure 6.1 Extract from the Network Graphic for the Archiving Object SD_VBAK (Sales Documents)

Irrespective of the question concerning system consistency, the retention periods to be applied determine a sequence that needs to be considered. This arises in cases where data without or with shorter retention periods has to be stored due to associated data having longer retention periods; the necessary proof of data accuracy otherwise wouldn't be possible. This applies in particular to master data that is used for many different purposes and can therefore only be deleted after the end of the last valid purpose of referencing application data. See Chapter 4, Section 4.1, for information on how to set this up for business partners in SAP Business Suite and SAP S/4HANA.

Organization of deletion

Regardless of the sequence based on the retention periods, the organizational *deletion process* still remains. In a business process, the different steps are assigned to different processors and are also defined functionally in the authorization concept. All steps necessary to complete a business process must therefore also be carried out at the right time by these processors. To do this, you'll have to determine the necessary steps and settings; documentation of the relevant deletion functionality of the application will provide you with the necessary information.

Example of a deletion sequence

For a business process involving the sale of goods, the following steps are necessary to complete the business process logically and enable archiving as part of the blocking and deletion process:

- **Material documents**
  For archiving material documents with the archiving object MM_MATBEL (Materials Management: Material Documents), there are no mandatory steps. In Transaction OMB9 (Change Document Lives), the document lives for each plant and transaction type can be set to the days according to which archiving is allowed.
- **Shipping costs**
  You can archive shipping costs with the archiving object SD_VFKK (Shipment Costs) if the material documents are archived. If purchase orders exist for the acquisition of sold products, these must also have been archived in advance. The status for complete invoicing, account assignment, and shipping must also be closed. Residence times after the last change up to the point of archiving can be set for each company code and shipment cost type in Transaction VORI (Archiving Control Shipment Costs).
- **SAP ERP Sales and Distribution (SD) transport**
  You can archive SD transport using the archiving object SD_VTTK (SD Transport). To do this, the relevant shipment costs must already have been archived. Furthermore, all related deliveries must be fully planned, goods movements completed, and delivery costs calculated in full.

- **Deliveries**
  You can then archive the delivery using archiving object RV_LIKP (Deliveries). In turn, the residence times set in Transaction VORL (Archiving Control for Delivery) for each sales organization and delivery type must have expired. The archiving preprocessing program only sets the corresponding deletion flags if the related billing documents have been completed, however.
- **Billing documents**
  After shipments and deliveries, billing documents can also be archived using archiving object SD_VBRK (Billing Documents). To do this, the overall processing status must be set to **Complete** or **Not Relevant**.
- **Sales documents**
  The final step prior to the master data being archived (e.g., customers with archiving object FI_ACCRECV or vendor master data) is the archiving of sales documents with archiving object SD_VBAK (Sales Documents). Residence times from the last change to the point of archiving can be set for this object, for each sales organization, and for sales document type in Transaction VORA (Archiving Control for Sales Doc.). In addition to archiving the required documents, such as those for deliveries, there may also be no individual sales order stocks or open physical inventory (PI) count documents.
- **Accounting documents**
  Accounting documents can only be archived after all other documents with archiving object FI_DOCUMNT (Financial Accounting Documents). The most important factors are the closing of the current fiscal year, the corresponding expiration of residence times for each company code and document type in accordance with Transaction OBR8 (Maintain Document Type Life), and the status of the documents.

Identification of the delete functions

In the example, the assignment of applications and SAP ILM objects is of course comparatively simple due to their familiarity. If you're following our procedural model described in Chapter 3, you'll already have identified all relevant SAP ILM objects. In other cases, such as Transaction DB15 (Data Archiving: Database Tables), means can be used to help identify existing archiving objects based on a table name. Other sources of information include the documentation of the application using archiving and deletion functions.

With the necessary knowledge of relevant applications, the data can then be grouped according to the applicable retention periods. This first abstract step is followed by the use of SAP ILM transactions for maintaining rules. Once again, the LOAs and POAs are decisive.

6.1 Data Controller Rule Framework

In addition to the standard transactions, as of SAP NetWeaver 7.5 SPS 07, a rule framework for the data controller (*Data Controller Rule Framework*) is available to help simplify the maintenance of residence and retention periods. It provides the definition of purposes as a basis for processing data, while also taking the business processes used and the relevant business objects into account. In the definition of data controllers, LOAs are assigned that represent the data controller in the system. As shown in Figure 6.2, the maintenance of the rules for a retention period is based on the data controller and the purposes defined for a data controller.

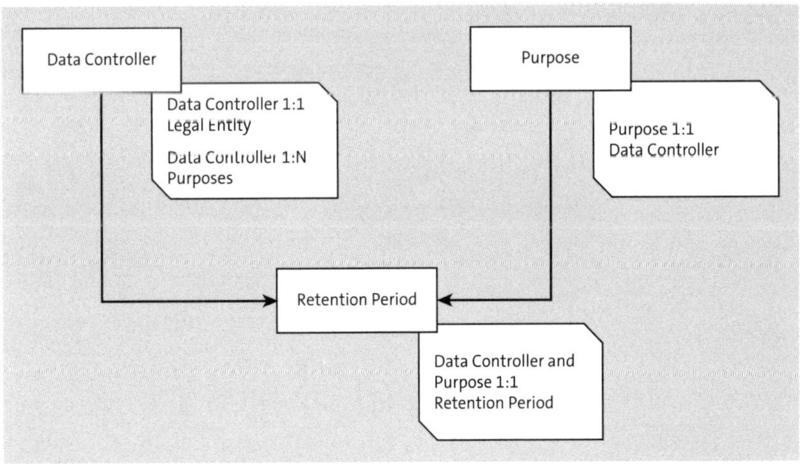

Figure 6.2 Data Controller, Purpose, and Their Connection to the Retention Period

The data controller and the purposes are connected to the data in the system and the SAP ILM objects. Activating maintained rules creates the required SAP ILM configurations and sets of rules for each assigned SAP ILM object based on the individual settings.

Individual maintenance in SAP ILM objects

Consequently, the prerequisite for this is the existence of SAP ILM objects that define the criteria and conditions for maintaining the rules. This is also the main reason for using the new framework. Because each application offers its own and usually varying condition fields for defining rules, the maintenance of the rules must also be tailored to the SAP ILM object. As we've learned, however, the deadlines that have to be maintained are tied to a data controller and purpose of use; this general information must therefore be translated into all corresponding values of the condition fields in the application.

In Figure 6.3 and in the explanation of Figure 5.12, described in Chapter 5, Section 5.4, you can see how the data controllers and purposes defined in the Data Controller Rule Framework connect to your line and process organization and how they are brought together for the definition of retention periods.

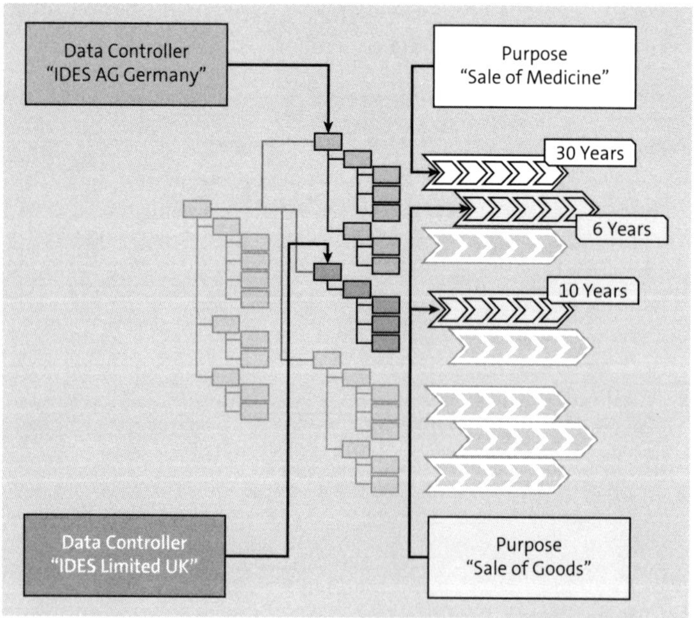

Figure 6.3 Data Controller, Purpose, and Retention Periods in Relation to Line and Process Organization

Generating rules for easy maintenance

In addition to the difficulty of assigning data controllers and purposes to the data using the condition fields of SAP ILM objects, creating rules also means maintaining a large number of individual rules. Generating a large number of rules in all assigned SAP ILM objects for the same period of time thus simplifies maintenance considerably. A further side effect is a higher data quality of the rules due to the fact that unintentional manual maintenance errors can be reduced.

6.1.1 Configuration of the Data Controller Rule Framework

Central functions that support the Data Controller Rule Framework (see Figure 6.4) are grouped together in Customizing under the following path: **SAP Customizing Implementation Guide • SAP NetWeaver • Application Server • Basis Services • Information Lifecycle Management • Retention Management • Data Controller Rule Framework.**

Figure 6.4 Configuration Options of the Data Controller Rule Framework

> **Further information**
>
> For more information about the following SAP Reference Implementation Guide (IMG) activities, please see the system documentation for the respective IMG activity.

Using the organizational structure

The IMG activity **Define Organization Entity** provides you with the various organizational structures necessary for mapping the data controllers. This is where you'll find the different types of LOAs. These refer to the organizational units that you've already maintained in the system, which you usually define and assign to each other in Customizing under **SAP Customizing Implementation Guide • Enterprise Structure**, as also shown in Figure 6.5. Additionally, further organizational units from industrial solutions or add-ons may also be needed.

The definition of organization entities is always connected with a specific implementation of the interface `IF_LRM_OE_DATA_PROVIDER`. These entries are used to make the different organization units known in the framework and to connect them in a uniform or reusable way. The entries are predefined by SAP and will be supplied to you in the system.

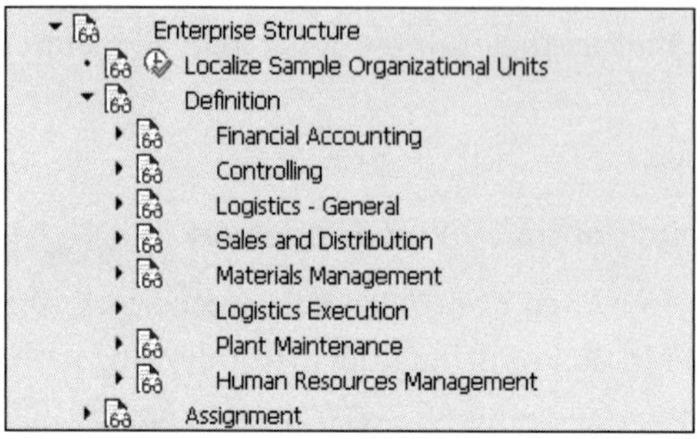

Figure 6.5 Definition and Assignment of Organization Units

Relation to company code

It's always important to have a clear link to the controller (legal entity) and thus to the company code. As shown in Figure 6.6, the entities that are used as condition fields in the SAP ILM objects are predefined by SAP. This enables you to define the data controller, starting from the company code. IMG also allows you to add your own organization entities.

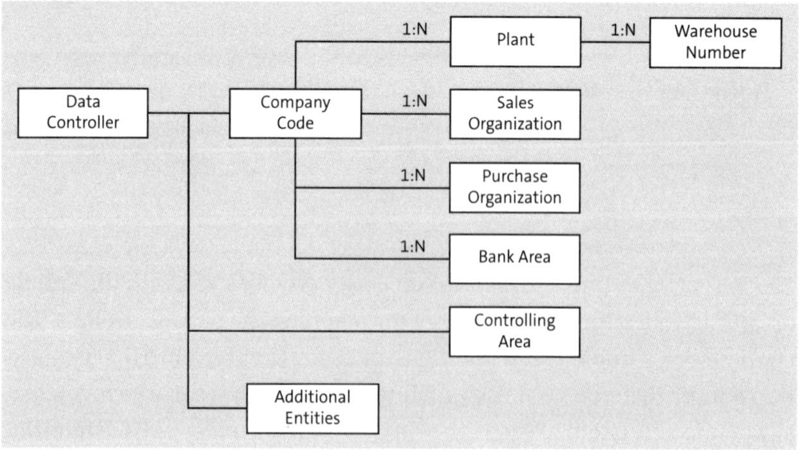

Figure 6.6 Organization Structure with Reference to the Company Code

Which condition fields are organization entities?

In addition to defining organization entities, this activity also includes the assignment of the corresponding condition fields of the SAP ILM objects. This helps to identify the corresponding entity; a programmatic assignment isn't possible due to the use of different names and data elements. You may also add your own SAP ILM objects.

Define data controller

In the IMG activity **Define Data Controller**, you can identify the data controllers that are relevant for your organization units, as shown in Figure 6.7.

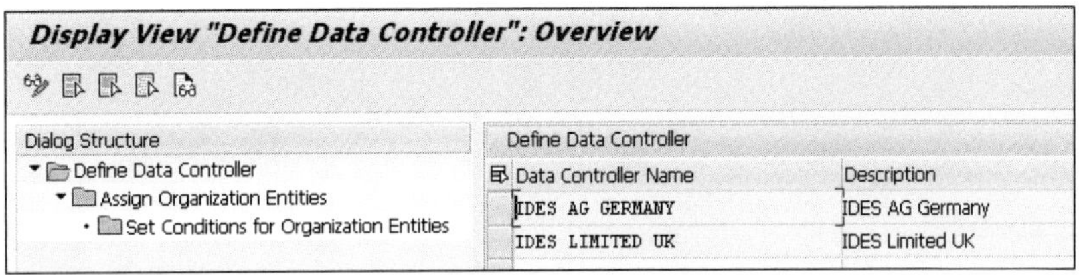

Figure 6.7 Overview of Data Controllers

Grouping of organization units

Various attributes that were previously defined as an organization entity (e.g., company code) will be grouped together. In accordance with the organization units that have been maintained, further assigned organization units are automatically determined and stored in the data controller (e.g., sales organizations within a company code).

Figure 6.8 illustrates the assignment of the organization entity *Company Code* (BUKRS) for the data controller **IDES AG Germany**.

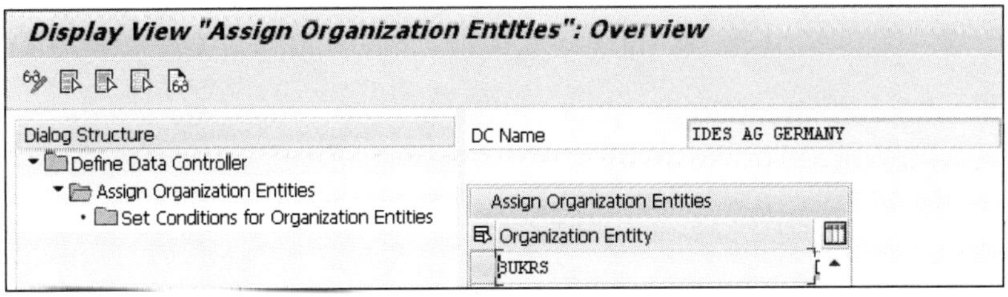

Figure 6.8 Directly Assigning Organization Entities

Determined organization units

As shown in Figure 6.9, for the directly assigned organization entity *company code*, the value for the organization unit **DE01** has been assigned. As a result, all subordinate organization units will also be assigned. When generating SAP ILM rules with reference to this data controller (e.g., for an SAP ILM object with the condition field **Plant**), therefore, all values of the plants in the generated rules that are assigned to company code DE01 will be entered.

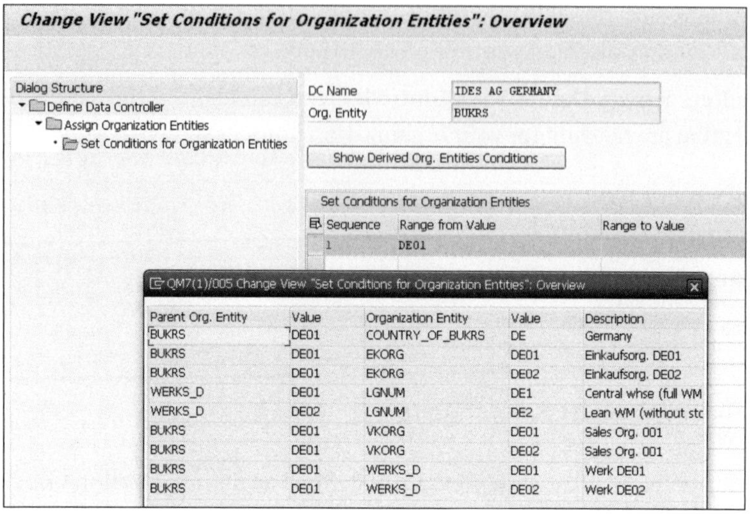

Figure 6.9 Assigning Organization Units for the Data Controller IDES AG Germany and Displaying the Selected Subordinate Organization Units

For comparison, Figure 6.10 shows the subordinate organization units determined for the data controller **IDES Limited UK** in relation to company code **UK01**.

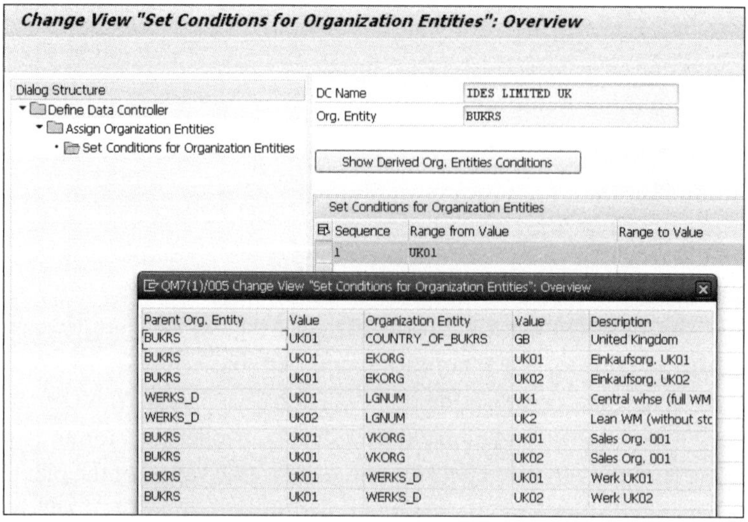

Figure 6.10 Assigning Organization Units for the Data Controller IDES Limited UK and Displaying the Selected Subordinate Organization Units

Define purpose

In the IMG activity for defining the *purpose* (see definition in Chapter 1, Section 1.2.1), you can create entries for mapping your business processes with the relevant POAs. These are used when defining retention rules in SAP ILM or when providing information about personal data. The purpose groups together the SAP ILM objects used in a business process for which the same residence and retention periods apply.

Figure 6.11 shows the definition of two purposes: **Order to Cash Processing** and **Order to Cash Processing Medicine**.

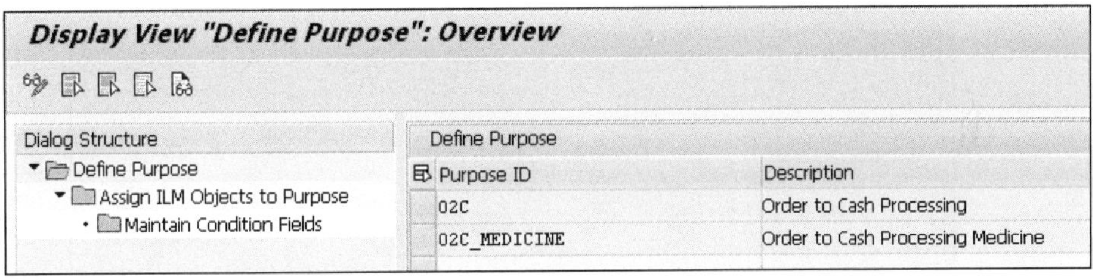

Figure 6.11 Defining Purposes

Identical SAP ILM objects in multiple purposes

Both purposes serve to document the sales process of goods and group together the same SAP ILM objects shown in Figure 6.12.

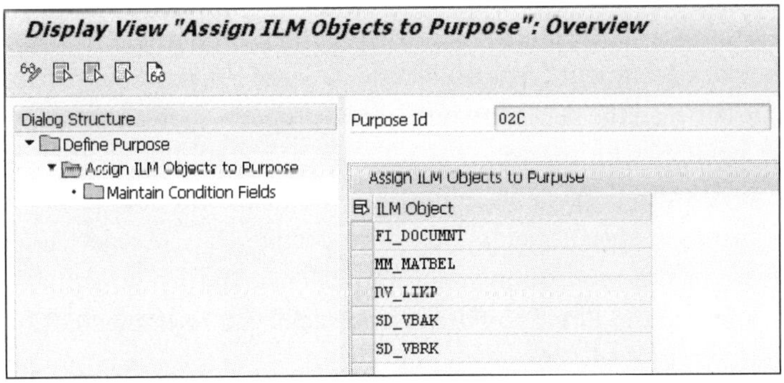

Figure 6.12 SAP ILM Objects Grouped by Purpose

In our example, we're assuming that the retention periods associated with the purpose **Order to Cash Processing** are valid for all goods. This means that a restriction to POAs, that is, to the corresponding condition fields of the grouped SAP ILM objects, isn't necessary. Consequently, when generating SAP ILM rules later on, these periods are valid for all data with reference to the data controller being used. This also applies to data with more specific purposes, as in our second example, **Order to Cash Processing Medicine**. This only makes sense if such unrestricted purposes have shorter retention periods.

Restricting to POAs

As mentioned previously, the purpose **Order to Cash Processing Medicine** has its own extended retention period and is restricted to certain values for POAs. As an example, Figure 6.13 illustrates this for sales document type **MED** in SAP ILM object **SD_VBAK** (Sales Documents).

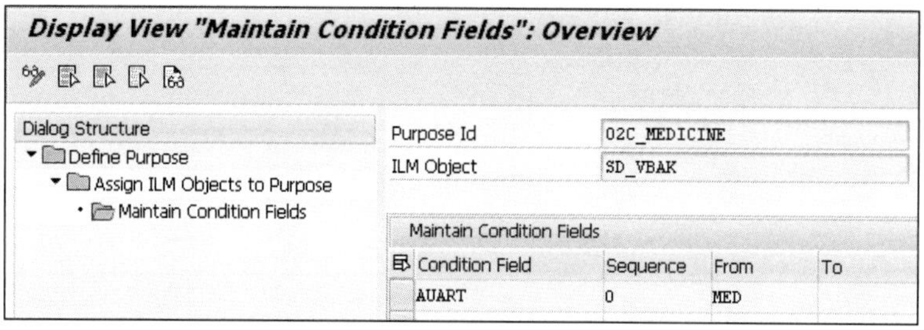

Figure 6.13 Restriction to a POA in One Purpose

The restriction should be made for all SAP ILM objects grouped in the purpose. This calls for the prior identification of the condition fields that are to be used. The answer to the question of whether the values used—as is the case for the sales document types of sales documents—make it possible to differentiate between the necessary purposes is probably more interesting. If this isn't possible with the values you use for the condition fields provided by SAP, it's also possible to define more suitable condition fields—if necessary, customer-specific fields—for the respective SAP ILM object as an alternative to the time-consuming relocation of data. The assignment and value determination in RM in SAP ILM can be achieved by implementing the Business Add-In (BAdI) definition `BADI_IRM_OT_FLD` in the enhancement spot `ES_IRM_CUST`. Note, however, that you also need the differentiation according to purpose for consistent maintenance of authorizations. Adding additional fields to the SAP ILM objects may mean that you can't use these fields to differentiate between authorizations.

Time reference and time offset

With the IMG activity **Set Time Reference and Time Offset**, you can specify the standard time reference and time offset for an SAP ILM object. This setting is used to generate SAP ILM rules for each SAP ILM object. You can choose all time references for each SAP ILM object, as shown in Figure 6.14. If there are several values, select the value that, for your requirements, best represents the time for the end of the business process.

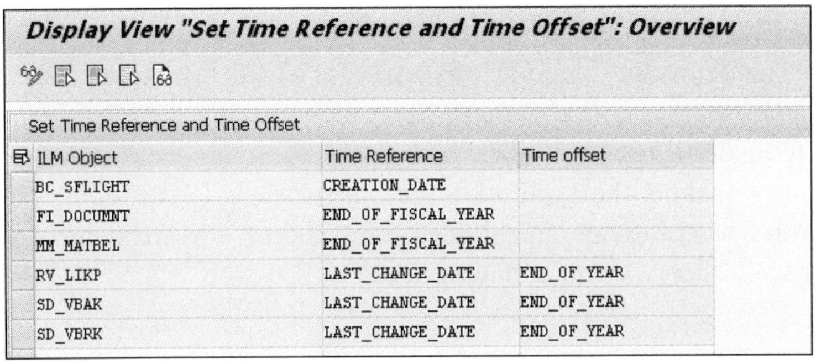
Display View "Set Time Reference and Time Offset": Overview

Set Time Reference and Time Offset

ILM Object	Time Reference	Time offset
BC_SFLIGHT	CREATION_DATE	
FI_DOCUMNT	END_OF_FISCAL_YEAR	
MM_MATBEL	END_OF_FISCAL_YEAR	
RV_LIKP	LAST_CHANGE_DATE	END_OF_YEAR
SD_VBAK	LAST_CHANGE_DATE	END_OF_YEAR
SD_VBRK	LAST_CHANGE_DATE	END_OF_YEAR

Figure 6.14 Set Time Reference and Time Offset for SAP ILM Objects

The *time offsets* enable you to use December 31 as the start time for residence and retention periods for all business processes terminated within the same year, for example, with the value **END_OF_YEAR**. This meets the requirements for the retention of documents and also offers advantages for archiving data; the archiving functionality creates a separate archive file with the same end of the retention period. This means that if you use the time offset **END_OF_YEAR**, all documents of the same year with the same retention period end up in the same file, and you avoid creating multiple archive files for each date.

Setting the default audit area

In a further IMG activity, you can set the *default audit area* that will be used to generate SAP ILM rules for retention periods. Figure 6.15 uses the **Audit Area GENERAL** (General Rules). SAP recommends that you instead use your own audit area, created under the customer name, to define SAP ILM rules for retention periods. You can define this by using Transaction ILMARA (Audit Area Processing).

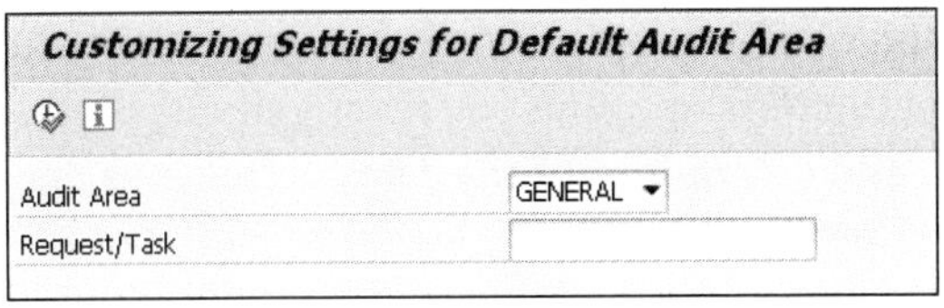

Figure 6.15 Setting the Audit Area for SAP ILM Rules on Retention Periods

Audit area ARCHIVING

In contrast to retention periods, the SAP ILM rules for residence periods are always generated for the SAP audit area ARCHIVING (Data Archiving). This audit area is subject to special use when archiving data. It only allows data archiving if the valid residence periods for the data to be archived have expired. This enables you to control the time at which the data can be archived (and therefore blocked); this is true for all SAP ILM objects linked to an archiving object that support the policy category RST (Residence Rules) for defining residence rules. This centralized solution based on SAP ILM rules enhances the application-specific solutions for defining residence rules, such as the aforementioned Transaction VORA (Archiving Control for Sales Docs.) with the archiving object SD_VBAK.

6.1.2 Rule Maintenance in the Data Controller Rule Framework

To create and activate rules in the Data Controller Rule Framework, you can use the SAP Fiori app Manage ILM Business Rules or use Transaction IRM-RULE (Business Rule Maintenance). Follow these steps:

1. Enter a **Rule ID** and a **Rule Description** in the **Business Rule** area.
2. Select the **Rule Start Date**. The selected date can't be earlier than the current date. You can use the start date to schedule changes to the rules and, for example, postpone activating the rule until this date has been reached.
3. The **Rule End Date** is automatically set to **31.12.9999**. If you want to replace an active rule with a new rule, you can restrict it to a specific end date.
4. You may specify an **Authorization Group**. This field can be used to apply SAP ILM rules for blocking archived data in business function ILM_BLOCKING. The values are used to determine which users are authorized to view blocked data during the relevant retention period when reading in the archive.
5. Assign the data controller for which you want to create the rule in the **Data Controller Name** field. At the same time, you're assigning all organization units maintained and determined in the data controller as line-specific attributes. This is used for the simulation and creation of SAP ILM rules in the SAP ILM objects assigned according to their purpose.

6. In the **Retention/Residence Fields** area, enter a suitable time unit (year, day, or month) into the **Residence Period** field. You should also maintain a **Retention Period** and the time unit to be used for this. When creating the rule, the system will ask you whether you want to maintain residence periods only, retention periods only, or both. These fields will be available according to the selection you make. You can use this to create rules that are valid for blocking only, deleting only, or both. This provides you with the necessary flexibility to create SAP ILM rules, even in special cases, such as when additional residence periods are required.

7. You can add one or more purposes to a rule. This assigns the SAP ILM objects defined in the purposes to the POAs for which the rule is later generated. By assigning several purposes, you have, for example, the necessary flexibility to maintain different purposes with identical retention periods in one rule, instead of several rules.

Figure 6.16 shows an example maintenance of a rule in Transaction IRMRULE (Business Rule Maintenance) for the data controller **IDES AG Germany** and the purpose **Order to Cash Processing Germany**.

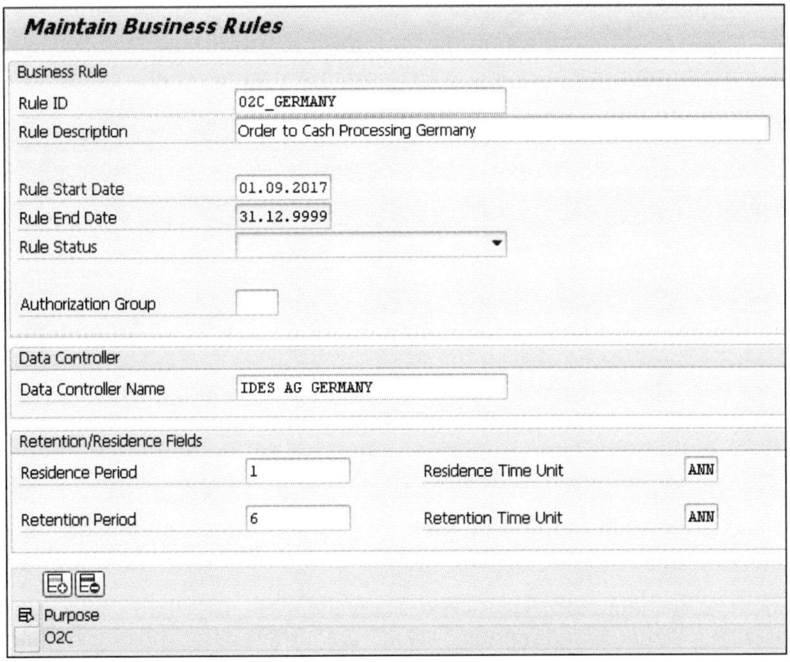

Figure 6.16 Example for Creating a Rule in Transaction IRMRULE

When saving the data, a business rule with the status **Draft** will be created. You can change or delete rules in this status at any time. The first screen of the transaction (see Figure 6.17) shows an overview of all the rules you've maintained.

Maintain Business Rules

Refresh Create Delete Display

Business Rule ID	Rule Description	Data Controller Name	Status	Res.Time	Unit	Ret. Time	Time Unit	Start Date	End Date
O2C_GERMANY	Order to Cash Processing Germany	IDES AG GERMANY	Draft	1	Year	6	Year	01.09.2017	31.12.9999
O2C_MEDICINE GERMANY	O2C_MEDICINE Germany	IDES AG GERMANY	Draft	1	Year	30	Year	01.09.2017	31.12.9999
O2C_UK	Order to Cash Processing UK	IDES LIMITED UK	Draft	1	Year	10	Year	01.09.2017	31.12.9999

Figure 6.17 Overview of Rules Maintained in Transaction IRMRULE

Simulating rules

For rules with the status **Draft**, you can simulate the creation of SAP ILM rules. As a result, the system displays a list of SAP ILM rules that would then be generated. Figure 6.18 shows the results of the simulation for all SAP ILM objects with the purpose **Order to Cash Processing** for data controller **IDES Limited UK**. The simulation results are based on a residence period of 1 year and a retention period of 10 years based on the time unit and the time offset.

ILM Rules

Number	Condition Field	From	To	Ret. ...	Retention Time Unit	Res...	Residence Time Unit	Time Reference	Time Offset	ILM Object	Pol...	Policy Name	Audit Area
1	BUKRS	UK01		10	Year	0		END_OF_FISCAL_YEAR		FI_DOCUMNT	RTP	R114114814	GENERAL
1	BUKRS	UK01		0		1	Year	END_OF_FISCAL_YEAR		FI_DOCUMNT	RST	R114114814	ARCHIVING
1	BUKRS	UK01		10	Year	0		END_OF_FISCAL_YEAR		MM_MATBEL	RTP	R114114135	GENERAL
1	BUKRS	UK01		0		1	Year	END_OF_FISCAL_YEAR		MM_MATBEL	RST	R114114135	ARCHIVING
1	VKORG	UK01		10	Year	0		LAST_CHANGE_DATE	END_OF_YEAR	RV_LIKP	RTP	R114114905	GENERAL
2	VKORG	UK02		10	Year	0		LAST_CHANGE_DATE	END_OF_YEAR	RV_LIKP	RTP	R114114905	GENERAL
1	VKORG	UK01		0		1	Year	LAST_CHANGE_DATE	END_OF_YEAR	RV_LIKP	RST	R114114905	ARCHIVING
2	VKORG	UK02		0		1	Year	LAST_CHANGE_DATE	END_OF_YEAR	RV_LIKP	RST	R114114905	ARCHIVING
1	BUKRS_VF	UK01		10	Year	0		LAST_CHANGE_DATE	END_OF_YEAR	SD_VBAK	RTP	R114114835	GENERAL
1	BUKRS_VF	UK01		0		1	Year	LAST_CHANGE_DATE	END_OF_YEAR	SD_VBAK	RST	R114114835	ARCHIVING
1	BUKRS	UK01		10	Year	0		LAST_CHANGE_DATE	END_OF_YEAR	SD_VBRK	RTP	R114114126	GENERAL
1	BUKRS	UK01		0		1	Year	LAST_CHANGE_DATE	END_OF_YEAR	SD_VBRK	RST	R114114126	ARCHIVING

Figure 6.18 Simulation Result for the Order to Cash Processing Purpose and the IDES Limited UK Data Controller

As configured, the retention periods will be generated in the SAP ILM objects of the audit area GENERAL (General Rules). Residence periods are only generated in SAP ILM objects RV_LIKP, SD_VBAK, and SD_VBRK; the other SAP ILM objects don't support the policy category RST (Residence Rules). As described earlier, the retention periods are always assigned to the audit area ARCHIVING (Data Archiving). The condition fields assigned to the SAP

ILM objects have been filled with the organization units maintained and determined in the data controller. The purpose isn't restricted to other condition fields; the SAP ILM rules for each organization unit therefore aren't combined with other condition fields.

In comparison, Figure 6.19 shows the simulation result for the **Order to Cash Processing Medicine** purpose and the **IDES AG Germany** data controller. The time references and audit areas remain the same. However due to the differing data controllers, SAP ILM rules are determined for other organization units. Because restrictive values are maintained as POAs for the purpose, the SAP ILM rules determined for each organization unit are linked to these values. This ensures that such an SAP ILM rule is only applicable for data in the specific organization unit and for these POAs only.

ILM Rules

Number	Condition Field	From	To	Ret. ...	Retention Time Unit	Res...	Residence Time Unit	Time Reference	Time Offset	ILM Object	Pol...	Policy Name	Audit Area
1	BSCHL	ME		30	Year	0		END_OF_FISCAL_YEAR		FI_DOCUMNT	RTP	R124004814	GENERAL
1	BUKRS	DE01		30	Year	0		END_OF_FISCAL_YEAR		FI_DOCUMNT	RTP	R124004814	GENERAL
1	BSCHL	ME		0		1	Year	END_OF_FISCAL_YEAR		FI_DOCUMNT	RST	R124004814	ARCHIVING
1	BUKRS	DE01		0		1	Year	END_OF_FISCAL_YEAR		FI_DOCUMNT	RST	R124004814	ARCHIVING
1	BUKRS	DE01		30	Year	0		END_OF_FISCAL_YEAR		MM_MATBEL	RTP	R124004135	GENERAL
1	VGART	ME		30	Year	0		END_OF_FISCAL_YEAR		MM_MATBEL	RTP	R124004135	GENERAL
1	BUKRS	DE01		0		1	Year	END_OF_FISCAL_YEAR		MM_MATBEL	RST	R124004135	ARCHIVING
1	VGART	ME		0		1	Year	END_OF_FISCAL_YEAR		MM_MATBEL	RST	R124004135	ARCHIVING
1	LFART	MED		30	Year	0		LAST_CHANGE_DATE	END_OF_YEAR	RV_LIKP	RTP	R124004905	GENERAL
1	VKORG	DE01		30	Year	0		LAST_CHANGE_DATE	END_OF_YEAR	RV_LIKP	RTP	R124004905	GENERAL
2	LFART	MED		30	Year	0		LAST_CHANGE_DATE	END_OF_YEAR	RV_LIKP	RTP	R124004905	GENERAL
2	VKORG	DE02		30	Year	0		LAST_CHANGE_DATE	END_OF_YEAR	RV_LIKP	RTP	R124004905	GENERAL
1	LFART	MED		0		1	Year	LAST_CHANGE_DATE	END_OF_YEAR	RV_LIKP	RST	R124004905	ARCHIVING
1	VKORG	DE01		0		1	Year	LAST_CHANGE_DATE	END_OF_YEAR	RV_LIKP	RST	R124004905	ARCHIVING
2	LFART	MED		0		1	Year	LAST_CHANGE_DATE	END_OF_YEAR	RV_LIKP	RST	R124004905	ARCHIVING
2	VKORG	DE02		0		1	Year	LAST_CHANGE_DATE	END_OF_YEAR	RV_LIKP	RST	R124004905	ARCHIVING
1	AUART	MED		30	Year	0		LAST_CHANGE_DATE	END_OF_YEAR	SD_VBAK	RTP	R124004835	GENERAL
1	BUKRS_VF	DE01		30	Year	0		LAST_CHANGE_DATE	END_OF_YEAR	SD_VBAK	RTP	R124004835	GENERAL
1	AUART	MED		0		1	Year	LAST_CHANGE_DATE	END_OF_YEAR	SD_VBAK	RST	R124004835	ARCHIVING
1	BUKRS_VF	DE01		0		1	Year	LAST_CHANGE_DATE	END_OF_YEAR	SD_VBAK	RST	R124004835	ARCHIVING
1	FKART	ME		30	Year	0		LAST_CHANGE_DATE	END_OF_YEAR	SD_VBRK	RTP	R124004126	GENERAL
1	BUKRS	DE01		30	Year	0		LAST_CHANGE_DATE	END_OF_YEAR	SD_VBRK	RTP	R124004126	GENERAL
1	BUKRS	DE01		0		1	Year	LAST_CHANGE_DATE	END_OF_YEAR	SD_VBRK	RST	R124004126	ARCHIVING
1	FKART	ME		0		1	Year	LAST_CHANGE_DATE	END_OF_YEAR	SD_VBRK	RST	R124004126	ARCHIVING

Figure 6.19 Simulation Result for the Order to Cash Processing Medicine Purpose and the IDES AG Germany Data Controller

Activating the rules

After the selected start date has been reached, you can activate a rule. If the rule's start date is still in the future, the business rule is saved with the status **Scheduled for Activation**. In all other cases, the SAP ILM rules are generated, and the rule is saved with the status **Active**.

You can use Transaction IRMRULE_ACTIVATE (Activate Scheduled Business Rules) to activate the scheduled business rules. In this transaction, you'll only be able to display rules that have the status **Scheduled for Activation** and whose start date is earlier than or the same as the current date.

When you've activated the rule, the data discussed in the following paragraphs will be generated in RM of SAP ILM.

Activating audit areas

The SAP ILM objects assigned to the purposes of use will be activated (if necessary) for the audit area selected for the retention rules. The same applies to the audit area ARCHIVING (Data Archiving) if the residence periods are of relevance. You can see the outcome in sequence in Transaction ILMARA (Audit Area Processing), as shown in Figure 6.20 and Figure 6.21.

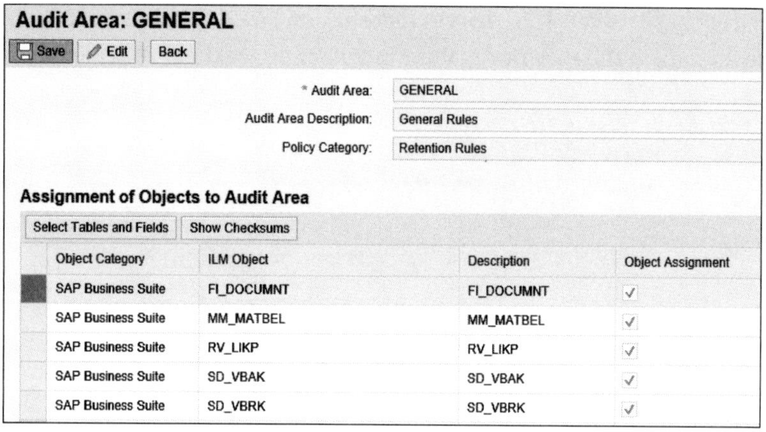

Figure 6.20 Activated SAP ILM Objects for Audit Area GENERAL

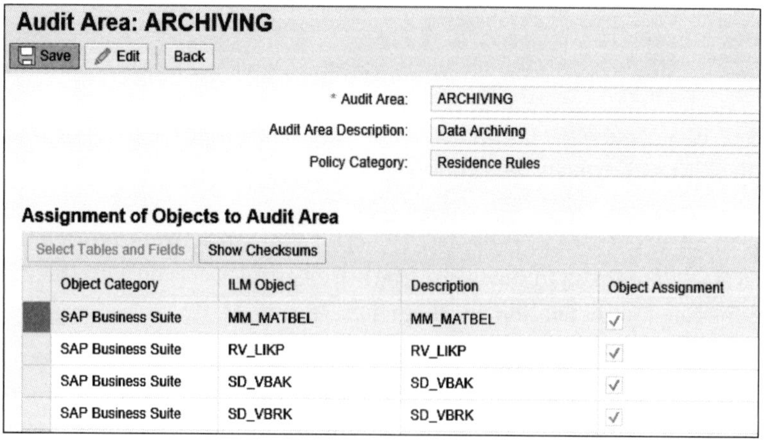

Figure 6.21 Activated SAP ILM Objects for Audit Area ARCHIVING

Generating rule groups

In Transaction IRM_CUST_CSS (IRM: Customer-Specific Settings), an object group with assigned rule groups can be generated. As you can see in Figure 6.22, the rule groups contain the defined deadlines and units of time. Rule groups will be generated for both retention periods and residence periods. The object group is assigned to the SAP ILM objects, which are then also set to active for the use of rule groups, as demonstrated in Figure 6.23.

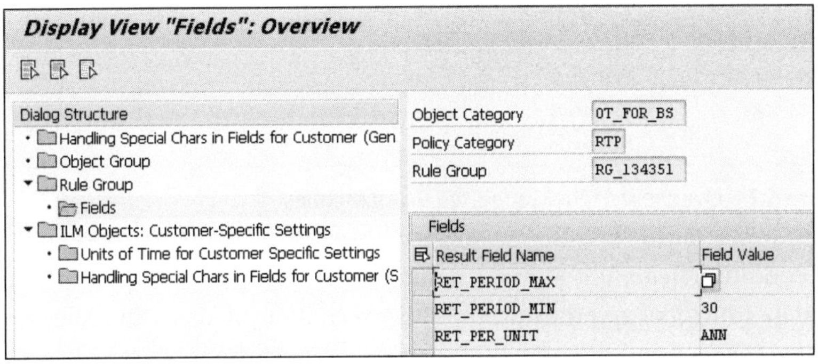

Figure 6.22 Rule Group Created for the Retention Period

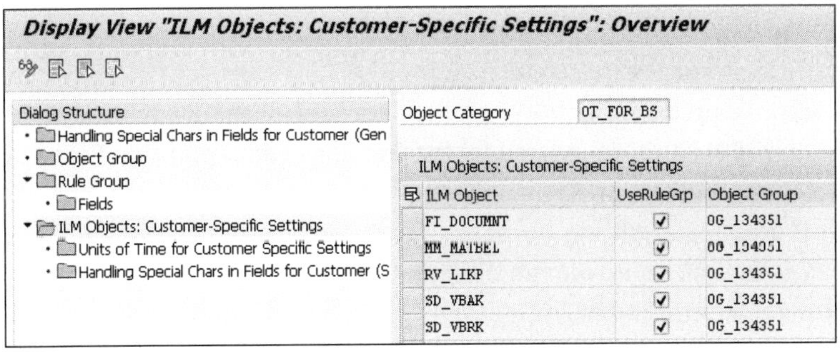

Figure 6.23 Activated Use of Rule Groups for SAP ILM Objects

Generating SAP ILM rules

SAP ILM rules are generated in Transaction IRMPOL (ILM Policies). As you can see in Figure 6.24, this is the case for the object category OT_FOR_BS (**SAP Business Suite**), the selected audit areas for the **Policy Category** RST (Residence Rules) or RTP (Retention Rules), and the assigned **Audit Area**.

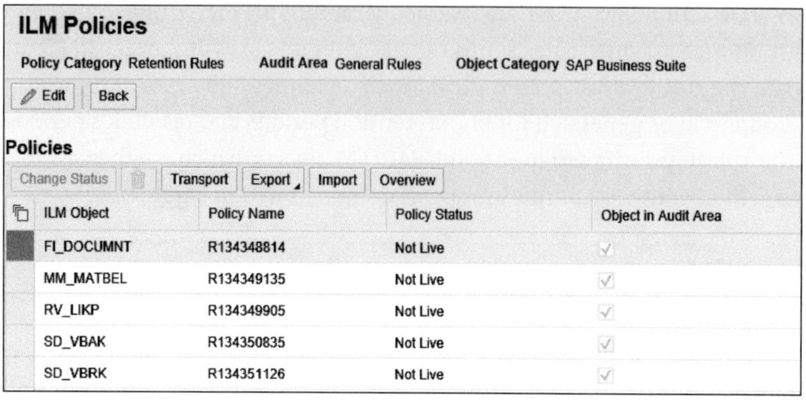

Figure 6.24 Overview of the Generated SAP ILM Rules

The condition fields are assigned to the SAP ILM objects in accordance with the data controller and the purposes for which they are used, and rules are created for each combination of these values. The periods are available via the assigned rule group; the time references and time offsets will also be copied. You can also supplement the ILM Store where the archive files are to be stored later.

Figure 6.25 shows the rule created for the SAP ILM object `FI_DOCUMNT` (Financial Accounting Documents). From the data controller IDES AG Germany, the value **DE01** has been entered for the **Company Code** condition field. The value **ME** in the **Posting Key** condition field was copied from the **Order to Cash Processing Medicine** purpose. The generated rule group RG_134351 with the minimum and maximum retention period of **30** years, along with the time reference **End of Fiscal Year**, has now been assigned.

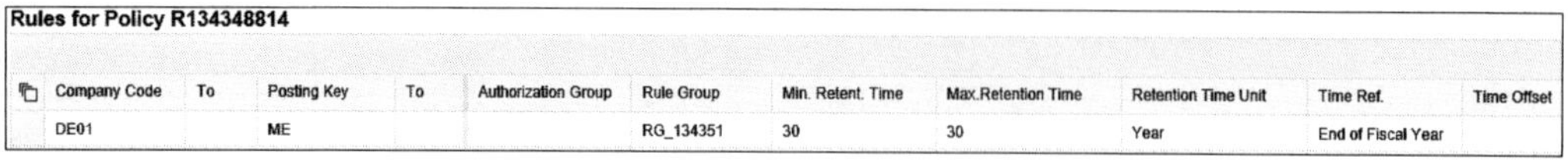

Figure 6.25 Generated Rule for SAP ILM Object FI_DOCUMNT

The rules are saved in the rule group status **Not Live**. After you've checked that the generation result is correct, you can set the status to **Live** so that you can use the rules in future archiving runs (Transaction SARA – Archive Administration) and data destruction runs (Transaction ILM_DESTRUCTION – Data Destruction).

Active and historical rules

In Transaction IRMRULE (Business Rule Maintenance), you can copy rules with the status **Active**. In this case, a follow-up rule with the status **Draft** is created for the copied rule; this rule will be saved with the status **Historical** and can no longer be changed. The end date of the historical rule is set to the current date. The SAP ILM rules generated for the previously active rule won't be changed.

For rules with the status **Active** or **Historical**, you can also display the generated SAP ILM rules in Transaction IRMRULE (Business Rule Maintenance). This allows you to later determine which SAP ILM rules were created for which data controller and for which purposes. Note that manual changes and the deletion of SAP ILM rules are possible in Transaction IRMPOL (ILM Policies), which means that this information would no longer be available for your control and proof obligations.

6.2 Summary

Structuring the end involves various aspects such as the sequence for deleting the data and how this can be determined. This is influenced not only by the length of the applicable retention periods but also by the functionality of the applications, which ensures consistent data deletion. To illustrate the different activities that need to be organized for archiving data, we used the example of the customer sales order process.

With the Data Controller Rule Framework, we've also introduced an application that links your personal data used in business processes with the data controller, the purposes for which it's being processed, and the relevant residence and retention periods. This provides you with a clear overview of your personal data in the system and enables you to effectively differentiate between this data by assigning it to the LOAs and POAs.

By fully assigning your data to the purposes for which it's used and to the data controllers, you'll also receive confirmation on principle that all personal data can be deleted. For subsequent blocking and deletion, you can check whether the solution will work completely and consistently (e.g., which data isn't yet included, which dependencies exist, etc.).

By using the Data Controller Rule Framework, you can also simplify maintenance considerably. Our assessment of all SAP ILM rules that need to be maintained for an organization with 200 subsidiaries and full use of the SAP Business Suite amounts to more than 1 million entries. You can use the Data Controller Rule Framework to create these SAP ILM rules with considerably less administration work.

Chapter 7

Authorization Concept

For a long time, authorizations were the only thing many customers thought about when it came to data protection. Of course, a well-defined authorization concept will continue to play an extremely important role in data protection in the future. However, a large number of adjustments to the concepts may be necessary.

This chapter will provide you with a brief introduction to the role-based access control concept (RBAC). This serves as a basis for showing you how a purpose-based separation can be made within the authorization concept by using line organizational attributes (LOAs) and process organizational attributes (POAs). Finally, we'll describe abstractly how to make risk definitions and introduce a new risk assessment.

7.1 Users and Authorizations: An Introduction

To display how the principle of minimization and purpose limitation can be realized in authorizations, you'll need at least an overview of users and authorizations. The following explanations are based on the book *Authorizations in SAP Software* by Lehnert and Stelzner (SAP PRESS, 2010, *www.sap-press.com/2316*).

7.1.1 Users

Different types of users

For a (natural) person to be able to perform actions in the SAP system, he needs a user to whom authorizations are assigned (see Figure 7.1). Each person ❶ has ❷ a user ❸; one (or more) roles ❹ are assigned to the user. A role ❺ has a menu ❻ that contains applications ❼. In relation to these applications, authorizations ❽ are included in the role. The individual authorizations are of an authorization object ❾.

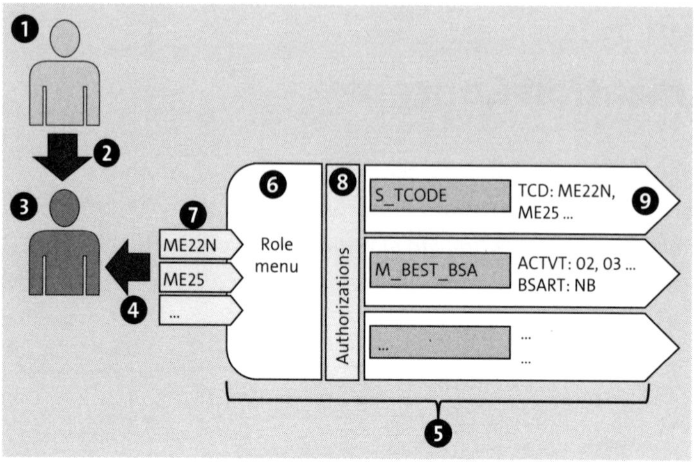

Figure 7.1 Person, User, and Role in Authorizations

All of the actions in the SAP system are performed by users. There are different user types for different types of actions, as follows:

- **Dialog user**
  Dialog users are personalized for natural persons who use the graphical user interface, SAP GUI, to log on to the SAP system. The dialog user is the main user type and therefore the focus of this book.
- **Service user**
  Service users are used, for example, for the anonymous access of several users in web services. For this reason, the authorizations for this user type should be restricted considerably. A user logs on using the SAP GUI; it's possible that the user will log on more than once. The status of the password of a service user is always productive, which also means that only a user administrator can change the password.
- **Communication user**
  Communication users are person-related users who log on, not using the SAP GUI, but rather by means of a remote function call (RFC). The user can change the password. The system checks whether the password has expired or is new. Depending on whether the user has logged on interactively or not, the password may have to be changed.
- **System user**
  System users are needed in technical processes, such as batch runs. The

user doesn't log on using the SAP GUI. Multiple logons are possible when working with system users. Passwords don't have to be changed.

- **Reference user**
  The reference user is a means of simplifying authorization administration. It's not possible to log on to the SAP system with this user. The reference user is used to pass on authorizations.

The business authorization concept also has to contain information about the users displayed. For reasons of rule conformity, you can only grant technical users the authorizations that are required, which makes it all the more important that this principle applies to all users that allow people to access the system.

7.1.2 Authorizations

Authorizations are necessary to start SAP ERP system applications and execute their functions. The following sections explain the structural properties and the use of authorizations in ABAP programs.

ABAP programs include authorization checks to protect the execution of a business function from unauthorized persons. When the programs are executed, the system determines whether the user is allowed to process the application-specific data as required.

Authorization field

To map a business process from the perspective of authorization, you first have to define a parameter for each characteristic value involved in the process. This parameter is called an *authorization field*. Because several parameters are normally involved in a business transaction, you'll need to have the right combinations of authorization fields.

Authorization object

These combinations are called authorization objects. An *authorization object* consists of a maximum of 10 authorization fields and is assigned to an authorization object class. After you assign values to the fields contained in an authorization object, an authorization is created. In the following sections, we'll look at two examples of authorization objects.

Example: Authorization Object M_BEST_EKO

Figure 7.2 shows a simple example of an authorization object `M_BEST_EKO` (Purchasing Organization in the Purchase Order).

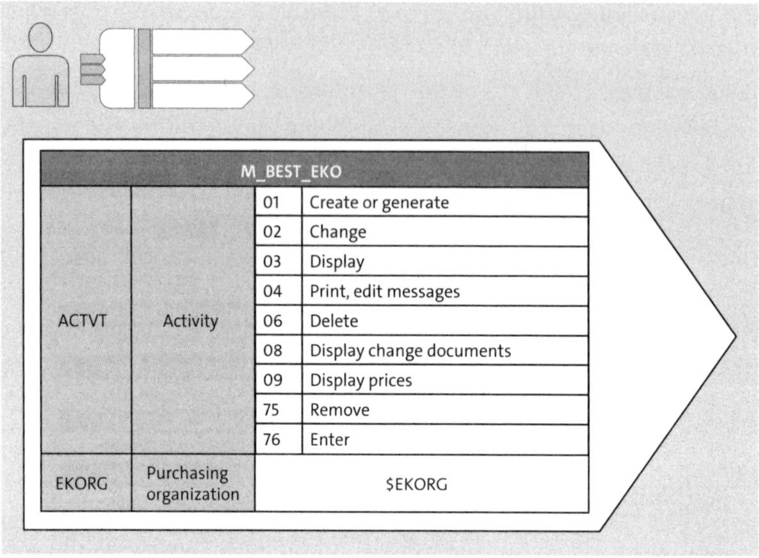

Figure 7.2 Example of an Authorization Object

The object contains the authorization fields **ACTVT** (**Activity**) and **EKORG** (**Purchasing Organization**). You can use the authorizations for this object to specify which types of processing (e.g., creating purchase orders) members of a particular purchasing organization can perform within a given application (e.g., purchase order).

ACTVT is one of the most frequently used authorization fields, and appears in objects in very different application areas.

LOAs

EKORG (**Purchasing Organization**) is the field in which you define the purchasing organizations these authorizations should apply to. Chapter 5, Section 5.2.1, already covered the purchasing organization as a *line organizational attribute (LOA)*. At this point, you can also maintain this exact characteristic (and the other LOAs mentioned in Chapter 5) in the authorizations.

Example: Authorization Object M_BEST_BSA

POAs

The situation is similar for authorization objects such as `M_BEST_BSA` (Document Type in Purchase Order), which are suitable for including *process organizational attributes (POAs)*, as previously described in Chapter 5, Section 5.3.

The authorization objects consist of two fields. If you choose to display this authorization object in Transaction SU21 (Maintain Authorization Objects), you'll see a screen similar to Figure 7.3.

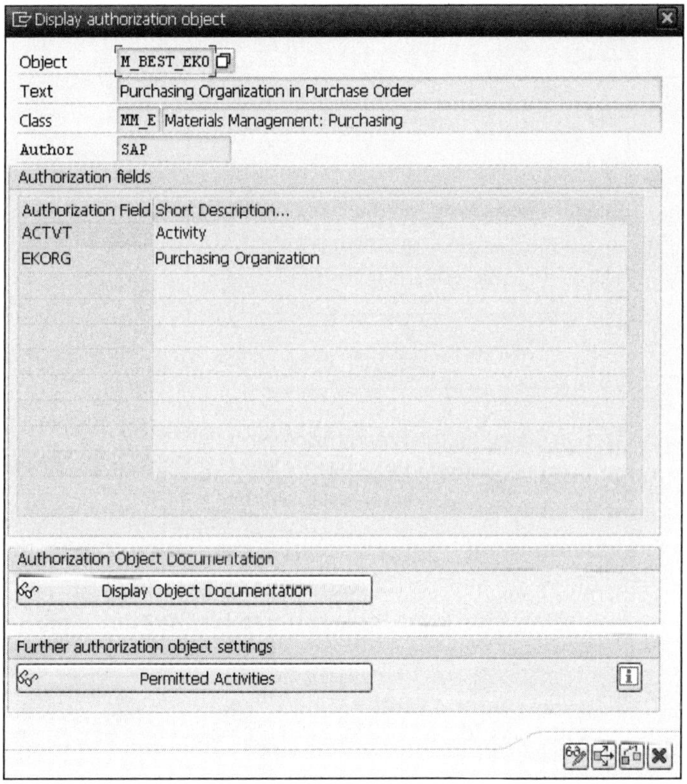

Figure 7.3 Authorization Object M_BEST_BSA

Authorization check during program execution

If the authorization objects have been specified, corresponding authorizations will be generated that will always be based on the role in this model. Both authorization objects are used to control which activity is possible, in which purchasing organization, and in which document type. Depending on the complexity of the program, several authorizations will be checked step by step, starting with a start authorization check. The checking sequence of the technical process in Transaction ME21N (Create Purchase Order) is simplified and schematized in Figure 7.4.

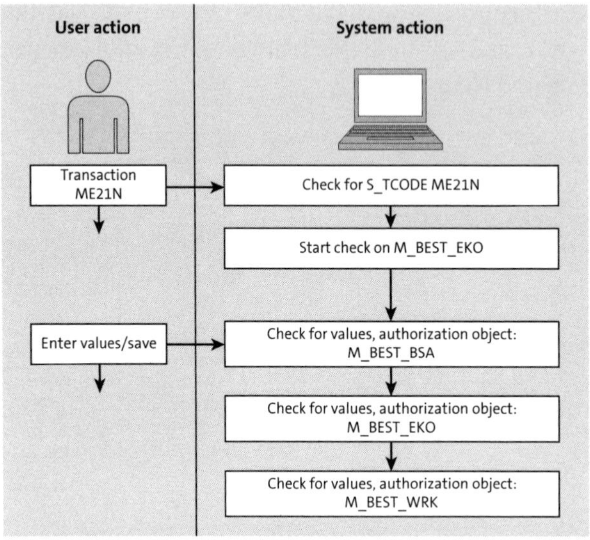

Figure 7.4 Authorization Checks in the Program Sequence

The first check shown in the graphic for S_TCODE (Transaction Code Check at Transaction Start) is also possible for other start authorization objects; the object S_SERVICE (Check at Startup of External Services) is particularly important for SAP S/4HANA because this is required for SAP Fiori apps.

[»]

Access Restriction via LOAs and POAs

A user is assigned to a person, and roles are assigned to this user. The roles contain authorization objects that—as soon as the role has been generated—constitute the authorizations of the user concerned. A sequence of authorization checks takes place in a number of programs, for example, in business applications. It's therefore possible to sufficiently restrict the user's access using LOAs and POAs by differentiating the access in a relevant way.

7.2 Rethinking Organizational Levels

To complete the picture, a few more details about the organizational levels are necessary. For roles, the organizational levels are strong organizational differentiators that are validated in numerous authorizations. In many cases, the organizational levels correspond to the characteristics described in Chapter 5, Section 5.2.1, such as company code or purchasing organization.

Existing organizational levels

The organizational levels available in the system are shown in table USORG (Organizational Levels for the Profile Generator), as shown in Figure 7.5. In principle, authorization fields for organizational levels can also be "raised." Organizational levels are initially also authorization fields in an authorization object. Their special feature is their status and the possibilities that arise from it. Organizational levels are required for the derivation concept. As you go through the defined organizational levels, you'll find that not all organizational levels are LOAs as defined in this book.

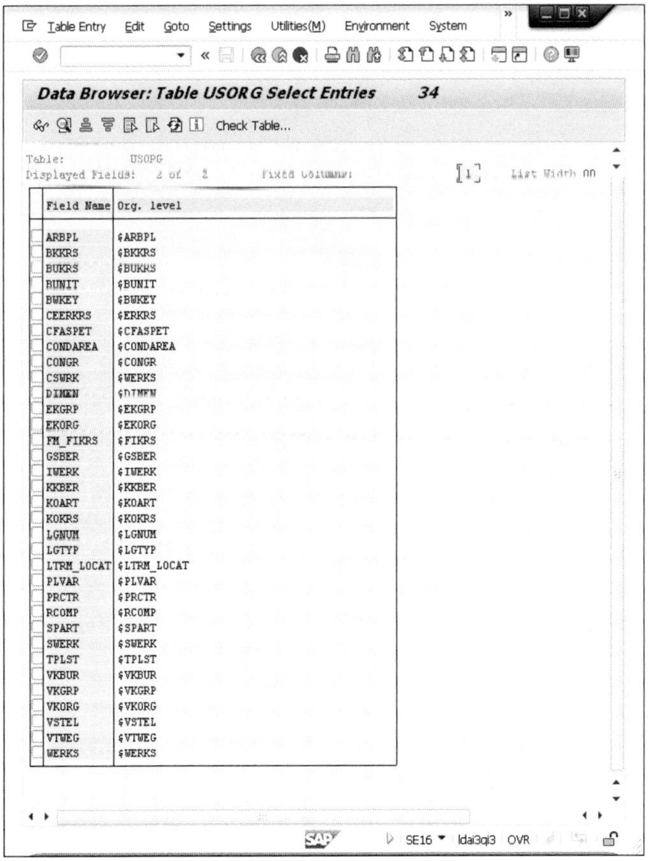

Field Name	Org. level
ARBPL	$ARBPL
BKKRS	$BKKRS
BUKRS	$BUKRS
BUNIT	$BUNIT
BWKEY	$BWKEY
CEERKRS	$ERKRS
CFASPET	$CFASPET
CONDAREA	$CONDAREA
CONGR	$CONGR
CSWRK	$WERKS
DIMEN	$DIMEN
EKGRP	$EKGRP
EKORG	$EKORG
FM_FIKRS	$FIKRS
GSBER	$GSBER
IWERK	$IWERK
KKBER	$KKBER
KOART	$KOART
KOKRS	$KOKRS
LGNUM	$LGNUM
LGTYP	$LGTYP
LTRM_LOCAT	$LTRM_LOCAT
PLVAR	$PLVAR
PRCTR	$PRCTR
RCOMP	$RCOMP
SPART	$SPART
SWERK	$SWERK
TPLST	$TPLST
VKBUR	$VKBUR
VKGRP	$VKGRP
VKORG	$VKORG
VSTEL	$VSTEL
VTWEG	$VTWEG
WERKS	$WERKS

Figure 7.5 Organizational Levels in Table USORG (Organizational Levels for the Profile Generator)

Derivation concept

The derivation concept is the central technical vehicle of the authorization concept. The system also recognizes the need to differentiate roles along clear organizational boundaries. As shown in Figure 7.6, roles can be derived from a central reference role that has its own specific organizational level characteristics and LOAs. Assuming there are three legally independent units, these can each be mapped with one set of LOAs; when deriving the roles, these values are entered in the derived role.

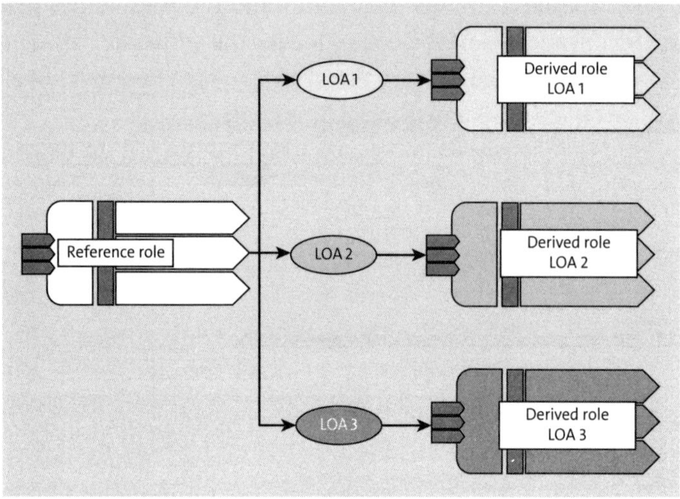

Figure 7.6 Derivation Concept and LOAs

As described in Chapter 5, as a general rule, we assume that the purpose of processing personal data is to be considered specifically for a legally independent entity. Accordingly, it's also important that the organizational model is reflected in the use of the organizational levels. Chapter 12 deals with the control measures that are necessary to achieve this. An essential question in this context is how the organizational levels were defined in the roles.

Procedural model as a basis

If you've been following our procedural model (see Chapter 3), you've seen a comprehensive overview of the line organization differentiation requirements simply because you also need these attributes for blocking and deleting and when providing information. If you also use the business retention Data Controller Rule Framework, you'll have a representation there that can be used accordingly with the authorization concept.

If, however, you want to start with authorizations as your first step of implementation, you have no other option than to determine the relationships outlined in Chapter 5, Section 5.2.1. This section will also show you where you can evaluate the assignments in the enterprise structure. You'll have to determine which assignments are maintained and evaluate whether the relationships refer uniquely to a controller (usually the legal person). The controller is usually represented by the company code. **Alternative approach**

After you've traced this assignment, check table USORG (Organizational Levels for the Profile Generator) to see which organizational levels are available for authorizations in your system. The next step requires an actual analysis; you'll have to examine the actual assignments to the authorizations in table AGR_1252 (Organizational Levels). You should also consider the manual values of these fields in table AGR_1251 (Authorization Data for Activity Group). Together, these two specifications provide information on which line-organizational differentiations currently exist for you in the roles. Entries made to these fields in table AGR_1251 (Authorization Data for Activity group) are also proof that your authorization concept doesn't comply with the standard.

[!]

No Generic Maintenance

Generic maintenance with "*" or comprehensive intervals "0001–9999" aren't generally useful as a means of differentiation.

[«]

Is the Data Processed Separately for Each Purpose?

Our regular discussions with SAP Consulting often deal with the question of whether or not data can actually be processed separately. In such cases, our standard response is that a brief look at the organizational differentiation of roles will provide a rapidly identified and weighty indicator.

7.3 Defining Process Attributes

POAs were already addressed in Chapter 5, Section 5.3. In doing so, we also clarified our assumptions in the process and gradually presented the elements of an exemplary process: customer, order, delivery, and billing document. These business objects are regularly protected by relevant authorization objects that allow you to differentiate according to POAs. As an example, refer to authorization object V_VBAK_AAT (Sales Document: Authorization for Sales Document Types) (see Figure 7.7).

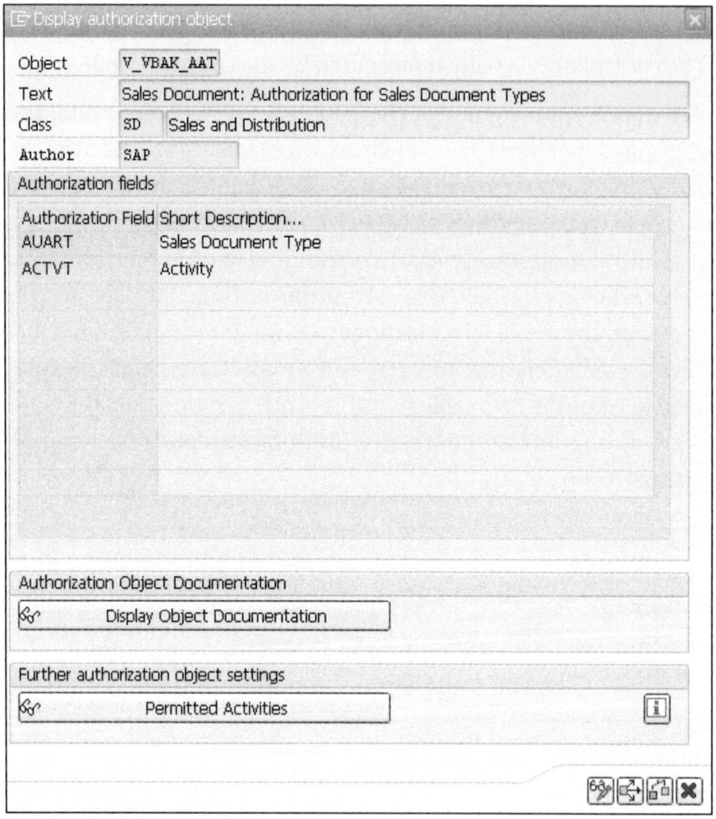

Figure 7.7 Authorization Object V_VBAK_AAT (Sales Document: Authorization for Sales Document Types)

Authorizations for handling a sales order are also assigned in SAP ERP Controlling (CO) (e.g., product cost estimate). From a data protection perspective, an application-related solution should be sought; this is achieved using the two authorization objects in Figure 7.8.

Authorization object V_VBAK_AAT allows you to differentiate between different sales document types. A detailed description of such attributes can be found in *Authorizations in SAP Software* by Lehnert and Stelzner (SAP PRESS, 2010, *www.sap-press.com/2316*).

Procedural model as a basis

With regard to POAs, it's also important that you've already identified the most important POAs in our procedure model because you'll also need these attributes for blocking and deleting. Likewise, when using the Data Controller Rule Framework, the model should have already been mapped in its essential parts.

7

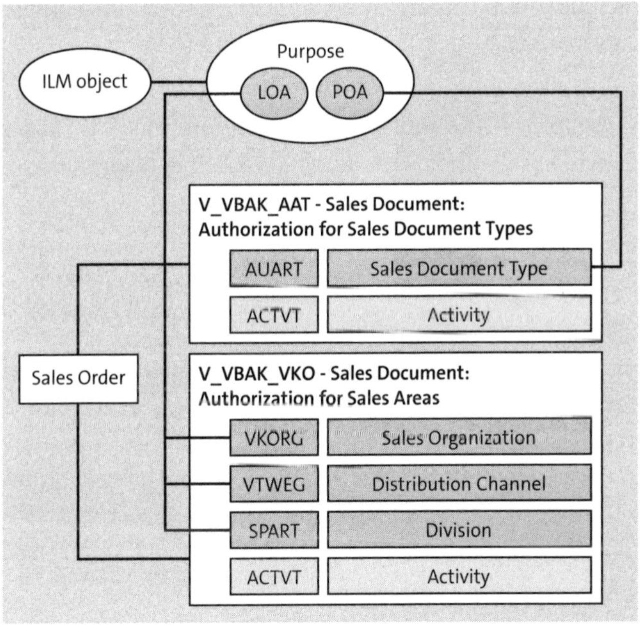

Figure 7.8 LOAs and POAs in the Authorization Objects for the Sales Order

Alternative approach

An alternative procedure in this case is much more complex, as there are far more possible fields and approaches. However, experience with the customer has shown that a differentiation has usually already been made for purely business-related and internal organizational reasons; this differentiation must be examined and, where necessary, modified.

One possible starting point is again the characteristic value of the roles, which can be analyzed using table AGR_1251 (Authorization Data for the Activity Group). This time, however, it's not just the small number of organizational levels that need to be considered but rather other numerous fields. You can further facilitate your work by describing the respective activities in the fields. For example, you may add the term "Exclude activity" to the field **ACTVT**.

7.4 Authorization Risks

As previously explained in Chapter 1, Section 1.2.4, authorizations must follow the strict principle of data minimization. All access beyond the purpose of processing is a violation of the minimization principle.

Data protection perspective

Risks in the authorization system are usually defined and evaluated. The classic approach is ultimately a principle of prohibition, which is simply based on the following principle: a user should not be able to execute certain actions or certain combinations of actions.

The principle of minimization is, however, a principle of requirement. A user should only be allowed to perform actions that correspond to the purpose of processing.

To highlight this (in a simplified way) with quantity structures, consider that of the approximately 60,000 business transactions, several thousand transactions (approximately 2,500 in the SAP Access Control rules) are listed in the classical risk definition logic and are regarded as risky. However, in terms of the minimization principle of data protection, any transaction that is suitable for exposing personal data is a risk if this isn't needed for the specific purpose. Realistically, this is 20 times the amount.

All too risky?

This, however, not only leads to considerable challenges in terms of the amount of risk definitions but also in terms of the number of hits (again simplified). After all, every one of the users in the system deals with personal data in one way or another, and this is precisely what the number of hits would cover. It's therefore almost worthless to say that almost every user deals with personal data. The question is therefore, what do we have to prove? We have to prove which users have access for which processing purposes.

Activity-related risks

From a user authorization perspective, activity-related risks can be divided into three different types of critical access into the system:

- **Segregation of duties (SoD) conflicts**
  SoD conflicts are the result of a combination of two activities. For example, the combination of supplier maintenance and order processing is critical. However, depending on rules, procedures, and Customizing settings, an SoD conflict can also be displayed within a transaction if the set of rules stipulates an SoD between entering and releasing a posting. The technical control of these various activities allows for an operation-oriented SoD; that is, a separation of the entry and release processes can be configured.
- **Critical actions**
  Critical actions affect a single activity (execution) leading to a risk. Maintaining metadata preferences, for example, is a critical action because it can result in the production system being opened for unauthorized modifications. A critical action is defined as the connection of an application, for example, of a transaction with an authorization object.
- **Critical authorizations**
  Critical authorizations are critical in themselves, without the type of access to this authorization needing to be defined already (technical definition: authorization object without connection to a specific transaction). One example is debugging in change mode.

This is what the "classic" risk perspective has to offer! What about the risks based purely on data protection law?

SoD in data protection

In data protection, the SoD is particularly important for system-related activities, such as the segregation of user administrator and authorization administrator, or the SoD in transportation management.

[«]

Transportation Management

By transportation management, we mean the management of transport requests between development and production systems.

SoD requirements explicitly linked to business management should be borne in mind, for example, when customers or suppliers are unblocked. The allocation of a special bonus and the initiation of payment are still a risk of SoD in terms of business management; this risk doesn't have to be subject to any data protection considerations. The risks involved in the

SoD, therefore, play a rather marginal role in data protection in terms of volume.

Critical actions in data protection

Critical actions also exist in data protection. Naturally, technical actions are more serious. The previously mentioned general maintenance of metadata preferences is also an explicit data protection risk. Specifically, with regard to data protection, it should also be noted that unlimited access to tables generally constitutes a massive violation of the minimization principle and the principle of purpose separation.

Critical authorizations in data protection

The definition of critical authorizations in data protection is much more important than in classic risk assessment. For example, access to internal vendors (e.g., travel expenses) is a risk for all users, regardless of the type of access, who aren't explicitly authorized for the purposes relating to internal accounts payable.

Purpose risk

The requirement to only provide authorizations if the access is covered from the purpose of the processing leads to a new category. The latter must be in a position to provide information as to whether the separation of purposes in the user's authorizations has been carried out in such a way that the user only has authorizations resulting from the purposes for which he has to be authorized. The term *purpose risk* has been introduced to describe this risk.

[»]

Purpose Risk

A purpose risk is a general, purpose-oriented risk definition using the authorization objects assigned to individual artifacts within a purpose, as well as the LOAs and POAs of a purpose. The purpose risk is therefore made up of a set of all critical authorizations as defined by data protection law in relation to all artifacts of a processing purpose.

Let's begin by taking a look at the graphic in Figure 7.9. In this context, the sales order is protected by two essential authorization objects: **V_VBAK_AAT** (**Sales Document: Authorization for Sales Document Types**) and **V_VBAK_VKO** (**Sales Document: Authorization for Sales Areas**). The division, distribution channel, or sales organization may be used as LOAs. The POA is the order type. The activity is negligible for this assessment.

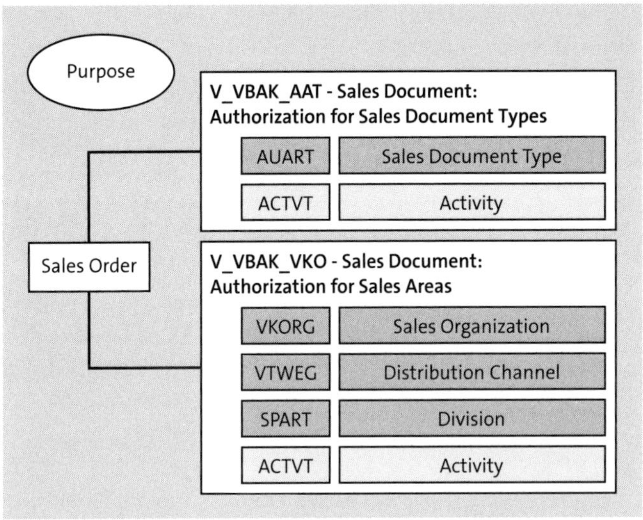

Figure 7.9 Relationships among Purpose, Artifact, and Authorization Object in the Risk Definition

Given that sales organization n:1 is linked to the company code, a potential risk definition is as shown in Table 7.1.

Field Name	Field Description	Value
V_VBAK_AAT (Sales Document: Authorization for Sales Document Types)		
AUART	Sales document type	Each within the scope of the purpose
ACTVT	Activity	
V_VBAK_VKO (Sales Document: Authorization for Sales Organization)		
VKORG	Sales organization	Controller
ACTVT	Activity	

Table 7.1 Risk Definition (Combination of "Critical" Authorizations)

This artifact-related observation must now be repeated for each artifact in the purpose until all risks have been defined.

The cumulative total of all risk definitions (which are in fact definitions of critical authorizations) represents the entire purpose risk. Thus, two levels can be represented: one general level that provides information about the purpose, and a concrete level that also identifies the artifacts in relation to the purpose (see Table 7.2).

User	Purpose (General Level)	Artifact (Specific Level)
Miller	Sale of cough syrup	Customer master, sales order, billing document
Miller	Sale of peppermint tea	Customer master

Table 7.2 Two Levels of Purpose Risk

Procedural model as a basis

Again, if you've been following our proposed procedure model, where significant values have already been determined, they must also be applied accordingly. To do this, you'll have to prepare the artifacts for their SAP ILM objects, for which you've already created rules. If you've already set up the Data Controller Rule Framework, you'll find yourself in the comfortable position of having POAs, LOAs, and SAP ILM objects already assigned to the purpose.

7.5 Summary

The topic of authorizations is technical and not necessarily trivial. It's also important for a more system-remote data protector to know that authorizations are generally checked at several levels, that the line organization and the process organization must be observed, and that there is a close relationship between the rules for deletion and the authorizations. It's unlikely that a data protector of this kind will make technical risk definitions independently. They might also be able to consult those responsible in IT as to which risks are defined and how POAs and LOAs are to be taken into account.

In this chapter, we've shown the authorization-affine IT specialists that they can ultimately—albeit in the guise of data protection—expect a familiar field of activity with a generally substantial need for action.

Chapter 8
Information Retrieval Framework

Requirements for transparency are a major part of the new data protection law. The information retrieval framework not only serves to satisfy the right of access to information but also supports the requirements for advance information and the creation of a record of all processing activities.

In this chapter, we'll explain the information retrieval framework (a *new* product feature), which supports both the obligation to provide the data subject with access to information and also the use of the framework for the right of data portability.

In Chapter 4, Section 4.1, we explained that personal data can be deleted via SAP Information Lifecycle Management (SAP ILM) and that SAP ILM objects are a prerequisite for this. Considering that information must also be provided for the personal data deleted via SAP ILM, the Information Retrieval Framework also has access to the SAP ILM objects, which means that a congruence between deletion and the provision of information can be achieved.

The basic ideas behind the preceding statements are as follows:

- We know of all relevant person-related SAP ILM objects.
- An information retrieval framework data model can be generated automatically from these database tables, whereby the information retrieval framework uses the functionality of the Generic Smart Search (GSS).
- The information retrieval framework data model is revised manually.
- Based on the information retrieval framework data model, GSS automatically extracts all data for each purpose.
- The GSS results can be sent to the requestor after a final check by the data protection officer.

Because the product functionality is very new, some of the figures used in this chapter were only available with entries made in the German language when this book went to print. We'll provide translations where necessary.

8.1 Transparency: Access to Data and Information

In Chapter 1, Section 1.1.6, we already addressed the subject of transparency of data processing in detail. You learned there that the requirements for transparency are in fact included in the data subjects' rights and are also very comparable in terms of structure and content.

Access to data and advance information

With regard to the data subjects' rights, we've made a distinction between their right of access to data in accordance with Art. 15 GDPR and their right to advance information in accordance with Arts. 13 and 14 GDPR. There are several overlaps, however, as listed in Table 8.1.

Specifications Pursuant to Art. 15	In Art. 13 (Paragraph) (Letter)	In Art. 14 (Paragraph) (Letter)
a) Purposes of processing	(1)(c)	(1)(c)
b) Categories of personal data	–	(1)(d)
c) Recipients/categories of recipients/ Recipients in third countries/ international organizations	(1)(e) (1)(f)	(1)(e) (1)(f)
d) Retention periods	(2)(a)	(2)(a)
e) Rectification, deletion, the right to object, blocking	(2)(b)	(2)(c)
f) The right of appeal with a supervisory authority	(2)(d)	(2)(e)
g) Source of the data		(2)(f)
h) automated decision-making, including profiling	(2)(f)	(2)(g)

Table 8.1 Access to Data and Advance Information

One very important but logically justified difference between the advance information and the right of access to data is that for access to data, the data itself must also be accessed.

This comparability naturally leads to the assumption that the person who can provide information pursuant to Art. 15 GDPR should be in a position to provide the necessary advance information pursuant to Arts. 13 and 14 GDPR. In Chapter 1, Section 1.1.6, we also outlined the basic comparability of some of this information with the information for the records of processing activities pursuant to Art. 30 GDPR.

Data portability and access to data

Furthermore, in Chapter 1, Section 1.1.9, we also explained that a report that can output all personal data is also sufficient to formally fulfill the right to data portability under Art. 20 GDPR, provided that it converts the data into a machine-readable format. We've also made it clear that we hope for a standardization or standards to ensure the effective usability of this data.

A report that can provide suitable information (obviously excluding purely organizational data) is also able to support advance information and the record of processing activities.

Information and procedural model

If you follow our procedural model, you'll have already identified and linked the relevant artifacts by implementing blocking and deletion with SAP ILM. You'll also have taken a look at your data model with regard to its intended purpose and adapted it where necessary. There is therefore no further reason why you shouldn't be able to provide information for a specific purpose.

8.2 Setup of the Information Retrieval Framework

To use the information retrieval framework, it's necessary to perform several tasks, as explained in the following sections.

8.2.1 Activating the Business Function

Start Transaction SPRO (Customizing – Edit Project), and select **Activate Business Functions**. On the next page, select the business function **CA_DTINF_FW** (Information Framework Business Function) and activate it, as shown in Figure 8.1.

[!]

Client-Independent Setting

The activation of the business functions is a client-independent setting that is valid for the entire SAP system.

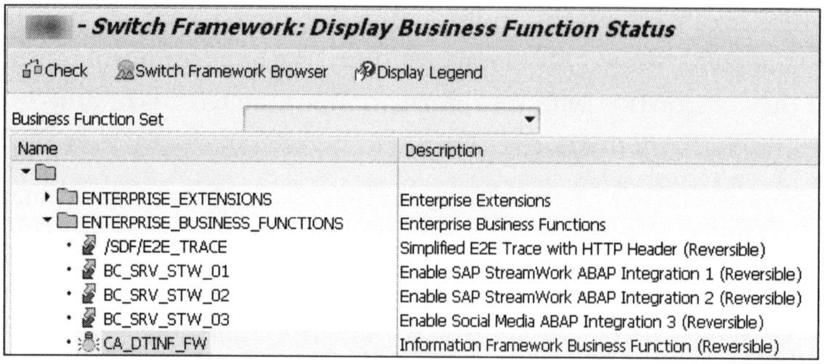

Figure 8.1 Activating a Business Function

8.2.2 Determining the System Status

The next step is to define the system status; this specifies the functionality of the information retrieval framework in each client (unlike the business function). In Customizing, select **Maintain system status** (see Figure 8.2).

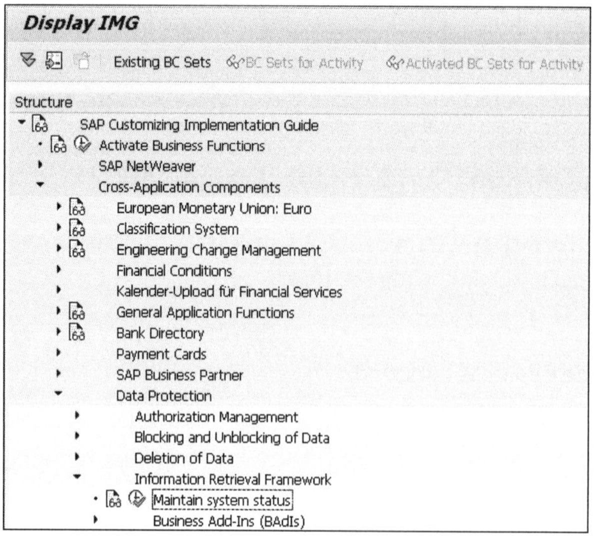

Figure 8.2 System Status in the Menu

A new page opens, as shown in Figure 8.3.

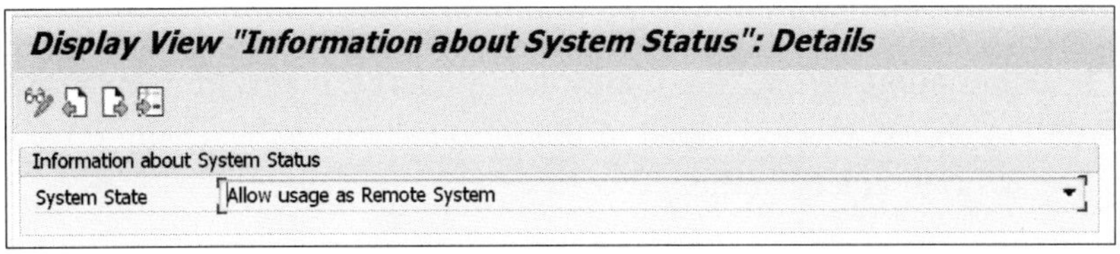

Figure 8.3 Defining System Status

System state

Three system states are available:

- **Disallow usage**
  This is a standard setting. Even if the business function is active, the information retrieval framework can't be used in the client.
- **Allow usage as Remote System**
  The information retrieval framework can be used, but its functionality is restricted to this client and the SAP system.
- **Use System as Central Instance**
  Although the functionality of the information retrieval framework is limited, you can search for personal data in all systems that are connected by remote function call (RFC). This is explained in greater detail in Section 8.6.

This book focuses on the remote system.

You'll also need to activate the OData services and set up the SAP Gateway. Refer to the SAP documentation for information retrieval framework for more information.

8.2.3 Assignment of Authorizations

You can find all the possible information retrieval framework authorization objects in Transaction SU21 (Maintain Authorization Objects) as `S_INF*`, for example, `S_INF_MAIN`, to change the data model. Different activities can be assigned to almost every authorization object, depending on requirements. To find out which authorizations are required for the examples described here, refer to the documentation for each authorization object.

8.3 SAP ILM Objects in the Information Retrieval Framework

The information retrieval framework data model generated from (relevant) SAP ILM objects was explained in the introduction to this chapter. We'll now take a closer look at this.

BC_SFLIGHT We'll now use an example that may trigger a déjà vu for some readers: We'll take a look at the flight data model, which is also used in SAP training courses on ABAP development. For this data model, you'll find an SAP ILM object BC_SFLIGHT. In turn, SAP ILM objects are assigned to archiving objects or SAP ILM destruction objects.

Archiving object Starting at the lowest level—the archiving object—we'll check which tables are assigned to this object. Start Transaction AOBJ (Archiving Object Definition), find and select the entry **BC_SFLIGHT**, and then click on **Structure Definition**. The overview is shown in Figure 8.4.

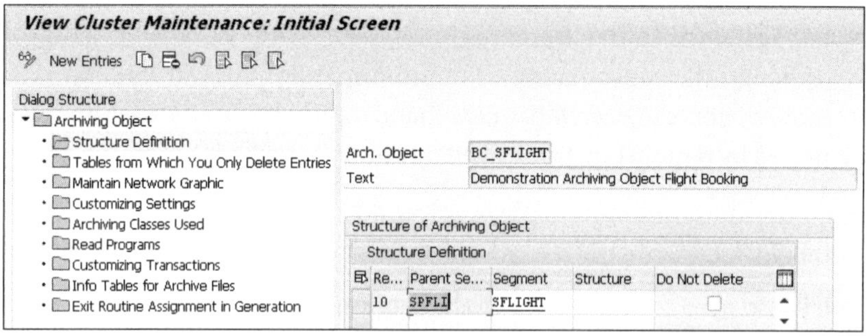

Figure 8.4 Archiving Object BC_SFLIGHT

Only two tables are relevant: table SPFLI as the output table (Parent Segment) and table SFLIGHT as the dependent table (Segment). The data from table SFLIGHT is dependent on table SPFLI; in other words, the data from table SFLIGHT is determined based on the data from table SPFLI. We therefore also have an understanding of the hierarchy—output tables and the tables dependent on these tables—which is important information for the information retrieval framework data model.

Archiving an object BAdI

Archiving objects can be changed using *Business Add-Ins (BAdIs)*. We can find out what this means by starting Transaction DB15 (Data Archiving: DB Tables) and entering "BC_SFLIGHT" in the **Tables in Object** field. Figure 8.5 shows how the result may look.

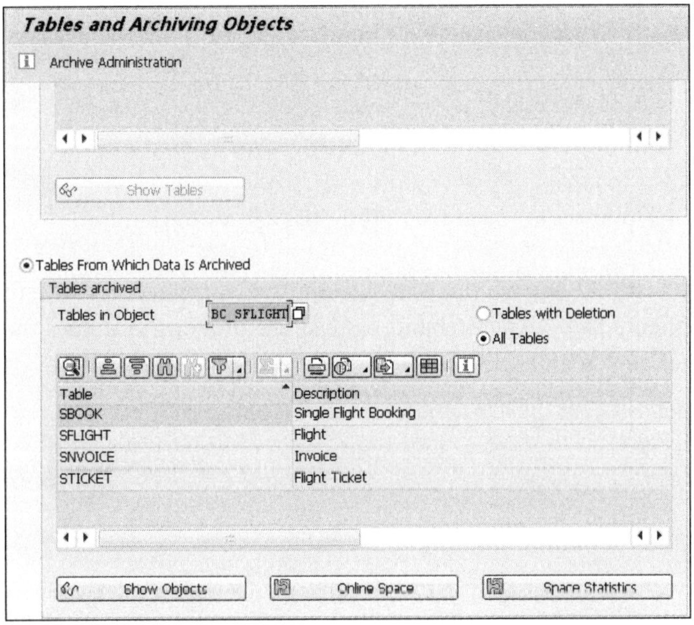

Figure 8.5 Tables and Archiving Objects, Including a BAdI

The result is already different from that in Transaction AOBJ (Archiving Object Definition). As you can see, three more tables have been added (tables SBOOK, SNVOICE, and STICKET), table SPFLI has disappeared, and we no longer see the hierarchy.

SAP ILM objects and information retrieval framework

We'll now check what the information retrieval framework can determine. Start Transaction DTINF_ADJUST_MODEL (Adjust Inf. Retr. FW Model). A workbench request must be selected, which you may still have to generate. Every change to the information retrieval framework data model is logged in this request, and all changes are client-specific. After entering a valid workbench request, a user interface (UI) will appear, as shown in Figure 8.6.

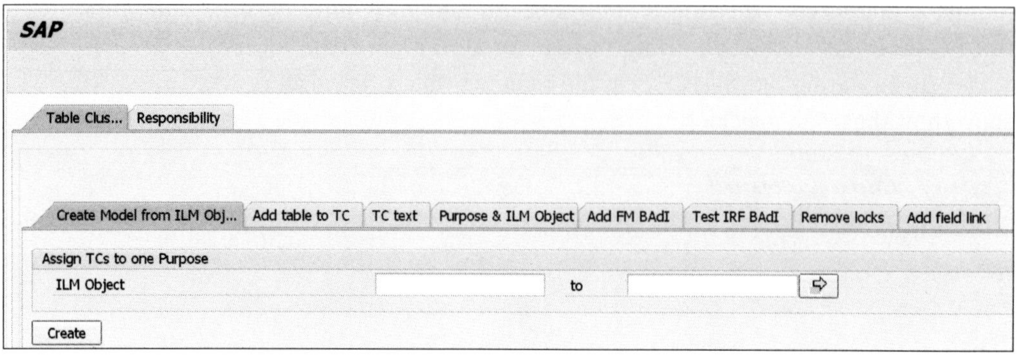

Figure 8.6 User Interface in Transaction DTINF_ADJUST_MODEL

Test IRF BAdI tab

Click on the **Test IRF BAdI** tab. Don't let this confuse you: you don't have to have implemented a BAdI beforehand. Instead, the program evaluates the SAP ILM object and with it the BAdI.

Enter "BC_SFLIGHT" in the **ILM Object** text field (see Figure 8.7).

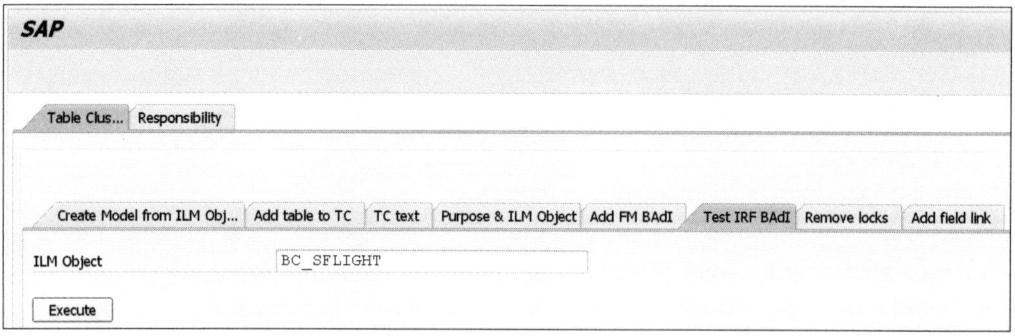

Figure 8.7 Test IRF BAdI Tab

Click on **Execute**. On the next page, click **Execute** again, and you'll be presented with the results, as shown in Figure 8.8.

Check BADI_DTINF_ILM_OBJ_TABLES implementation

Check BADI_DTINF_ILM_OBJ_TABLES implementation

Father	/	Son
	/	SNVOICE
	/	SPFLI
SPFLI	/	SFLIGHT
SFLIGHT	/	SAPLANE
SFLIGHT	/	SCARR
	/	STICKET
STICKET	/	SBOOK
STICKET	/	SCARR
STICKET	/	SCUSTOM
STICKET	/	SFLIGHT

Figure 8.8 Tables Used by the Information Retrieval Framework for the SAP ILM Object BC_SFLIGHT

Hierarchy of tables

These results provide information about the tables and their hierarchy from which the information retrieval framework data model would be generated (this is described in Section 8.4). You can see the output tables on the left side and the dependent tables on the right side. The tables are as follows:

- Table SPFLI represents a starting point because it's displayed as dependent table without an output table (line 3).
- Table SFLIGHT is dependent on table SPFLI (line 4).
- Table SFLIGHT is also the output table for table SAPLANE and table SCARR (lines 5 and 6).

Check tables

Why does the result show table SCARR, table SBOOK, and other tables, although these weren't listed in either of the previous two transactions? The information retrieval framework also determines check tables for the fields of each table and uses this data to automatically extend the model.

BADI_DTINF_ILM_OBJ_TABLES

You can implement the BAdI BADI_DTINF_ILM_OBJ_TABLES for an SAP ILM object to enhance the data model at the time of its creation, for example, to include additional tables. This particular BAdI is also used by SAP to remove obsolete tables from the data model without adjusting the archiving objects. It's important, however, that there is still consistency between the data on which information is provided and the data that is deleted.

8.4 Creating an Information Retrieval Framework Data Model

Create model from SAP ILM object

Now that we've clarified which database tables are used by the information retrieval framework for an SAP ILM object, let's generate an information retrieval framework data model. In Transaction DTINF_ADJUST_MODEL (Adjust Inf. Retr. FW Model), which you've already used, enter the SAP ILM object "BC_SFLIGHT" on the **Create Model from ILM Object** tab. (Note: You can also enter more than one SAP ILM object at a time.) Then, click **Create**, and you'll see the message informing you that the model has been created. Now let's take a closer look at the model in the following sections.

8.4.1 Display Information Retrieval Framework Data Model

Viewing the model in your browser

To access the modeling tool that opens a browser window, start Transaction DTINF_MODELING (Launch Galilei UI in Browser). We recommend Google Chrome as this browser offers the best performance (as of September 2017). After successfully logging in, you'll see the browser screen shown in Figure 8.9. Select **BC_SFLIGHT** in the **ILM Object** field.

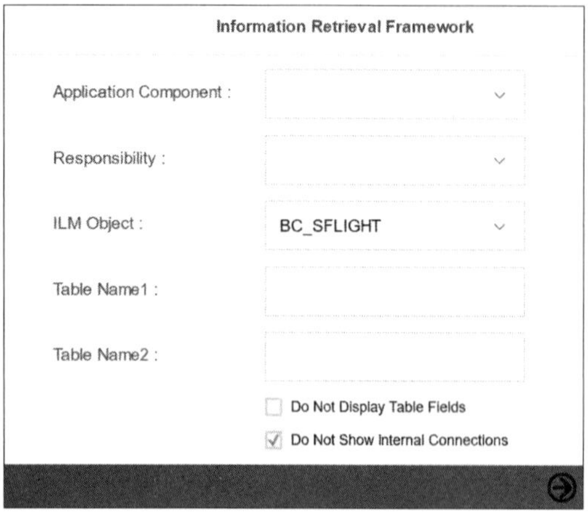

Figure 8.9 Modeling Tool: First Page

Modeling tool

Now click on the **Next** button at the bottom right. The window shown in Figure 8.10 will appear.

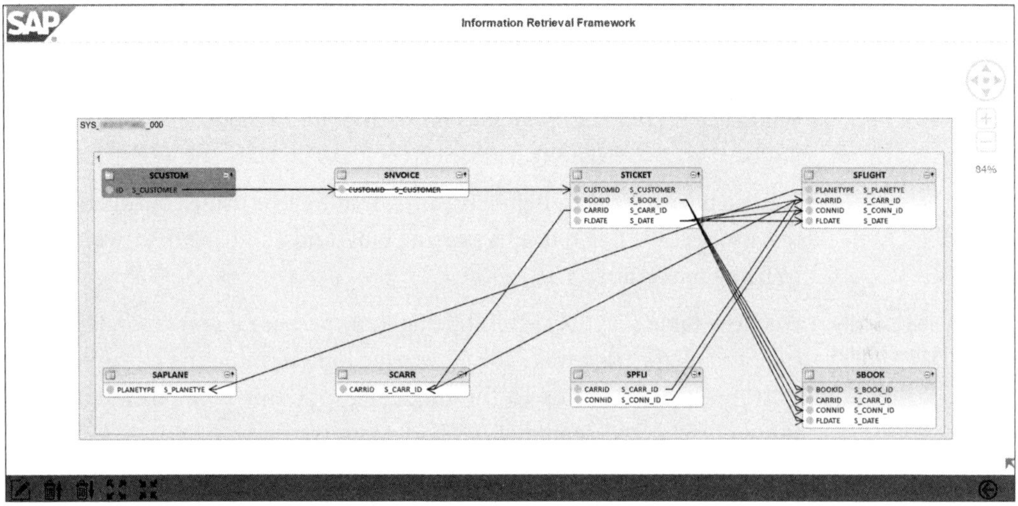

Figure 8.10 View of an SAP ILM Object in the Modeling Tool

This display shows the following:

- We're working on the system **SYS_<ID_Mandant>** (blue box).
- All previously identified tables are located in table cluster **1** (in beige).
- All of the tables have connections that are marked with arrows.
- For each table, you'll see all of the fields relevant for a connection. (The field **ID** from table SCUSTOM is linked to the **CUSTOMID** field in table STICKET.)
- The direction of the arrows corresponds to the hierarchy shown in Section 8.3.
- Table SCUSTOM is highlighted because it's the only table that only links to other tables. It can be regarded as the starting table for this particular table cluster.

Table cluster

Table clusters should contain tables that are logically related. The starting tables of a table cluster are the entry points when searching for data; they also represent the output tables for all other tables within the table cluster.

8.4.2 Selecting a Data Record for the Provision of Information

Generate example data

Before we move on to the iterative process of checking and modifying the information retrieval framework data model, we need to know which data record we want to search for—in our case, this is a flight customer. To do this, we'll need data from the relevant database tables. For our example, we can execute Transaction SA38 (ABAP: Program Execution) and the reports SAPBC_DATA_GENERATOR and SFLIGHT_DATA_GEN one after the other.

We also have to select a flight customer that we'll be using continuously for this process. We'll also need a starting table and a starting field, which we'll be using in Section 8.4.3.

Check and identify starting table and starting field

We'll use table SCUSTOM as the starting table because it corresponds specifically to a flight customer. You now have to determine the corresponding starting field. According to the modeling tool, this is the **ID** field, which should be checked again beforehand. Start Transaction SE11 (ABAP Dictionary Maintenance), and then enter "SCUSTOM" in the **Database table** field (see Figure 8.11).

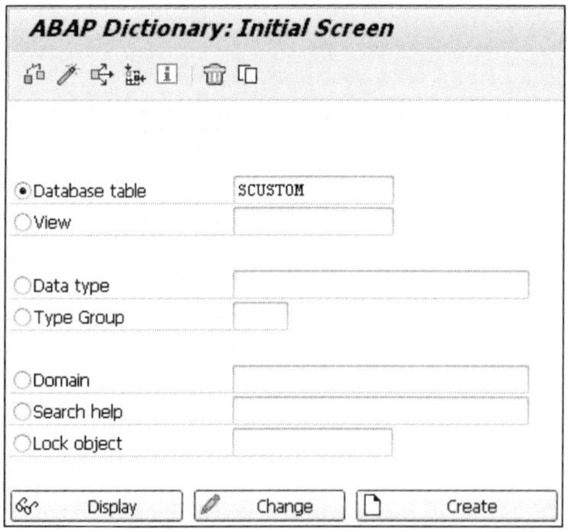

Figure 8.11 Opening the Starting Table

Click on the **Display** button to open the window shown in Figure 8.12.

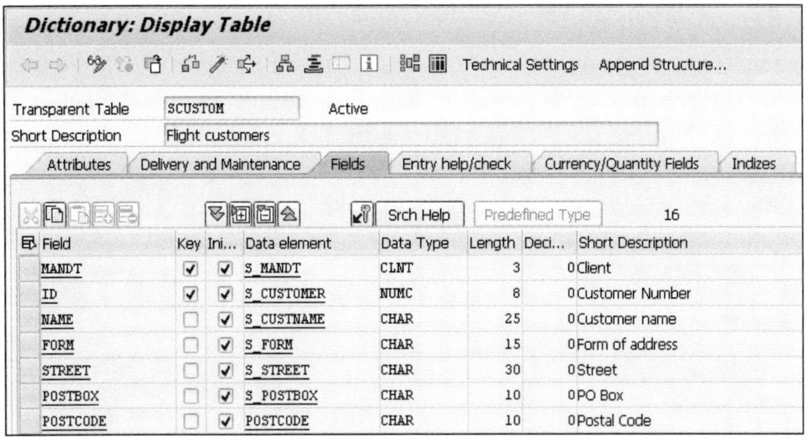

Figure 8.12 Identifying the Starting Field

Determining a data record for the search

The only highly relevant field is **ID**; **Customer Number** in the **Short Description** column also seems promising. This is therefore the starting field. The question now arises as to which data record—that is, which customer number—should be searched for. To do this, click **Contents** (the symbol to the left of **Technical Settings**) in the menu bar. Transaction SE16 (Data Browser) opens. On the following page, click **Execute**. In our example, a screen will open that may differ from your screen (see Figure 8.13).

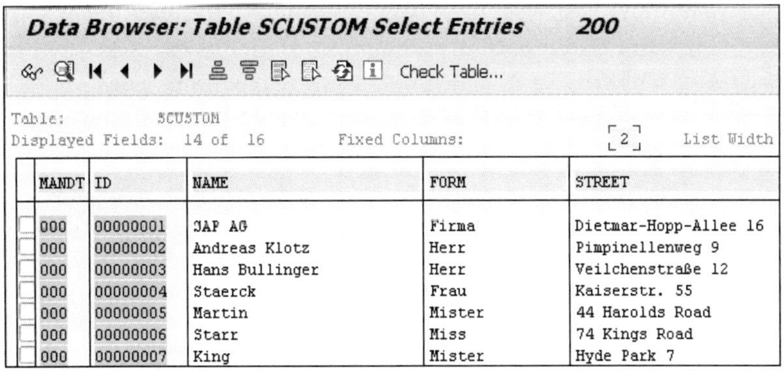

Figure 8.13 Database Contents of the Starting Table

We're using customer number 7 for our example (you can ignore the preceding zeros).

8.4.3 Assigning an SAP ILM Object to a Purpose

SAP ILM object and purpose

To search for the data, we have to specify and define a purpose. To do this, start Transaction DTINF_ADJUST_MODEL (Adjust Inf. Retr. FW Model), and select the **Purpose & ILM Object** tab (Figure 8.14).

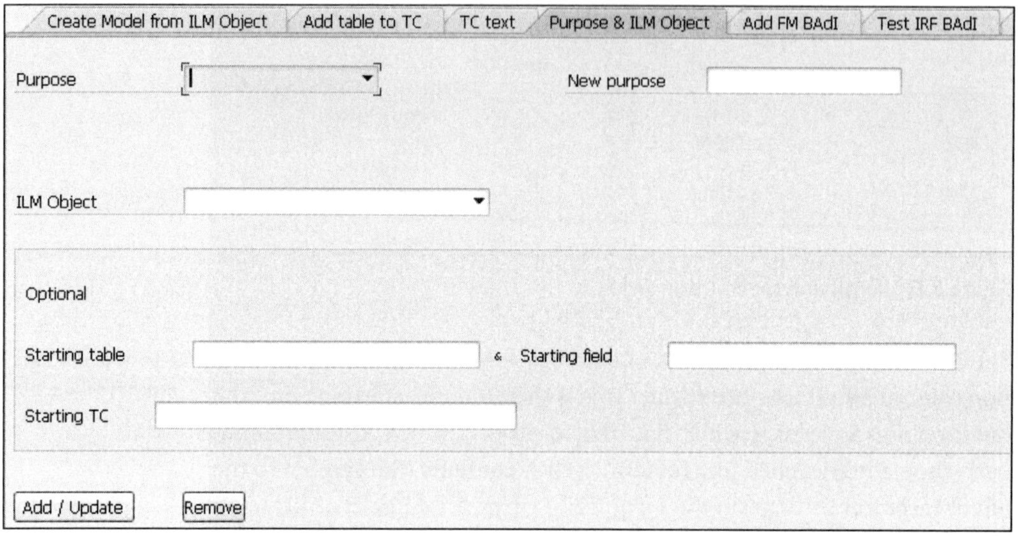

Figure 8.14 Purpose & ILM Object Tab

Because a purpose hasn't yet been defined, you have to create a new purpose. In the **New purpose** field, enter "TEST_FLIGHT". You also have to select the SAP ILM object to which you want to assign this purpose (**BC_SFLIGHT**) from the **ILM Object** dropdown list.

[»]

> **List of SAP ILM Objects Displayed**
>
> This list only contains SAP ILM objects for which a data model was previously created.

While continuing to maintain and update the starting table and the starting field, you'll see the results shown in Figure 8.15.

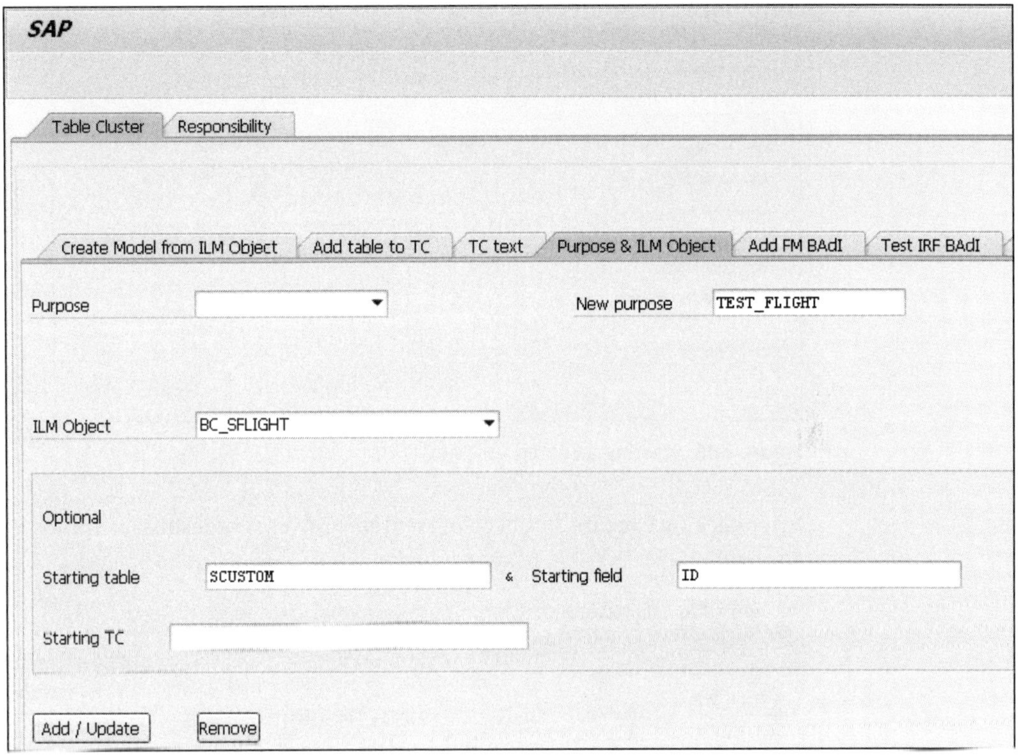

Figure 8.15 Assigning an SAP ILM Object to a Purpose

Click **Add/Update** to assign the SAP ILM object to the purpose.

Assigning several SAP ILM objects

By selecting an SAP ILM object and an existing purpose, you can assign this SAP ILM object to the selected existing purpose, and thereby update the assignment.

Use the **Remove** button to remove a purpose.

8.4.4 Search for a Flight Customer

After all of the basic settings have been defined, you can start the iterative process. To do so, start Transaction DTINF_TEST_MODEL (Information Ret. FW – Test Model), and enter the values and data shown in Figure 8.16.

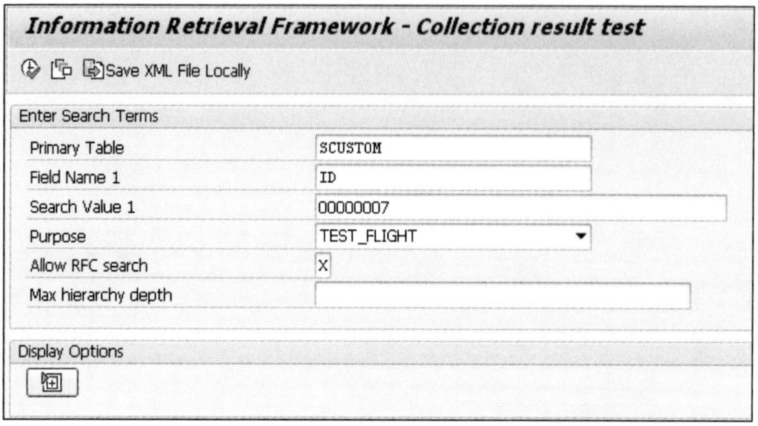

Figure 8.16 Starting a Search for Data

After clicking **Execute**, you'll be presented with a list of results, as shown in Figure 8.17.

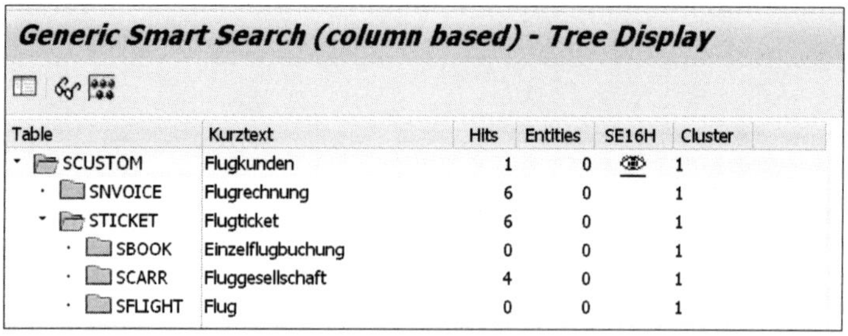

Figure 8.17 Results of the Initial Data Search

You'll see the anticipated table hierarchy and also that several data records for that customer have been found (e.g., **1** hit for **SCUSTOM** and **6** hits for **SNVOINCE** based on the entries in the output table `SCUSTOM`).

By clicking on the **Hits** of each line, the view changes, and you can see which data has been obtained. Click on the **4** for the table SCARR where the airline information is stored (**Fluggesellschaft**). The results are shown in Figure 8.18.

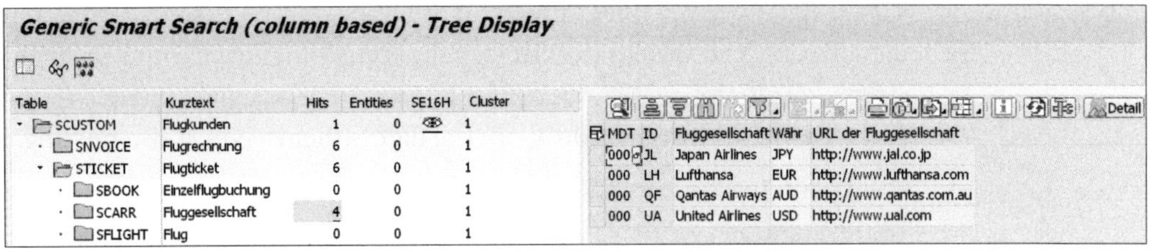

Figure 8.18 Data Found in a Table

Data used in a data selection

If we click on the abacus icon, we'll see how the data was selected from this table (see Figure 8.19).

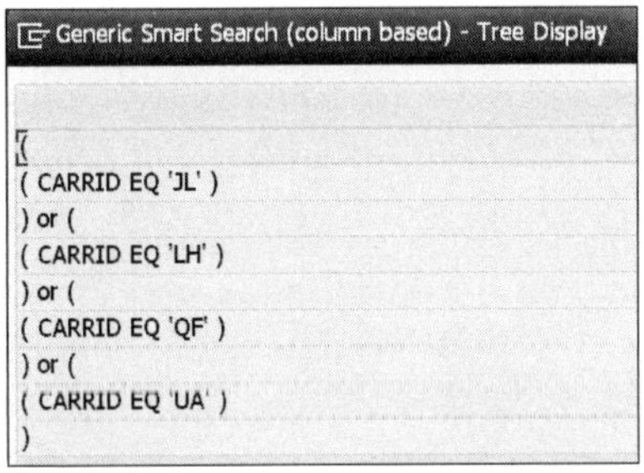

Figure 8.19 Selection Condition between Tables

Data obtained from a table

Four different entries were searched for. The entries are derived from the data in the output table STICKET where information on the flight ticket is stored (**Flugticket**), as shown in Figure 8.20. The above entries can be found there as well.

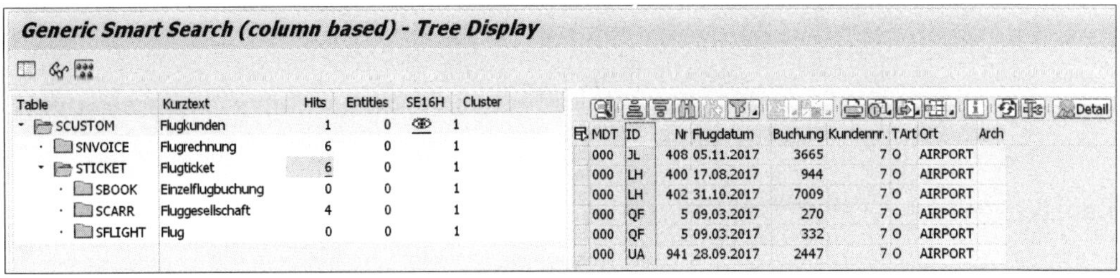

Figure 8.20 Table of the Selection Condition

Inconsistencies in the model This result, however, doesn't seem to be completely consistent. You would actually expect bookings to exist for a flight customer from which the flight tickets result; you would not expect a ticket to be assigned directly to the flight customer. Information about the flights themselves is also missing.

To explain the reasons for this, we'll take another look at the information retrieval framework data model in the modeling tool, which was shown earlier in Figure 8.10. For the sake of simplicity, it's shown again in Figure 8.21.

You can see that the flight customer (**SCUSTOM**) is linked to the ticket (**STICKET**) but not to the booking (**SBOOK**). In turn, the booking is linked to the ticket.

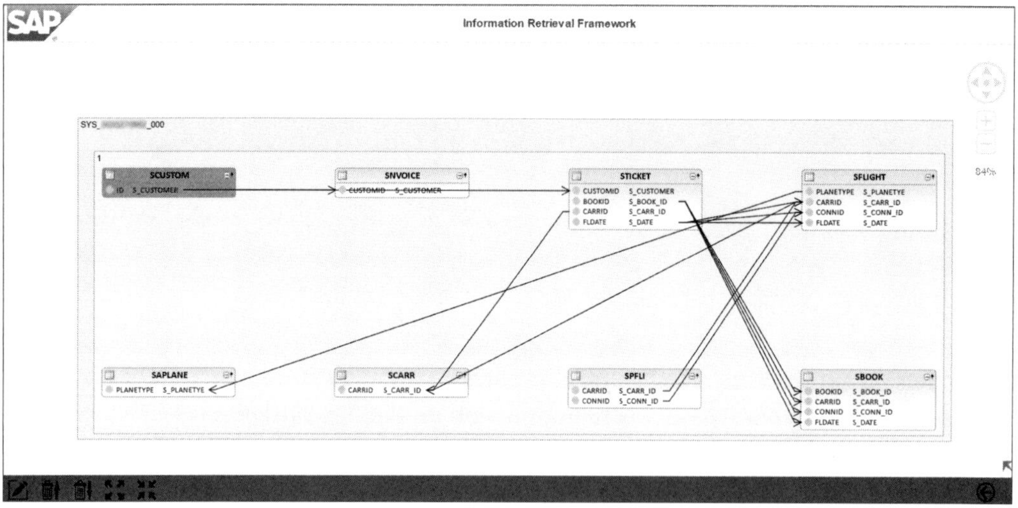

Figure 8.21 View of the SAP ILM Object in the Modeling Tool

8.4.5 Making Corrections to the Information Retrieval Framework Data Model

We'll now correct the previously mentioned facts in the modeling tool. You have to change the view because it isn't possible to edit an SAP ILM object as displayed here. Click on the **Back** button at the bottom right.

Using an application component On the previously described page (refer back to Figure 8.9), select the **Application Component BC-DWB-TND** (these entries are generated automatically when creating an information retrieval framework data model), and click—as done previously—on **Next**. The next screen is similar to the one shown previously (see Figure 8.22).

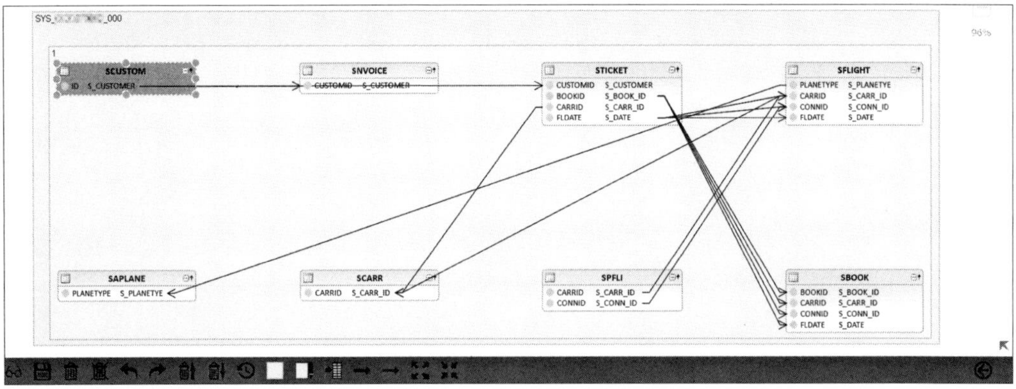

Figure 8.22 Modeling Tool: Initial Situation

The difference between selecting an **Application Component** or a **Responsibility** for an SAP ILM object is that all table clusters assigned to this SAP ILM object will be displayed. This is a very complex representation that can quickly lead to the loss of overview.

The **Application Component** or **Responsibility** (a combination of several application components that can be created by the user) represents only a small section of all the assigned table clusters and their connection to other table clusters. At this level, it's possible for different people to work simultaneously, for example, on the data model of one (or more) SAP ILM objects, without blocking each other.

Editing

You can now click on the **Edit** button and enter a new workbench request. All changes that are now made will be included in an order.

Expand table

Table SCUSTOM currently can't be connected to table SBOOK because there is no suitable field in table SBOOK. You'll have to expand this table. To do so, after selecting table SBOOK, click the **Expand** button, which results in a new display (see Figure 8.23). (Because the only change is to the table cluster, the following figures will focus on this and hide the rest.) All fields in table SBOOK are now available for selection; you'll now also find the **CUSTOMID** field.

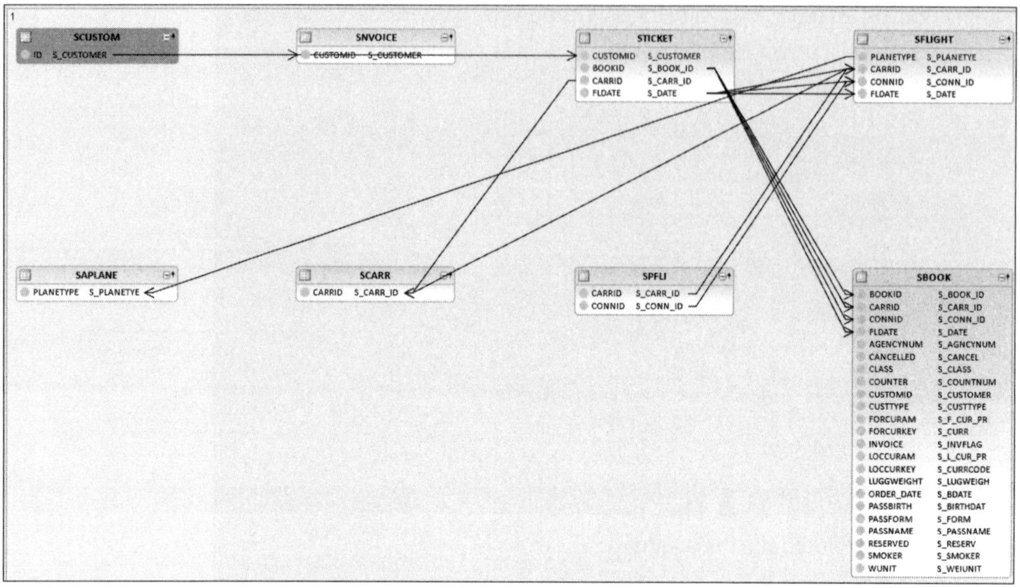

Figure 8.23 Expanding a Table in the Modeling Tool

Making changes to the model

You can now modify the information retrieval framework data model by following these steps:

1. To remove the link between **SCUSTOM** and **STICKET**, click the **Delete** button or press the `Delete` key.
2. To connect the **ID** field of table **SCUSTOM** to the **CUSTOMID** field of table **SBOOK**, click the **Join** button.
3. Select the table **SBOOK**, and click on the **Collapse** button.

This results in a new information retrieval framework data model, as shown in Figure 8.24. It's also noticeable that the order of the tables has changed, which happens automatically.

To save the current version, simply click on the **Save Model** button.

To turn the focus onto tables **SBOOK** and **STICKET**, begin by expanding the table **STICKET**. The result is shown in Figure 8.25.

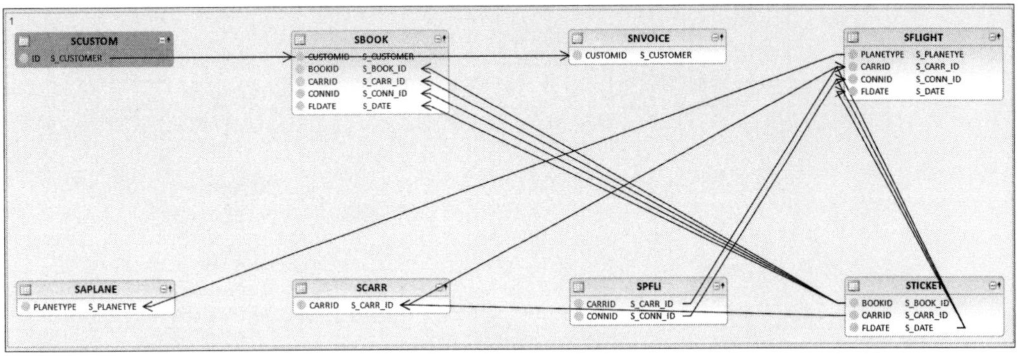

Figure 8.24 Modifying the Connections in the Modeling Tool

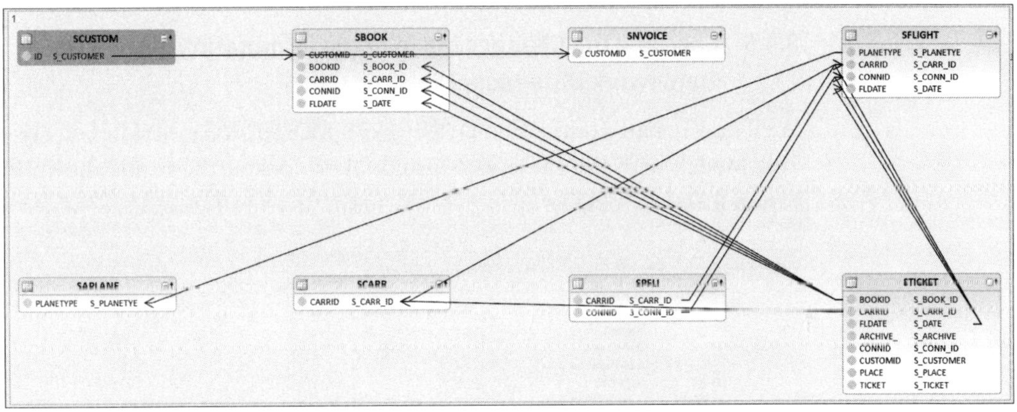

Figure 8.25 Expanding Table STICKET in the Modeling Tool

Complete the following steps:

1. Remove all four links from table **STICKET** with **SBOOK**.
2. The fields **CUSTOMID**, **BOOKID**, **CARRID**, **CONNID**, and **FLDATE** from table **SBOOK** are linked to the fields of the same name from table **STICKET**.

After saving, the result will appear as shown in Figure 8.26.

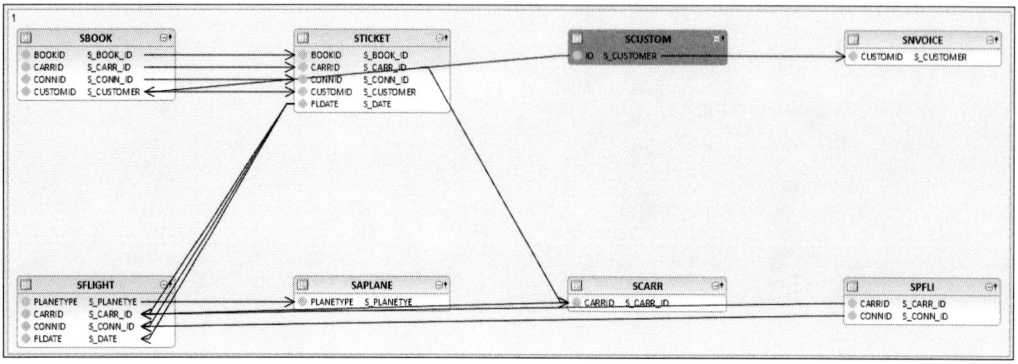

Figure 8.26 Table STICKET and Table SBOOK Connections in the Modeling Tool

8.4.6 Checking the Changes Made to the Information Retrieval Framework Data Model

We'll now restart Transaction DTINF_TEST_MODEL (Information Ret. FW – Test Model) with the same values and take a look at the result shown in Figure 8.27.

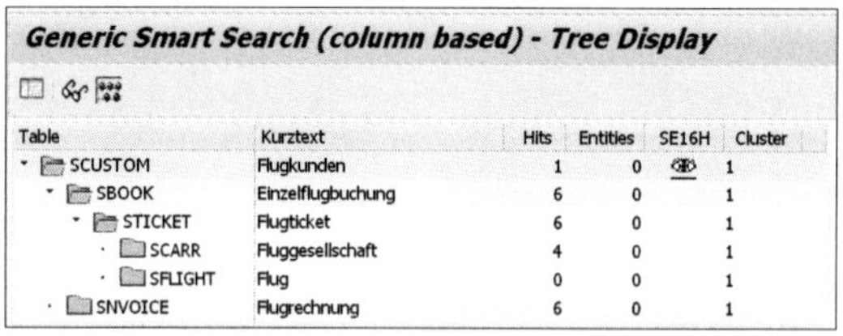
Generic Smart Search (column based) - Tree Display

Table	Kurztext	Hits	Entities	SE16H	Cluster
SCUSTOM	Flugkunden	1	0		1
SBOOK	Einzelflugbuchung	6	0		1
STICKET	Flugticket	6	0		1
SCARR	Fluggesellschaft	4	0		1
SFLIGHT	Flug	0	0		1
SNVOICE	Flugrechnung	6	0		1

Figure 8.27 Data Search after the First Modification

Further errors in the model

This corresponds to what we previously felt to be an inconsistency.

Table SFLIGHT is still incorrect because it doesn't contain any hits, and table SPFLI is missing entirely. You should therefore change the information retrieval framework data model as follows:

1. Remove the three connections from **STICKET** to **SFLIGHT**.
2. Create links from **STICKET** to **SFLIGHT** for the fields of the same name **CARRID**, **CONNID**, and **FLDATE**.
3. Delete the link between **STICKET** and **SCARR**. **SCARR** has already been identified by **SFLIGHT** and is therefore redundant. We believe that the airline is also better suited to a flight rather than a flight ticket.

4. Reverse the connections from **SPFLI** to **SFLIGHT** (delete the connections and reconnect).

The results are shown in Figure 8.28.

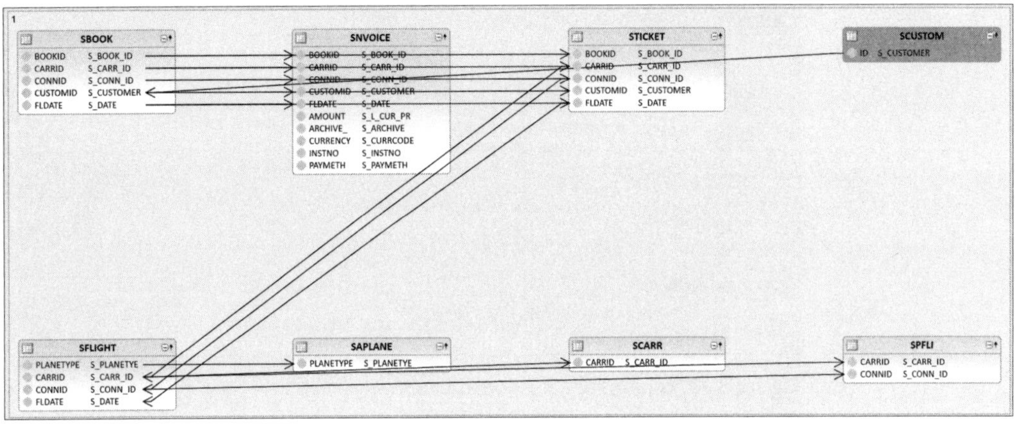

Figure 8.28 Final Information Retrieval Framework Data Model in the Modeling Tool

Renaming table clusters

We're now going to make two more changes. In the modeling tool, click the number **1** that contains the current description of the table cluster but doesn't provide information about what this means. Now you have to enter a new name. To do this, click on the number **1** again, enter "FLIGHT CUSTOMER" (**FLUGKUNDE**) in the text field that appears (see Figure 8.29), and press the Enter key. Subsequently, you need to save the model.

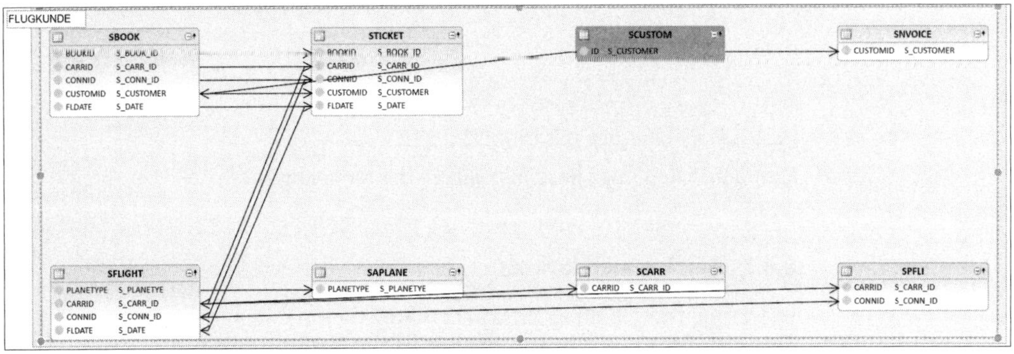

Figure 8.29 Renaming a Table Cluster in the Modeling Tool

You should now exit the modeling tool and restart Transaction DTINF_ADJUST_MODEL (Adjust Inf. Retr. FW Model).

Renaming the Responsibility

Click on the **Responsibility** tab, and enter the data as shown in Figure 8.30.

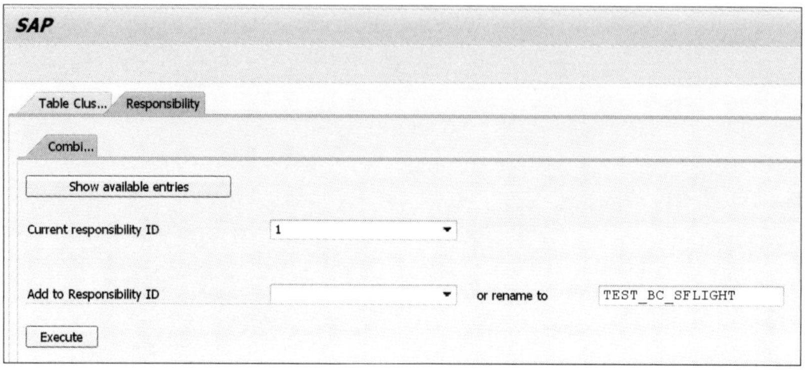

Figure 8.30 Renaming a Responsibility

After clicking the **Execute** button, **Responsibility 1** will be renamed **TEST_BC_SFLIGHT**. If you now reopen the modeling tool, you'll see this entry in the field **Responsibility**, making it much easier to find (see Figure 8.31).

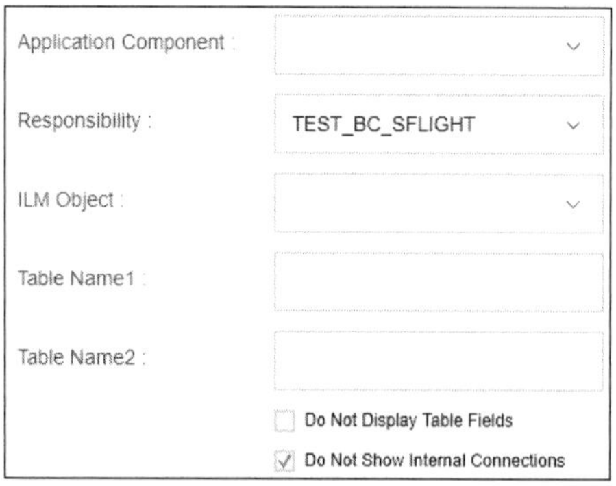

Figure 8.31 Renamed Responsibility in the Modeling Tool

8.4.7 Final Search Results

Executing the search again will produce the final result, as shown in Figure 8.32.

Generic Smart Search (column based) - Tree Display

Table	Short Text	Hits	Entities	SE16H	Cluster
SCUSTOM	Flight customers	1	0		FLUGKUNDE
SBOOK	Single Flight Booking	6	0		FLUGKUNDE
SNVOICE	Invoice	6	0		FLUGKUNDE
STICKET	Flight Ticket	6	0		FLUGKUNDE
SFLIGHT	Flight	5	0		FLUGKUNDE
SAPLANE	Plane	3	0		FLUGKUNDE
SCARR	Airline	4	0		FLUGKUNDE
SPFLI	Flight schedule	5	0		FLUGKUNDE

Figure 8.32 Collected Data after Final Revision

8.5 Handling a Data Subject Request

Now that the information retrieval framework data model meets the requirements (and in a realistic case, the workbench request has been released by transport to the quality or productive system), we'll assume that a customer wants to receive information from your company about his personal data.

Data Controller Rule Framework

If you use the Data Controller Rule Framework (see Chapter 6), you don't need to have defined any purposes because the information retrieval framework interacts with the Data Controller Rule Framework and determines the maintained and updated purposes and the corresponding SAP ILM objects. You would otherwise have to enter all purposes, including the SAP ILM objects, manually.

Transaction DTINF_START_COLL

To provide information, start Transaction DTINF_START_COLL (Start Data Retrieval). The search criteria are more restricted than was previously the case in Transaction DTINF_TEST_MODEL (Information Ret. FW – Test Model); for example, you can only search by business partner numbers, customer numbers, or vendor numbers. The starting table you previously defined in Section 8.4.2 and the manually defined starting field are already stored for each selection in the SAP system.

To explain the previous example, the authors modified the search so that it can also be performed for a flight customer.

As before, we're using **Flight Customer 7**. Because the language of the data subject is German, the output should be in German. Enter the data as shown in Figure 8.33.

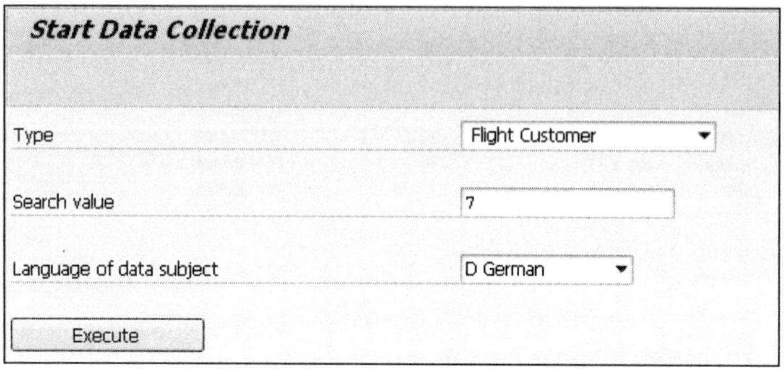

Figure 8.33 Starting the Information Request

Further processing can be triggered by pressing the Enter key. We'll then receive confirmation that the search has been initiated.

In the background, a job is continuously being executed, which is responsible for the provision of information. A few minutes later, the GSS for data will be started in the background.

Transaction DTINF_PROC_COLL

If you start Transaction DTINF_PROC_COLL (Process Data Collection Results), a screen as shown in Figure 8.34 appears. As you can see, the search for flight customer (**Flugkunde** in our example) **7** will appear in yellow.

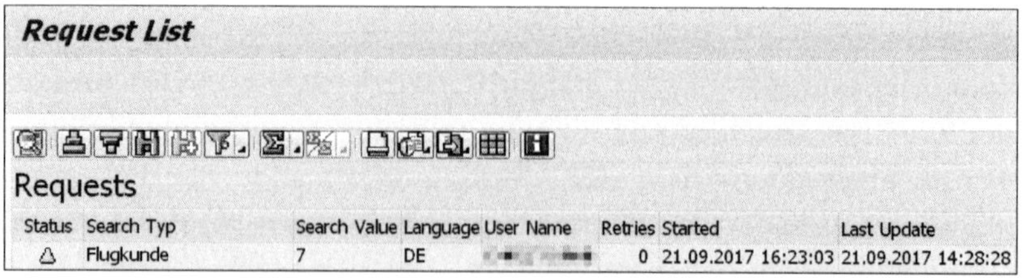

Figure 8.34 Search Query: Waiting

After a few more minutes, restart the transaction. The search has been completed, and the window will show a green square for the search query (see Figure 8.35).

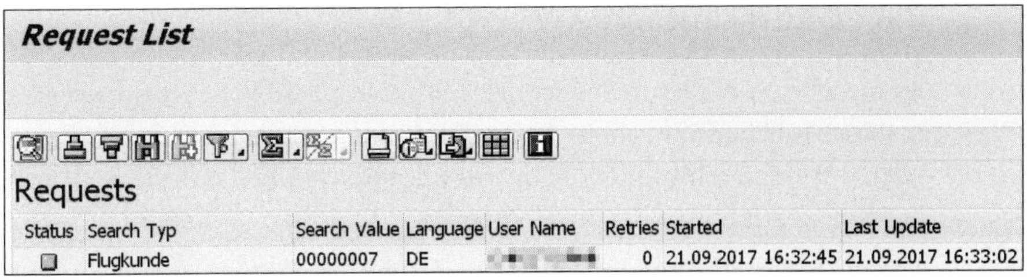

Figure 8.35 Search Query Completed

Double-clicking will open a new page (see Figure 8.36). On the left side of this page, you'll see all the purposes for which a search has been performed (in our case for **TEST_FLIGHT** only). This result corresponds to the result that was previously determined using Transaction DTINF_TEST_MODEL, albeit with a different representation. The hierarchical table tree can be expanded, and all entries for a hit will be listed on the right.

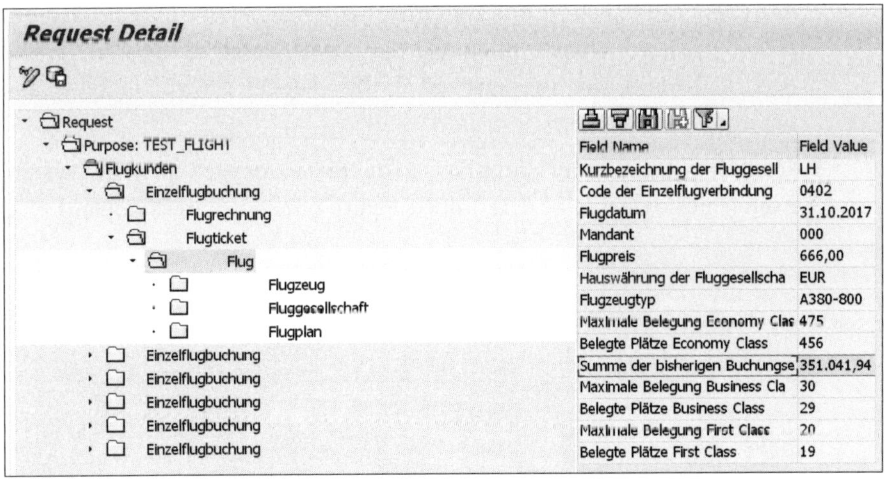

Figure 8.36 Result of an Information Request

If the user has the appropriate authorization, the result of the search can be downloaded as a text file by clicking the **Download** button. This can then be revised manually. How this data is delivered to the customer is at the company's discretion.

8.6 Central Instance

Subject to confirmation As mentioned earlier in Section 8.2.2, it's also possible to set up a central instance (CI), which enables you to determine personal data from all connected systems. This functionality may not be available at the time of publication, as it is still under development.

The possibilities of the information retrieval framework, when using this kind of CI, go beyond the options considered here. The CI makes it possible to determine personal data for an entire business process. This means, for example, that not only is the data determined for the SAP Supplier Relationship Management (SAP SRM) application but also the corresponding data from the application components SAP ERP Materials Management (MM), SAP ERP Financials (FI), and SAP ERP Controlling (CO), resulting from the business process, is also consulted.

Security aspect user To perform this cross-business process search, it's necessary to set up a CI. As a client can only have one system status, a new client will be needed. For security reasons, this client should only be available to those users who need it (from a security perspective, this reduces the vulnerability and potential security risks).

From this CI, RFC connections have to be created for each client in a system from which data is to be determined. Figure 8.37 shows an example.

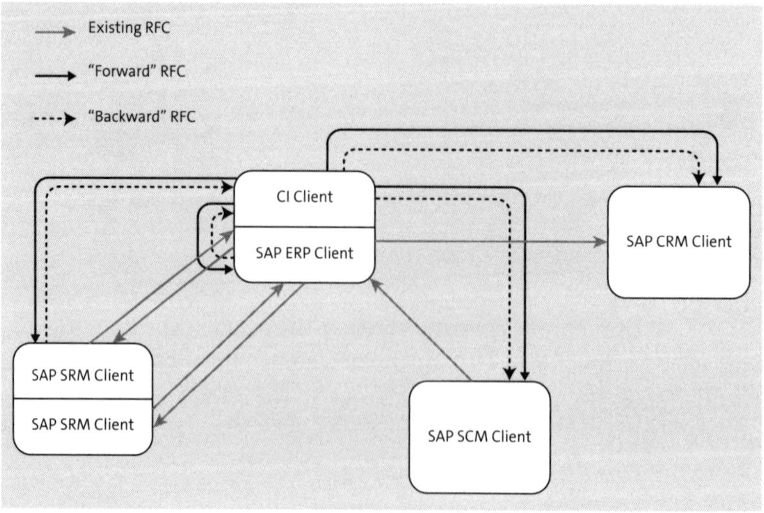

Figure 8.37 RFC Connections of a CI

Existing RFC connections

The system landscape consists of four different systems: SAP ERP, SAP Customer Relationship Management (SAP CRM), SAP Supply Chain Management (SAP SCM), and SAP Supplier Relationship Management (SAP SRM) with two clients. In the past, a total of six RFC connections were created for this purpose, which are required by the applications and are referred to as existing RFC connections.

Forward RFC

A total of five forward RFC connections must be created from the CI: one RFC connection per client per system. Although the CI runs on the same system as the SAP ERP system, RFCs must still be set up.

Backward RFC

All affected systems must in turn receive a backward RFC connection to the CI client. In this case, however, one connection per system is sufficient because RFC connections are available to every client in the system.

In this way, the CI can communicate with each application via the new RFC connections. For example, if there are follow-up documents in SAP ERP in the business process SAP SRM, the GSS on the CI will ensure that these follow-up documents are identified in the SAP ERP system by triggering this using a forward RFC connection. If the SAP ERP system has completed the search, it will inform the CI of this by means of the backward RFC connection.

Security aspect RFC user

These new RFC connections should be provided with new users of the user type "System" in the target systems. Reusing existing RFC connections is a potential security risk in view of the powerful capabilities of the information retrieval framework.

For more information, please see the SAP documentation.

8.7 Further Technical Information

We want to take this opportunity to provide you with some further information:

- Read the SAP documentation. We don't deal with the other icons within the modeling tool, nor with the other options found in Transaction DTINF_ADJUST_MODEL (Adjust Inf. Retr. FW Model).
- You shouldn't work with SAP ILM objects in the modeling tool. It may be interesting to look at the generated data model. However, for SAP ILM

objects of applications, this can be very extensive and very confusing. You're not allowed to change anything in this mode anyway.

- Don't forget to save the changes in the browser regularly.

BAdI enhancement spot ES_DTINF

- Take a look at the BAdIs that are available in Transaction SE18 (BAdI Business Add-Ins: Definitions) in enhancement spot `ES_DTINF`. In particular, the possibility of using functional modules to influence the search process can be extremely helpful and may also be necessary in some situations. If needed, SAP delivers several BAdI implementations that you can have a look at.

8.8 Summary

In the past, it was necessary to understand or be familiar with a large number of different reports, transactions, or UIs to implement a request for information. This involved a lot of manual work and possibly without the direct support of the business processes. You've now seen that this can be carried out almost fully automatically by using SAP ILM objects, and the entire procedure may already be automated in a form that is comprehensible to the applicant as is demanded by the GDPR.

However, this doesn't work without your help: A correct data model can only be created through the iterative process of manually revising the information retrieval framework data model and analyzing the search result.

Where exactly the limit lies—between the minimum you could send to the requestor (a page of paper that probably isn't sufficient) and the possible maximum (hundreds or thousands of pages of paper)—will have to be decided individually.

Chapter 9
Read Access Logging

When you think about data protection, you might start by thinking that it's also about protecting people from surveillance. However, to effectively protect personal information, you must be able to survey all system users one by one.

In 2013, SAP introduced Read Access Logging (RAL) in SAP NetWeaver, which can also be used in SAP Business Suite and in SAP S/4HANA. However, this tool has been used only hesitantly for three reasons:

- Efforts incurred with implementation and utilization
- The tension area between data protection and behavioral control
- The slowly developing willingness of companies to actively shape their data protection activities

After a short description of possible requirements and a practical description of a sensible utilization, this chapter will explain the structure and maintenance of RAL.

9.1 Scope of Read Access Logging

You've already familiarized yourself with the logging of read access as a means of monitoring access in Chapter 1, Section 1.2.4.

A two-edged sword

Logging user activities definitely has two sides. It may serve to protect personal data, but, at the same time, it also generates personal data that must also be assessed to be a behavioral control measure pursuant to Section 87 (1)(6) Works Constitution Act (BetrVG in German law).

The necessity to log changes of data and access to the system, even access to individual software programs, is widely undisputed because neither the consistency of posting contents nor the system's security could be ensured otherwise. RAL, however, offers another dimension of possible behavioral control.

The authorities' point of view

Due to this complex tension, the Federal Commissioner for Data Protection in Germany introduced some decisive requirements in his 14th Activity Report, which—in a similar form—are also included in the *Guideline on Logging* by the German supervisory authorities (Working Group "Technical and Organizational Data Protection Issues"/"AK Technik," 2009):

- Logging is only permissible in cases where it's actually necessary.
- The necessity also determines the actual evaluation.
- If logging exclusively serves the purpose of maintaining data protection and data security, the log files may also be used exclusively for these purposes.

The *Guideline on Logging* by the German supervisory authorities (Working Group "Technical and Organizational Data Protection Issues"/"AK Technik," 2009, p. 4–5; see *http://deacademic.com/dic.nsf/dewiki/94630*; only available in German language) recommends logging the following activities:

- Authentication and authorization
- Entering and changing of data
- Data view
- Data transfer
- Data destruction

Don't log at random

In his 14th Activity Report, the Federal Commissioner emphasized that, from a data protection law perspective, random logging of all user activities is a cause for concern. Instead, it's essential that activities with an increased need for protection be logged.

With regard to the logging procedures in SAP Business Suite and in SAP S/4HANA, we'll assume that these requirements are met. SAP delivers sample configurations for particularly sensitive data.

The data of special categories (see Chapter 1, Section 1.1.4), as well as specifications concerning bank accounts, should be considered sensitive data. Beyond the sample configurations, you can also set up your own configurations for data that you consider to be particularly sensitive in your system.

[«]

Procedural Model

If you follow our procedural model (see Chapter 3), you should already have collected essential information related to the personal data.

RAL supports a range of channels in which end users of the system can carry out a logging procedure (user interface [UI] channels) and which can be used when communicating between systems (remote application programming interface [API] channels).

To find out which channels are supported by RAL, refer to SAP Note 1969086: Availability of RAL and Prerequisites (Kernel and SAP-GUI Version). This will also provide you with an overview of the current status of SAP NetWeaver releases and support packs (SPs), including the required kernel versions. SAP Notes will be extended when new RAL channels are available, or there will be references to other notes concerning new RAL channels.

Available RAL channels

At the time this book went to print (June 2018), the following RAL channels were supported:

- UI channels
  - Dynpro
  - Web Dynpro
  - CRM Web UIF (WebCUIF)
- Remote API channels
  - SAP Gateway (for OData/SAPUI5/SAP Fiori)
  - Remote function call (RFC)
  - Web services

9.2 Setup and Maintenance

Having explained which RAL channels are available in the previous section, and having provided you with the knowledge as to what can be logged, we'll use this section to outline how RAL needs to be configured so that you can log data. To use RAL, you'll need to assign authorizations and activate RAL.

9.2.1 Operation

Deletion of read access logs

In relation to UI channels, RAL logs exactly which user looked at a certain data record at which point in time. This information is stored in RAL logs. The related data can be deleted via SAP Information Lifecycle Management (SAP ILM) and the RAL-specific SAP ILM objects (SRAL, SRAL_ELOG, SRAL_EXP) in an automated procedure.

However, it would be wrong to log everything. This would reduce the system's performance considerably, and it's also not advisable because this would result in the random logging of all user activities, as described in Section 9.1.

For these reasons, and to keep track of suspicious cases, logging should be restricted to data that enables you to search for certain criteria at a random point in time. Those criteria may be an account number, a credit card number, or a customer.

If, for example, you logged the customer number (and also logged, e.g., the transaction in the Web Dynpro channel), and you're able to identify the point in time when the entry was generated in RAL logs, you can look up what the user saw at that point in time by using the change documents related to the respective transaction or application. You should, however, keep in mind that the user possibly wasn't able to view all of the data you managed to reconstruct with the change documents. This may be the case when some of the coding errors aren't displayed in Web Dynpro or when they have been deactivated in the system by using Business Add-Ins (BAdIs).

In the RAL configurations, you can store the fields that should be logged. We'll elaborate further on these configurations in Section 9.5.

If you want to log the UI channels, you first need to create RAL recordings so that, from these, you can subsequently generate RAL configurations. This will be discussed further in Section 9.4.

9.2.2 Authorizations

Transaction SU21

To run RAL you'll need the required authorizations. All possible RAL authorizations can be found in Transaction SU21 (Maintenance of the Authorization Objects) as S_RAL*, for example, S_RAL_REC for recording configurations.

These authorizations must be assigned correspondingly. The authorizations required for the examples described here can be found in the documentation of the respective authorization objects.

9.2.3 Activation

Authorization S_RAL_CLIS

Having assigned the authorization S_RAL_CLIS, you can start Transaction SRALMANAGER (Read Access Logging Manager). The browser window as shown in Figure 9.1 opens.

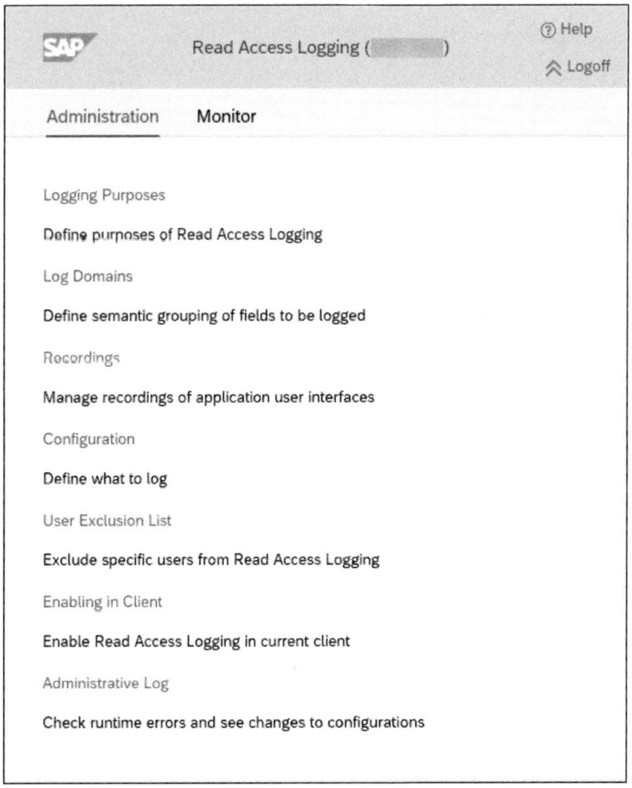

Figure 9.1 Transaction SRALMANAGER in a Web Browser

One click on **Enabling in Client** will open the screen displayed in Figure 9.2.

The **Enable Read Access Logging in current client** field must be activated. If you want to use RAL for the RFC channel, you can also enable the respective systems here.

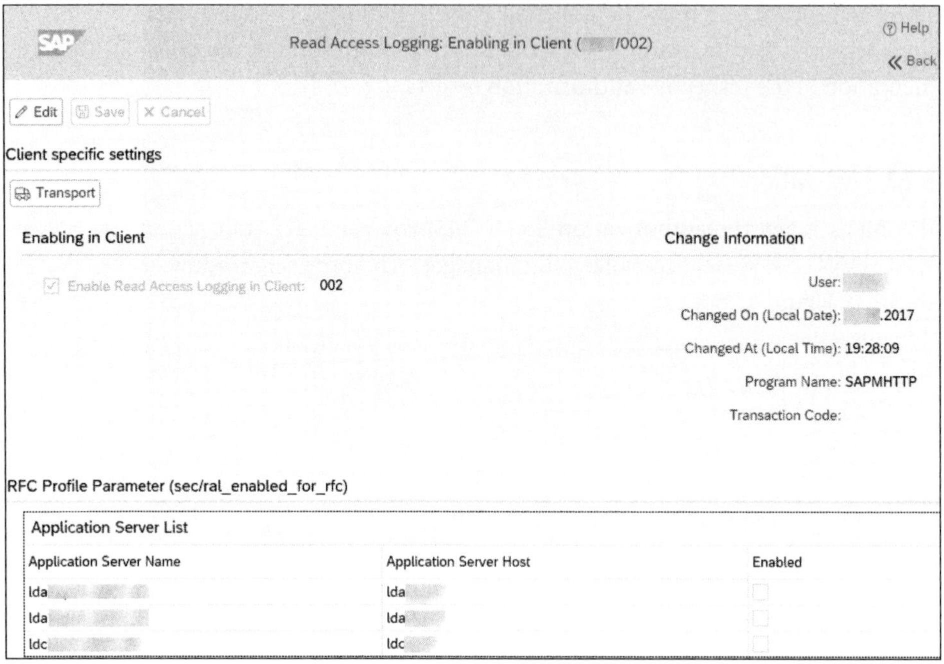

Figure 9.2 Activation of RAL

9.3 Logging Purpose and Domains

Before we get down to the actual work in RAL, two further steps, which will be explained in the following section, are necessary.

9.3.1 Logging Purpose

As the name implies, the logging purpose defines the purpose of generating a log. You can store as many logging purposes as required or desired. Therefore, click on **Logging Purposes** in Transaction SRALMANAGER. This will open a screen as shown in Figure 9.3. If you click the **Create** button, a new screen will open.

Because we're working with an example of a customer in this chapter, we'll assign a purpose (Figure 9.4) and then click **Create**.

The image previously displayed in Figure 9.3 will then show the newly created entry (see Figure 9.5).

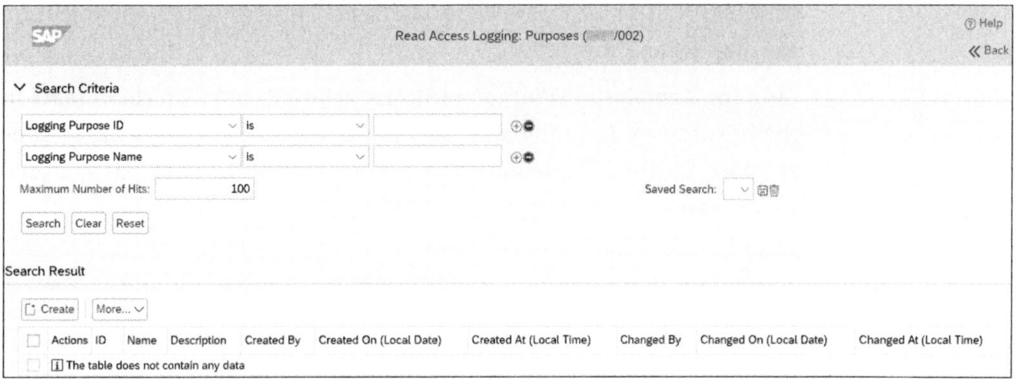

Figure 9.3 Screen for Purposes of Logging

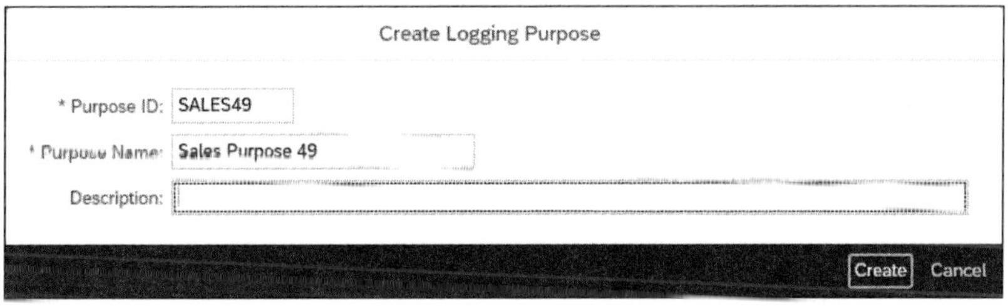

Figure 9.4 Adding a Logging Purpose

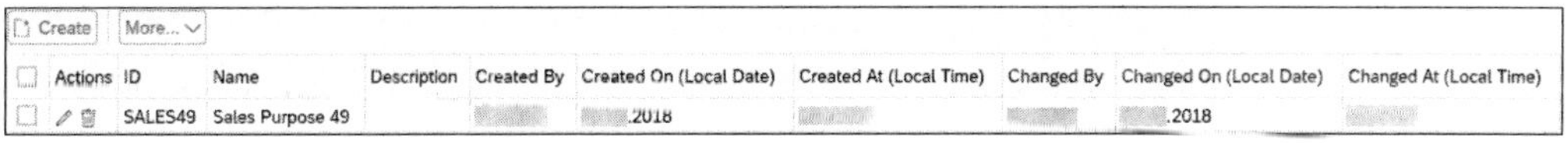

Figure 9.5 Storing the Logging Purpose in the System

9.3.2 Log Domains

Consistent specification

Log domains enable you to define the type of field for the fields you're going to log later on. This could be a vendor number, for example, or a bank account number. These log domains are also written in the RAL logs.

If you specify the log domains for the corresponding fields consistently, the respective log domain will enable you to search the RAL logs for a certain log domain (bank account number) and a value (**2811...**)—and this works across all RAL channels! A search like this would thus detect all entries, irrespective of whether they were viewed in a Web Dynpro-based application or in SAP Customer Relationship Management (SAP CRM), or they were transferred via a web service.

Click **Log Domains** in Transaction SRALMANAGER, and then click **Create** in the next screen. A combination of a name and the business area must be specified for the log domain. We'll use the entries in Figure 9.6 and then click **Create**.

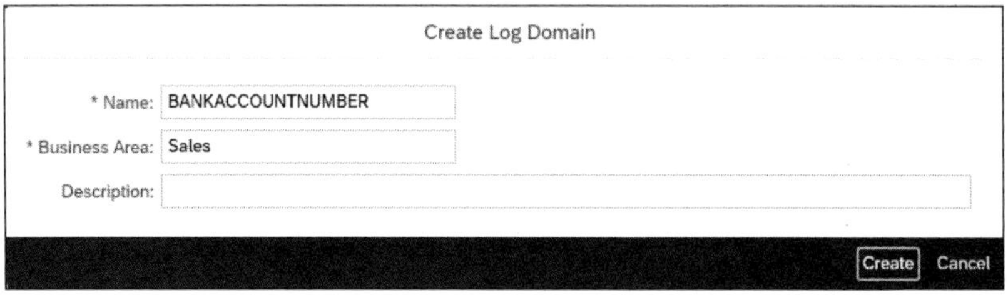

Figure 9.6 Create Log Domain

Subsequently, the newly created entry will be displayed (see Figure 9.7).

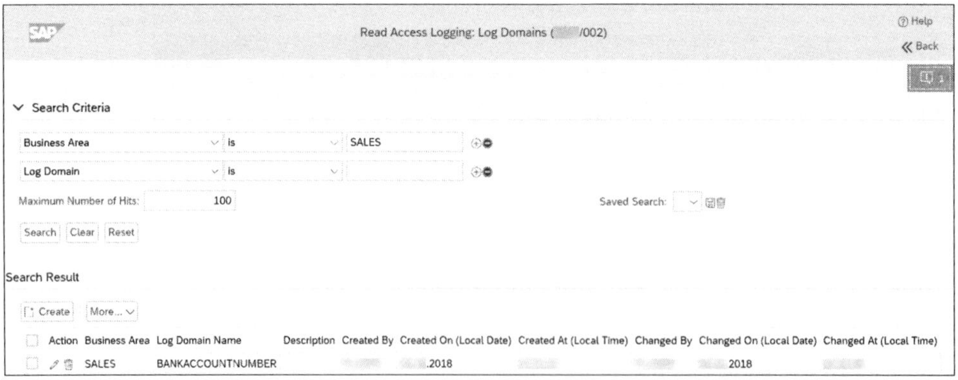

Figure 9.7 Log Domain Stored in the System

We can now turn our attention to the actual work, that is, the creation of records and configurations.

9.4 Recordings for User Interface Channels

Recordings for UI channels

For UI channels, you need to manually define the fields of the UI to be logged by following these steps:

1. Click **Recordings** in Transaction SRALMANAGER.
2. To record some fields allocated to the Dynpro channel using RAL, click **Create.**
3. Enter the data according to Figure 9.8, and then click **Create** again.

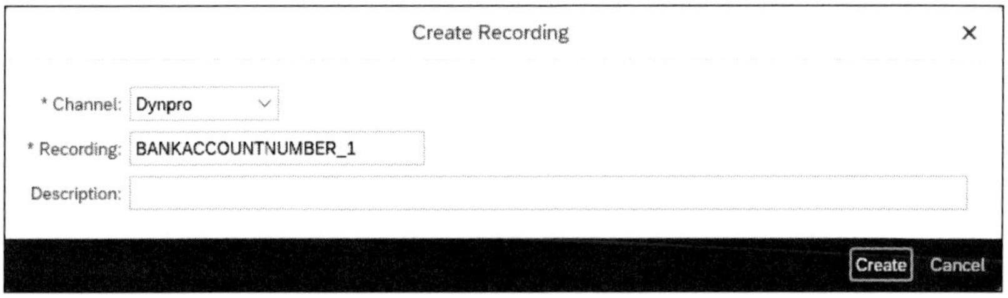

Figure 9.8 Creating a Recording

The next screen will show the recording you've created (see Figure 9.9). The stop sign indicates that this recording is currently active. The related recording user (i.e., our user) will now be able to log in on the SAP GUI and include the fields in this recording.

Figure 9.9 Started Recording

You'll need to log in to the system (again) via the SAP GUI and open the business partner via Transaction BP (Maintain Business Partner). Here, you'll have to choose a customer who is also a business partner, and open the **Payment Transactions** tab. The screen shown in Figure 9.10 appears.

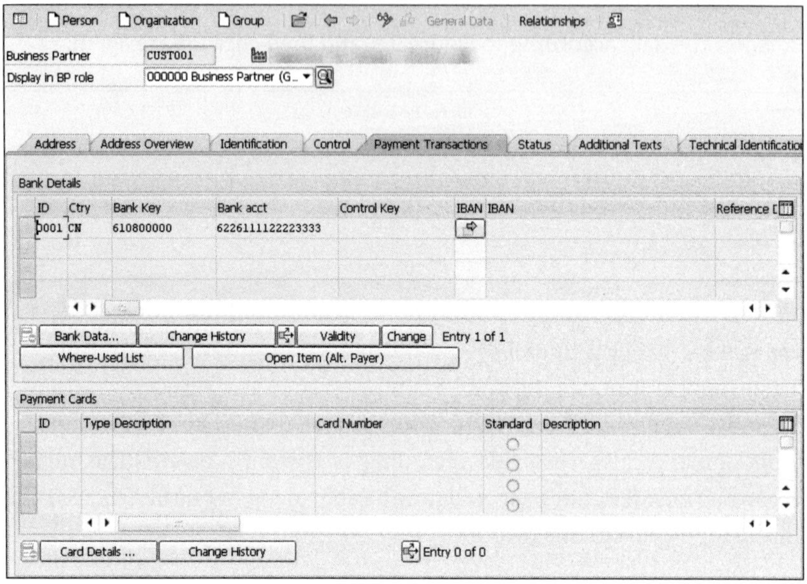

Figure 9.10 Payment Transactions of a Business Partner

Record field

Select the entry **CN**, right-click to open a popup window (see Figure 9.11), and select **RAL: Record field** from the menu.

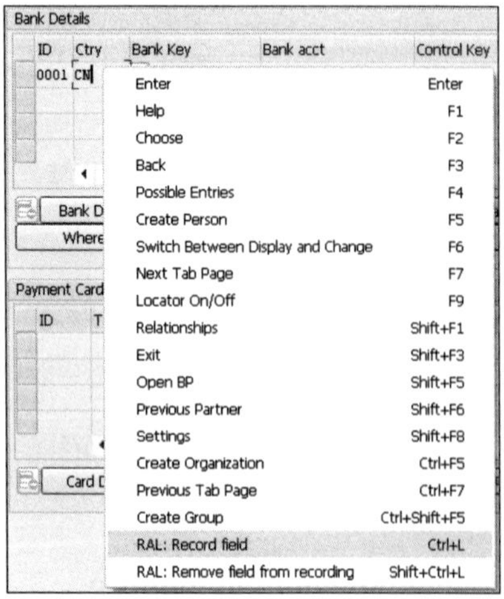

Figure 9.11 Record Field in RAL Recording

Recording will be confirmed by a system message (see Figure 9.12).

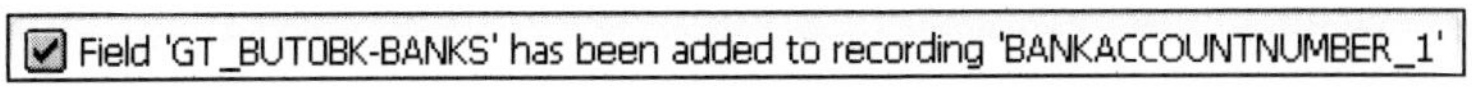

Figure 9.12 Message: Field Successfully Added to Recording

We'll repeat this for the bank key, the bank account, and the IBAN.

Remove field from recording

If you want to remove a field again, click on **RAL: Remove field from recording** (refer to Figure 9.11). You can also remove this field from Transaction SRALMANAGER at a later time; we'll describe this in further detail later.

At this point, we complete the recording. You can therefore click **Recordings** in Transaction SRALMANAGER (Read Access Logging Manager) again. The system will confirm this, and the screen displayed in Figure 9.13 will appear.

Figure 9.13 Recording Stopped

You can open, start, or delete a recording via the icons. Delete enables you to delete a recording. Start can be understood in the same manner as continue—any user can continue an existing recording. This is useful for when you didn't manage to complete all the work and want to continue with it a day later.

Now click the **Open** button. Select the first entry on the follow-up screen, which is displayed in Figure 9.14.

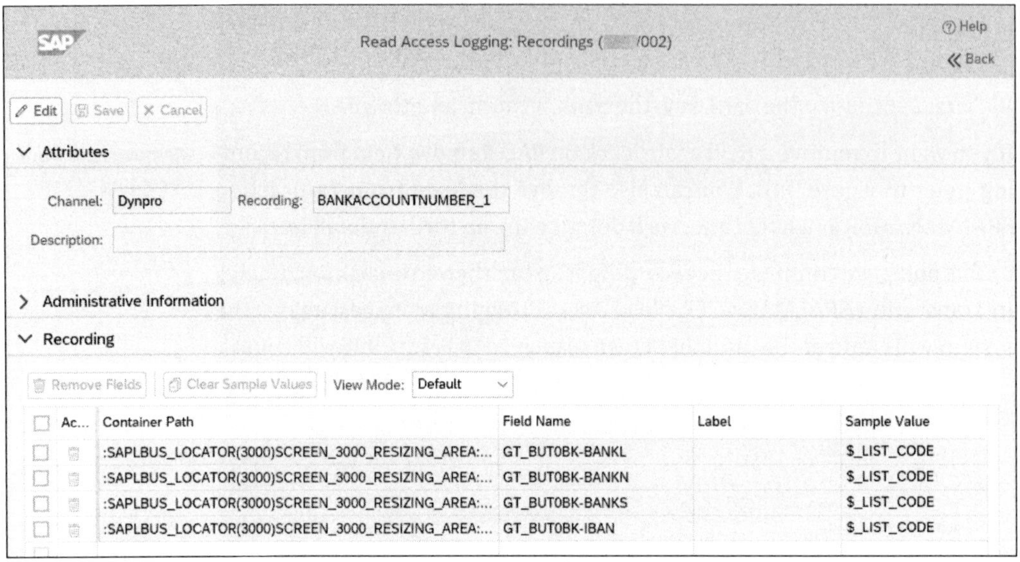

Figure 9.14 Display of the Recording

You may recognize the field names as they correspond to the field names in Figure 9.12.

The **Container Path** provides the related technical information regarding where the corresponding field is located. The path in our example is too long to be displayed in full (and it's absolutely irrelevant for your understanding). You can also see the transaction under which this field has been recorded.

If you select **Edit**, for example, you can remove fields; however, we'll skip this part for now.

The procedure for Web Dynpro and SAP CRM Web UIF corresponds to the proceedings described in this section, so we'll skip this and turn our attention to the RAL configuration.

9.5 Configuration

RAL configuration

The RAL configurations define what should be logged. In this section, we'll deal with a step in a configuration that has to be taken after a recording, so that you can follow this process more easily. How to carry out a configuration for remote API channels will be described in Section 9.7.

To work with the RAL configurations, click on **Configuration** in Transaction SRALMANAGER. The screen displayed in Figure 9.15 opens.

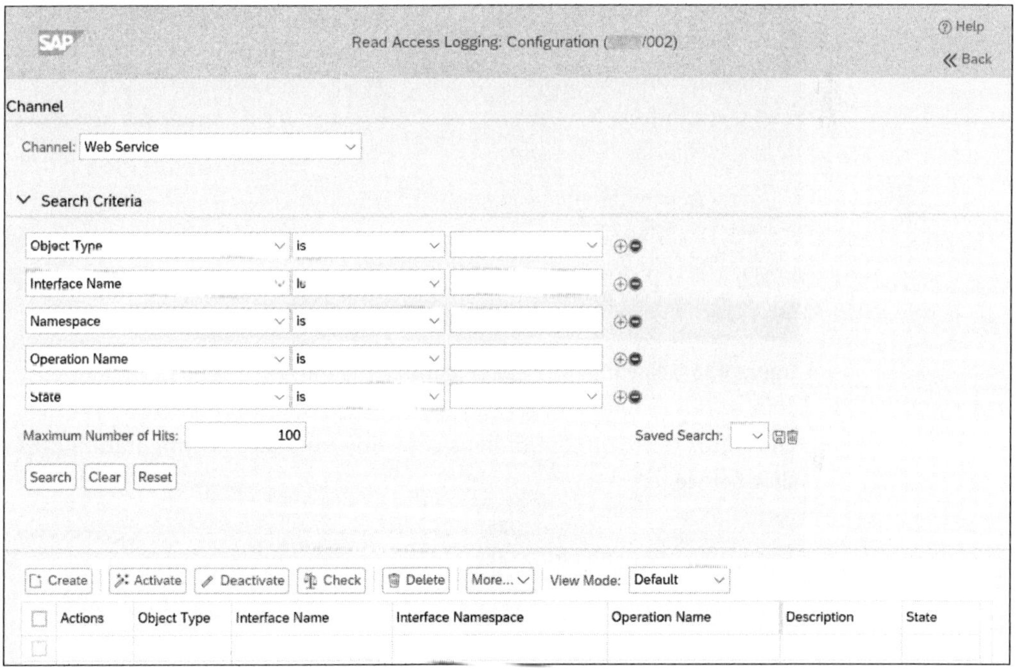

Figure 9.15 RAL Configuration in a Web Browser

The search criteria displayed are equal to the channel's criteria, in this case, the web service. Switch to **Dynpro** via the dropdown menu **Channel**, and then click the **Create** button. In the next screen, you can enter the name of your recording (**BANKACCOUNTNUMBER_1**) and then click the **Search** button (see Figure 9.16).

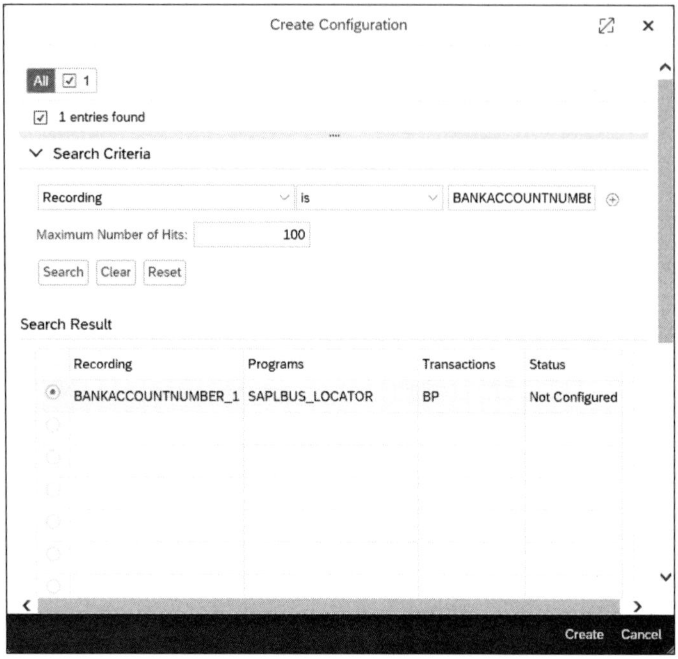

Figure 9.16 Selecting the Recording for Configuration

The status tells you that there is currently no related configuration. Next, click **Create**.

[»]

Recording and Configuration

A recording can be used for several configurations; a configuration, however, consists of only one recording.

In the next screen, click **Create Log Group** to create a group of logs, select **Sales Purpose 49** from the **Purpose** field, and click **Create** (see Figure 9.17).

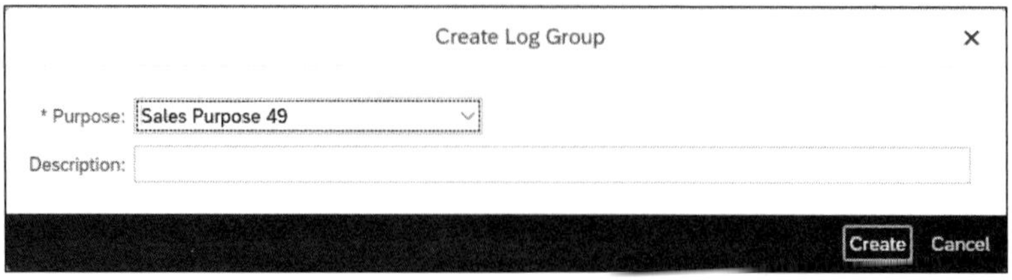

Figure 9.17 Create Log Group

The screen will change, and you can now drop the fields into a table (see Figure 9.18).

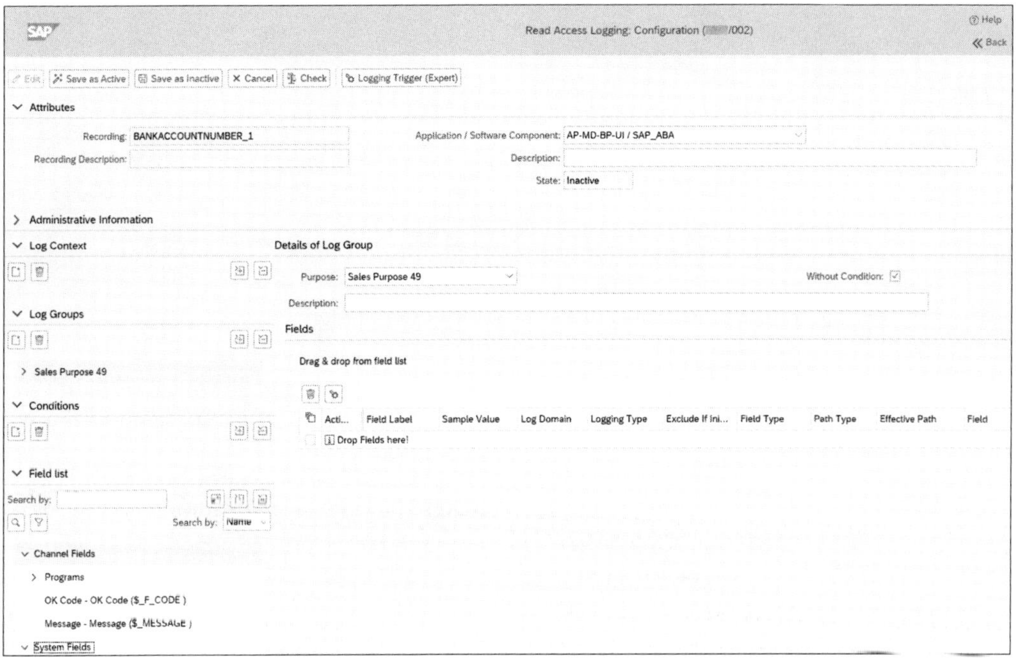

Figure 9.18 Adding Fields to a Configuration

The fields you can transfer to the table are displayed at the bottom left. Drag the transaction code, the user name, the OK code, and the message into the table using drag and drop.

At this point, it's still lacking your previously defined fields. Now, you can either open the tree below **Programs** and keep continuously opening the tree, which will then be built up below until you reach the fields, or you can simply drag **Programs** directly into the **Fields** table to integrate all fields (see Figure 9.19).

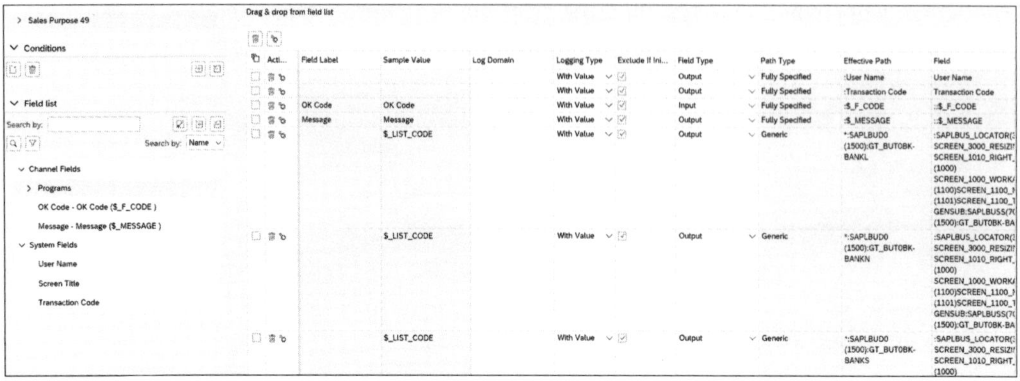

Figure 9.19 Adding All Fields to the Configuration

Assigning the log domain

A log domain can be assigned to the first four fields. However, we didn't create log domains for these fields or categories, so leave these blank (for the moment).

To the remaining four fields, assign the bank account number by selecting **SALES/BANKACCOUNTNUMBER** via the search functionality. Next, you can copy the text from the column and adopt the remaining three entries. The sample value may help you decide which logging domain you should specify (see Figure 9.20).

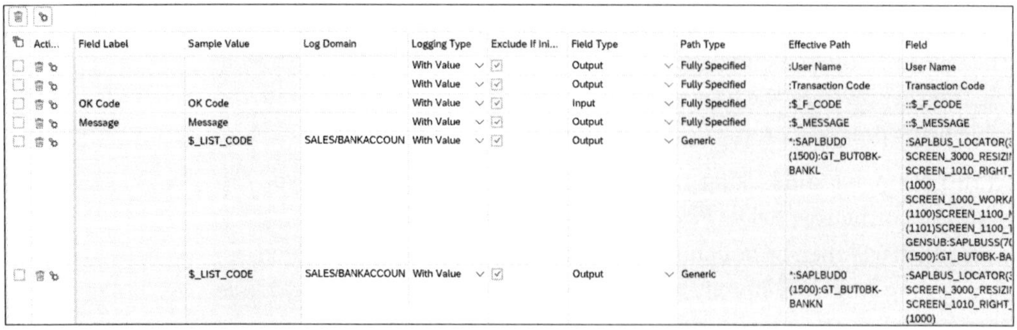

Figure 9.20 Setting Fields Related to the Logging Domains

Field type

The field type can be used to determine when a field will technically be logged. It can accept the following values:

- **Output**
  Output (at the time of output) means that only the information displayed will be logged.
- **Input**
  Input (at the time of input) allows logging of the value in an input field.
- **Both**
  Both leads to logging both the case of an **Output** and the case of an **Input**.

Logging type

With the logging type, you can define whether the value will be logged or not. We obviously suggest that you log the entries that are relevant for the identification of a data record – further fields, of which you only want to log the fact that they were viewed, i.e. logged without a value. The reason for this is that these values can be traced back via change documents. We explained this in more detail in Section 9.2.1.

For instance, you might log employees' access to a patients' data because you want to know who saw that some patients had been diagnosed with HIV. Therefore, you would have to log (besides the user) the patient (with a value) and the HIV diagnosis (without a value). You'll need the patient to know whose patient data has been viewed; the diagnosis itself is irrelevant for logging (and viewing it should be strictly avoided because this is a sensitive, personal data record) and can be derived from the change documents if necessary.

Activating the configuration

Adopt the other previous settings, and click **Save as Active**. From this point on, the configuration will be activated. It will now be evaluated at runtime and may possibly lead to a logging procedure.

All fields of configuration are evaluated separately, and, should a field be displayed to a user, this will be logged. This can be influenced by RAL conditions (Section 9.8), however. The following section will show why this might be necessary.

9.6 Evaluation of Logs

In our example, a configuration has been activated that will log the users' activities where applicable. This section will address the issue of checking the logs and, where necessary, adjusting the configuration.

9.6.1 Manual Evaluation

Creating and viewing log entries

You may now want to check whether anything from our example is logged in RAL and what this includes. To do so, you'll have to rerun Transaction BP (Edit Business Partner), which you've already used in Section 9.4. You'll need to click through a few tabs, switch to Transaction SRALMANANGER, and open the link to the read access log via the **Monitor** tab. As **Source**, use the **Raw Database**, and as **Date/Time**, use **Last Three Hours**. Finally, click the **Search** button (see Figure 9.21).

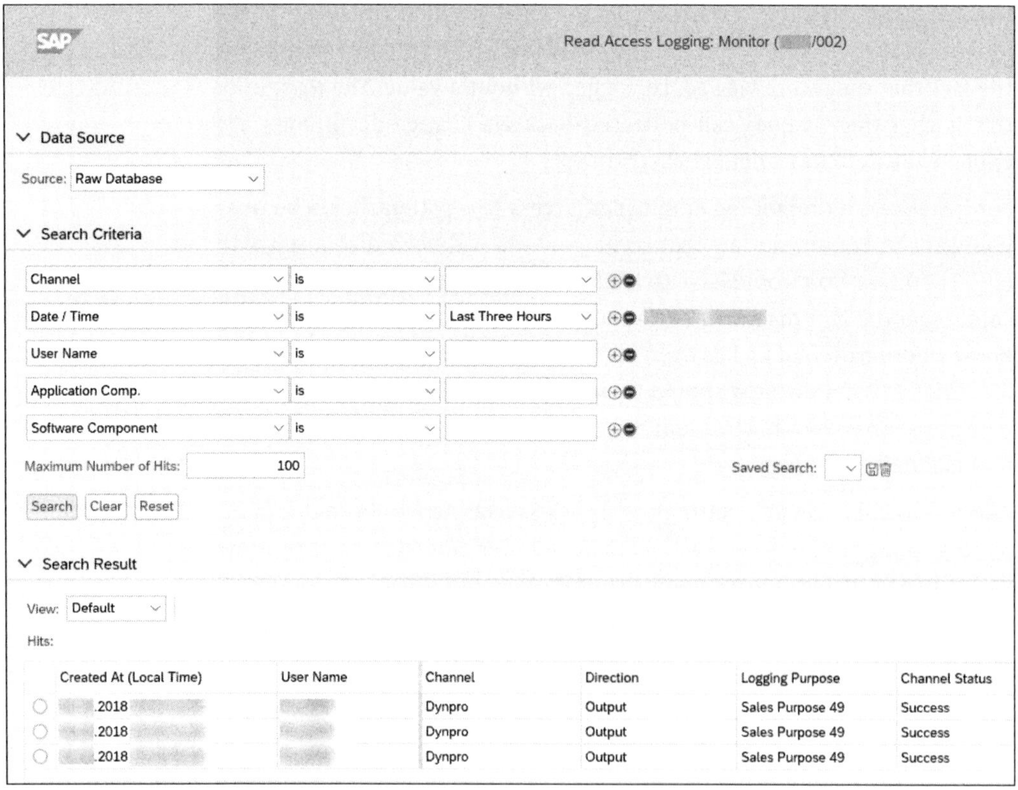

Figure 9.21 Overview of System Accesses in the Read Access Log

Logged entries

Next, we'll select the oldest (the final) entry. Figure 9.22 shows that everything has been logged just the way we configured it.

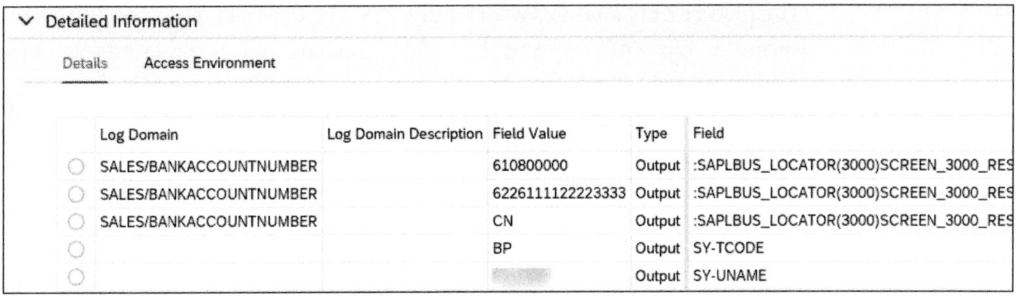

Log Domain	Log Domain Description	Field Value	Type	Field
SALES/BANKACCOUNTNUMBER		610800000	Output	:SAPLBUS_LOCATOR(3000)SCREEN_3000_RES
SALES/BANKACCOUNTNUMBER		6226111122223333	Output	:SAPLBUS_LOCATOR(3000)SCREEN_3000_RES
SALES/BANKACCOUNTNUMBER		CN	Output	:SAPLBUS_LOCATOR(3000)SCREEN_3000_RES
		BP	Output	SY-TCODE
			Output	SY-UNAME

Figure 9.22 Log at the Start of the Transaction

If you open the second oldest entry, you'll see fewer fields—you were on a different tab without relevant fields for the logging; and you'll also see that the user triggered a function code to continue to the next tab (see Figure 9.23). This is missing in the first case because the transaction opened a tab directly.

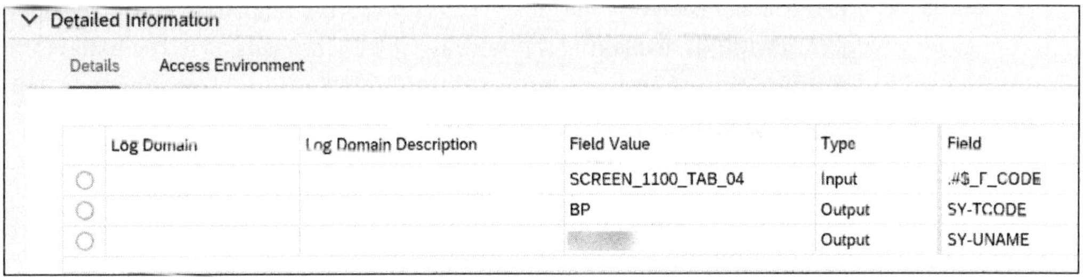

Log Domain	Log Domain Description	Field Value	Type	Field
		SCREEN_1100_TAB_04	Input	:#$_F_CODE
		BP	Output	SY-TCODE
			Output	SY-UNAME

Figure 9.23 Log after Switching to a Different Tab (TAB_04)

A similar picture is displayed in Figure 9.24—a user activity without any relevance for logging.

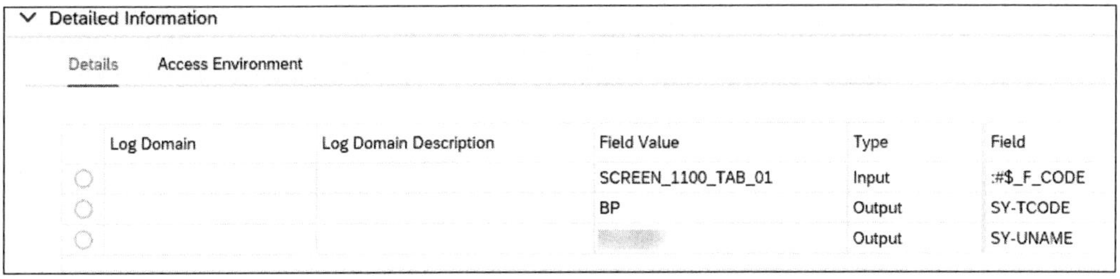

Log Domain	Log Domain Description	Field Value	Type	Field
		SCREEN_1100_TAB_01	Input	:#$_F_CODE
		BP	Output	SY-TCODE
			Output	SY-UNAME

Figure 9.24 Log after Switching to a Different Tab (TAB_01)

The picture only changes with Figure 9.25: The user has reopened the corresponding tab (TAB_05), and the log now reveals that data related to a bank account number and the related values were displayed to the user.

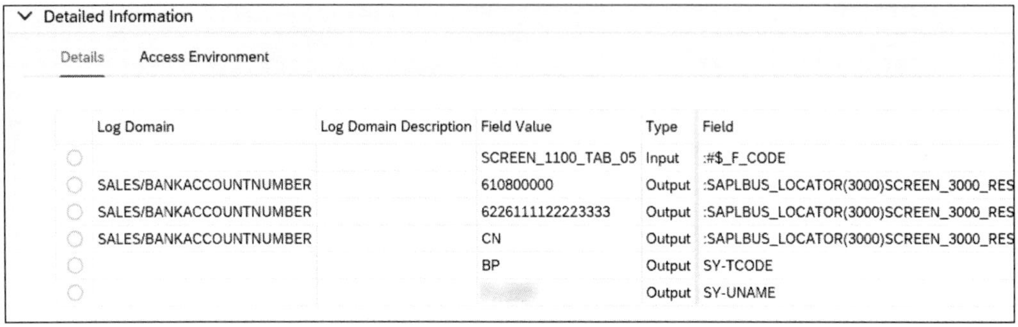

Detailed Information

Details | Access Environment

	Log Domain	Log Domain Description	Field Value	Type	Field
○			SCREEN_1100_TAB_05	Input	:#$_F_CODE
○	SALES/BANKACCOUNTNUMBER		610800000	Output	:SAPLBUS_LOCATOR(3000)SCREEN_3000_RES
○	SALES/BANKACCOUNTNUMBER		6226111122223333	Output	:SAPLBUS_LOCATOR(3000)SCREEN_3000_RES
○	SALES/BANKACCOUNTNUMBER		CN	Output	:SAPLBUS_LOCATOR(3000)SCREEN_3000_RES
○			BP	Output	SY-TCODE
○				Output	SY-UNAME

Figure 9.25 Log in the View of Payment Transactions

Visible behavioral monitoring

As you can see, logging has been carried out correctly. However, you can also see that each one of this user's activities has been logged in this transaction without displaying the relevant field. This leads us to the behavioral monitoring that was previously addressed in Section 9.1: too much is definitely being logged here!

We also need to take into account that with every action, RAL will save a random identification number, which is generated when a transaction is started. Each step taken by a user within a transaction can be logged by means of this identification number. In some cases, this may be necessary because the knowledge needed to understand and classify a case can only be acquired by understanding the chain of actions that led to a particular event. At this point, you should refer to the RAL conditions that can be stored with each configuration in RAL (Section 9.8).

9.6.2 Automated Search in Read Access Logging Logs

You can use the RAL logs via the UI to search for relevant entries; however, this requires a considerable amount of manual effort. Understanding what a user has done in the system can quickly push you to the limits of your understanding.

Evaluating logs with ABAP code

We therefore suggest developing code that will, depending on requirements, search the RAL logs in an automated manner and provide the results in a processed form. However, because the RAL logs are only available in an internal RAL format, you can't evaluate or read them via database queries as usual. Instead, you'll have to resort to the RAL API. For instance, the class `cl_sral_simple_reader` includes the method `if_sral_simple_reader~read_data_unpacked`, which you could use. The rest is a matter of your imagination.

9.7 Configurations for Remote API Channels

As opposed to the UI channels, the remote API channels are easily set up. We'll demonstrate this with an example for the RFC channel; the other channels behave in a similar way.

Configuration of an RFC function module

You'll have to select this channel in the configuration and click **Create**. Next, you need to select the function module `BAPI_BUPA_BANKDETAIL_GETDETAIL`, and click the **Search** button. A screen like Figure 9.26 appears.

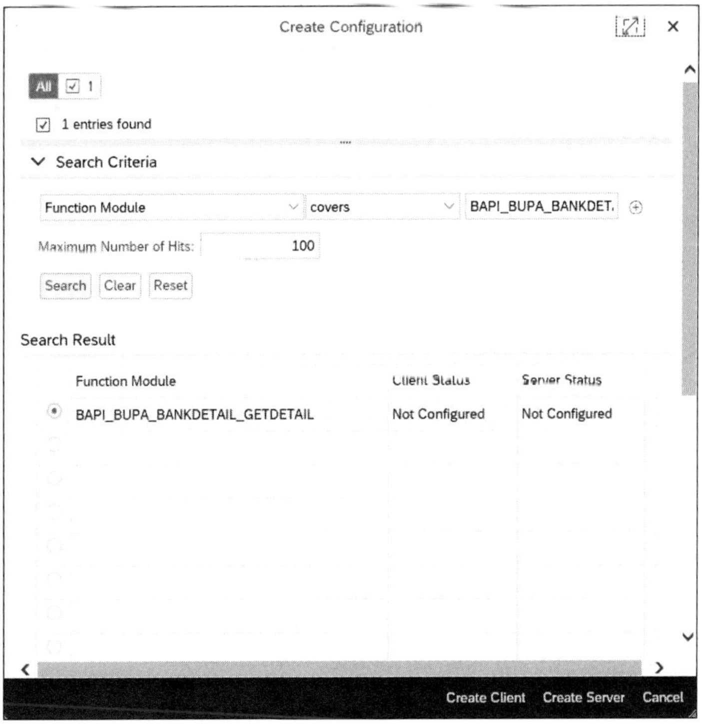

Figure 9.26 Configuration Variant for the RFC Function Module

RFC client or RFC server

Two button are available for selection, as follows:

- **Create Client**
  This creates a configuration for a new RFC client; it's also the system from which the RFC is initiated (the client's functionality is limited, so it's not discussed here in any further detail).
- **Create Server**
  This creates a configuration for the RFC server that prompts the system to respond, and which then delivers a response.

You can now click **Create Server** and generate the log group as described in Section 9.5. The screen that appears is similar to Figure 9.27.

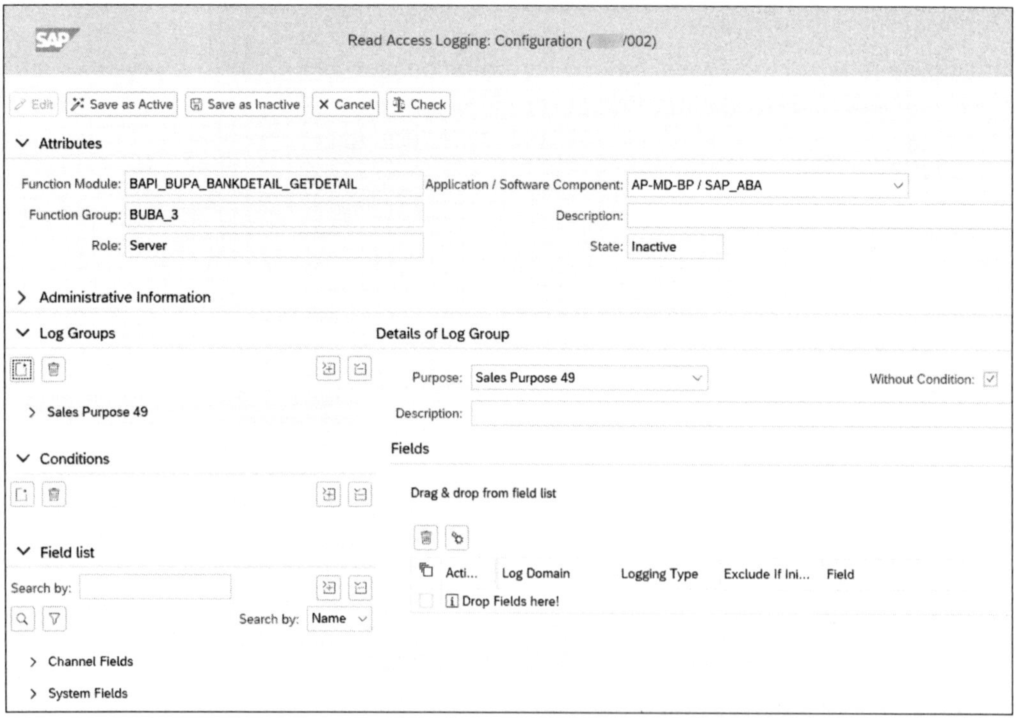

Figure 9.27 Creating a Configuration for the RFC Server

Clicking on **Field list** opens a tree with all fields that are available in the interface parameters of an RFC (**Importing**, **Exporting**, **Changing**, and **Tables**) and can be added to the configuration.

Adding fields to the configuration

Select the necessary fields used by the RFC to select the data (of the business partners), the fields that have been transferred, and also the error messages that may have occurred. Configuration can then be created, as displayed in Figure 9.28 (for a better view, some fields were removed before creating the image).

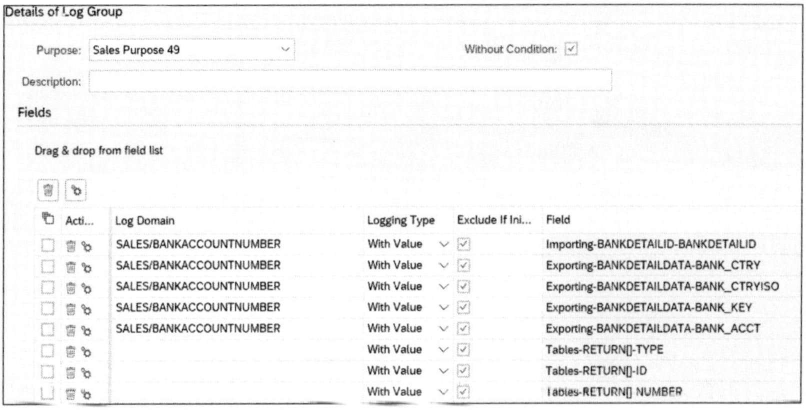

Figure 9.28 Adding Parameters of the RFC Function Module

Limitation of RFC logging

After this configuration has been saved as active, a logging procedure will be performed because an RFC was triggered by another system. An RFC from the same system in a different client doesn't trigger a logging procedure.

9.8 Conditions

Limitation of logging via conditions

In this section, we'll explain how you can set up the logging functionality so that logging will only be performed only under certain conditions. To do so, you'll need to add conditions to a configuration. We'll continue to illustrate this using an example. In Section 9.5, we created an RAL configuration for the bank account number, and logging was carried out successfully.

Logging the business partner and bank account number

Instead of only logging the bank account number, as we did previously, it may also be important to log which business partner viewed the bank account number. You'll therefore have to generate a new business partner log domain as described in Section 9.3.2. You can subsequently continue the recording `BANKACCOUNTNUMBER_1`.

Next, you can select the same business partner and again start Transaction BP (Edit Business Partner). Open this business partner, and add the related business partner number to the RAL recording (see Figure 9.29).

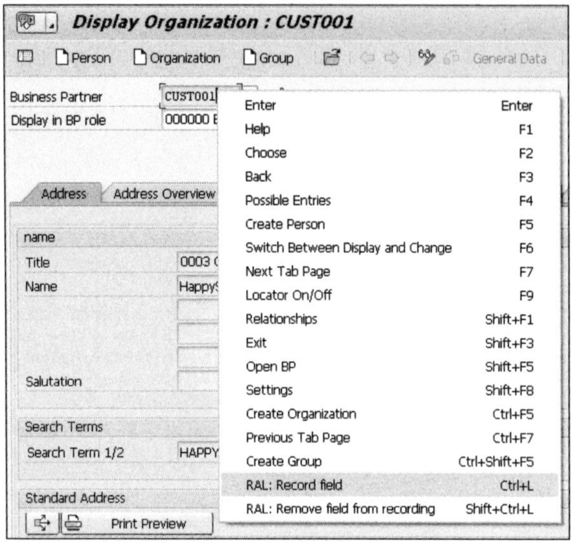

Figure 9.29 Recording the Business Partner

A message will confirm that the field has been added to the recording (see Figure 9.30).

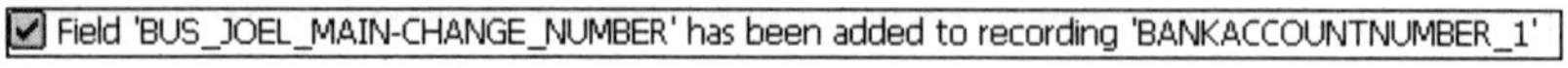

Figure 9.30 Field Business Partner Added to Recording

You can then terminate the RAL recording and open the same RAL configuration as previously described in Section 9.5.

Apply new fields from recording in the configuration

One more time, you can drag the entire **Programs** tree to the screen area on the right and drop it there. Error messages will occur as there are already many fields in the configuration. You can, however, see our previously recorded field at the end of the table, and you can define the log domain (see Figure 9.31).

After the RAL configuration has been activated, in addition to the bank account number (and other fields, as explained in Section 9.6.1), the business partner has been logged.

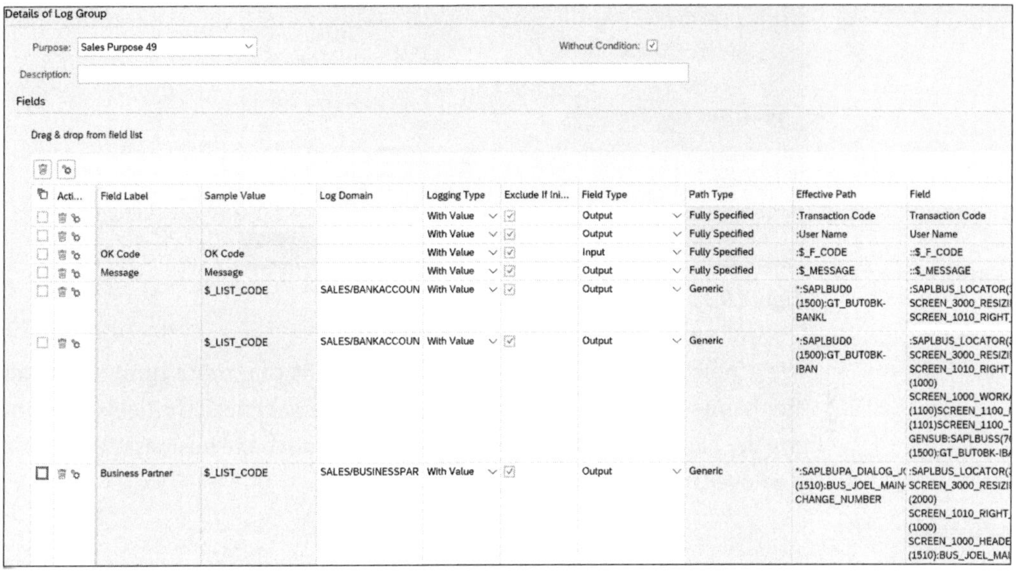

Figure 9.31 Business Partner Added to Configuration

The fact that logging a business partner (or all other related fields) is only necessary when the bank account number is displayed to the user illustrates the necessity to apply RAL conditions.

Creating a condition

To create a condition, click on **Create Condition**, enter the data as shown in Figure 9.32, and click **Create**.

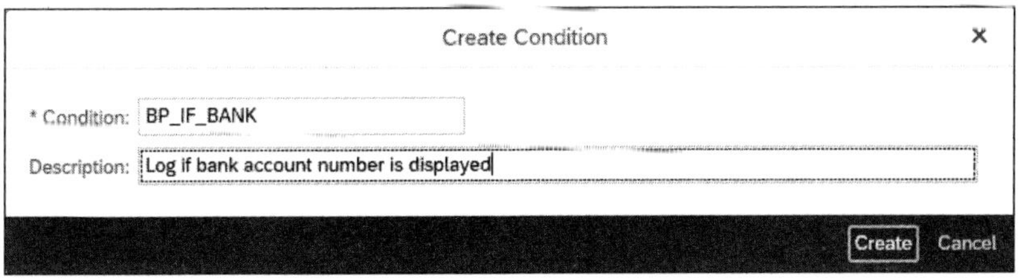

Figure 9.32 Create Conditions

The conditions will open in the new screen, where you need to click **Create**, enter the value for the expression as shown in Figure 9.33, and, finally, click **Create** to confirm.

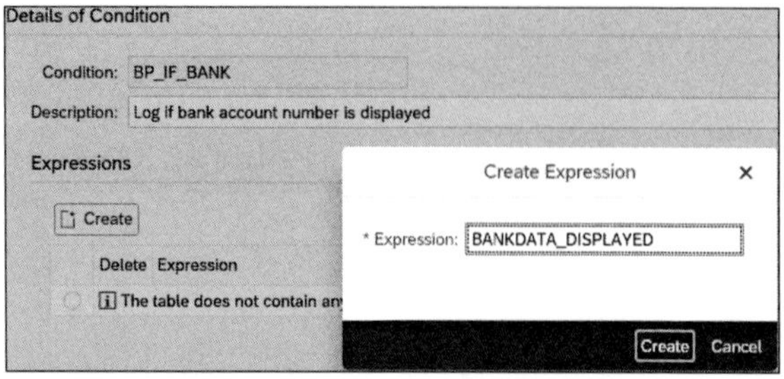

Figure 9.33 Create Expression of the Condition

We'll now drag the **Programs** tree to the right one more time. Again, all fields are shown (see Figure 9.34). However, we only need the fields containing the bank details. Consequently, we can remove the business partner via **Remove Line**.

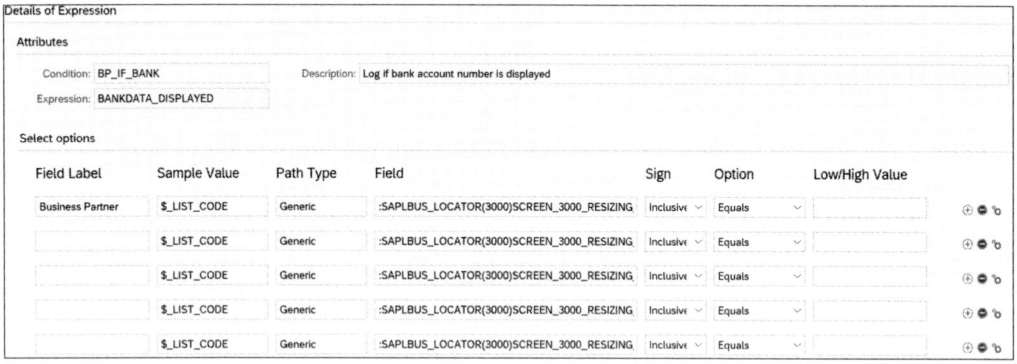

Figure 9.34 Fields for the Condition

Defining selection options

Our objective is to only log information when the bank account number is displayed. You can achieve this using the selection options shown in Figure 9.35.

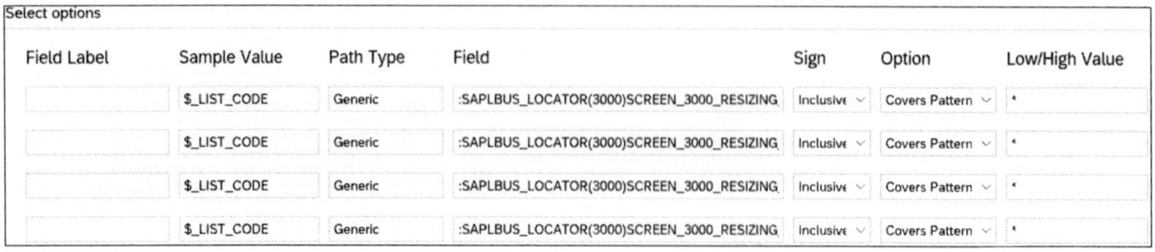

Figure 9.35 Defining Selection Options

You can then go back to the log group and deactivate the field **Without Condition** (see Figure 9.36).

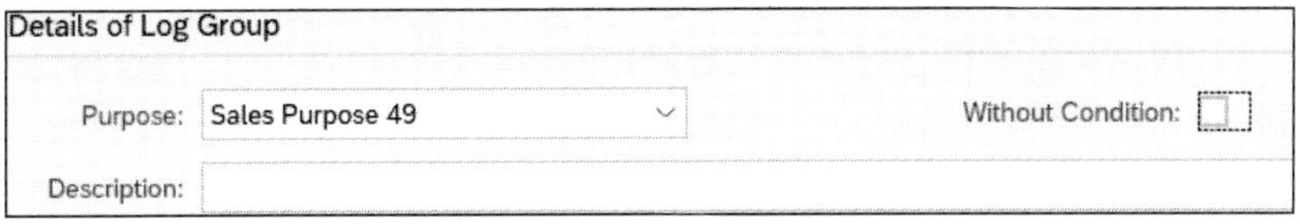

Figure 9.36 Allowing Conditions for the Log Group

Below the table of fields, a new area named **Assigned Conditions** will open. Click on **Assign Condition**, and select our previously created condition **BP_IF_BANK** from the dropdown list of the **Condition** field. You'll also have to activate the status. The result should look like Figure 9.37.

Figure 9.37 Activate Condition

Testing a new configuration with conditions

After activating the configuration, start Transaction BP (Edit Business Partner) again. Here, you should open the business partner as you've done previously, click the different tabs, and view the RAL. Instead of receiving a large number of entries like before, logging is only performed when the bank account number has been viewed (you'll also be able to see the business partner by whom it was viewed), as shown in Figure 9.38.

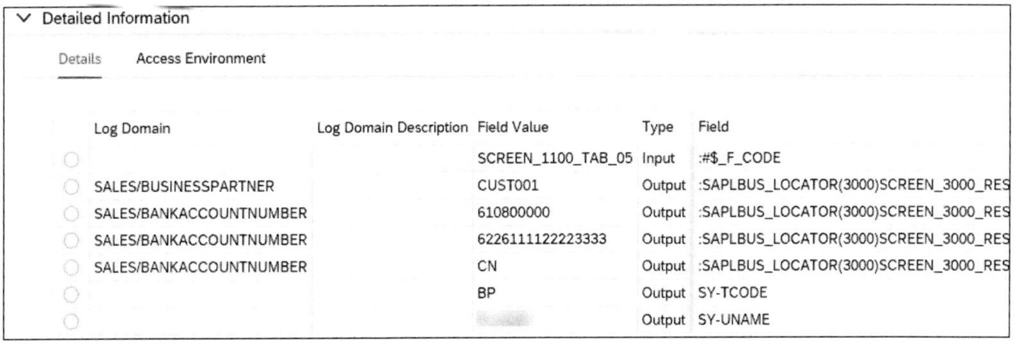

Figure 9.38 Log with Condition in the Configuration

Logging of fields without their value

We've now managed to significantly reduce the number of log entries.

You can still round out the entire functionality by changing the fields of the bank account number in the RAL configuration by setting the logging type to **Without Value**. In that case, you would create a log where you could see which user viewed a business partner's bank account number and at which point in time this occurred. You can't see the bank account number, but because this can be looked up in the change documents, you avoid an unnecessary replication of data. Searching for this bank account number is of course no longer easily possible in such a configuration.

9.9 Transport, Import, and Export

Transportation of generated RAL Customizing

RAL is configured in a Customizing client. To use this data in the productive system, it must be transported. To do so, you need to select your created purposes, log domains, and configurations in the respective screens, and click **Transport** via the **More** icon, where you then need to select a transport request. Following this, you can release it as usual.

You may have noticed that the list of information to be transported doesn't include the recordings. You don't have to take care of this because the recordings are automatically transported in conjunction with the respective configuration.

Importing and exporting RAL Customizing

In analogy to transporting, it's also possible to save entries in a local file via export, and then import this file into another system. Perhaps you would also like to save the current status to be able to return to this status whenever necessary.

9.10 Summary

In this chapter, you learned how you can use RAL to log the data that was displayed to a user. The data covered by this is something you yourself will need to define (although SAP partially delivers sample configurations).

You've also learned how to set this logging functionality up for the end users who work with the system, as well as which systems requested data from your system via system connections.

You've also seen that RAL provides in-depth logging to an extent that might require a check for compliance with legal regulations. We've also discussed which conditions can be linked to this logging procedure to limit the amount of data being logged.

Chapter 10
SAP Master Data Governance

By Reiko Enghardt and Christian Geiseler

Various sections of this book deal with data structures and how they can be set up for specific purposes. The thematic focus is therefore the purpose-related management of data.

10

The provision of high-quality master data is an important prerequisite for managing business processes in a transparent, efficient, and data-protection-compliant manner. This is explained, among other things, for data in general, in Chapter 1, Section 1.1.3. Master data is by its very nature a focus of data protection law because it may have to be kept for a long time. In the corresponding operational and analytical processes, master data is constantly referenced, so that deficiencies in these processes not only lead to a lack of purpose-orientation and to errors in these business processes or reports but also often to manual follow-up work and consequently lower efficiency. Corrections are often only made once for the purpose of successfully executing the transaction; however, the master records are neither corrected nor analyzed to determine why such errors could occur when master data is created.

Tracking processes

For numerous business, organizational, or regulatory requirements, it's becoming increasingly important to ensure transparency in business processes, data sets, and the movements thereof. This is supported in several ways for master data using SAP Master Data Governance (SAP MDG), which defines and documents precisely who carried out which creation/change and when during the centrally governed maintenance process. This can help prove who released a new SAP General Ledger (G/L) account for use for which fiscal month, when a change was made to a supplier's bank data, or who created or changed data records containing personal data for end users or contact persons. Proactively, this also means that it's exactly this kind of data access that can be controlled centrally via SAP MDG. In other words, it's not only retrospectively traceable, but from the very beginning, only very specific access requests are permitted for individual users or authorized roles.

Avoiding lack of quality

Proactivity is also at the forefront for data quality with SAP MDG. Process interruptions and subsequent corrections (if deliveries didn't arrive due to incorrect address data or if incorrect products or the same products were delivered several times and under different conditions due to duplicate material data) can be reduced using SAP MDG because high data quality is initially achieved by cleansing and deduplication and can also be maintained by the centrally controlled maintenance process with its quality mechanisms.

In this way, SAP MDG enables you to meet the high demands of a company-wide system landscape with regard to the accuracy of master data, transparency in its processing, and central control of data provisioning mechanisms.

In this chapter, we begin by explaining the scenarios for master data management and then finish by highlighting the importance of data quality assurance.

10.1 Master Data Maintenance Scenarios

There are two basic scenarios for managing master data: decentralized maintenance and centralized data maintenance.

Decentralized data maintenance

When maintaining data locally on several systems, there are usually no uniform standards for data model extensions, formats, numbering, or nomenclature, and often there is no transparency regarding which users or roles are involved in which steps of maintenance. Similarly, master data records are often stored redundantly in several systems, but they can't easily be identified as being the same due to the lack of standards. This lack of transparency also leads to problems relating to data protection law, and it's very likely that it will be difficult to obtain all of the information required. To provide central applications with a unified version of these nonstandardized and/or redundant data sets, mechanisms are needed that can convert the source data into a consolidated data set based on identified similarities/uniformity.

Central data maintenance

The second scenario involves centrally controlled data maintenance in which all users follow the same standards and rules to create or change master data. Group-wide or division-wide standards for the respective data models and extensions will need to be defined, including the following, for example:

- Rules for permitted field contents and checking them during maintenance
- Transparent maintenance processes that make it easy to track all changes that have been made

SAP MDG

SAP MDG is an SAP master data management application that supports both scenarios. In the first versions, SAP MDG was designed to support central governance (central workflow control, central and decentralized users); in later versions, support for the consolidation scenario was added. SAP MDG is a cross-domain application, which means that it uses the same application framework for different data domains (e.g., customer, vendor, and material) or financial master data (e.g., G/L account, cost center, or profit center). The respective data models in SAP MDG are based on the standard data models in SAP ERP and provide extensive coverage for the available fields and structures. We'll discuss the two scenarios in additional detail in the following sections.

10.1.1 SAP Master Data Governance Central Governance

Temporary storage: SAP MDG staging area

The basic idea behind the central governance scenario in SAP MDG is based on staging, so that any data records that have been partially maintained, checked, or approved are only stored and made visible in SAP MDG staging. They are only activated and distributed to the relevant target systems after all quality checks and all necessary approval steps have been successfully completed. This prevents incomplete, qualitatively inferior data records from being left behind in operative systems, where they either aren't used or trigger subsequent errors in operative processes when used.

SAP MDG maintenance process

The SAP MDG maintenance process is based on a basic sequence of requests using different approval levels, in which the required or permitted scope of data maintenance is offered at each stage and assigned to the respective roles. The number of participants can be structured in a very flexible manner and determined dynamically based on implementation using a set of rules. In this way, it's possible to map not only highly standardized simple maintenance processes but also very complex and dynamic maintenance processes. An example of a simple, two-step workflow for a request for a new and approved cost center with attribute maintenance is shown in Figure 10.1.

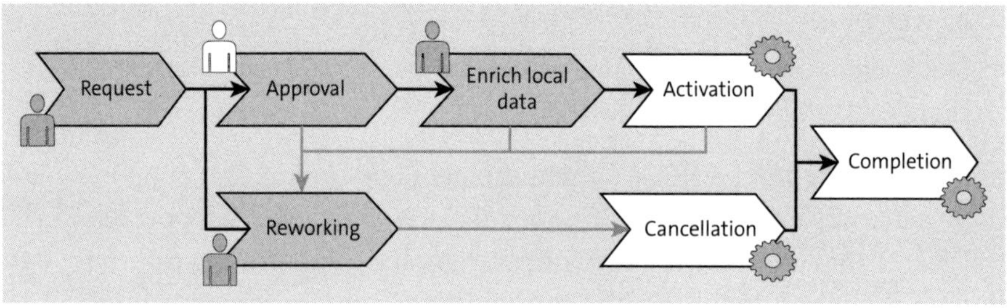

Figure 10.1 Simple Process for Adjusting Cost Centers

An example of a more complex workflow is a request for a new material of the type "Merchandise" with a data specialist enriching the basic data and with the approval of product management. Material master data for SAP ERP Sales and Distribution (SD) and its release takes place in parallel to the process parts for purchasing data with the check and maintenance of material requirements planning (MRP) data and valuation data. The final approval by the central product management completes the processing procedure, which is managed by the SAP MDG system on the basis of rules. Activating the data and then distributing it allows for consistent data storage in all receiver systems. Figure 10.2 shows a simplified representation of the process.

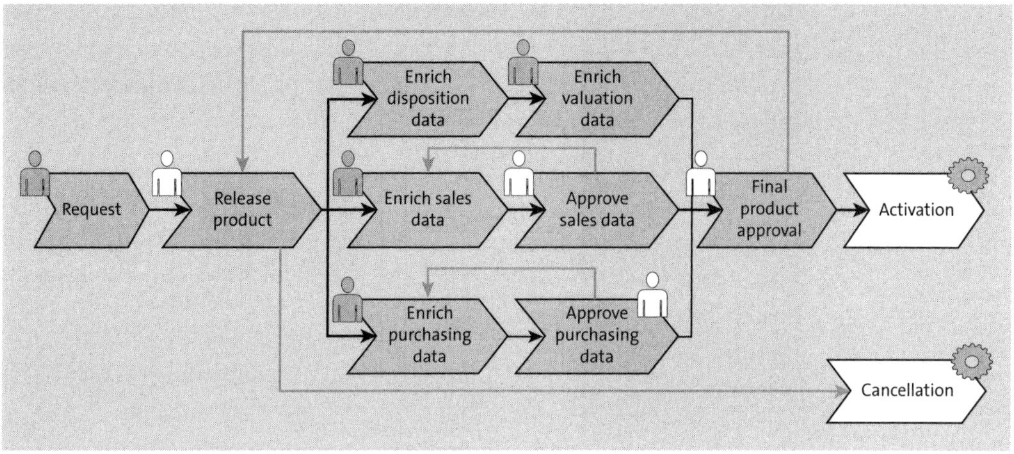

Figure 10.2 Material Creation Request Process

Ensuring the quality of data

Validation mechanisms at every step ensure that the only content which meets the predefined and internal quality requirements is stored in the data set and later duplicated in the operational systems. These mechanisms also offer the possibility of automatically supplementing your own data via third-party provider data, for example, address data obtained from postal data offerings.

After final approval or completion, the newly created or changed data records are automatically distributed to the respective target systems using a standardized data replication mechanism. This process can be controlled by workflow or by scheduled reports. Manual replication is also supported by the distribution mechanisms available in SAP ERP (e.g., Application Link Enabling [ALE]/IDoc, web services, remote function call [RFC], or file transfer) and enables data distribution to both SAP and non-SAP systems.

10.1.2 SAP Master Data Governance Consolidation

Data import into the SAP MDG import area

SAP MDG consolidation is based on a process model that starts when data is imported from various source systems into the SAP MDG import area. In addition to maintaining vendors, customers, and business partners, it also allows you to edit material master data. The use of consolidation for custom-built master data objects is also supported. SAP MDG consolidation is used to harmonize data from different source systems with the SAP MDG data set. Depending on the type of master data, slightly different processes may be used. We'll restrict this presentation to business partners that may include customers and suppliers, as these are of particular importance in the context of data protection.

The process flow chart shown in Figure 10.3 outlines a standardized process flow of a consolidation process for business partners, which is often only marginally deviated from in practice. The option of guaranteeing a segregation of duty (SoD) in various critical phases makes it possible to set up data-protection-compliant processes.

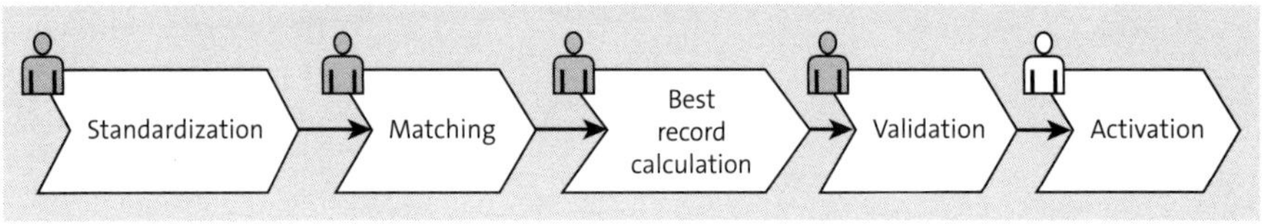

Figure 10.3 Consolidation Process for Business Partners

For the corresponding Customizing for this consolidation process, see Figure 10.4.

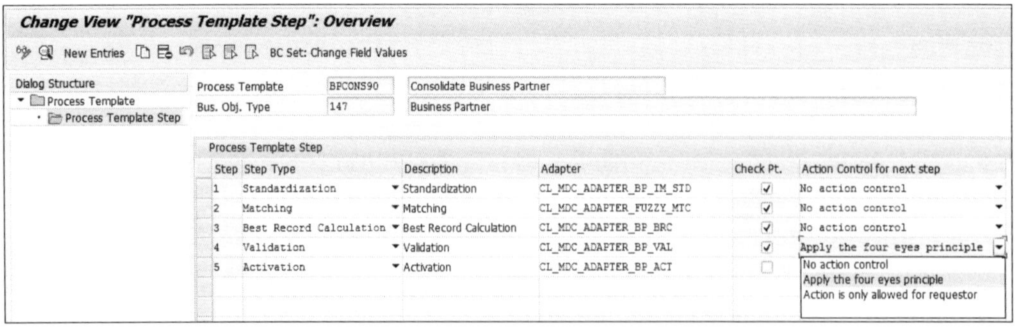

Figure 10.4 Customizing the Consolidation Process for Business Partners

SAP MDG is the first step in consolidation to standardize the data. This is where the transferred data is prepared for optimal comparability.

Avoiding redundancy

The next step is to use an error-tolerant search algorithm to compare each data record with the other data records and check for similarities. Any similarity here will contribute to a match score based on a set of rules for the weighting, which ultimately provides an indication of the similarity for each comparison. The aim is to determine and merge all data records that have been identified as being identical. If the match score is very high, this can be done automatically. If the score is high but insufficient, it can be assessed manually and corrected where necessary. In this type of processing step, it's also possible, for example, to extract data records into other processes for further processing.

Consolidating best record

Based on these matching results—and, if necessary, manual intervention—the data records from each group that were identified as being the same are then merged into one best record. A further set of rules can be used to control which content should be adopted in the event of competition. This is necessary if the source data contains different information for the same attribute. The authorized user also has the option of starting process steps with different settings and repeating them whenever necessary to improve data quality results.

Transparency at every step

Actions of this kind are logged and can be read in detail in the auditing log, as shown in Figure 10.5.

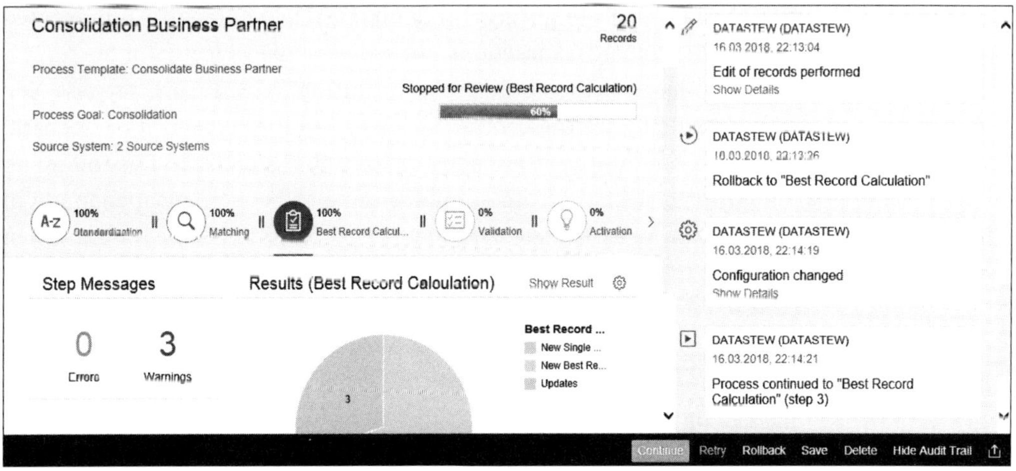

Figure 10.5 Auditing in the Business Partner Consolidation Process

Validate and activate

The consolidated data is then checked (validated) for completeness and correctness by SAP MDG to ensure that the new best records meet the expected quality requirements. An optional workflow step for enrichment or approval can also be included during this step, which also enables incorrect data records to be removed. After the final check, the consolidated data records are activated directly from consolidation or transferred to central governance via an SAP MDG change request and thus made available to the subsequent central governance processes. If necessary, further postprocessing and a repeated or alternative mass approval can be carried out in these processes.

10.1.3 Combining Scenarios

Both of the scenarios described previously are often combined as developments in a group-wide master data management system, as discussed in the previous section. Defining and introducing central sets of rules also requires a great deal of organizational preparation. This means that the use of consolidation can initially ensure that an adjusted and duplicate-free master data set is available for a scheduled period to, for example, clearly support a central finance or reporting scenario.

Activating central maintenance

As soon as the centrally controlled maintenance process (central governance) can be applied in the company, this scenario is activated in SAP MDG—additionally requiring that decentralized maintenance is prevented in SAP ERP standard transactions. Further data maintenance for the respective data objects is then only performed using the SAP MDG process. You can continue to use the central data set from the consolidation scenario because it has already been adjusted to central standards. Depending on the business scenario, both scenarios can also be used independently of one another, for example, for different data objects or business areas. When using the central maintenance scenario, a new source system may also be connected via the consolidation process at any time, so that, for example, following a company acquisition, the new data can be consolidated with the existing data so that the same customers, suppliers, or products can be merged or new data records can also be made available centrally and in a timely manner.

10.2 Maintaining Sensitive Data

Worth protecting: employee data

SAP MDG also supports the processing of objects requiring special protection, such as employee data. Employees with travel activities are often required as vendors in the SAP ERP system to reimburse travel expenses and other expenses. These are processed as business partners with SAP

MDG in the same way as other vendors. The need for authorization-based separation—for example, via the vendor account groups—can be ensured with SAP MDG in both central governance and consolidation.

Self-services

The extent to which release is required for employee data processes must be clarified in the requirements analysis. For example, if the employee maintains his bank data and/or address data using self-services, an additional approval may not be necessary if the data is validated with appropriate methods. This can be done, for example, by means of the IBAN check, which practically prevents the entry of incorrect bank data. Address data can also be checked, as explained in Section 10.4.

SAP MDG also allows processes, in particular those involving sensitive data, to display only the data that is absolutely necessary and to, for example, hide sensitive data. This is illustrated in Figure 10.6 and Figure 10.7, which show an example of the requester's view and the approver's view, respectively.

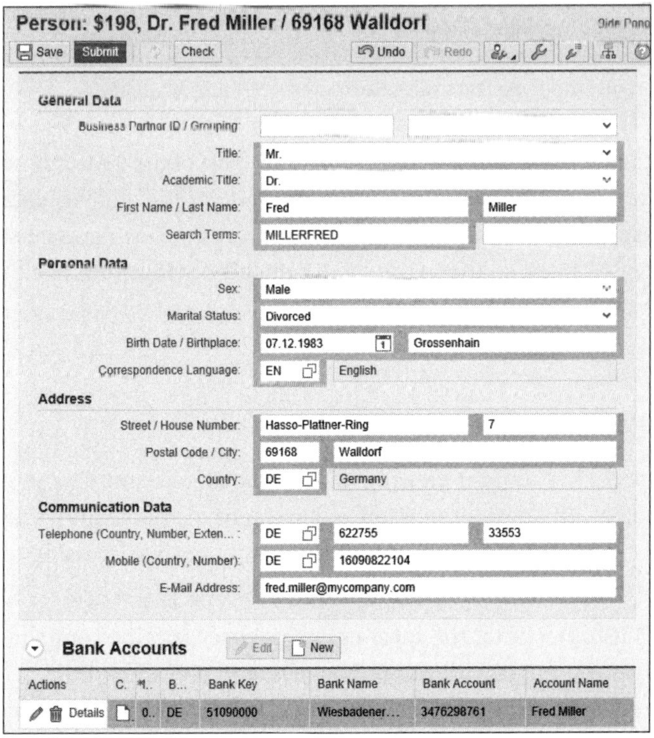

Figure 10.6 Requesting Changes to Employee Data

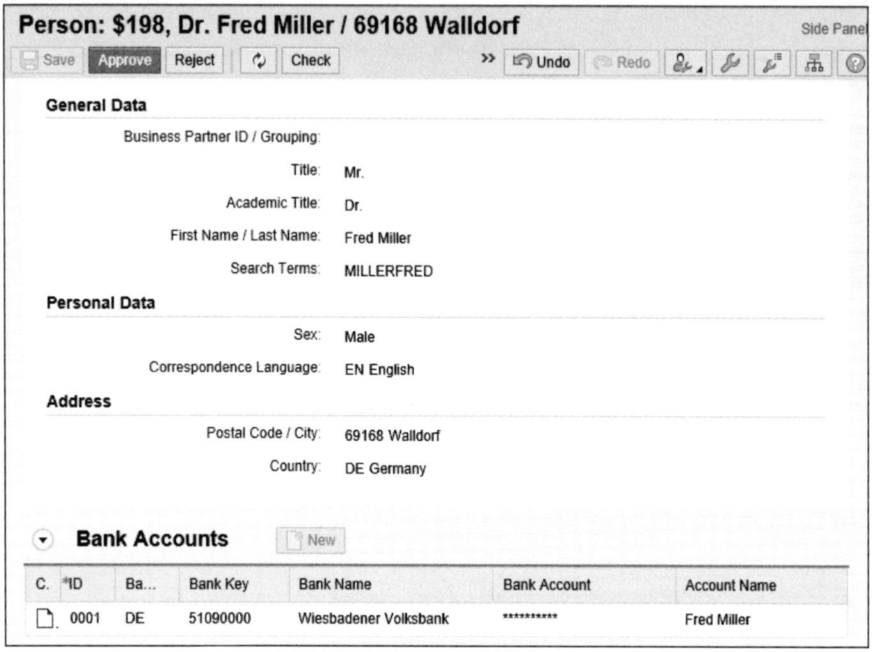

Figure 10.7 Approve Employee Data with Restricted Attribute Visibility

Hide sensitive data The approver can't change the data and can only see part of the data that he needs for the verification. The marital status, birth data, and address data either aren't displayed or are only displayed incompletely. Bank data is displayed in encrypted form, so that although it remains obvious that one or several bank details exist, details worthy of protection aren't visible.

10.3 Organizational Separation

SAP MDG is the central tool for viewing and editing all relevant data in a master data object. The data protection requirement also demands that organizational separations be made and that comprehensive accessing of clearly locally assigned data stocks be prevented.

In the case of customer data, the local organizational data for company codes, sales organizations, distribution channels, and divisions shouldn't be visible to process participants who don't belong to these organizations.

Authorization control in SAP MDG master data

SAP MDG enables this using the standard means of authorization control on the master data objects themselves, which remain active and valid without needing additional configuration. The following measures allow the necessary differentiation of access:

- No access
- Creating the data
- Changing the data
- Displaying the data
- Change blocking indicator
- Edit deletion indicator

Suppression of authorization control

For certain request processes, it may be useful to suppress this authorization control if, for example, a new customer needs to be created centrally for many organizations at the initial request stage. However, if the scheduled requester isn't allowed to regularly maintain any of the organizational data, the subsequent efficient parallelization of local enhancement activities in the process can only be considerably simplified if the authorization check is first deactivated. If this isn't done, separate requests have to be created for each organization or alternative methods have to be implemented. The function for initially deactivating the authorizations is shown in Figure 10.8.

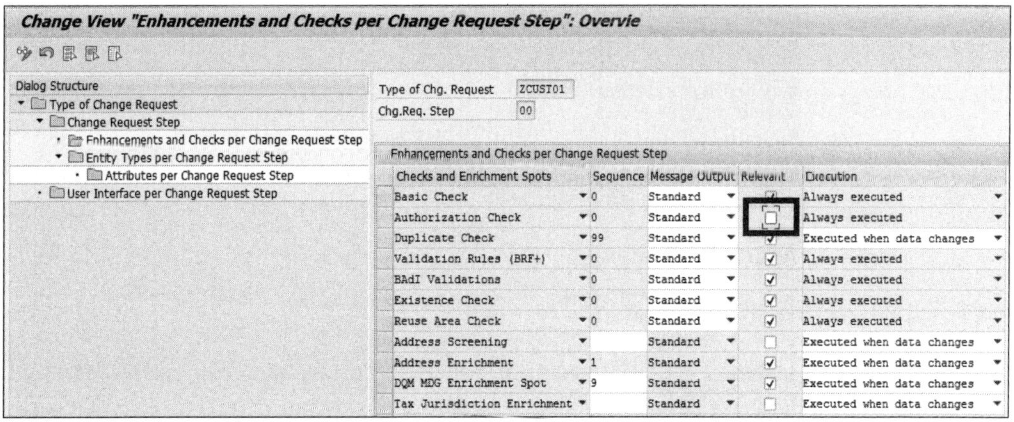

Figure 10.8 Settings for Deactivating the Authorization Check for One Change Request Step

The corresponding **Relevant** indicator is deactivated for the step **00** (Request) in process **ZCUST1** (Request New Customer).

In such cases, it should be ensured that the requester can only provide the absolutely necessary information and that the required enhancement is carried out by authorized users at a later stage.

10.4 Data Quality Assurance Using Services

Data quality assurance options

One of the core tasks of SAP MDG is to ensure adequate data quality. In addition to the subsequent use of SAP ERP standard Customizing (e.g., input help and validity checks), other methods may be used. The options provided by the Business Rules Framework (BRF), which enables SAP MDG-specific configuration of derivations (preassignment of fields under specified conditions) and validations (checks under specified conditions), are regularly used in SAP MDG projects. Other options include the integration of customer-specific coding and the integration of external services—often in combination.

10.4.1 Key Services

A number of external services are also available for different use cases. The services regularly used in many projects are as follows:

- Address validation
- Duplicate detection
- Sanction party list screening/business partner screening
- Enrichment against public data directories

Address Validation

The address validation service is also used, for example, to support the standardization steps described in Section 10.1.2. Such services can be installed and operated on internal systems as well as integrated as cloud-based services. They enable the address to be standardized, making it easier to compare different spellings, for example, for street ("Street," "St," "St.").

In addition, these services enable a comparison of the specified address with a public data directory. This results in a high-quality address entry, as missing or incorrect data is supplemented, corrected, or renewed, and at the same time, compared. Figure 10.9 shows this kind of integration in the SAP MDG application for vendors.

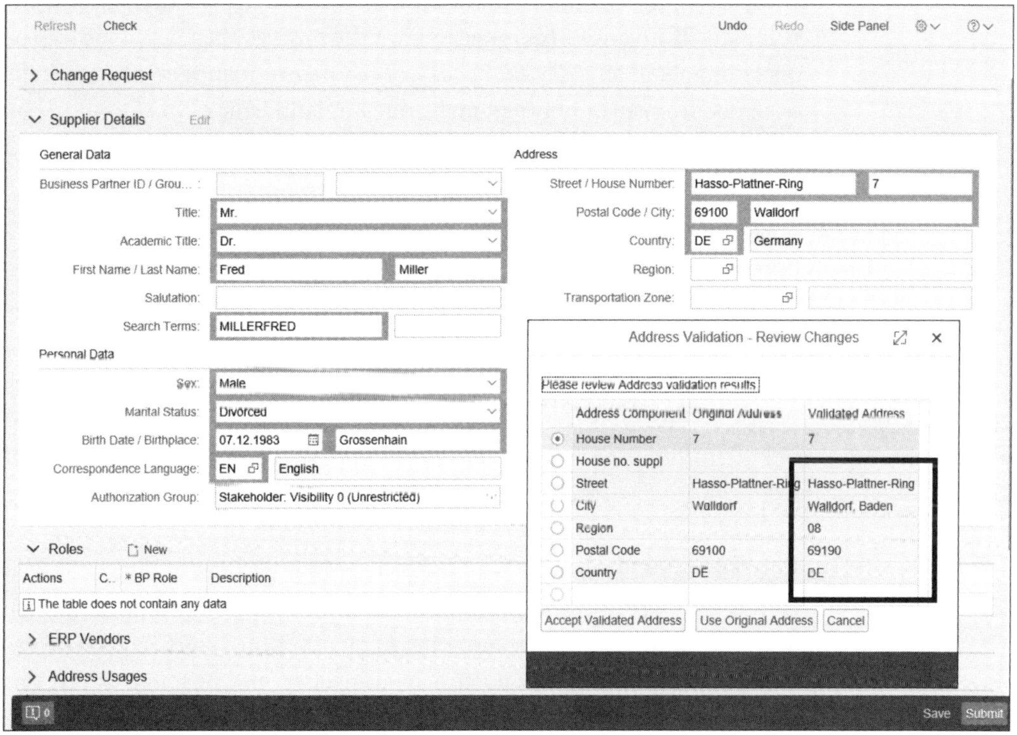

Figure 10.9 Address Validation within an SAP MDG Change Request Step

Duplicate Detection

The use of such address validation mechanisms is also an important prerequisite for improved identification of duplicates for business partners, customers, and suppliers. One of the goals of central governance is to avoid such duplicate entries in the master data, which lead to the problems described in Section 10.1.1 in transactional processes.

Screening

Another important service is sanction party list screening, which can also be integrated into the SAP MDG application. It allows you to prevent business relationships with potential candidates shared on sanction party lists at an early stage because potential candidates can be restricted to vendors and customers within the framework of master data maintenance in the company in advance. This is necessary if the business partners appear to be questionable in any way or, by way of regulatory requirements, are to be excluded from all or only certain business relationships.

Various sources can be used for the sanction party list screening. These may be external sources (e.g., legislatures, the European Union, supranational organizations, or the security authorities of one or more countries). In addition to the sources mentioned, internal instructions (management decisions or decisions made by affiliated companies or partners) must often be observed. It should be noted that sanctions against business partners may be time-related and/or of a geographical nature and that the restriction may therefore not be globally or permanently applicable. SAP MDG enables the involvement of suitable specialists in the request processes for master data.

Data Enrichment

Dun & Bradstreet is one of the best-known providers of data enrichment services. These services are also offered by other providers. OneKey IQVIA (formerly IMS Health) for doctors, pharmacists, and hospitals is just one example. The quality and reliability of such services should be reviewed before use. Their core functionality often lies in verifying the specified data with a central public database. In most cases, their identification numbers are also stored in SAP MDG to enable quicker detection. This helps improve the quality of your own data repository for a fee, without having to invest in manual processing yourself. Such services can be integrated into the system landscape using the enhancement features provided by SAP MDG.

10.4.2 Proxy Provider

Proxy provider for services

There are services that act as a proxy, tunneling the requests to the actual provider, for example, to conceal a member's customer/supplier contacts from the external provider. At the same time, the members of the association can inform each other about concerns regarding individual specific business partners. This may also be questionable in terms of data protection compliance and needs to be taken into account when making a sustainable decision.

[!]

Risks with External Services

From a data protection perspective, it should be noted that the use of all the external providers' options described in this chapter may pose a risk. With regard to traceability and observability, it may be possible, under certain circumstances, for service providers to draw conclusions about their own business activities.

Each call to external services may send sensitive information about existing or potential new business partners to external third-party sources for data verification. This may be a potential gateway for competitors or other malicious third parties. We want to expressly point out that the use of such services also falls under the necessity of the relevant data protection legitimation.

10.5 Summary

As described in Chapter 5, among others, all personal data must be kept in a clear form for the purposes for which they are collected. This is necessary to fulfill authorizations, simplified blocking and deletion, and information and other transparency obligations.

Duplicate data or data with missing or incorrect purpose attributes can cause considerable difficulties in terms of data protection obligations, including the actual impossibility of achieving and proving data protection compliance.

Personal data must be correct, up-to-date, and attributed to a specific purpose, which calls for an adequate central management. SAP MDG helps fulfill these requirements.

Chapter 11
SAP Test Data Migration Server

By Dr. Boris Hoffarth

SAP Test Data Migration Server (SAP TDMS) was initially developed to minimize the use of hardware. Today, it's used to minimize data in accordance with current data protection guidelines. This chapter will show you the options available for achieving this.

An essential requirement of data protection is that personal data may only be used and stored for the intended purpose. Consequently, personal data may not be located on test, training, or other nonproductive systems. A simple system copy—as used up to now—therefore isn't permitted. However, after sensitive data has been made anonymous, it's no longer considered to be personal data (General Data Protection Regulation [GDPR], Art. 4, Rec. 26). As complete anonymization is difficult to achieve, we recommend pseudonymization be used as an alternative means of complying with data protection obligations (Art. 4, Rec. 28 GDPR).

In Chapter 1, Section 1.1.12, under the sections about anonymization and pseudonymization, we commented in detail on the problems of depersonalization.

SAP Test Data Migration Server (SAP TDMS) is an SAP product originally developed for SAP ERP systems to reduce the volume of test systems. It's based on project and development experience from SAP's System Landscape Optimization department, which specializes in system-wide migrations. Although it's not SAP S/4HANA-ready at this time, the scope of SAP TDMS has extended beyond SAP ERP. Its functionality has also gone beyond the creation of simple test data.

Real data for test systems

Even today, one of the main application areas of SAP TDMS is the efficient provisioning of clients from productive data for testing, training, or development. In addition, central client administration and, in particular, the use of SAP TDMS for pseudonymization or anonymization, have been added.

Scrambling as a technically neutral term

In this chapter, we'll focus mainly on the technology. Whether or not changes made to the data also take the various data protection requirements into account depends on the individual case. This is why we won't use the terms anonymization or pseudonymization here, but instead, the neutral expression *scrambling*.

In addition to the fields of application, this chapter also describes the structure and functions of SAP TDMS. In Section 11.3, you'll learn how SAP TDMS can be integrated into a more extensive system landscape and what functions are available. Section 11.4 deals specifically with the use of SAP TDMS for data protection.

[»]

Complete Documentation

For the purpose of complete documentation, reference is also made to existing SAP TDMS manuals (which can be found centrally under *http://support.sap.com/tdms*).

Here, the focus is on the standard cases, which also form the basis for scrambling systems or filling them with scrambled data.

11.1 Use Cases

This section describes the most important use cases for SAP TDMS. We won't discuss special cases any further at this point, although some are already included in the SAP TDMS delivery. However, there are still many other individual customer-related cases that can be derived from the general concept as described in Section 11.2.

11.1.1 Setting Up Test Clients

First delete the client and then fill selectively

The basic scenario of SAP TDMS is to create a test client from the productive client or from a copy that comes close to the production. The target client is initially deleted and then filled again with the data records from the source.

During this process, transactional data—but only the most recent data (e.g., three months)—is included.

A special feature is that system-specific entries remain unaffected by this procedure. In this way, test system user data remains unchanged and isn't overwritten by the production data during migration. This applies in particular to the authorization settings, too.

11.1.2 Setting Up Clients for Training

Training clients can be set up with SAP TDMS in the same way as test clients. It's often necessary to repeatedly make such a client available and in an identical manner.

Training systems with several clients

Because such a client is much smaller than a system copy, it's possible to create several clients in the training system. One client serves as a training master, which you then copy within the system to one or more training clients. Due to the small size of the client, you can copy the data using system tools. Alternatively, you can also use SAP TDMS for these client refreshes. You also have the option of temporarily storing all of the data in files. This eliminates the selection for the new provision of clients, and the client is provided identically each time.

11.1.3 Setting Up Clients for Development

There is hardly any production-related test data in a development system. SAP TDMS can be used to provide an additional client that includes realistic test data. The existing development environment remains unchanged, and, at the same time, you can test all program changes almost in the same way as in production.

11.1.4 Alternating Test Clients

Testing without system reset interruptions

Organizational problems often arise when it comes to finding a time window in which you can reset a test system and update it with current data from the productive system. SAP TDMS allows you to update two clients alternately (see Figure 11.1). Even if you've already determined a new client to be the official test client, long-running processes can still be completed in the old client without time pressure. In Figure 11.1, the new test client in current use is client **200**, which replaces client **100**. There is also no time pressure for setting up the test clients themselves.

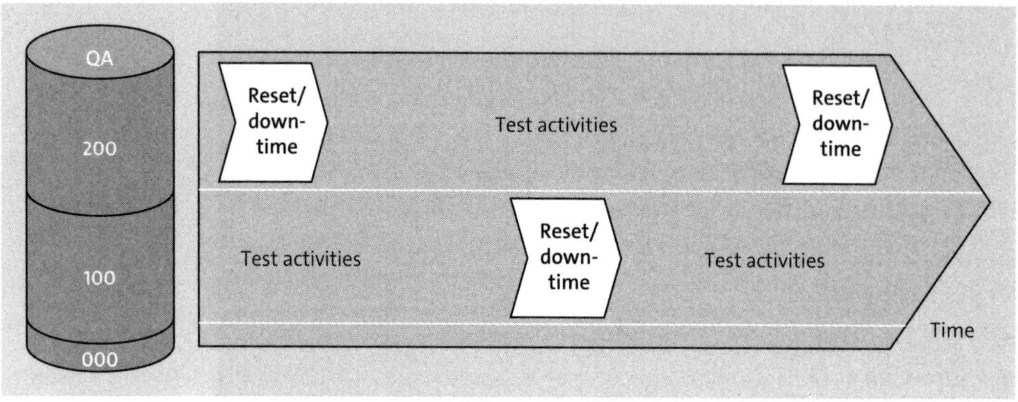

Figure 11.1 Alternating Test Clients

11.1.5 Transfer of Selected Test Cases

Object-oriented approach

In some cases, it's sufficient to transfer individual test cases, for which SAP TDMS offers the option of migrating individual objects under the name *Business Process Library* (BPL). SAP ships objects for various types of master data and for related processes.

11.1.6 Conversion and System Scrambling

When setting up a new client after a system copy, you'll have to adjust the logical system names in various tables, including larger ones. This conversion is also known by Basis administrators as a *BDLS run* (in reference to Transaction BDLS).

You can also perform this conversion in parallel with SAP TDMS. In doing so, your hardware is used to the greatest extent.

Scrambling, which you set up via a separate interface, works very similarly. You can find further information about this in Section 11.2.6.

11.1.7 Standard Range of Functionalities

The various SAP TDMS options mentioned previously and their availability in various SAP applications are shown in Table 11.1.

SAP TDMS options

In addition, there are also other special options for some applications, such as migrations per object for SAP ERP Human Capital Management (SAP ERP HCM) and several industry solutions which we won't address in further detail.

SAP TDMS Option	SAP Application
Client copy with time-based reduction	SAP ERP, SAP Business Warehouse (SAP BW), SAP Customer Relationship Management (SAP CRM), SAP Supply Chain Management (SAP SCM), SAP Supplier Relationship Management (SAP SRM), SAP for Oil & Gas (SAP IS-OIL)
Client copy with time based and company code reduction	SAP ERP
Client copy without transactional data	SAP ERP, SAP CRM
Entire client copy	SAP ERP, SAP CRM, SAP SCM, SAP SRM, SAP Global Trade Services (GTS)
Data import through temporarily stored files	SAP ERP, SAP ERP HCM, SAP BW, SAP CRM, SAP SCM, SAP SRM
Ready-made BPL objects	SAP ERP
Standalone scrambling without migration	SAP ERP, SAP ERP HCM, SAP CRM, SAP SRM

Table 11.1 Availability of SAP TDMS Options

11.2 Structure and Functionality

SAP TDMS consists of the following components:

Components

- User interface (UI)
- Process control

- Migration Workbench (MWB) for data records
- MWB for objects
- Conversion Workbench (CWB)
- Scrambling control

These components are described in further detail in the following subsections. Special elements such as the Process Execution Monitor won't be dealt with here.

11.2.1 User Interface

You can access the initial screen for working with SAP TDMS using Transaction TDMS (SAP TDMS Control Center). This will take you to the SAP TDMS **Portfolio** UI (see Figure 11.2).

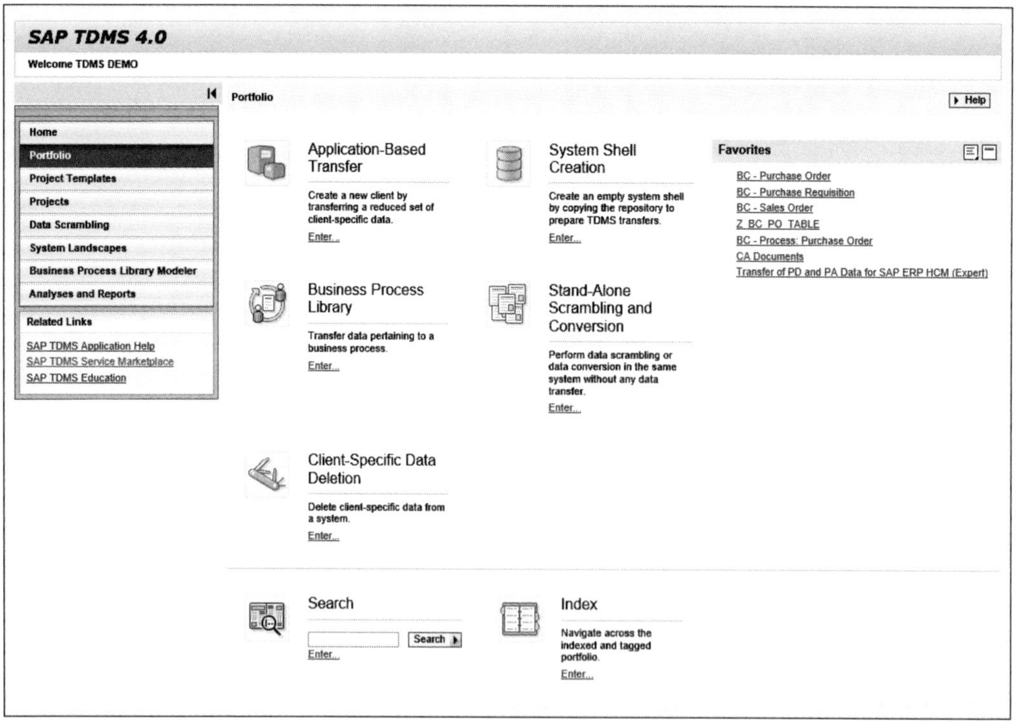

Figure 11.2 SAP TDMS Portfolio UI

From here, you can access various areas of SAP TDMS. You can select and create the previously mentioned scenarios using a guided process control.

The client copies are application-specific and can be selected under **Application-Based Transfer** (see Figure 11.3).

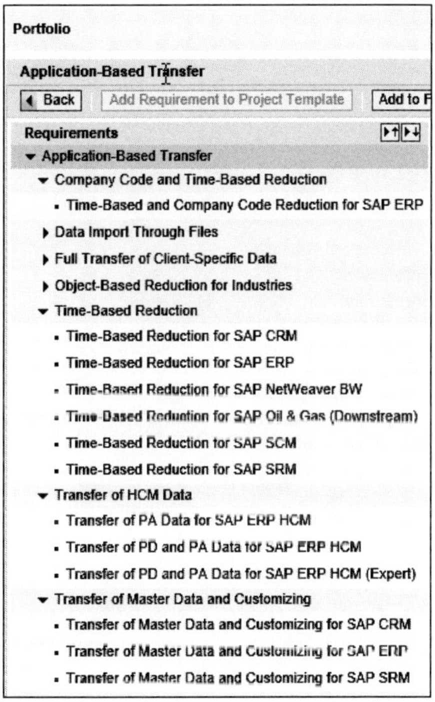

Figure 11.3 Application-Based Transfer

When you select such a transfer, an SAP TDMS package is created internally. All SAP TDMS activities and information are then held together under a package ID.

11.2.2 Process Control

Using the *Process Control Layer (PCL)*, all steps belonging to a package are executed in a controlled sequence or—if permitted—in parallel.

As you can see in Figure 11.4, the status of the individual steps of a package and the associated details and logs are also provided. When processing in parallel, details can also be displayed from here.

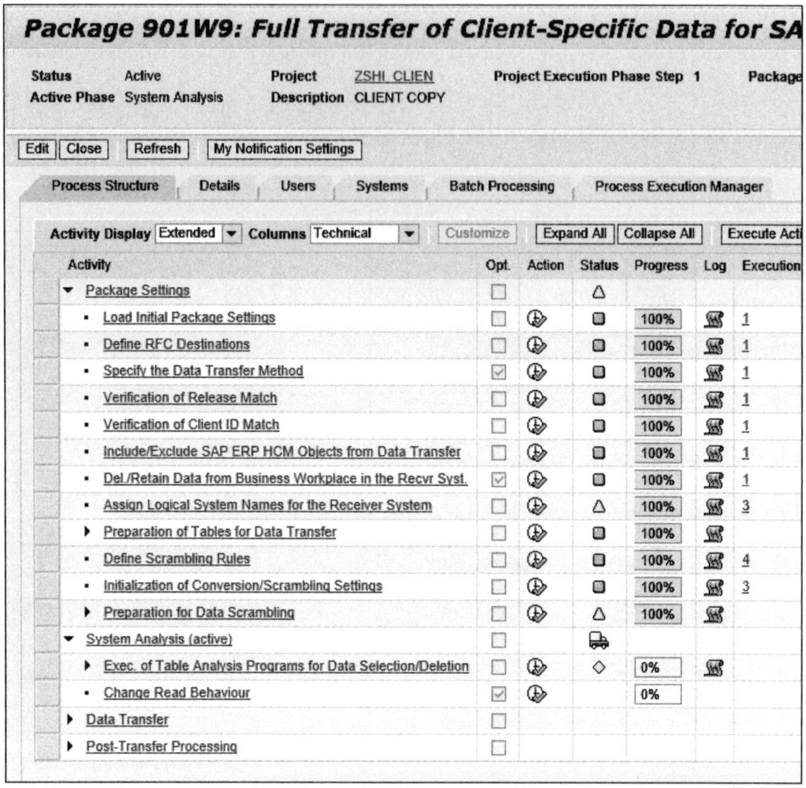

Figure 11.4 Process Control

11.2.3 Migration Workbench for Data Records

The *Migration Workbench (MWB)* for data records is used to read data records selectively from a source system, transfer them to the target system, and save them to the target system. With this machine, new clients can be completely populated with data after their deletion so that they can be used directly.

One common additional requirement is to achieve the highest possible level of performance because large systems in particular require test systems of a reduced size. Another important auxiliary requirement is consistency. Errors found in a test system should point to problems in the original system and not to shortcomings in the test system landscape.

Architecture of the migration procedure

Migration consists of reading the data records on the source system, controlling them via the control system, transferring them by the central system, and saving them in the target system. Both the control system and the central system have remote function call (RFC) connections to the source and target systems. The number of connected systems is unlimited (see Figure 11.5).

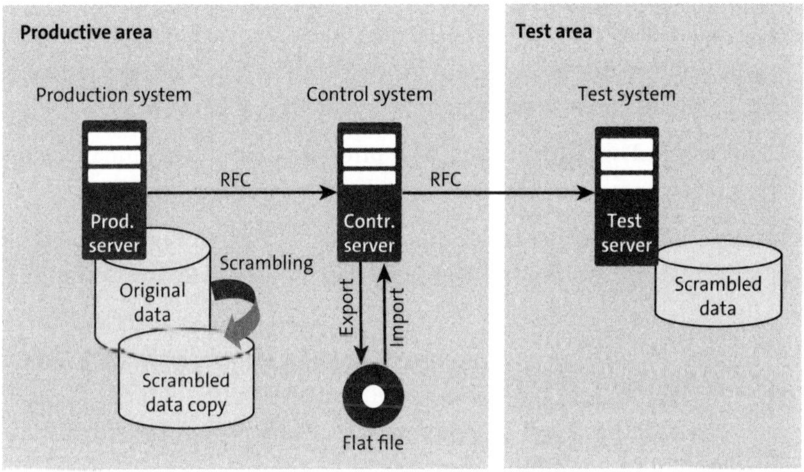

Figure 11.5 Architecture (Dr. Boris Hoffarth, 2018)

Separate routines are generated for reading and writing for each table, thus ensuring that any differences in the structures between the two systems can also be managed. This architecture also enables the migration of different installations—such as Unicode/non-Unicode, on-premise system/cloud, or any standard database/SAP HANA—as long as the versions released are compatible.

Selection procedures

To create a new target client, the MWB only ever selects data records from one client. This only takes client-specific tables into account. In addition, tables that aren't typically required for test systems, such as temporary data, logs, or change documents, aren't selected.

Selection is determined by the chosen scenario. There are four scenarios to choose from:

- Selection based on time
- Selection based on company code

- Complete transfer
- Special case of object-based selection

Regardless of the chosen scenario, all Customizing data and all master data is always selected. Because the volume of this data is typically less than 10%, this method has paid off.

The time-based variant selects the transactional data that is valid after a selected date. For reasons of consistency, in certain constellations, dependent documents that lie further in the past are also read. The typical goal is, for example, to create a test system with data from the past three months.

Selection based on the company code directly reduces the company code-dependent transactional data to the selected company codes.

During a full transfer, all tables that are regarded as relevant and all their data records are selected. As described earlier, user data, for example, is excluded.

In the area of *industry solutions* (e.g., IS Utilities, IS Banking, and IS Retail), these procedures can't always be used effectively. For this purpose, a hierarchical selection has been programmed in certain areas. This special case won't be discussed further at this point.

The selection results are either stored in the form of the relevant keys or intervals, or the completely imported data records are compressed in a cluster and stored in the same system.

Transfer procedure

The data records are transferred via *RFC interfaces*. This ensures that the data is transferred to the relevant database in the correct format. A Unicode conversion, if required, is integrated here, for example.

The transfer takes place table-wise, in small blocks that are managed individually. This allows for improved parallelization and, in case of errors, restarting at the beginning of a block so that the entire table doesn't have to be transferred again.

Writing procedure

When writing the data records, you can control the writing behavior for each table. In the standard system, the data is inserted in blocks without overwriting it. You can, however, also specify that the data is to be migrated record by record and overwritten. This setting is often selected after an error has occurred.

An SAP TDMS run reads and writes 20%–30% of all data records in a system in the typical time-based scenario. If you want to execute such a run within a reasonable time, you generate a high load for the systems and databases involved. This applies equally to large systems as it does to small systems because the hardware equipment is usually also adapted to the system sizes. SAP TDMS accordingly offers various options for optimizing performance.

At the table level, you may choose between writing single records or blocks. The standard procedure is to start writing in blocks and only switch to single-record processing if problems occur.

Performance

To optimize performance, you can specify how many parallel processes SAP TDMS can use on each system. In particular, the load on a productive source system can be limited so that the running operation is only impaired to an acceptable extent.

Consideration in the magic square

You must consider the following factors in the settings:

- Total runtime
- Impairment of the running operation
- Efforts for one run
- Consistency of the system to be made available

[!]

Runtime versus Data Quality

For consistency, it's advisable to lock production for the duration of the run or ensure that a system copy is available. Otherwise, inconsistencies may occur because tables are migrated regardless of running processes. It's also advisable to fix the data immediately during selection by directly buffering the data at the source.

To reduce the overall runtime, however, start writing to the target as early as possible because this particular process takes the longest; this is possible due to block processing.

11.2.4 Migration Workbench for Objects

As an alternative to table-oriented transfer, you have the option of migrating single data records and their associated data records for a specific object (see Section 1Section 11.1.5). Ready-made objects can be selected for migration directly from the portfolio entry page under **Business Process Library** (see Figure 11.6). In addition to a range of typical master data and transactional data, we also offer compilations of data for entire process chains.

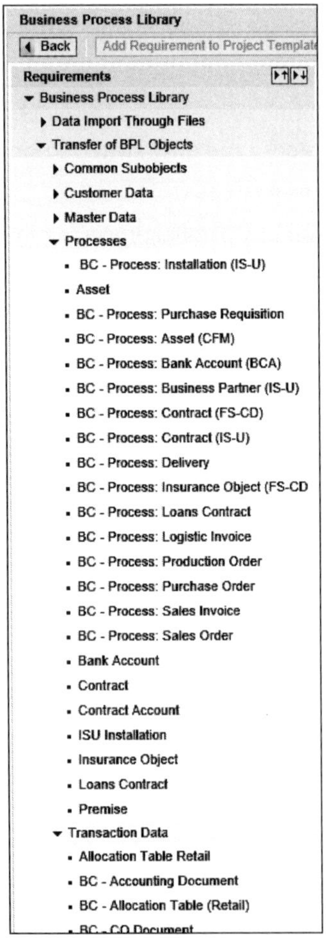

Figure 11.6 BPL Objects

The corresponding tables for all these objects are stored together with the necessary links. As a matter of course, these table links can only be made for the SAP standard version. You can use the *Business Process Library Modeler* (BPL Modeler) to adapt the linked selection to your installation, which may also include additional tables (see Figure 11.7).

Figure 11.7 BPL Modeler

The BPL Modeler allows you to add your own tables to the objects provided. You don't need to specify your own additional argument fields. SAP TDMS processes them automatically.

11.2.5 Conversion Workbench

The *Conversion Workbench* (CWB) is able to convert data performantly in parallel within a system. The conversion can take place in two different ways: either the data is changed directly in the system (standalone), or the data selected and buffered in a cluster (Section 11.2.3) is changed there before actual migration. **CWB**

For each system structure from a different system, you need to adjust at least the logical system names. The list of system names will be suggested, allowing you to assign the original names of the production data to those of the test landscape (see Figure 11.8).

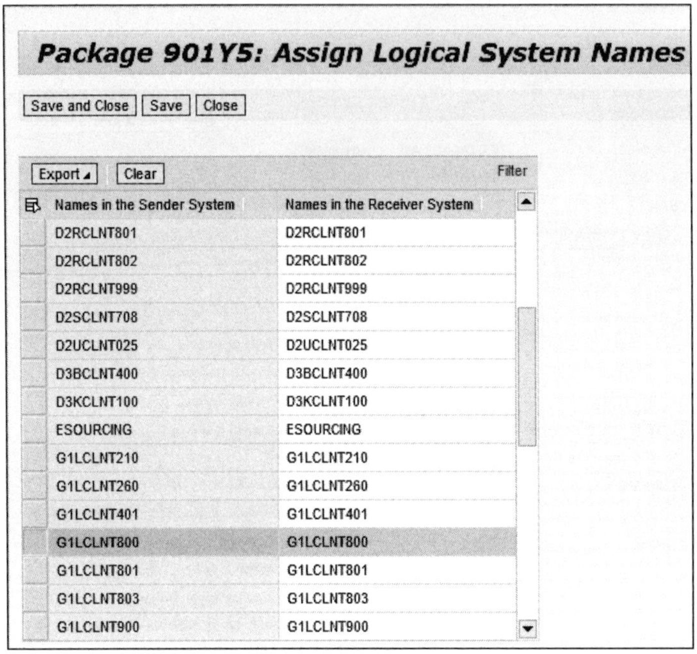

Figure 11.8 Scrambling of Logical System Names

11.2.6 Scrambling Control

Data scrambling

The *scrambling* of data is, technically speaking, also a conversion. It's also performed accordingly by the conversion machine described earlier. This means that you can also perform the scrambling here as part of a migration or simply on a system itself (standalone).

As a rule, simple assignment tables aren't sufficient for scrambling, so a separate interface is provided for this purpose. With the increasing importance of scrambling, this control system in particular is undergoing intensive further development. In the future, this may lead to possible deviations from the process presented.

To apply scrambling rules consistently to all field occurrences across different tables, they are stored in a hierarchical structure.

Within a solution category, such as **SAP_ERP**, these rules are combined into groups, which in turn are combined into supergroups (see Figure 11.9).

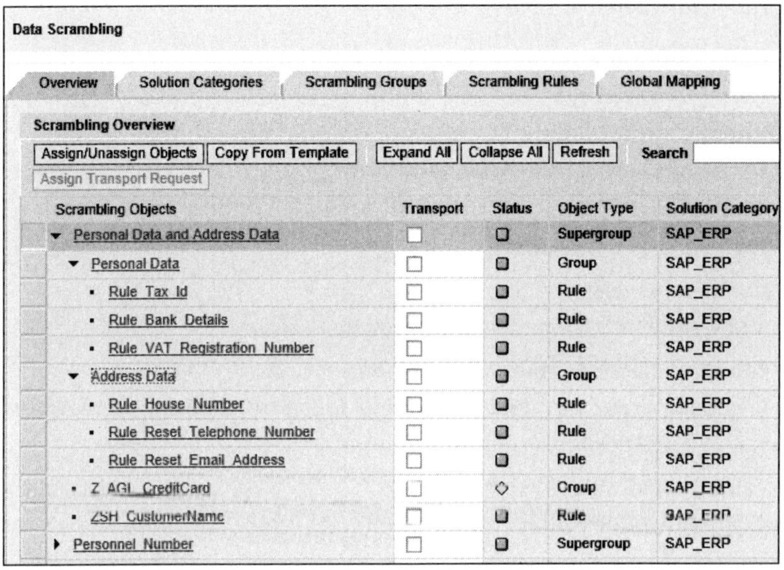

Figure 11.9 Scrambling Overview

A rule is assigned to a type that determines processing (see Figure 11.10).

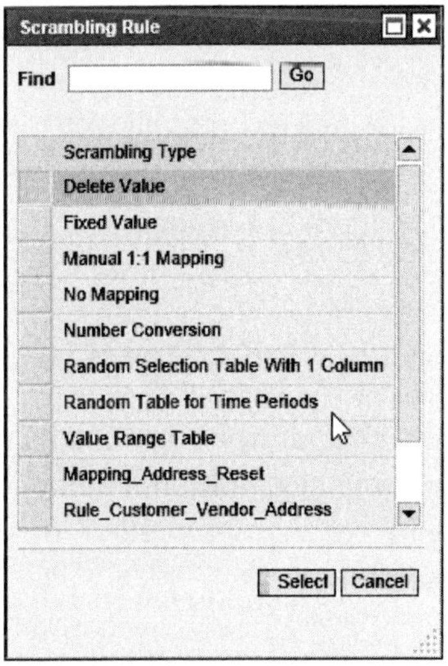

Figure 11.10 Scrambling Types

Depending on the type, the following standard conversions are possible:

Standard conversions

- **Delete Value**
  The field is deleted.
- **Fixed Value**
  A field is returned with a fixed value.
- **Manual 1:1 Mapping**
  The value is taken from a mapping table.
- **No Mapping**
  The field is left unchanged.
- **Number Conversion**
  A new number assignment is generated.
- **Random Selection Table with n Columns**
  A value or group of values is randomly taken from a list of valid related values (e.g., for address fields).
- **Value Range Table**
  A random value is drawn from an interval. There are different variants for this.

[»]

Further Information

Further variants or special types aren't discussed here. Consult the how-to-guide "How to Scramble Data" at *http://support.sap.com/tdms.*

If you want certain rules to be applied to specific data records only, you can control this using condition groups. For example, you can define country-specific rules for postal codes.

11.3 Integration of the System Landscape in SAP TDMS

Your test landscape should reflect the productive landscape as accurately as possible. You should therefore create all production application systems as test systems. To ensure that they are consistent with each other, they should, wherever possible, be set up at the same time.

SAP TDMS is designed to allow you to control all activities in the entire landscape with one single control and central system. To do so, you'll have to connect the various systems to this SAP TDMS system using RFC connections (see Figure 11.11). In this context, each client acts as a system, as clients are logical systems and are addressed via RFCs individually. Depending on the situation, you can also run the SAP TDMS system on the source or target hardware. Alternatively, if you have more hardware, set up separate central systems so that you can migrate your various SAP applications in parallel.

Central SAP TDMS system for your system landscape

The data isn't temporarily stored in an SAP TDMS system. The only space necessary here is that needed for log and Customizing data.

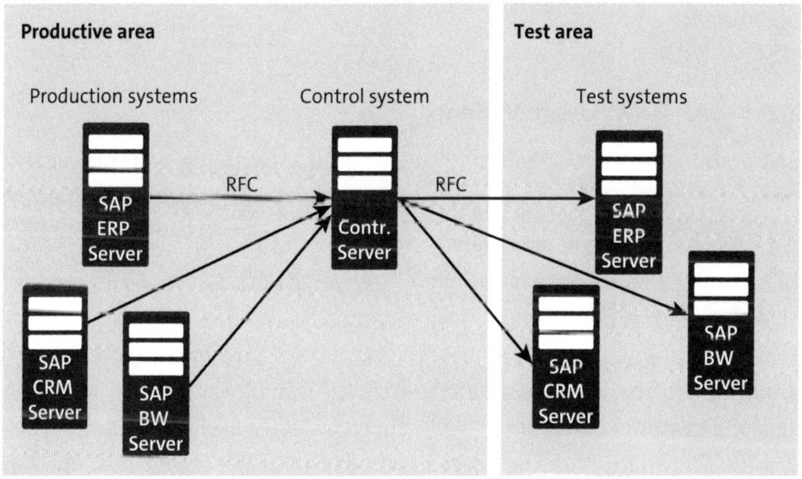

Figure 11.11 SAP TDMS System Landscape

11.4 Data Protection with SAP TDMS

How can you use SAP TDMS for data protection? SAP TDMS offers you a range of technical options for changing data within a system or during system configuration, as described earlier. Whether or not the various requirements of data protection are taken into account depends on the individual case. This is why the preceding explanation wasn't about anonymization or pseudonymization, but instead about scrambling.

Differential privacy versus pseudonymization

The scrambling presented in Section 1.2 only ever changes the data records individually. Another way to achieve data protection compliance is *differential privacy*, in which the result of a database query is given a certain amount of blurriness, so that the result is only roughly correct. For example, the system could return the neighboring address or a comparable one, but not the person-specific case from a group of similar cases. Such methods are successfully used for statistical or scientific evaluations. This procedure, however, isn't suitable for fulfilling data protection requirements for test or training systems in which a process may have to be tracked across several systems; in these cases, you'll have to scramble the data records so that they still work without technical errors, but their content is no longer meaningful.

11.4.1 SAP TDMS Usage Variants

Clean separation of systems

SAP TDMS offers two different procedures for scrambling systems: scrambling an existing system and scrambling in combination with a migration.

A test system is often set up by copying the production and then scrambling it. Until scrambling is completed, personal data is stored on a test system. During this phase, you'll have to temporarily restrict the access to the system strongly. However, the safer alternative is to not export the personal data from the productive system in the first place. SAP TDMS ensures that the personal data doesn't leave the productive system at all by applying the scrambling rules for data record copies in the source system. This can happen despite the scrambling rules being maintained in the control system.

11.4.2 Setting Up Scrambling

Check your free-text fields

When setting up the scrambling, the first thing you think of is direct personal data, such as address and bank details in the SAP ERP system. Predefined scrambling rules are delivered with the SAP TDMS standard for scrambling this data. The SAP ERP system also contains additional data that is directly linked to the SAP ERP business partner, such as additional communication data, credit card numbers, or insurance numbers. You also need to check whether you've created additional fields of your own containing personal data. In addition, fields in your system could be used for diverse other purposes and may contain sensitive data that doesn't actually belong there. Pay particular attention to open-text fields.

To achieve a legally compliant test system, you must first identify which field contents are to be scrambled.

[!]

There Are Many Data Traces

Note that many types of data can be used to identify people. Just think about shopping behavior. For example, the combination of products purchased by an otherwise anonymous person may be used to identify the person. For all the systems you run, you therefore need to check what exactly may be considered personal.

Argument values

As long as the sensitive data is in *argument fields* and not in the key of a data record, you can simply replace the data with other values. Make sure that these values are also valid. If the country key and postal code format don't match, your system will later be inconsistent. Selection tables with several columns in which valid field combinations—for example, for addresses—can be stored are part of the SAP TDMS scrambling functionality. A random generator can then be used to select a line from which the interdependent fields are transferred. In this way, you can populate this table with all data records. As a rule, however, a considerably smaller number is sufficient. Although this leads to many duplicates, it's usually irrelevant for a test system.

[+]

Mark Scrambled Data

It has been proven useful to mark scrambled data explicitly as such. If everyone has "test" in their name, everyone knows immediately which system they are in and aren't likely to search for real data.

Depending on how intensively you want to test the various fields in the systems, you can opt for more or less elaborate scrambling rules. In many cases, a fixed value or simply a deleted field is sufficient.

Amount values

Amount values, such as prices or invoice amounts, are themselves generally not suitable for identifying a person. This changes when extraordinary values are involved. You can't, however, simply change these values because the system uses them for calculations, and you can influence values or aggregates by changing them elsewhere. There are two ways of dealing with amounts that can be realized with a reasonable amount of effort:

- Set all values to zero. This is quite possible, but drastically limits the usability of the system.
- Filter out the outliers; however, you'll also lack exactly these special cases for testing.

In limited areas, it's possible to change values consistently. Here you have to decide on a case-by-case basis.

Communicated key values

System keys are another critical element associated with personal data. Such keys are, for example, contract or account numbers that you use in communication with customers and that serve as central keys for the system. The CWB is capable of scrambling such keys. However, you must approach this with increased caution. The rules may not merge two data records into one data record. To do so, you could select the number conversion (refer to Figure 11.10).

11.4.3 Scrambling Across Systems

In the case of scrambling, you have to consider not only the consistency within a system but also the cross-system consistency for processes that run through several systems in a landscape. In particular, the scrambled keys must have an identical value in all systems.

A basic strategy of SAP TDMS is that the original data is already scrambled in the original system, which means the central system can no longer generate consistent scrambling across systems. Instead, the procedure must be identical in all systems.

One strategy for consistent scrambling across systems is to use the same random tables in all systems. For example, a function can determine the identical result for one or more original values, that is, a key used across systems (injective function). With this result, the same entry is selected from the random table in all systems. With a one-to-one relationship, tracking is possible; with a one-to-*n* relationship, it's no longer possible. The latter is only suitable for argument fields, not for key fields. Regardless of which variant you choose, the information about the scrambling of cross-system keys must be made known by one system to the next system—whether as a clear function or as a clear mapping table. Traceability is thus ensured as long as this information exists. It must therefore be considered to be very sensitive.

Functions for distinct scrambling

Functions are often preferred for scrambling, as they can be used across the board without any problems. Wherever possible, they should not be reversible. As a rule, data protection is generally achieved by doing so. If such a function still depends on a random value that is assigned covertly by the central system, even the programmer can no longer easily determine the real data.

11.5 Summary

Tailor your project to your demand

As explained in this chapter, SAP TDMS provides extensive technical options for scrambling data. Whether you have to make personal data anonymous or just pseudonymous depends on your data protection concept. SAP TDMS can help you achieve data protection compliance. The chapter has given you an indication as to what is possible and what should be considered in the context of scrambling data. You should plan a suitable project carefully. Ultimately, however, it's up to you how you use SAP TDMS.

Chapter 12
Accountability: Protection, Audits, Controls, and Documentation

When it comes to data protection audits, reference is made very quickly to standards such as ISO/IEC 27018 on data protection in the cloud or the BSI basic protection catalogue. This isn't wrong; however, we assume that it's necessary to develop the requirements from the legal situation before referring to the named ISO/IEC 27018 or other standards of the ISO/IEC 27 series.*

12

The cornerstone of the subject of controls is Art. 5 General Data Protection Regulation (GDPR), as it describes the principles of processing. One of the key requirements here is compliance with accountability pursuant to Art. 5 (2) GDPR. In this chapter, we'll use legal bases to develop a comprehensive control framework. It's obvious that these controls, especially in the area of integrity controls, are highly consistent with the controls already in place in the *internal control system* (ICS). Please regard the data protection controls as an integral part of your ICS.

[Ex]

Imagine ...

The supervisory authority carries out an audit (see *https://ico.org.uk/for-organisations/resources-and-support/audits/*), and the question arises as to which technical and organizational measures are being used to ensure that the processing of data is secure. To provide information, most readers of this book don't necessarily need to be able to set up these controls; however, you do need a basic understanding and an overview of them. With the help of this chapter, you'll be able to ask your IT department about specific data security aspects, which will enable you to provide the supervisory authority with information.

12.1 Control Frame and Principles of Processing

In Figure 12.1, we return to the control circle/proof circle that was introduced in Chapter 1.

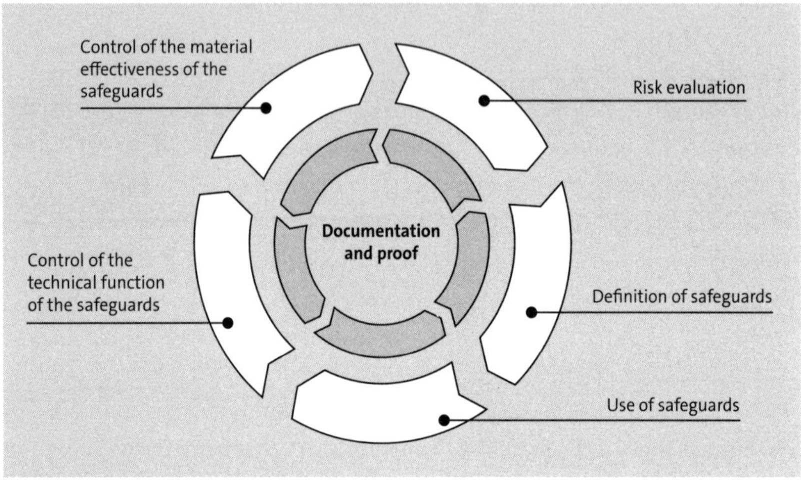

Figure 12.1 Control Circle/Proof Circle

This circle is intended to make it clear how Art. 5 (2) in conjunction with Art. 24 (1) GDPR specifically triggers an endless control circle. In this chapter, we'll take a closer look at the subject of controls based on the requirements of the GDPR.

Art. 5 (1) GDPR generally specifies the requirements to be met when processing personal data. Art. 5 (2) establishes full accountability with regard to these requirements. This is shown in an overview in Figure 12.2.

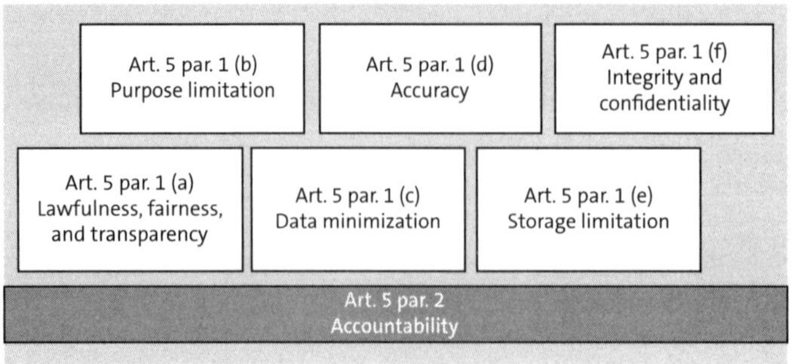

Figure 12.2 General Control Frame

In practice, the question now arises as to how, for example, it can be proven that processing has been carried out *fairly*. The following explanations will help answer these questions.

12.2 Lawfulness, Fairness, and Transparency

In this section, we'll show you which requirements can be derived from Art. 5 (1)(a) GDPR with regard to necessary controls, as this article calls for a systematic interpretation.

As outlined in Figure 12.3 and presented in this section, the requirement of lawfulness refers to the lawfulness of processing pursuant to Art. 6 GDPR; in turn, Art. 6 GDPR mentions consent as the basis for processing, which is detailed in Art. 7 GDPR and should be considered systematically and obligatorily in conjunction with Art. 8 GDPR, which regulates consent for children. Furthermore, the requirement of lawfulness is a general clause; it enforces compliance with all GDPR requirements to prove lawfulness.

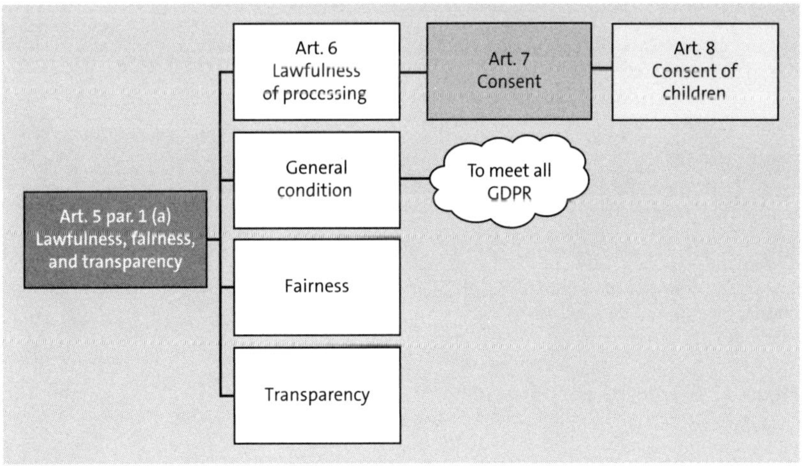

Figure 12.3 Conclusions from Art. 5 (1)(a) GDPR

Conclusions from Article 5 (1)(a)

The lawfulness of processing results on the one hand from Art. 6 GDPR, which lists the possible grounds for processing (consent, performance of a contract, legal obligation, vital interests, public interest, and legitimate interest). Consent is substantiated again in Art. 7 GDPR to then be further defined by special conditions for the consent of children (Art. 8 GDPR).

Inherent compliance

On the other hand, Frenzel (2017) states in Art. 5 marg. 14–16 with reference to recital 40 GDPR that the processing itself must be lawful, that is, based on the requirements of the GDPR. In simple terms, even if the basis of the processing is lawful, it's still necessary for it to be carried out in conformity with the law, that is, in accordance with the GDPR.

The requirement of transparency was discussed in detail in Chapter 1, Section 1.1.6. As a reminder, it's shown again in Figure 12.4.

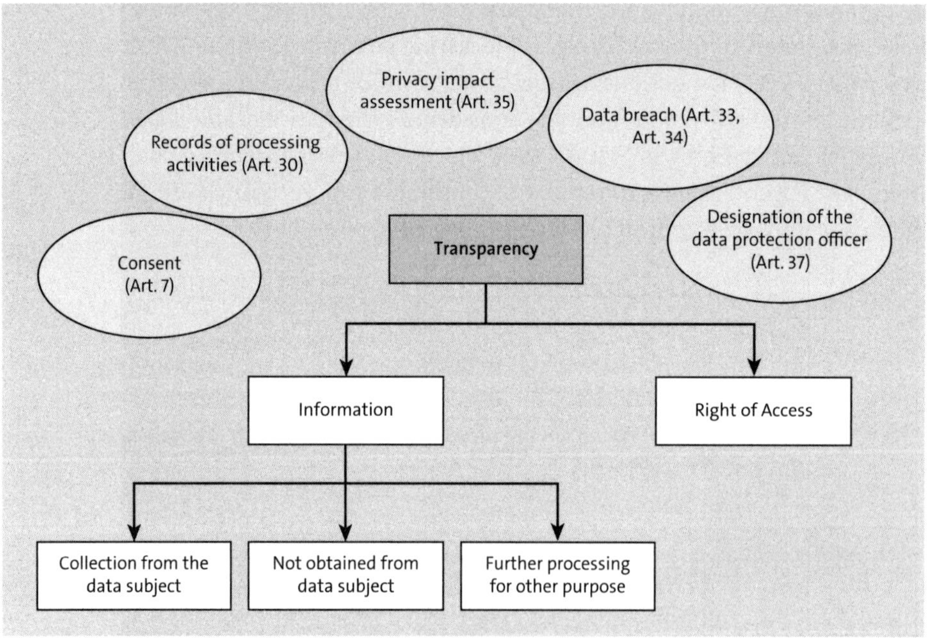

Figure 12.4 Transparency Requirement in a Broader Sense

Control Options for Art. 5 (1)(a)

Now let's discuss the controls more precisely. Table 12.1 provides an overview of possible controls.

Requirement	Content	Control
Lawful processing – basic principle	Proof of the respective legal grounds	Organizational control
Lawful processing – general clause	Comprehensive accounting for technical and organizational measures	Organizational control; technial control
Fairness	Fairness	Assessment on a case-by-case basis
Transparency	Accounting for the advance information and the right of access	Technical control, whether available and technically complete

Table 12.1 Controls according to Art. 5 (1)(a)

12.3 Purpose Limitation

The purpose limitation has already been addressed in Chapter 1, Section 1.2.1, and in Chapter 5. Our conclusions from Art. 5 (1)(b) GDPR are outlined in Figure 12.5 and are presented in the following sections.

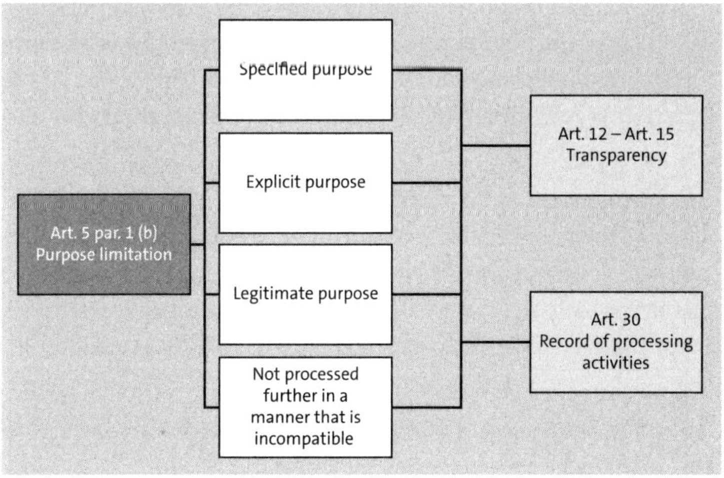

Figure 12.5 Conclusions from Art. 5 (1)(b)

Conclusions from Article 5 (1)(b)

The aforementioned provisions concerning the purposes of processing are specified, among other things, in Arts. 13 and 14 GDPR. Accordingly, the purposes of the processing must be the subject of the data subject's information at the start of the processing. As previously explained in Chapter 1, experts are currently discussing the notion of purpose. The question of unambiguity is something that could provide for an interesting discussion, but we would quickly end up in the field of semantics. The concept of semantics itself could then be considered from various perspectives such as linguistics, philosophy, law, and finally computer science, which would possibly lead to a number of different conclusions.

Unambiguity in the software

From the point of view of standard software, two main questions arise, that are well worth following: How can the use be clearly determined for a specific purpose, and how can the use be clearly proven for a specific purpose?

"Unambiguous" would have to be expanded on with "or multiple unambiguous uses": In Chapter 5, we addressed central master data such as the customer master record. This must also be clearly related to the respective purposes. However, because it can serve several purposes, it must be possible to account for each individual purpose.

We believe that we've just provided an answer to the first question in Chapter 5: personal data must be identified by line organizational attributes (LOAs) and process organizational attributes (POAs) in such a way that processing for different purposes can take place separately. The answer to the second question results from the answer to the first question (see also Chapter 8).

Legitimate?

The recurring emphasis on the legitimacy of the purposes doesn't, in our view, lead to any further need for control. This applies in particular because the purpose definition remains, in total, an organizational act not included in the software, which can at best be supported by compliance software such as the SAP Governance, Risk, and Compliance (SAP GRC) suite.

Reconcile further processing with the purpose?

Depending on how you want to define the purposes, the question of further processing within the purposes already arises in the applicable retention regulations. If, for example, you define the retention as your own purpose within the framework of commercial accounting regulations (and define ex ante as such), no further processing would take place that is compatible with the purpose, but rather the processing was carried out for the purpose of retention within the framework of commercial retention regulations. Our interpretation, which locates the purpose in the actual business core process, would mean that retention would constitute further processing that is strictly compliant with the original purpose . . . so much for the abstract discussion!

Further processing of data

The question of further processing becomes more specific wherever data leaves the system. The probability that a transfer to the SAP Business Warehouse (SAP BW) is in fact a type of further processing should be obvious. The same applies to all other interfaces, including the transfer of data to Microsoft Excel, which we already described as problematic. More specifically, if a list of employees is extracted from the system in Excel as a list of voters for the works council, it may well be permissible to assume that this can still be understood as *data processing for employment purposes* as defined by Section 26 German Data Federal Protection Act (BDSG-new). The next imminent question, however, would be how the company can ensure that the Excel list is only used for this purpose, that is, that the personal data will only be processed further for this purpose.

The handling of the purpose limitation is also explicitly regulated in Art. 25 (2) GDPR; this is discussed in further detail in Section 12.4.

Control Options for Article 5 (1)(b)

After this general outline, we need to define the controls more precisely. Accordingly, Table 12.2 provides an overview of possible controls.

Requirement	Content	Control
Specified purposes	Have the purposes been defined (previously)?	Technical control if the purposes have been defined. ▪ Data Controller Rule Framework ▪ Information retrieval framework
Unambiguous purposes	Accounting for unambiguousness	Organizational control

Table 12.2 Controls according to Art. 5 (1)(b)

Requirement	Content	Control
Unambiguous purposes	Accounting for a purpose-related retention of data	Technical control ▪ Data Controller Rule Framework ▪ Information retrieval framework ▪ Control in SAP Reference Implementation Guide (IMG)
Legitimate purposes	Assessment on a case-to-case basis	Assessment on a case-to-case basis
Further processing pursuant to the purpose	Proof that further processing is only carried out pursuant to the purpose	Retention related to separate purposes Interface control

Table 12.2 Controls according to Art. 5 (1)(b) (Cont.)

12.4 Data Minimization

Our conclusions from Art. 5 (1)(c) GDPR are outlined in Figure 12.6: data minimization requires data to be adequate, relevant, and limited to the extent necessary for the purpose. This must be ensured by appropriate technical and organizational measures (TOMs). In the following, we'll specify these requirements in more detail.

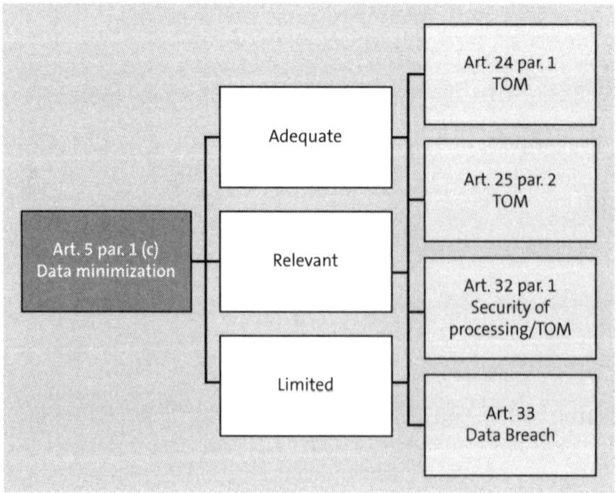

Figure 12.6 Conclusions from Art. 5 (1)(c)

Conclusions from Article 5 (1)(c)

The data must be adequate and relevant to the purpose. We'll now take a closer look at what is considered to be adequate and relevant.

Adequate for the purpose

The only data that may be collected is that which is adequate for the scope of the processing. As to adequacy, Pötters (2017, marg. 15) states: "Processing is adequate if it's proportionate in the narrower sense." A good example for several European countries is the processing of trade union memberships on the obvious pretext that all trade unions have certain information and access rights under the various Works Constitution Acts in Europe (e.g., BetrVG). To grant these, one must know which trade unions are represented in the company. It's evident that a list of trade unions represented in the company is indeed necessary. However, it makes sense for a company to do this by means of other instruments that intervene significantly less in the fundamental rights of its employees. In our view, therefore, it would be reasonable to reject the idea of trade union membership for every employee as this is *inadequate for the purpose under the principle of proportionality*. The company simply need not be interested in whether Doris Delaney is a member of trade union X; the only thing the company needs to know is that trade union X is represented in the company.

Relevant for the purpose

The data necessary for processing within the scope of the purpose is relevant for this purpose. If a contract has been concluded in which the service provider is entitled to collect the payment using the IBAN procedure, the IBAN number is significant for this purpose, as it's absolutely necessary. The transaction can't be concluded without the IBAN number. In the previous example, specifying whether a specific person is a member of a trade union isn't relevant for the purpose. Not even if this person were the only member of the trade union in the company.

Processing limited to the extent necessary

While the first two terms are primarily an evaluation of which data may be processed, the limitation to the necessary extent is much more comprehensive. The processing of personal data is therefore subject to the following:

- Time aspects, that is, at which points in time processing is necessary
- User-related aspects, that is, which user must be allowed to process the data according to his fulfillment of duties

Pötters (2017, Art. 5 Marg. 22), goes so far as to also problematize the frequency of use:

> *This means that multiple evaluations of data that contain largely the same information are illegal. As so often, however, this is initially a legal opinion that is by no means uncontroversial.*

For instance, Böhm and Ströbel (2017, Art. 5 Marg. 19) take a different view:

> *Unlike the term data minimization implies, Art. 5 (1)(c) GDPR does not restrict data processing to the absolute minimum. Whether data processing violates the principle of data minimization depends rather on a test for adequacy.*

TOMs Art. 24 GDPR now stipulates that "appropriate technical and organisational measures must be implemented." Art. 25 (2) GDPR clarifies that "by default only personal data which are necessary for each specific purpose of the processing are processed." In turn, Art. 32 stipulates that for the security of processing, "appropriate technical and organisational measures must be implemented to ensure a level of security appropriate to the risk."

We've already explained TOMs in Chapter 1, Section 1.2.4. With regard to data minimization, these measures are likely to be the following:

- Physical access control
- Data medium control
- Storage control
- User control
- Access control
- Transfer control
- Transport control
- Order control
- Separability

In any event, in addition to the TOMs, the following should also be mentioned:

- Blocking and deleting personal data
- Encryption

For the reasons stated in Chapter 1, Section 1.1.12, we take a critical view of the pseudonymization mentioned in Art. 32 (1)(a) with regard to its actual realizability and therefore prefer the term *depersonalization*. A very good example is the depersonalization of test data as described in Chapter 11.

Control Options for Article 5 (1)(c)

Now let's take a more detailed look at the controls. Accordingly, Table 12.3 gives you an overview of possible controls.

Requirement	Content	Control
Adequate for the purpose	Collected data must be adequate in the sense of proportional.	■ Organizational control
Relevant for the purpose	The data must be relevant in the sense of necessary.	■ Organizational control; technical control on a case-to-case basis; conceivable: proofs of use
Limited to the extent necessary	Processing may be carried out only in relation to the purpose.	■ Retention according to separate purposes ■ Technical control ■ Data Controller Rule Framework ■ Information retrieval framework ■ Control in IMG
Limited to the extent necessary	Corresponding restriction of access is required.	■ Organizational controls: – Organizational instructions ■ Technical controls: – Authentication – Minimal principle in the authorization concept – Memory control – Access logging – Transfer log – Transport control – Encryption

Table 12.3 Control according to Art. 5 (1)(c)

12

Requirement	Content	Control
Limited to the extent necessary	Depersonalization of data is required.	■ Technical controls, for example,, depersonalization of test systems
Limited to the extent necessary	The time-related access must be shaped accordingly.	■ Technical controls: – Blocking data when they need to be retained for legal reasons – Deleting data when both the purpose and the legal reasons for retention have expired

Table 12.3 Control according to Art. 5 (1)(c) (Cont.)

12.5 Accuracy

Our conclusions from Art. 5 (1)(d) GDPR are outlined in Figure 12.7. The accuracy of the data can be divided into three categories: the accuracy of the data, the up-to-dateness of the data, and the need to correct or delete data that isn't correct for the purpose. This appears to be explicit according to Arts. 16 and 18 GDPR.

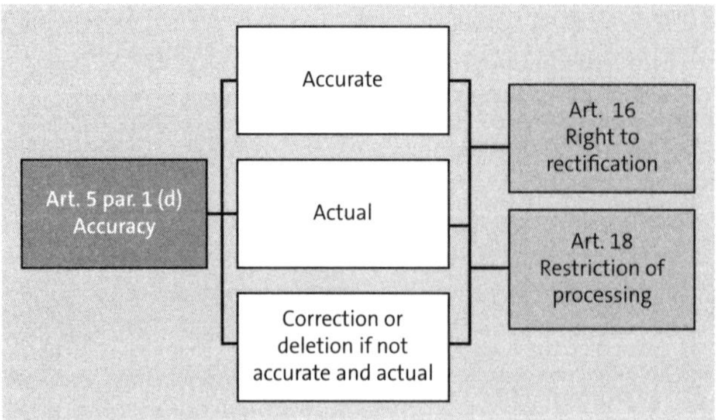

Figure 12.7 Conclusions from Art. 5 (1)(d)

Conclusions from Article 5 (1)(d)

The requirement that personal data must be accurate and, if necessary, up to date already seems to be inherent in an SAP ERP solution for business reasons. Finally, personal data is processed in an SAP ERP system to make decisions and conduct business on a rational basis. In this sense, from a business point of view, incorrect data can become expensive data. Data protection, however, isn't about the entrepreneurial risk of incorrect data, which can lead to wrong decisions, but about the rights of those affected. Incorrect data related to a person can lead to incorrect assessments or even decisions about that person. The loan not granted due to an incorrect credit rating is only one such example.

Accuracy

For this reason, the GDPR defines the general requirement that data must be factually correct. In addition to common errors, such as the incorrect spelling of a name, other significantly more problematic information can also be incorrect. For example, the information about a credit rating may be incorrect and, in the event of an unjustifiably poor credit rating assessment, may have negative consequences for the person concerned (e.g., the person concerned may be offered worse payment terms).

Up-to-dateness

A frequently occurring problem arises from personal data relating to relatives. If these aren't corrected after a divorce, various undesirable results such as transfers to the ex-partner may occur. The creditworthiness mentioned under "Accuracy" must also always be regarded as time-dependent. A negative scoring from the past doesn't necessarily reflect the current payment behavior of the person concerned. From a business point of view, this naturally also applies the opposite way around.

Right to rectification

In connection with the right to accuracy and up-to-dateness, the legal claim of the person concerned is that incorrect personal data be rectified. This legal claim is stipulated in Art. 16 GDPR.

Restriction of processing

The right to restriction of processing is also defined, among other things, in the event that the data subject disputes the accuracy of the data processed (Art. 18 (1)(a)).

Control Options for Article 5 (1)(d)

Now let's take a closer look at the controls. Table 12.4 provides an overview of possible controls.

Requirement	Content	Control
Accuracy	The data must be accurate for the purpose.	Organizational controls: ▪ Authorization procedure Technical controls: ▪ Duplicate test ▪ Master data management
Up-to-dateness	The data must be up to date for the purpose.	Organizational controls: ▪ Authorization procedure Technical controls: ▪ Duplicate test ▪ Master data management ▪ Procedure to determine when scoring values become invalid
Right to rectification	The data must be rectified.	Organizational controls: ▪ Authorization procedure

Table 12.4 Control according to Art. 5 (1)(d)

12.6 Storage Limitation

Our conclusions from Art. 5 (1)(e) GDPR are outlined in Figure 12.8: due to storage limitation, it's essential to restrict the identifiability of the individual to a specific period of time, for example, by deletion. If this isn't done, it may be assumed that there has been a breach of protection in the processing event. This time limitation is also covered indirectly by Art. 32 GDPR. The right to restrict processing may lead to the opposite effect of data being blocked before access and cause data to be available for a longer period of time. We'll now take a more detailed look at this.

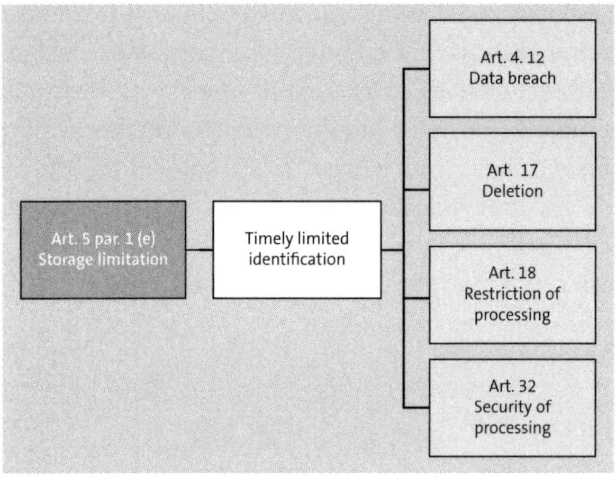

Figure 12.8 Conclusions from Art. 5 (1)(e)

Conclusions from Article 5 (1)(e)

The purpose of storage limitation is to ensure that personal data is only ever processed for as long as is necessary to fulfill the specified purpose. As we've already pointed out on several occasions, the requirement is also relevant for storage that is deemed necessary within the framework of legal obligations.

Frenzel (2017, Art. 5 marg. 45) discusses separating data for which purpose-related processing is no longer necessary from data for which justifying grounds continue to exist.

We work on the assumption that the storage limitation is accompanied, when interpreted in a legal system, by an obligation to block. This would ultimately also cover Frenzel's assumptions within the concept of simplified blocking and deletion (see Chapter 4).

Figure 12.9 illustrates our assumption of temporary use in the context of the GDPR. If storage is erroneously unlimited, a violation of protection (Art. 4 (12) GDPR) may arise. Furthermore, failure to block or delete the data is probably also a violation of processing security pursuant to Art. 32 (1). The need to block the data also arises from the principles pursuant to Art. 5 GDPR, namely purpose limitation and data minimization. A special type of blocking results from Art. 18 GDPR (Restriction of Processing), which stipulates that—under certain conditions—data is effectively to be blocked at the request of the data subject and that this also means blocking to prevent deletion. The storage limitation also includes pseudonymization, which in accordance with Art. 5 (1)(e), is described as "kept in a form which permits identification of data subjects for no longer than is necessary for the purposes for which the personal data are processed." In our opinion, this can be understood for both pseudonymization and anonymization. As we explained in Chapter 1, Section 1.1.12, real pseudonymization or real anonymization simply can't be achieved with valuable data; we also introduced the alternative term of depersonalization.

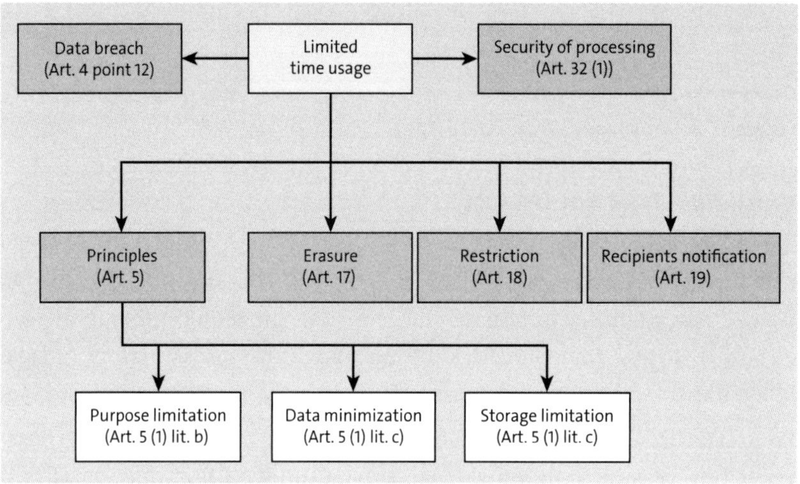

Figure 12.9 Storage Limitation: Blocking and Deleting

Control Options for Article 5 (1)(e)

Table 12.5 shows an overview of possible controls.

Requirement	Content	Control
Storage limitation	Time-limiting of use and/or identifiability	Technical controls: ▪ Verify rule-based deletion ▪ Verify rule-based data blocking ▪ Depersonalization

Table 12.5 Controls in accordance with Art. 5 (1)(e)

12.7 Integrity and Confidentiality

Our conclusions from Art. 5 (1)(f) GDPR are outlined in Figure 12.10.

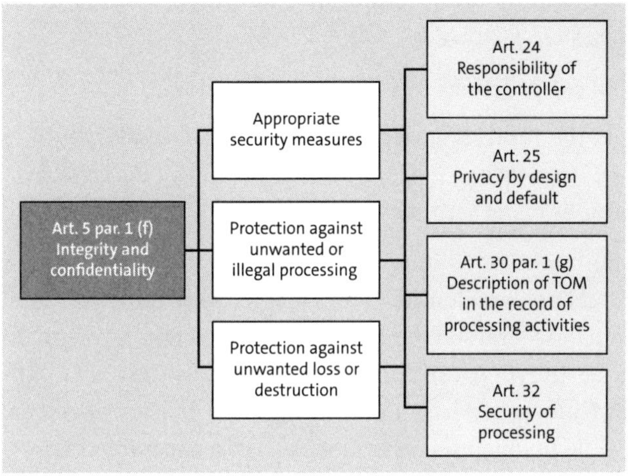

Figure 12.10 Derivations from Art. 5 (1)(f)

Three main areas can be identified systematically: adequate security of processing, protection against unlawful or unauthorized processing, and protection against accidental loss, destruction, or damage. These three areas are specified in further articles of the GDPR. The requirements are described in further detail in the following subsections.

Conclusions from Article 5 (1)(f)

The conclusions of Art. 5 (1)(f) can be summarized in one sentence: provide for suitable technical and organizational measures! These are also required in Arts. 24, 25, and 32 GDPR, and, pursuant to Art. 30 (1)(g) GDPR, should be included in the list of processing activities.

But what do integrity and confidentiality mean? The Federal Office for Information Security (BSI) (2013) defines integrity as follows:

> *Integrity means ensuring the correctness (integrity) of data and the correct functioning of systems. When the term integrity is applied to data, it expresses that the data is complete and unchanged. In information technology, however, it is generally interpreted in a broader sense and applied to information. The term information is used for data, to which*

certain attributes, such as author or time of creation, can be assigned, depending on the context. The loss of information integrity can therefore mean that it has been altered without permission, that information about the author has been falsified, or that time data has been manipulated in order to produce it.

Additionally, the BSI (2013) defines confidentiality as follows:

Confidentiality is the protection against unauthorized disclosure of information. Confidential data and information may only be accessible to authorised persons in the permissible manner.

The German BSI definitions aren't unique or only applicable in Germany or Europe. Requirements on confidentiality and integrity are quite common and are documented in several standards or rules. For reference, you might check the Summary of the HIPAA Security Rule provided by the U.S. Department of Health & Human Services. Even though this is about personal health information, it might provide evidence that comparable requirements are discussed in relation to integrity and confidentiality.

First, however, let's focus on the issue of integrity, and then conclude by looking at the points that still need to be highlighted in the context of confidentiality.

Control Options for Article 5 (1)(f)

In the following we'll provide you with an overview of possible controls but with the help of graphic representations. Figure 12.11 shows what we consider to be the obvious control points for the *integrity* buzzword.

[»]

> **Only a General Overview of the Essential Requirements**
>
> The options shown here are intended to provide you with an overview. This overview doesn't go into technical detail. For specific questions, always check the security guides at *https://help.sap.com*.

Vulnerabilities in the code

We'll start with the question of how secure your code is. SAP checks its own code with *code scans* that check whether there are any *vulnerabilities*, that is, weak points in the code. Examples include hard-coded passwords, backdoors, and cross-site scripting.

[«]

Cross-Site Scripting

Cross-site scripting is the exploitation of a vulnerability in web applications where information from an untrusted page is simply inserted into a trusted page. An attack can then be launched from the trusted site.

Vulnerabilities will occur time and again, even in the customers' own code. For example, authorization checks aren't used very often in customer-defined programs. Therefore, although it's helpful that SAP closely monitors its own code, customer-specific code must be subjected to comparable procedures.

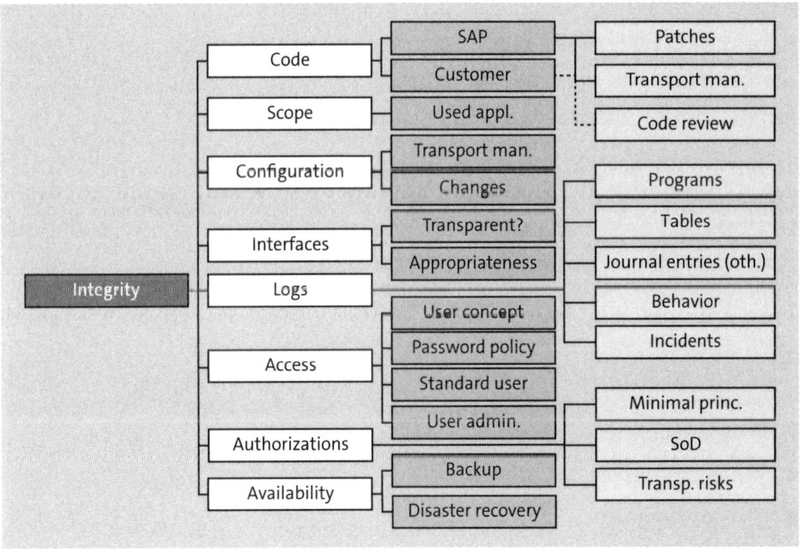

Figure 12.11 Integrity Checkpoints

SAP has been implementing a security response process for years to be able to immediately address postdelivery vulnerabilities. For this purpose, SAP delivers *patches*. A patch is usually a smaller software update to close gaps or correct errors. If they are relevant, they also have to be imported.

Transport Management System

All code changes in a production system can generally be accessed from the production client via the Transport Management System (TMS). This is necessary to be able to prove and check changes in the system or, in the sense of data protection law, in the procedure.

Scope of use SAP Business Suite and SAP S/4HANA provide numerous applications for various business processes. Transparency in their use is vital to secure your procedure. This applies to both the overview of usage and the overview of the release status.

Configuration System configuration is the combination of all desired settings. Every change to the configuration should always be made using transport requests. In other words, the TMS is also important in this respect. Furthermore, client settings have to be made to ensure that changes in the productive client aren't possible, but rather that the system can be accessed via the controlled transport route.

Interfaces: inventory and appropriateness We've mentioned the challenge of interfaces at various points, mainly with regard to data transmission control. Interfaces can also pose a risk because information reaches the client via interfaces where—in the worst-case scenario—malicious code may also enter the system. For this reason, it's also important that interfaces are fully listed and adequately checked for their appropriateness. Appropriate in this context means that the only data/data types allowed into the system are those that are relevant for the purpose of processing. To do this, it's necessary, among other things, to define the authorization concept for the interfaces accordingly.

Logging SAP Business Suite and SAP S/4HANA offer numerous logging options. We'll discuss how you can check whether these are "switched on" later. In terms of integrity, the following options should be mentioned:

- Program changes
- Table logging
- Change logging
- Behavioral logging
- Event logging

Logging changes to programs Because program changes can only reach productive clients via the TMS, any changes made must also be tracked via the TMS and version management.

Logging changes to tables Table logging is used to log changes to tables, provided that these tables are flagged accordingly and table logging is activated. Table logging is primarily aimed at changing configurations, and not so much at changing business data; separate change logging is provided for this. Because configurations are usually only to be made in a previous client and not in a production client, you'll have to activate your own table logging in the TMS. Both logs provide an overview of changes made to the configuration.

Logging changes

In SAP Business Suite and SAP S/4HANA, extensive change logs are generally activated. As far as the subject of system integrity is concerned, the contents play less of a role than the proof of logging itself. The contents of the changes protocols are, among other things, significant for the rights of those concerned. The logs relate to documents and master data.

Behavioral logging

Like any orderly system, SAP Business Suite and SAP S/4HANA allow user behavior to be logged in various protocols. In our view, these records are mandatory under data protection law. The working group Technical and Organisational Data Protection Issues (2009) at the Conference of Data Protection Commissioners of the German federal and state governments recommends the following:

> *The purpose of the logging is to make the procedure for processing personal data so transparent that it can be proven that the processing of personal data is fully compliant or that it violates the rules. The logged data should be able to provide information such as who has processed personal data, when it was process, which personal data was processed, and in what way it was processed [...] They must correctly document the operations actually performed, the applications involved, machines and people with time reference.*

By default, the following are logged:

- All logins to the system and changes of password
- Transactions/programs run
- Table changes
- Entering and changing master data
- The result of the last authorization check

Read logging

In addition to these general logging options, a reading log has been provided to allow read-only access to personal data. These logs are described in detail in Chapter 9. In terms of integrity, this logging is also only significant to the extent that its function is part of the necessary scope of an integrated system. The contents are considerable, for example, to prove and control the principle of minimization.

Event logging

Events are generally logged at various points in the system. For verification of system integrity, the Security Audit Log should receive a special mention; this log is used for logging security-related events.

Access checks

System access should be restricted to named users. This is part of a user concept and also applies to technical users, for example, in the RFC interfaces. Because the technical user ID isn't the same as the user ID of natural persons, they require a relevant purpose-related naming concept. The user concept also includes regular checks to see whether these users are also being used. Nonutilized users are ultimately proof that persons have been granted rights in the system without there being a reason for doing so; thus, evidence exists that the purpose has been violated.

Password rules

If Single Sign-On (SSO) isn't used, the system needs to provide for sensible password rules. Both SSO and the password rules are subject to system parameters.

Special users

Special users are created during the installation process and have extensive and in some cases every possible authorization in the system. They are therefore critical users. SAP's explicit recommendations for these special users are discussed in the section entitled "Section ."

Authorization administration

We've taken the following section from the book *SAP Authorization System*, which also contains further information on user and authorization administration (Lehnert, Stelzner, Otto, and John, 2016, p. 736).

In terms of authorization management, SAP's security guides are unique: authorizations and users in the productive system may not be maintained by one single user. It's strongly recommended to separate functions for three participating users: Role administrator, user administrator, and profile administrator.

Additionally, you'll have to make sure that no user can change his own roles in the productive system via user groups.

Authorizations

Chapter 7 describes the authorization concept. As far as system integrity is concerned, it has already been established that both SAP Business Suite and SAP S/4HANA provide an authorization concept that sufficiently safeguards the integrity of the system. However, it's essential that appropriate controls are put in place.

We've dealt extensively with risk definitions in the authorization system in Chapter 7, Section 7.4. The information provided there describes the control framework sufficiently at this point.

Transparent risks: authorizations

Availability

The availability of data is probably one of the oldest issues known and has probably played tricks on all of us. Computer crashes will most probably, at some point during our studies, have resulted in the loss of a paper, parts of our diploma thesis, or other important work. Only after something like that has happened do most of us start thinking about regular backups. There are normally three approaches to availability:

- Backup
- Disaster recovery
- Business continuity

A backup is a "simple," usually periodic, external copy. The BSI defines the backup (or data backup) as follows (Federal Office for Information Security, 2013):

> *A data backup creates backups of existing data to protect against data loss. Data backup includes all technical and organizational measures to ensure the availability, integrity and consistency of the systems, including the data, programs and procedures stored on these systems and used for processing purposes.*
>
> *Proper data protection means that the measures taken, depending on the data sensitivity, enable an immediate or short-term recovery of the condition of systems, data, programs or procedures after a recognized impairment of availability, integrity or consistency due to a damaging event. The measures include at least the production and testing of the ability to reconstruct copies of the software, data and procedures in defined cycles and generations.*

Disaster recovery

The backup ensures that the systems are recoverable. The term *disaster recovery* goes even further; it's not only about recoverability but also the definition of all measures to restore the systems, including the necessary technical infrastructure.

Business Continuity Management (BCM)

The most far-reaching concept is that of *Business Continuity Management* (BCM). This is described by the BSI as follows (Federal Office for Information Security, 2013):

Business Continuity Management (BCM) refers to all organizational, technical and personnel measures that serve to continue the core business of an authority or company after an emergency or security incident has occurred. BCM also supports the successive continuation of business processes in the event of prolonged outages or disruptions.

Availability and WannaCry

Availability is a requirement that is equally as important for business requirements. Nevertheless, the consultancy has shown that even in this field, there are striking gaps. This once again became evident when the encryption trojan WannaCry (Society for Scientific Data Processing, 2017) spread in 2017. The vast effects of WannaCry could have been avoided if systems had been properly patched. On the other hand, the impact could have been significantly reduced if backups had been made sooner. As a reminder, in the United Kingdom, patients could not be treated because WannaCry encrypted their data, and backups had not been made in time.

Confidentiality

We'll now turn to the second requirement of Art. 5 (1)(f), the confidentiality of processing. What is immediately striking is that all measures that ensure the integrity of a system are also measures that ensure the confidentiality of data processing, as illustrated in Figure 12.12.

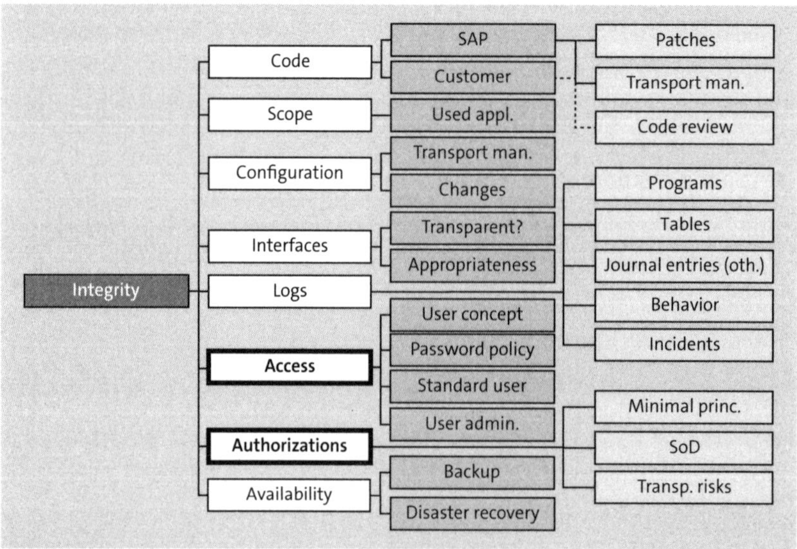

Figure 12.12 Checkpoints: Focus Confidentiality

In terms of the confidentiality of data processing, we believe that the technical requirements for system access and the requirements for the authorization concept should be particularly highlighted. We've already dealt with their contents in connection with the subject of integrity. In any event, in addition to the technical measures, organizational measures have to be specified. Persons entrusted with data processing have to be informed regularly about the requirements of confidentiality; this unfortunately still includes notification that users and passwords may not be shared.

12.8 Accountability

As we've already pointed out several times, including in the introduction to this chapter, it's not only necessary to take the correct technical and organizational measures but also to provide comprehensive proof of this in future (see Art. 5 (2) GDPR):

> *The controller shall be responsible for, and be able to demonstrate compliance with, paragraph 1 ('accountability').*

Infringements of accountability constitute administrative fines pursuant to Art. 83 (5)(a) GDPR (Böhm and Ströbel, 2017) and Art. 5 Marg. 42.

Both Böhm and Ströbel (2017) and Pötters (2017) insisted that accountability represents an important new GDPR requirement (Art. 5 (41) and Art. 5 Marg. 32, respectively). It certainly remains to be seen which requirements regarding accountability are specified by the supervisory authorities and by case law. The fact that a fine can be imposed makes it sufficiently clear that a consistent approach from risk assessment and measures to meaningful documentation will be required. Figure 12.13 shows our view of accountability.

First, the principles of Art. 5 GDPR have to be verified. Art. 24 (1) GDPR specifies this again by stipulating that the controller must be in a position to "demonstrate that processing is performed in accordance with this Regulation" (Art. 24 (1) GDPR). Art. 28 (3) GDPR also specifies the obligations of the contractor in this respect, including a right of review by the customer/controller. Art. 30 GDPR requires, as far as possible, that these measures are included in the record of processing activities.

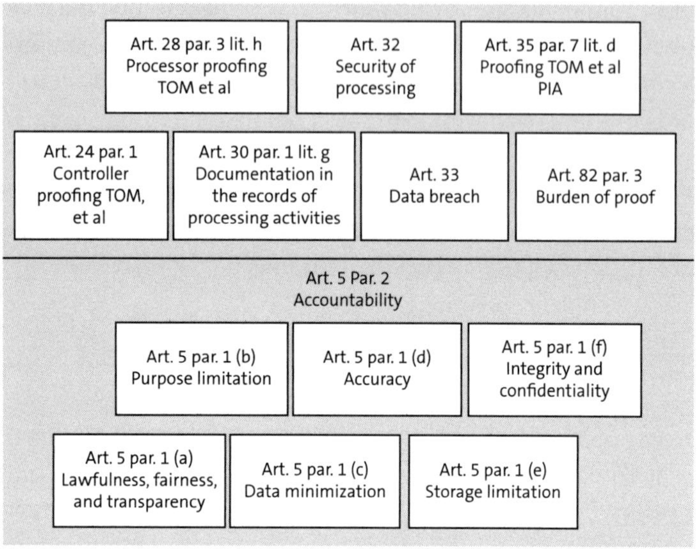

Figure 12.13 Accountability and Documentation

Art. 32 (1)(d) GDPR specifies measures for the security of processing and supplements the framework with a process "for regularly testing, assessing and evaluating the effectiveness of technical and organizational measures for ensuring the security of the processing."

Art. 33 GDPR stipulates that possible breaches of protection are subject to a notification procedure (*data breach*).

Art. 35 GDPR on the *privacy impact assessment* (PIA) requires that this should already document the measures taken to ensure the security of processing.

Finally, Art. 82 (3) GDPR contains a shift in the burden of proof because only if the controller and/or the contract processor can prove that "it's not in any way responsible for the event giving rise to the damage" is it exempt from liability.

12.9 Abstract Technical Controls

In the following, we'll systematize the control actions on a more abstract level. Because some control actions are suitable for supporting different control objectives, we'll also provide an overview, which will then be fully substantiated in Section 12.10. If we take the generally described controls mentioned earlier and reduce them to possible technical controls, the result would be as shown in Table 12.6.

Requirement	Control	ID
Lawful processing: general clause	Proof of appropriate technical and organizational measures	ALL
Transparency	Control information retrieval framework	1
Defined and unambiguous purposes	▪ Data Controller Rule Framework ▪ Information retrieval framework ▪ Attribution appropriate?	2 1 3
Further processing within the scope of the purpose	Separate data storage: ▪ Attribution appropriate? ▪ Check interface	 3 4
Data relevant to the purpose	Where-used lists	5
Limited to the necessary extent	Purpose-based separate data storage: ▪ Data Controller Rule Framework ▪ Information retrieval framework ▪ Attribution appropriate? ▪ Authentication ▪ The principle of minimization in the authorization concept ▪ Storage control ▪ Access logging ▪ Communication control ▪ Transport control ▪ Scrambling ▪ Depersonalization ▪ Block data if it's only kept for legal reasons ▪ Delete data if both the purpose and the legal reasons for retention have ceased to apply	 2 1 3 6 7 8 9 10 11 12 13 14 15

Table 12.6 Control Requirements

Requirement	Control	ID
Accuracy	▪ Duplicate check ▪ Master data management	16 17
Relevance	▪ Master data management ▪ Procedure when scoring values are no longer valid	17 18
Storage limitation	▪ Is data blocking based on rules? ▪ Is data blocking based on rules?	14 15
Code checks	▪ Patch management ▪ Transportation ▪ Code review	19 20 21
Scope of processing	Scope of processing	22
Configuration	▪ Transportation ▪ Modifiability: system and configuration	20 23
Interfaces	Interface checks Authorizations (also for technical users)	4 7
Logs	▪ Changes to the program ▪ Transport logs ▪ Changes to the table ▪ Document logging ▪ Behavioral logging ▪ Event logging	24 19 25 26 27 28
Access	▪ User concept ▪ Password rules ▪ Standard users ▪ User administration	29 30 31 32
Authorizations	▪ Principle of minimization ▪ Separation of functions ▪ Transparent risks	6 7 33
Availability	▪ Backup, disaster recovery	34

Table 12.6 Control Requirements (Cont.)

As you can see in Table 12.6, numerous monitoring requirements for different specifications are of considerable importance. In the following section, we'll discuss possible controls regarding the control requirements.

12.10 Technical Control Actions: Examples

In this section, we'll provide you with examples of technical control procedures. Some of these are part of standard system audits. However, these examples represent only a superficial fraction of the more than a thousand possible system audit controls. Data protection is based on technical security, which must be confirmed by means of a comprehensive system audit. Our examples are therefore far from adequate. They are merely food for thought in terms of technical security. From this list, we only see data-protection-specific control requirements in the following:

- Control requirement 1: Information retrieval framework
- Control requirement 2: Data Controller Rule Framework
- Control requirement 3: Attribution
- Control requirement 7: The principle of minimization in the authorization concept
- Control requirement 13: Depersonalization of test systems
- Control requirement 14: Data blocking
- Control requirement 15: Data deletion
- Control requirement 16: Duplicate check
- Control requirement 26: Document logging
- Control requirement 27: Behavioral logging

The Audit Information System (AIS) is available for the standard audit and can be used via Transaction SAIS (AIS – Workplace).

For a more in-depth study of audit/revision, refer to the relevant literature.

Control Requirement 1: Information Retrieval Framework

Proof of completeness

The information retrieval framework is used to provide information about a person's stored data in connection with the purposes you previously defined (see Chapter 8). When you activate the business function `CA_DTINF_`

FW, you document that use of the framework. The verification of the existence of customer-specific models with reference to all of the purposes you use is proof that you're able to provide full information about all personal data.

You can demonstrate that your organization actively uses the functionality by showing that search queries exist in the system. In a productive system, the completeness of the data found can only be checked at random. However, in a test system for business partners (that have been modeled accordingly) and the data created using test cases for business processes, you can prove that all data created in this way is also part of your data model and is fully included in the search result for the correct purposes.

Control Requirement 2: Data Controller Rule Framework

The Data Controller Rule Framework can be used to link the controllers and purposes you use with your data in the system and to simplify the maintenance of residence and retention periods for all grouped SAP Information Lifecycle Management (SAP ILM) objects (see Chapter 6). This functionality can be activated using the business function ILM_RULE_GENERATOR, which you can define as the first control point.

Responsible for all organizational units

The controllers defined in Customizing represent the organizational units relevant for the definition of SAP ILM rules in relation to the company code. Here you can check that for each company code you defined, at least one entry exists. By displaying the subordinate organizational units for each responsible unit, it's also possible to randomly check that all organizational units are linked to each other correctly.

Are there rules for all processes?

The defined purposes map your business processes and can therefore check the list of entries for completeness. The relevant SAP ILM objects are grouped together. By using the procedural model described in Chapter 3, you'll have created an overview list of your data, and you can now compare it with the data maintained in Customizing.

Verifying productive SAP ILM rules

Using your list of relevant business processes for each business area, you can also check the completeness of the maintained and active rules with the residence and retention periods. By viewing the generated SAP ILM rules, it's also possible to verify the existence of productive SAP ILM rules that are used in your blocking and deletion processes.

Control Requirement 3: Attribution

Checking the corporate structure

To determine whether an appropriate attribution is possible in the system, it's necessary to carry out an evaluation of the corporate structure. In Chapter 5, Section 5.2.1, we briefly explained where the assignments are maintained in the corporate structure in the IMG via **SAP Implementation Guide • Enterprise Structure • Assignment**.

The aim of the evaluation is to determine that significant organizational units have a clear relationship to the company code as independent accounting units and therefore generally as technical representatives of the controller.

Check POAs

In Chapter 5, Section 5.3, we introduced the process organizational attributes (POAs). We explained that these are characteristics, such as the account group or the sales document type. These attributes, like the line organizational attributes (LOAs), are indispensable for mapping the purpose of processing at the subclient level.

Procedural model as a basis

If you're following our suggested procedural model, you already know the main attributes because these are also required for blocking and deleting and for authorizations. If you use the Data Controller Rule Framework, the functional structure of the POAs and LOAs can be seen there.

Alternative procedure

To get an overview of the processes in the system landscape, compile the business artifacts used. Read the comments in Control Requirement 5, which explains how to verify the uses. Have the system determine which differentiation characteristics are used for these artifacts. Evaluate the sum of all POAs and LOAs to determine whether they are suitable for representing the purpose of processing.

Another way of checking the use of LOAs and POAs is to check the use of such attributes in the authorization concept in tables `AGR_1251` (Authorization Data for Activity Group) and `AGR_1252` (Organizational Levels for Authorizations).

Control Requirement 4: Interface Control

In Chapter 1, Section 1.2.4, we verified system interfaces. You need a complete list of the interfaces, the data that can be processed in these interfaces, and the technical measures that secure these interfaces, e.g., authentication mechanism, users, user types, authorizations, and encryption.

The DSAG states DSAG Data Protection Guidelines (Carlberg et al., 2014) address the following functions:

- Transaction SM59 (RFC destination)
- Transaction BD64 (distribution model maintenance)
- Basis services (BC-SRV) and SM54 (CPIC destination)
- Checking other connections (SAP Process Integration).

It's generally worth paying attention to Section 4.2.1.8 of the Data Protection Guide on this topic. Further documentation can also be found in the security guides under *https://help.sap.com* and in the Unified Connectivity (UCON) documentation. For the latter, also refer to the highly relevant Chapter 18 of *Authorizations in SAP Software* by Lehnert and Stelzner (SAP PRESS, 2010, *www.sap-press.com/2316*).

Control Requirement 5: Where-Used List

The search for blocked business partner data, for example, with Transaction SE16 (Data Browser), is only one of many options; many applications offer additional lists that you can use to verify data in the respective application (see Control Requirement 14 for more information on searching for blocked business partner data).

Where-used lists "domain" in tables As an application-independent tool, we also mention the report RSCRDOMA (Where-Used Lists for Domains in Tables). The report is part of the AIS, which can be used via Transaction SAIS (AIS – Workplace).

You can run the report for any Data Dictionary (DDIC) domain and data element names and find tables with contents that contain fields with reference to the selection criteria, as shown in Figure 12.14.

Report RPDINFO1 (Technical Overview of Infotypes), which allows SAP ERP HCM to perform a complete analysis of all infotypes used, is also worth mentioning. As shown in Figure 12.15, the number of entries is also specified.

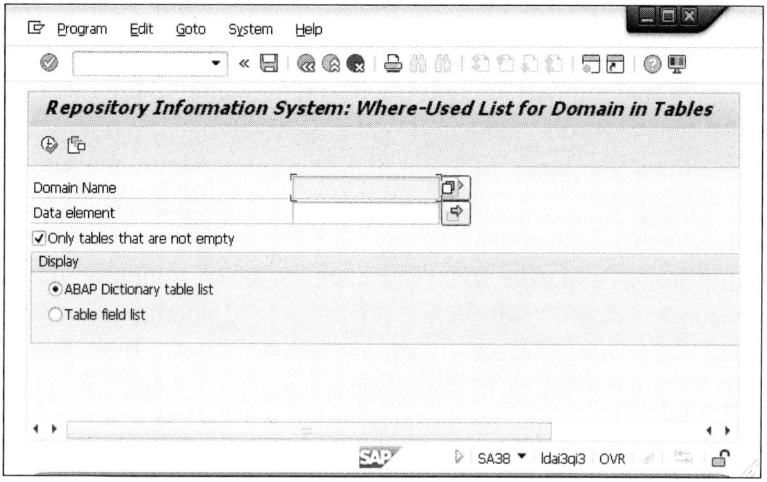

Figure 12.14 Report: Where-Used List for Domain in Tables

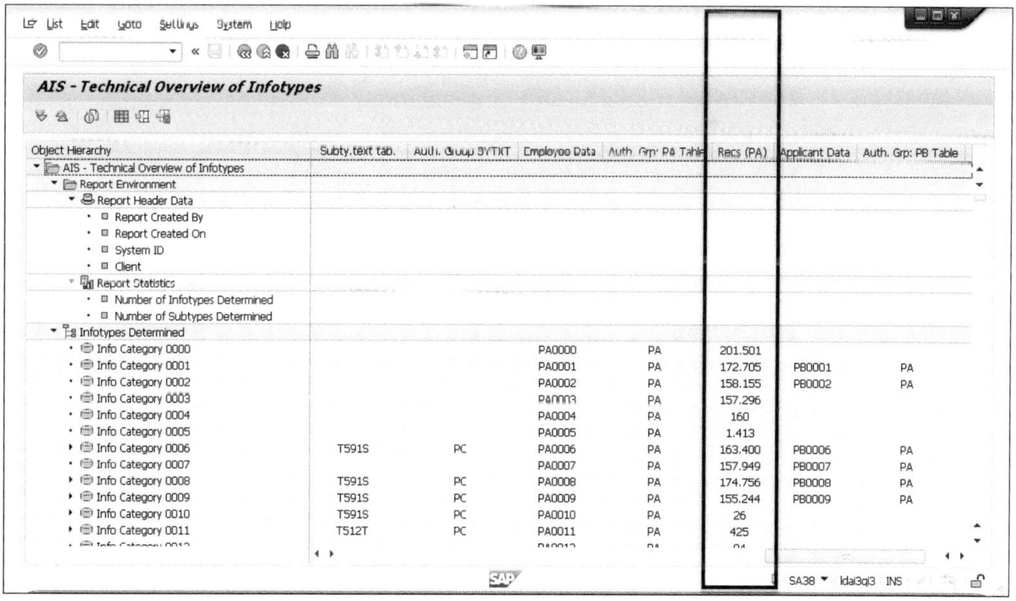

Figure 12.15 Technical Overview of Infotypes

Verifying archived data

You can usually list archived data using the archiving object display reports. These generally work by selecting existing archive files and outputting the key information for all archived data. Depending on the application, further important information may also be displayed.

You can also use Transaction SARI (Archive Information System) to read archived data. To do this, you have to create and activate archive information structures (supported, e.g., by SAP field catalogs) that enable you to search for specific data in all indexed archive files. Indexing can be done directly when the archive files are written, however, it's also possible to structure this at a later stage. For example, similar to Transaction SE16 (Data Browser), you can use Transaction SARE (Archive Explorer) to search for data for each archiving object and archive information structure. It's also possible to read the archive in other applications. For further information, see the corresponding application documentation.

Verifying data deletion

In Control Requirement 15, we describe how you can verify the deletion of data. The aim here is to prove that deletion was successful, that is, that it no longer exists in the database or the archive.

Control Requirement 6: Authentication

The unquestionable and unambiguous authentication of the user is ensured by appropriate procedures and parameters. In Chapter 1, Section 1.2.4, we explained the general requirements under the heading "User Control." The most important technical check to be performed at this point is the evaluation of the relevant profile parameters using report RSPARAM (Display SAP Profile Parameters), as shown in Figure 12.16.

Profile parameters

Profile parameters are explained in more detail in the system documentation. Also refer to SAP Note 2467 (Password Rules and Avoiding Incorrect Logons).

Note that depending on the configuration and authorizations in your development landscape, it may be possible to access the most productive system from these systems/clients. Therefore, also make sure to take care of the authentication parameters there.

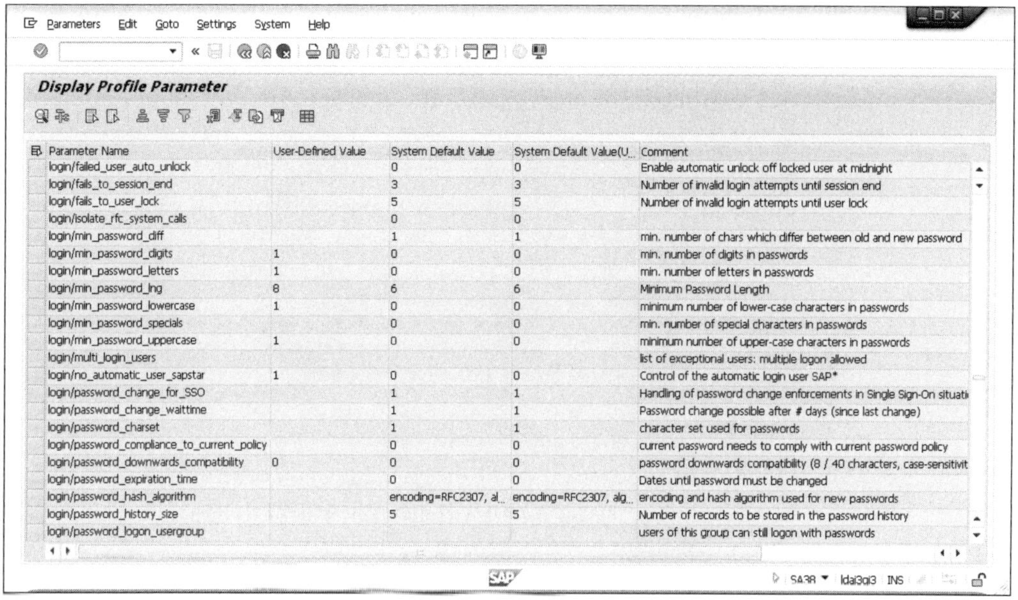

Parameter Name	User-Defined Value	System Default Value	System Default Value(U...	Comment
login/failed_user_auto_unlock		0	0	Enable automatic unlock off locked user at midnight
login/fails_to_session_end		3	3	Number of invalid login attempts until session end
login/fails_to_user_lock		5	5	Number of invalid login attempts until user lock
login/isolate_rfc_system_calls		0	0	
login/min_password_diff		1	1	min. number of chars which differ between old and new password
login/min_password_digits	1	0	0	min. number of digits in passwords
login/min_password_letters	1	0	0	min. number of letters in passwords
login/min_password_lng	8	6	6	Minimum Password Length
login/min_password_lowercase	1	0	0	minimum number of lower-case characters in passwords
login/min_password_specials		0	0	min. number of special characters in passwords
login/min_password_uppercase	1	0	0	minimum number of upper-case characters in passwords
login/multi_login_users				list of exceptional users: multiple logon allowed
login/no_automatic_user_sapstar	1	0	0	Control of the automatic login user SAP*
login/password_change_for_SSO		1	1	Handling of password change enforcements in Single Sign-On situati
login/password_change_waittime		1	1	Password change possible after # days (since last change)
login/password_charset		1	1	character set used for passwords
login/password_compliance_to_current_policy		0	0	current password needs to comply with current password policy
login/password_downwards_compatibility	0	0	0	password downwards compatibility (8 / 40 characters, case-sensitivit
login/password_expiration_time		0	0	Dates until password must be changed
login/password_hash_algorithm		encoding=RFC2307, al...	encoding=RFC2307, alg...	encoding and hash algorithm used for new passwords
login/password_history_size		5	5	Number of records to be stored in the password history
login/password_logon_usergroup				users of this group can still logon with passwords

Figure 12.16 Profile Parameters in Report RSPARAM (Display SAP Profile Parameters)

Control Requirement 7: Minimal Principle and Authorization Concept

In Chapter 7, Section 7.4, we considered the topic of risks in the authorization concept. Among other things, we looked at the purpose risk connected to the principle of minimization. Although we explained what useful risk definitions would look like, we didn't specify where they can be stored. In principle, these can be stored in a database that programs out the relevant data and verifies the risks. In SAP Business Suite, you can use the user information system (Transaction SUIM) or report RSUSR008_009_NEW (Critical Combination of Authorizations). This allows users and roles to be checked for defined risks. Maintenance of the definitions is shown in Figure 12.17.

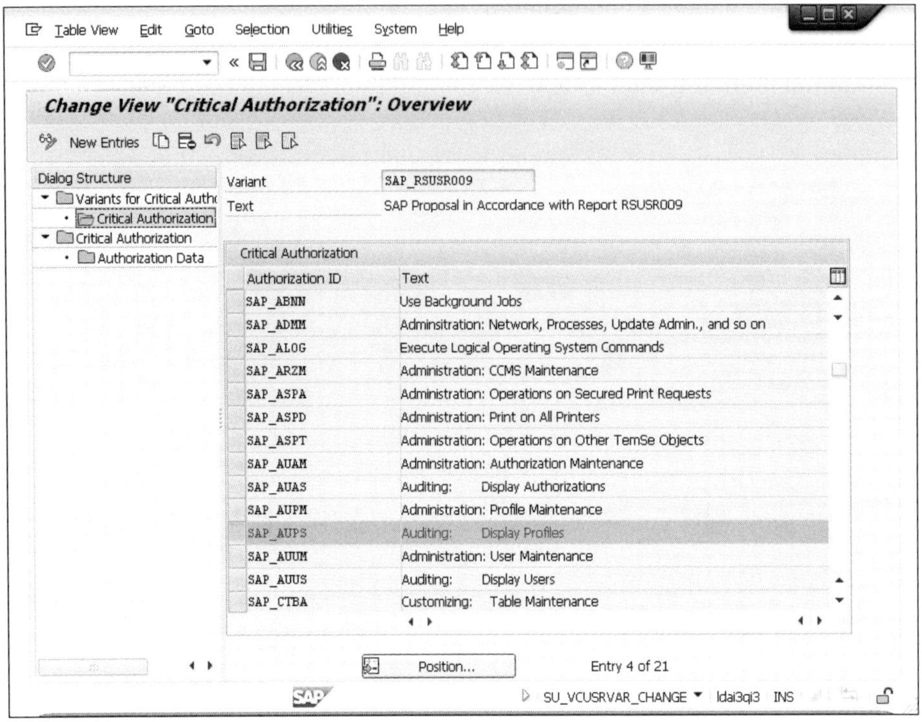

Figure 12.17 Maintaining Risk Definitions for Report RSUSR008_009_NEW (Critical Combination of Authorizations)

Can this be done comfortably? It's much easier to define risks and evaluate them using SAP Access Control in SAP GRC. This can help you set authorization assignments at a low risk from the very start.

However, note that explicit data protection risks aren't covered by the rule delivered by SAP with SAP Access Control. Similarly, there are also none in report RSUSR008_009_NEW (Critical Combination of Authorizations).

Additionally, neither of these instruments currently focus on the purpose risk; however, this can be verified by manual statements taken from the evaluations.

Random sample A simple sample of how well the principle of minimization has been taken into account is already outlined in Chapter 7, Section 7.2, using table AGR_1252 (Organizational Levels for Authorizations) and table AGR_1251 (Authorization Data for Activity Group).

Control Requirement 8: Storage Control

Storage controls are all measures that prevent unauthorized access to data storage containing personal data. While the storage in your server rooms are presumably effectively protected, it can also be assumed that there are numerous "wild" data stores on USB sticks and the like, which are no longer subject to this very control.

Furthermore, moving a nonencrypted hard disk with personal data, to another location—for whatever purpose—is unfortunately still a common practice.

Control Requirement 9: Access Control

As part of access control, you'll have to check the authentication (Control Requirement 6) and the authorizations (Control Requirement 7). Furthermore, you'll have to check the access logging (see Control Requirement 28), behavior logging (see Control Requirement 27), change logging (see Control Requirement 26), and finally any encryption measures (see Control Requirement 12).

Control Requirement 10: Transmission Control

As part of the transmission check, the interfaces have to be checked first (see Control Requirement 4). The verifications generated there must be added to in terms of the transmission control with the information about the data recipients and the logging of the transmission.

Application Link Enabling (ALE) is a standard procedure for transferring data within SAP system groups and beyond. The application systems of such a network are only coupled loosely. The data is exchanged asynchronously to ensure that it also reaches the receiving systems in the event that they can't be reached at the time of transmission. Intermediate documents (IDocs) are exchanged via ALE using RFC connections. An IDoc is essentially a containment. You can get an idea of what to expect from the framed area in Figure 12.18 where the field names and field contents of the transmission are displayed.

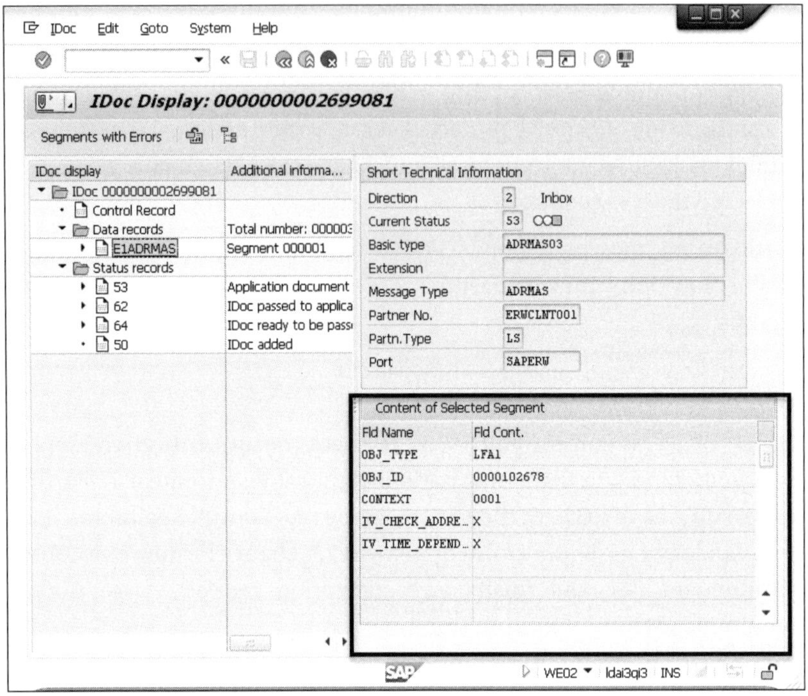

Figure 12.18 IDoc Display

The IDoc display was started from Transaction WE02 (Display IDoc). This transaction generally shows which IDocs were sent or received.

Control Requirement 11: Transport Control

The transport control is also made up of elements that are already partly known. As it's actually also a matter of physical transport, the first measures to be taken are storage control (see Control Requirement 8). It should also be mentioned that data transmission has to be encrypted (see Control Requirement 12). Secure Network Communications (SNC) enables you to establish secure connections between two SAP Systems. You can evaluate the SNC settings using the report RSPARAM (Display SAP Profile Parameters) shown earlier in Figure 12.16.

Control Requirement 12: Encryption

Encryption is possible in SAP Business Suite and in SAP S/4HANA via Secure Store and Forward (SSF). SSF, however, needs an external product to be able to encrypt effectively. You can check the settings in the IMG by selecting **SAP Implementation Guide • SAP NetWeaver • Application Server System Administration • Maintaining System Public-Key Information • Maintaining Application-Dependent SSF Information**.

Other products can also be used for encryption at the database level.

Control Requirement 13: Depersonalization

In Chapter 1, Section 1.1.12, we discussed the difficulties of anonymizing and/or pseudonymizing data. The first check in the event that this solution is invoked is therefore mandatory to verify the result. Refer to the literature listed in Chapter 1, Section 1.1.12.

As a substitute, we use the term *depersonalization* of data, which describes the goal and procedure and not the state of the data after changes are made.

One very important control action in terms of depersonalization is to check whether or not test systems have been treated adequately. Even today, we still have customers who use unchanged copies of their productive systems for testing. It's obvious that this generally can't be used within the scope of the original purpose of use. In our opinion, it's generally imperative to remove the personal reference to test data as far as possible. We assume that there is an obvious exception to this rule, namely when it comes to testing functions and procedures relating to data protection itself. In this case, the other protective technical and organizational measures would have to correspond, in all points, to the protective measures of the productive system, with the exception of test-relevant deviations, for example, in the authorization concept.

In Chapter 11, we provided an introduction to the SAP Test Data Migration Server (SAP TDMS). This allows you to effectively achieve depersonalization while maintaining the logical references.

Control Requirement 14: Data Blocking

As described in Chapter 4, Section 4.3, you can block transactional data, business partner master data, and time-dependent personal data in SAP ERP Personnel Administration (PA). You should also check the corresponding settings:

- SAP ILM
- Execution of the end of purpose (EoP) check for master data
- Archiving transactional data
- Configuration of the time-dependent authorization check in PA in SAP ERP HCM

SAP ILM residence rules for blocking by archiving

By making extensive use of the Data Controller Rule Framework (see Control Requirement 2), you've already demonstrated use of all the SAP ILM rules necessary for blocking transactional data. Because blocks are set after the residence periods have expired, you can also check the completeness of the productive SAP ILM rules for rule set category `RST` (residence rules) and the check area `ARCHIVING` in all SAP ILM objects provided for this purpose.

Use application-specific retention times

Some applications also offer additional Customizing for maintaining residence times that must be expired before archiving, such as Transaction VORI (Archiving Control Shipment Costs) for archiving object `SD_VFKK`. Because Customizing is always in the context of usage, a simple check for all possible transactions and their completeness isn't possible here. However, maintenance should be part of the archiving setup for each archiving object and can also be documented accordingly at this point.

Run archiving

Transactional data can be blocked by archiving the data and with it the access restrictions by reading it into the archive. You can check for the complete and periodic execution of archiving runs for personal data by displaying the statistics for data archiving in Transaction SARA (Archive Administration), as shown in Figure 12.19.

Archive all data

It's therefore not possible to check whether the choice of data to be archived includes all data. The variants of the write sessions used in archiving sessions provide all information necessary. In contrast to the archiving of mass data, it's necessary to regularly archive all personal data. This means that you're not allowed to archive only those objects or database tables with a particularly large amount of data.

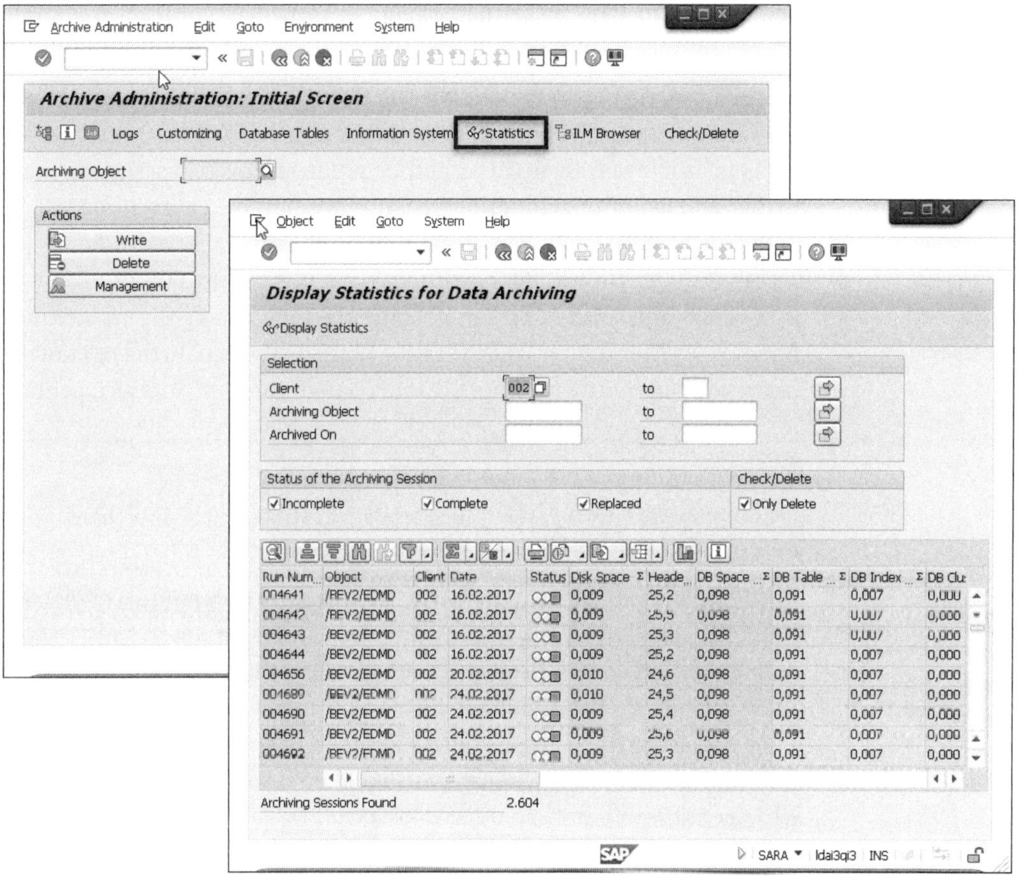

Figure 12.19 Statistics for Archiving

Storing the archive files

We won't go into more detail about how you can ensure the secure storage of archive files for your SAP ILM-certified WebDAV server because different measures may be required, depending on the option selected. As mentioned in Chapter 4, SAP ILM storage guarantees that the data won't be changed and that the retention periods will be respected.

Reading blocked data in the archive

You can only read data in the archive using the transactions designed for this purpose. This expressly includes application transactions that use the AIS (Transaction SARI). You can find out which these are, for example, in the documentation for the application. Transaction SARA (Archive Administration) also offers a **Read from Archive** option. By assigning these transactions and the associated authorizations to the roles of the users who actually need access to data from the archive, in principle, you can effectively restrict the blocking of data.

Read in archive by deadlines

You can use the business function ILM_BLOCKING not only to control read-only archive access but also to set up checks as to the periods in which reading is to be allowed. By defining authorization groups and assigning them to the valid retention periods of the SAP ILM object in Transaction IRMPOL (ILM Sets of Rules), you can create groups of users who are only able to access the archive for their respective check period. Data outside this period may still exist, but it can no longer be found using the archive read function. By checking the authorization object S_IRM_BLOC in the roles of the users, you can control for whom reading is permitted and in which periods.

[!]

Note the New Authorization Check

Authorization checks for archive access affect all access to the archive.

Archiving without blocking

Retention periods without assigned authorization groups are useful if, for example, as in the case of archiving mass data, data doesn't necessarily have to be blocked. Any user with access to the archive can read the data for these periods, even if simultaneously valid rules with assigned authorization groups exist. This makes separate control of such SAP ILM rules necessary. Our understanding is that this should only be set up for the shortest period of time.

Rules for blocking master data

Residence rules for blocking business partner master data, as described in Chapter 4, Section 4.2.3, were created in check area BUPA_DP and rule set category RST (residence rules) for the following SAP ILM objects:

- CA_BUPA (Business Partner)
- FI_ACCRECV (Customer Master Data)
- FI_ACCPAYB (Vendor Master Data)
- FI_ACCKNVK (Contact Person)

We don't expect you to have to configure this for each application name registered in the EoP check. However, productive SAP ILM rules should be available for the most important applications that characterize the business processes and also for the application names of the master data itself.

Configuring a business partner block

The IMG under **SAP Implementation Guide • Cross-Application Components • Data Protection • Locking and Unlocking Data** contains the necessary settings to be checked such as the definition of the next check period, the settings of the RFC connections for the leading master system and connected systems, and the definition of the authorization group for identifying blocked master data.

Authorization to access blocked master data

You can use the authorization groups assigned to the blocked business partners in particular to restrict users' ability to display blocked data using the authorization group-based authorization objects of the business partner master data. The roles of the users must therefore be checked to ensure that this special authorization group value is only contained for users who are actually authorized. Roles that contain for example, the value * for read access for all authorization group values should therefore only exist in exceptional cases. We recommend that you define these as critical authorizations, as described in Chapter 7, Section 7.4.

Check authorization object B_BUP_PCPT

The same applies to authorization object B_BUP_PCPT (business partner: business purpose fulfilled). This authorization object provides the valid activity 03 (Display), which also checks the display of blocked business partners in the system. The other activities 05 (Block), 49 (Request), and 95 (Unblock) are about the authorization to execute the EoP check or unblock master data and should, in our opinion, only be granted to a certain group of users.

Performing the EoP check

In our opinion, the EOP check for business partners should be carried out regularly. As this is usually mass data, it only makes sense to do this in the background. You can use Transaction SM37 (Overview of Job Selection) to control the scheduling and successful processing of jobs for the ABAP programs BUPA_PREPARE_EOP (Central Business Partner) or CVP_PREPARE_EOP (Customer and Vendor Master Data).

Evaluate EoP check log

Transaction SLG1 (Application Log: Display Logs) enables you to display the EoP check log for the central business partner for example, to check for errors. To do this, use object BDT_DATAARCHIVING with subobject BUPA_EOP.

You can use Transaction CVP_DISPLAY_LOG (Display Stored Application Logs for Customer and Vendor) to display the application log for the EoP check for customers and vendors in greater contextual detail at the log item level than in Transaction SLG1. To do so, use the object CVP_LOG with the subobjects CUSTOMER_BLOCKING (Block Customers) and SUPPLIER_BLOCKING (Block Vendors). Customer selection is shown in Figure 12.20.

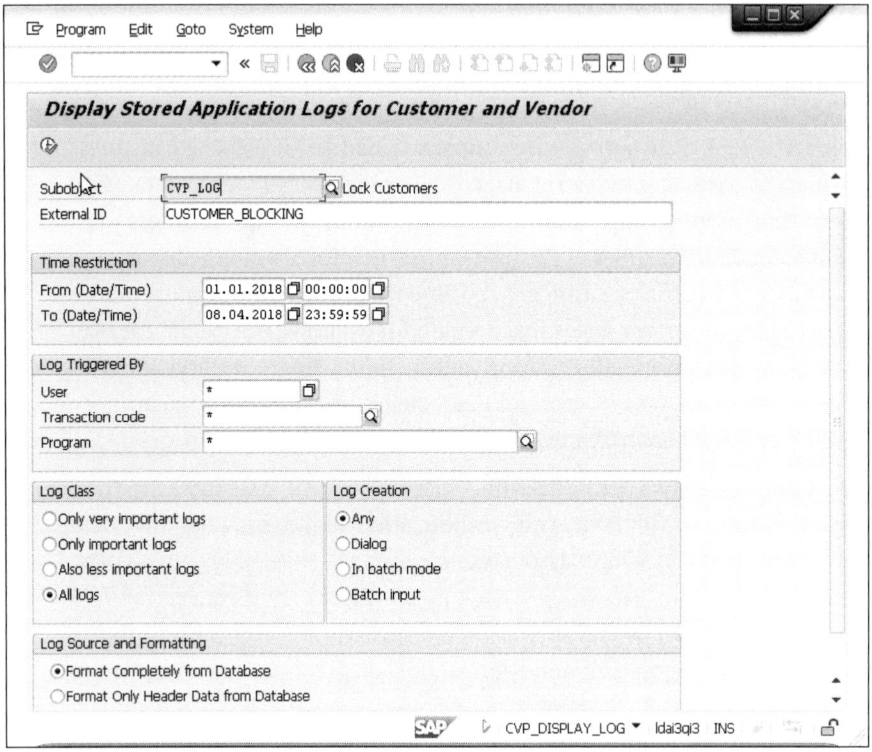

Figure 12.20 Check Application Log for EoP Customer

Check partner block

One last checkpoint on the subject of blocking business partner master data is to check whether the data has actually been blocked. To do so, you can use Transaction SE16 (Data Browser). You may select blocked data for the blocking indicator "X" in the tables as shown in Table 12.7.

Business Partner Object	Table	Field for Blocking Indicator
Central business partner	BUT000	XPCPT
Customer master (general part)	KNA1	CVP_XBLCK

Table 12.7 Business Partner Master Data Tables with the Relevant Field for the Blocking Indicator

Business Partner Object	Table	Field for Blocking Indicator
Customer master (company code)	KNB1	CVP_XBLCK_B
Vendor master (general part)	LFA1	CVP_XBLCK
Vendor master (company code)	LFB1	CVP_XBLCK_B

Table 12.7 Business Partner Master Data Tables with the Relevant Field for the Blocking Indicator (Cont.)

Blocking in connected systems

Don't forget that the blocking indicators are also communicated to the business partners in the connected systems and should therefore also be checked there to ensure that the blocking information is correctly available. As this is either synchronous or asynchronous using corresponding RFC function modules, SAP Enterprise Services, or ALE, you should also check the logs for inbound and outbound processing. Further information on interface controls is provided in the section on Control Requirement 4.

Time-dependent blocking: PA

The time-dependent authorization check requires active implementation of the Business Add-In (BAdI) HRPADAUTH_TIME (Time Logic in the PA Authorization Check). You can also check which users have assigned authorization object P_DURATION (Authorization periods for HCM Master Data) in their roles and whether this authorization covers correct infotypes/subtypes and periods. Similarly, you can also assign the setup IDs for the role-specific authorization periods from the Customizing activity **Assign ID for Role-Specific Authorization Periods (Time Period ID)** and check the periods set there for displaying personnel data in the past.

Control Requirement 15: Data Deletion

Final deletion, that is, the destruction of master and/or transactional data, can be carried out either in the database directly, or you can delete data that has been previously archived and is therefore no longer in the database, as described in Chapter 4, Section 4.4.

Deletion in the database

We'll first consider the options available to destroy data in the database, that is, data that hasn't been archived. As recommended in Chapter 4, Section 4.4.1, you can either use Transaction SARA (Archive Administration)—

execution of archiving with SAP ILM action **Data Destruction**—or Transaction ILM_DESTRUCTION (Data Destruction) for data destruction objects.

Deletion has to be planned—in the same way as with archiving—in the background; that is, you should therefore be able to document the existence and the success of the related background processes.

SAP ILM provides you with statistics to document the amount of deleted data in megabytes (MB) per run. According to Control Requirement 4, however, the check for the deletion of the data itself is a negative verification of use. This means that there should be no hits related to the deleted data. You can, however, verify which selections you used to carry out the destruction in the destruction procedures' administration.

Deletion in the archive You'll be able to delete data in archive files after the retention periods have expired. To do this, as described in Chapter 4, Section 4.4.2, use Transaction ILM_DESTRUCTION (Data Destruction) for the types Archive Development Kit (ADK) files or **Attachments and Print Lists**. Storage in your certified SAP-ILM ensures the data can't be deleted beforehand. Furthermore, Legal Case Management inhibits blocked data in a legal case from being deleted. Both procedures should also be documented.

You can also check and document the planning and success of the background processes for the destruction data sets maintained. The option described in Chapter 4, Section 4.4.2, of a dual control principle for performing the deletion should also be documented.

Ultimately, however, deletion in the archive is the same as deleting the corresponding files. Depending on the storage system, it should therefore also be possible to prove that the files were successfully deleted from there.

Critical authorization We recommend defining authorization for archiving and deleting to be critical authorizations as previously described in Chapter 7, Section 7.4. The documentation, for example, that of the Transaction PFCG template role `SAP_BC_ILM_DESTROY`, provides you with further information as to which authorization objects need to be checked for this.

Control Requirement 16: Duplicate Check

Detecting duplicates The functionalities concerning duplicate checks serve to validate the data entered and to monitor the creation of duplicate data records. This check can be set up separately for every change or creation of a central business partner (as well as for customer and vendor master data, and contact persons). However, it's also possible to run this in the background (particularly at the beginning of a consolidation process) to identify potential duplicates within the data that has already been saved.

Carrying out data cleansing

Data cleansing enables you to include, compare, and merge redundant business partner master records (potential duplicates) in the data cleansing cases. After the data cleansing process, you can use archiving to remove unneeded records from the system.

Options to identify duplicates

The following options to identify duplicates are available:

- Business Address Services (BAS) interface for embedding respective third-party software (search engines)
- Customer-owned software programs
- Business Information Provider (BIP) that searches through your data for potential duplicates
- Executing a duplicate check by means of match profiles in the application SAP Master Data Governance (SAP MDG)

Control Requirement 17: Master Data Management

In Chapter 1, Section 1.1.3, we briefly addressed the necessity of a data-protection-compliant management of master data. Chapter 10 deals with the SAP solution for master data management. A check is required as to whether personal data is accurate, up-to-date, and without duplicates. Thus, Control Requirement 16 is also part of the subject matter of this control requirement.

If you would rather not use a central solution for data management, potential checks can also be planned in the SAP Process Control in SAP GRC.

Control Requirement 18: Scoring Values

Scoring values or profiles as defined in Art. 4 (4) GDPR are to be regarded as values that may lead to automatic or semiautomatic system decision-making. They are determined, among other things, from a customer's payment history but also from ratings, for example, from SCHUFA (German credit bureau) and on the basis of ratings such as those provided by credit investigation companies.

Scoring in the financial supply chain

A process like this should be defined, for example, under **SAP Implementation Guide • Financial Supply Chain Management • Credit Management • Credit Risk Monitoring • Create Rule for Scoring and Credit Limit Calculation**.

Organizational measures must be taken to determine where such procedures are used. This also has to be checked technically. In addition to existence control, we have to check whether the data, such as payment behavior, leading to such a decision is kept up to date, accurate, and even still within the scope of the original purpose of use.

Control Requirement 19: Patch Management

The patches required for the actual system landscape, particularly security patches, can be checked in the application system recommendations in SAP Solution Manager. The patches installed and the notes installed for the ABAP instances will be taken into account.

An overview of the security patches can also be found at *https://support.sap.com/en/my-support/knowledge-base/security-notes-news.html*.

Control Requirement 20: Transport

In a system landscape, transport provides the necessary tools to transport changes to the configuration or to the programs from the development system to a test/quality management system and potentially further to the productive system. According to Chuprunov (2012, p. 201):

> *Experience has shown that there are very few complaints in the system landscape, as these do not only affect the requirements of auditors, but primarily the very interests of companies.*

Task of your auditing department

We assume it's sufficient to have a general description of the procedure and that you'll arrange for it to be regularly confirmed by the department responsible for auditing activities.

Control Requirement 21: Code Review

It's certainly state of the art that the software used is subjected to extensive tests before it's put to use. Such a test comprises several steps, starting with functional developer tests to determine that it works and process-related tests to determine that the effect specified in the design is achieved without unintentionally restricting other software functions.

Technical tests for customer-specific code

The tests then become much more technical. A code review can be carried out in various forms, including line-by-line manual checks by experts. A more effective way to find vulnerabilities is to use code scanners that use known vulnerabilities to scan the code. Unfortunately, the typical vulnerabilities are still user names and passwords that are permanently stored in the programs. It goes without saying that SAP uses appropriate procedures that comply with relevant industry standards. However, many customers still don't realize that customer code can also be hacked, meaning that their own developments have to be monitored accordingly.

Further task of your auditing department

Together with HP, SAP offers the following solution: SAP Fortify software by Micro Focus and SAP NetWeaver Application Server, add-on for code vulnerability analysis.

Again, it's our assumption that the data protector doesn't have to learn how to hack but can instead rely on the procedures that are already well-used in your company. If there is no such procedure for customer code, he should push for the introduction of relevant procedures, which are then, of course, also the subject to the company's own auditing activities

Control Requirement 22: Scope of Processing

The scope of processing was mainly established using the where-used lists (see Control Requirement 5). In some literature, reference is made to Transaction SPAM (Support Package Manager); here you can at least check which support packages (SPs) have been imported for which components. These may be interpreted as an indication of which components are used; however, we recommend that you always use correct where-used lists.

Control Requirement 23: Changeability of System and Configuration

In principle, productive systems may not be changeable. In addition to data protection issues (proof of integrity), this also results from accounting regulations and laws. A distinction must be made between the system change option and the client change option. You can view the system change option locally in Transaction SE06 (Set Up Transport Organizer).

In addition to the system change option being displayed locally, this can also be displayed centrally in the SAP Solution Manager in the Configuration Validation application.

The client changeability can be displayed locally for each client in Transaction SCC4 (Client Administration), as shown in Figure 12.21. These two views (system change option and client change option) are now combined in Transaction RSAUDIT_SYSTEM_ENV (Client and System Settings), which, with display authorizations only, provides a complete overview of all clients in the system.

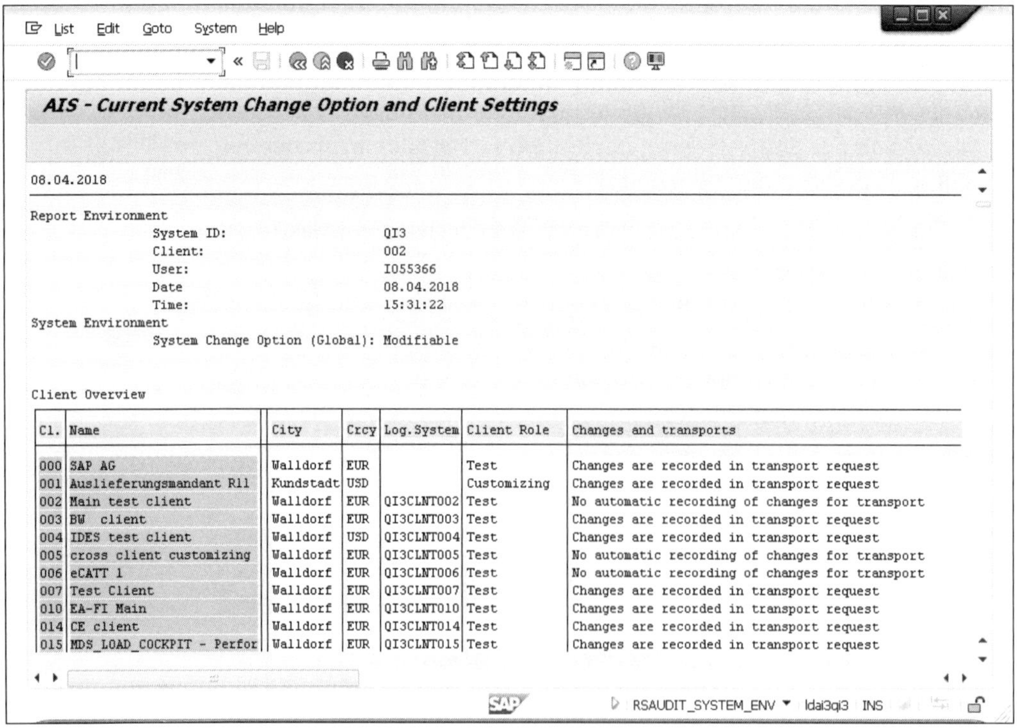

Figure 12.21 Client and System Settings

Also with regard to these settings, it should suffice for the data protector to have the settings explained and to document them. The department responsible for auditing should monitor these settings and report accordingly.

Another task for the auditing department

Control Requirement 24: Logging Changes to Programs

Program changes and internal revision

Program changes and configuration changes always reach the productive system via the TMS. Controlling the changes is therefore a two-step process in which the logs of the TMS and the version management of programs in the development system have to be synchronized.

In this respect, we also assume that, from a data protection perspective, it's necessary to document the basic procedure; however, control can and should be carried out by the internal auditing department.

Control Requirement 25: Changes to Tables

From a data protection perspective, changes made to the tables must be logged whenever configurations are involved that have an influence on personal data. Table logging should only be used as an exception, when necessary for logging transactional changes, because such logging can have a significant effect on performance.

In any event, you have to ensure that logging is active. You can check this by entering the profile parameter "rec/client" in Transaction RZ11 (Profile Parameter Maintenance) and prompting the display. Figure 12.22 shows the necessary settings.

Internal auditing again

In the selected field, you can see that not all clients are logged. In a productive system, the productive client must be switched on at a minimum.

Here, too, the profile parameter is presumably checked by your internal audit because logging is also required for other legal reasons. The general task of the auditing entity, however, is followed by the task of data protection to check whether relevant tables are scheduled for logging. This can be verified in report RDDPRCHK (Check Table Logging). You can evaluate the changes themselves using Transaction SCU3 (Table History). For more information, see SAP Note 112388 (Tables Requiring Logging).

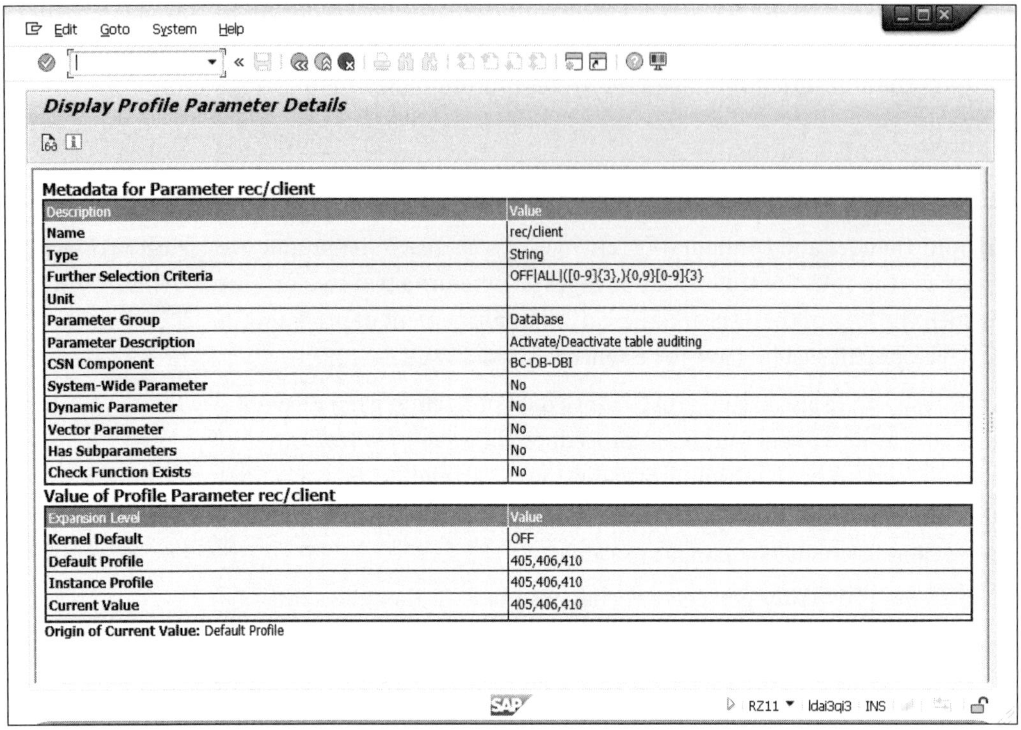

Figure 12.22 Profile Parameters for Logging Tables

Control Requirement 26: Logging of Documents

The general logging of changes made to personal data can be traced in the transactions. Figure 12.23 shows an example of this for user master records.

And in SAP ERP HCM?

You can also evaluate the changes using report CHANGEDOCU_READ (Read Change Documents from Archive or Database).

Report RPUAUDOO (Logged Changes to Infotype Data) is also available in SAP ERP HCM, as shown in Figure 12.24.

You can navigate forward to the detailed changes by double-clicking on the selected line.

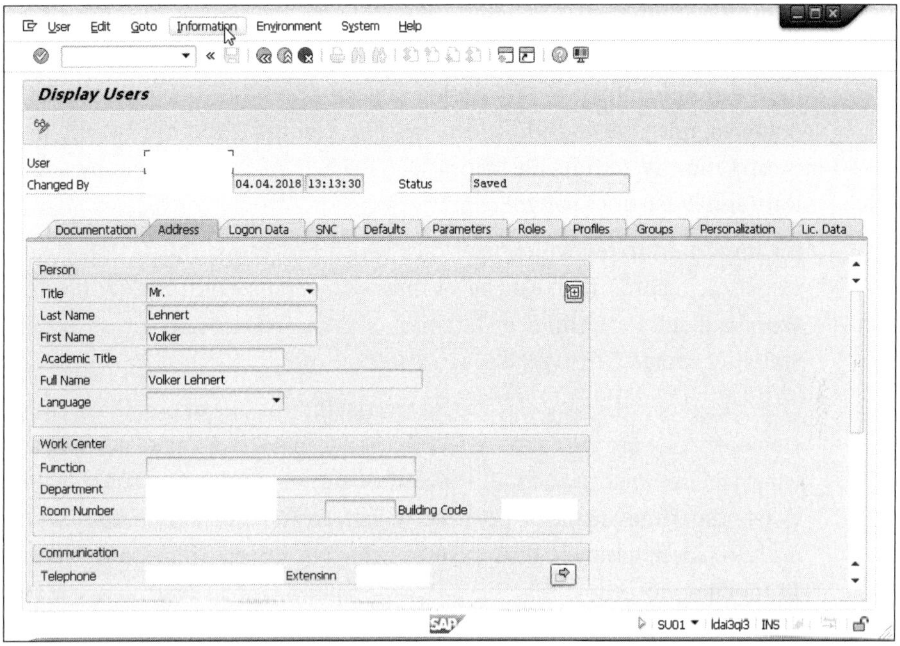

Figure 12.23 Change Documents for User Master Records

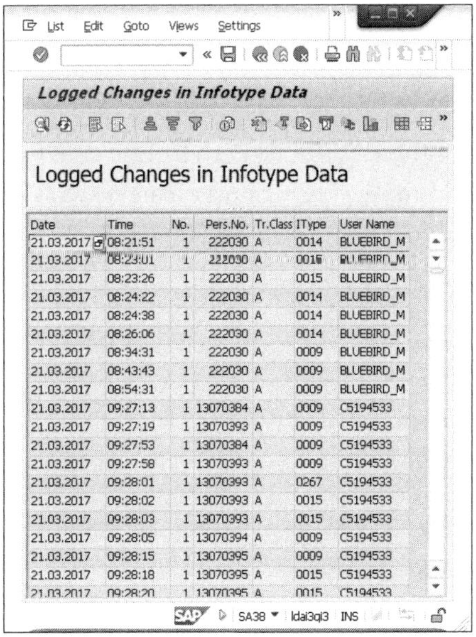

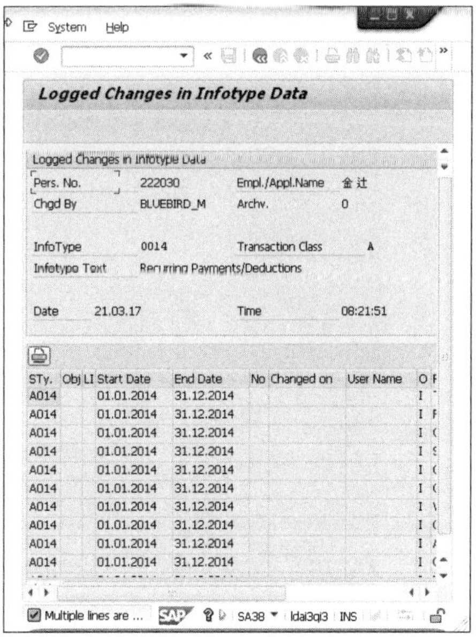

Figure 12.24 Logging of Changes in SAP ERP HCM

Control Requirement 27: Logging of Behavior

In our opinion, the logging of behavior is also one of the measures to be used and controlled in data protection. Among other things, a record is made when a user logs on to the system. You can check this in the user information system using Transaction RSUSR200 (List of Users by Logon Date and Password Change).

It's important to log which user calls which programs. This is done using statistical records that can be evaluated in Transaction ST03N (System Workload and Performance Statistics) or Transaction STAD (Cross-System Statistics Record Display) (see Figure 12.25).

The data generated here can provide initial indications of possible misuse. However, they are also used in SAP Access Control to evaluate periodically whether users really need all the authorizations they have. Such evaluations sometimes make it possible to reduce the amount of application authorizations assigned by up to 90%, which in any case represents a benefit for data protection. Also see SAP Note 548624 (FAQ: Performance Monitors, R/3 System Log, System Availability).

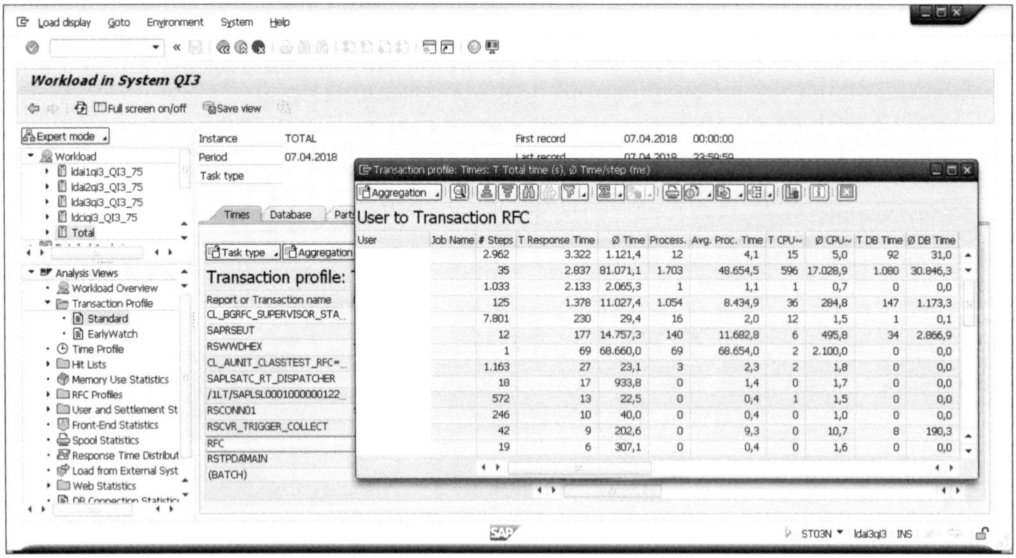

Figure 12.25 Evaluation in the System Workload Monitor

Another important behavioral protocol, Read Access Logging (RAL), was introduced in Chapter 9.

[!]

Logging Is Necessary and Problematic

Logging user activities is always an ambivalent procedure. On the one hand, it's subject to co-determination by the works council/staff council. On the other hand, however, logging is only permitted at all if there are any relevant legal grounds or if logging is for the purpose of system security or data protection. In the opinion of the supervisory authorities (Working Group "Technical and Organizational Data Protection Issues," 2009), it's only permitted if access is limited to the purpose of logging and if data is actually evaluated.

Control Requirement 28: Logging of Events

Exemplary control actions

Event logging covers all logs that are suitable for verifying that the system is being operated correctly or the potentially problematic events that may have occurred. The AIS, Transaction SAIS (AIS Workplace), contains numerous transactions that log events under **System Logs** and **Status Displays**. Again, we can only provide examples of the control actions.

In Control Requirement 10, we've already dealt with the ALE procedure; there we've shown how IDocs can be evaluated and also how transmission can generally be controlled.

In Control Requirement 14, we described how Transaction SLG1 (Application Log: Display Logs) can be used to verify that the EoP was processed correctly.

The Security Audit Log should also be mentioned in this section. The following can be verified here (*http://help.sap.com*):

- Successful and unsuccessful dialog logon attempts
- Successful and unsuccessful RFC logon attempts
- RFC prompts of function modules
- Successful and unsuccessful transaction starts
- Successful and unsuccessful report starts
- Changes to user master records
- Changes to the audit configuration

You can check the configuration in Transaction SM19 (Configuration Security Audit) and perform analyses using Transaction SM20 (Analysis of the Security Audit Log). The start of the analysis is shown in Figure 12.26.

Subsequent Transactions

As of SAP NetWeaver 7.50, Transaction SM19 (Configuration Security Audit) and Transaction SM20 (Analysis of Security Audit Logs) have been replaced by Transaction RSAU_CONFIG (Security Audit Log – Configuration), Transaction RSAU_READ_LOG (Analyze Security Audit Log), Transaction RSAU_ADMIN (SAL – Administration of Log Data), and others. See SAP Note 2191612 – FAQ: Use of the Security Audit Log as of NetWeaver 7.50.

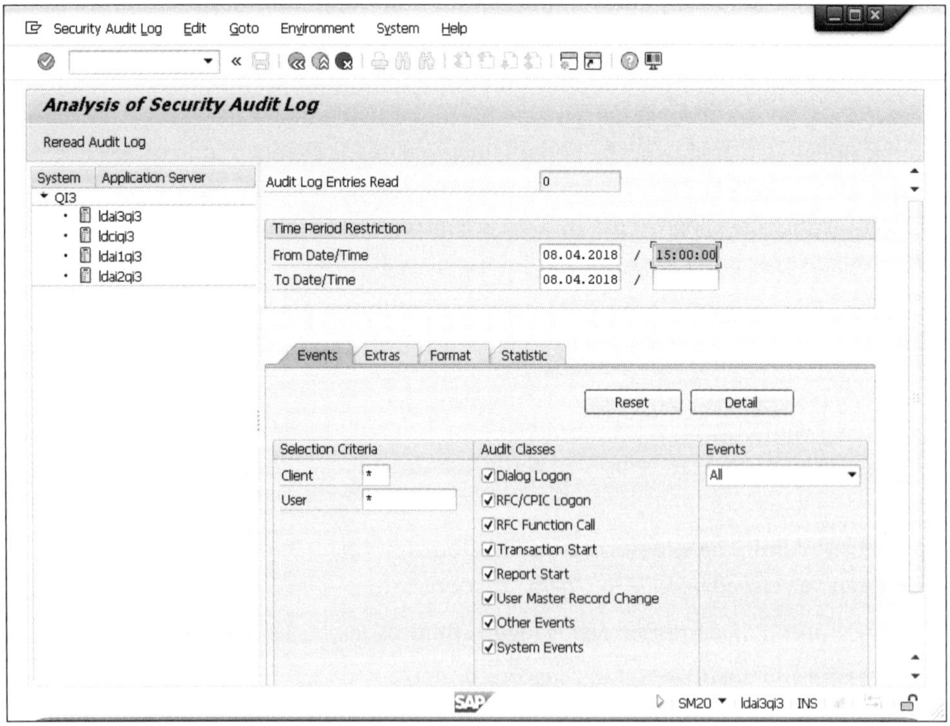

Figure 12.26 Analysis of Security Audit Logs

Events and internal auditing

In our view, complete control, far beyond the scope described, is also a matter of internal auditing; however, data protection should at least be able to and must at least present these measures generically.

Control Requirement 29: User Concept

In addition to the topics already discussed, only the following needs to be said about the user concept:

- Technical users must be created specifically for a purpose.
- Users for natural persons must be created individually.
- Every action in the system must always be traceable back to an identifiable user.

The fact is, however, that the sharing of user names and passwords is still quite common in many companies. Additionally, technical users sometimes have comprehensive authorizations and are used for numerous purposes.

You can run analyses in the user information system using Transaction SUIM (User Information System). A selection of relevant reports can be seen in Figure 12.27.

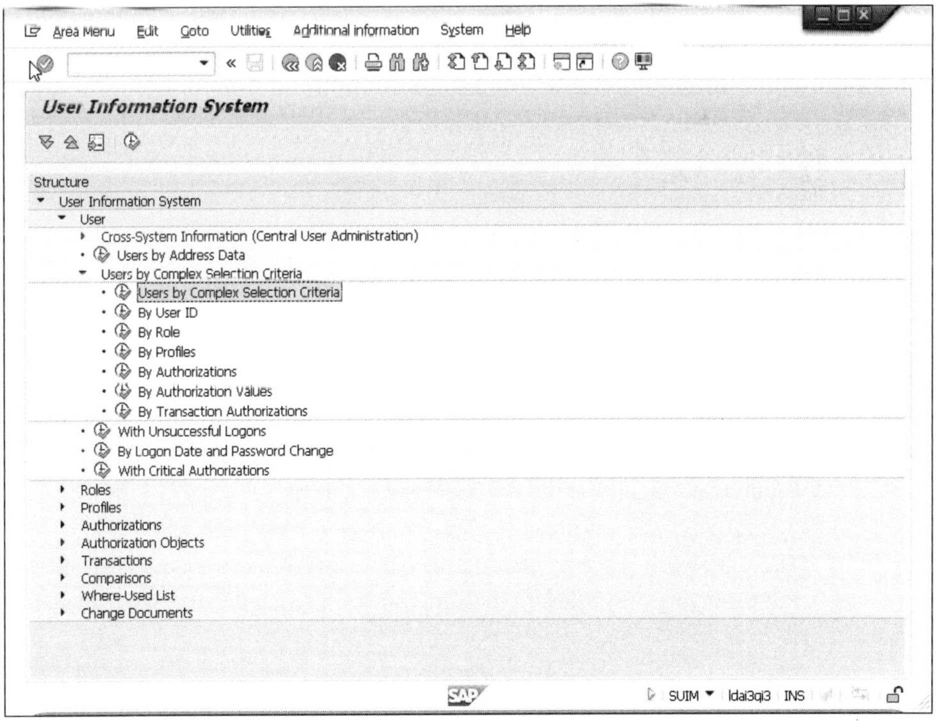

Figure 12.27 Selected Reports in the User Information System

Control Requirement 30: Password Rules

Significant changes have been made to the password rules. In addition to the definition of password rules using profile parameters, security policies have now been introduced. A security policy defines, among other things, the password rules that apply to a user assigned to this rule. In Transaction SU01 (User Maintenance) in the **Logon Data** tab in Figure 12.28, the position at which this data can be displayed in the user master record has been selected. A comprehensive analysis is possible using Transaction S_YI3_39000082 (Where-Used List for Sec. Policies).

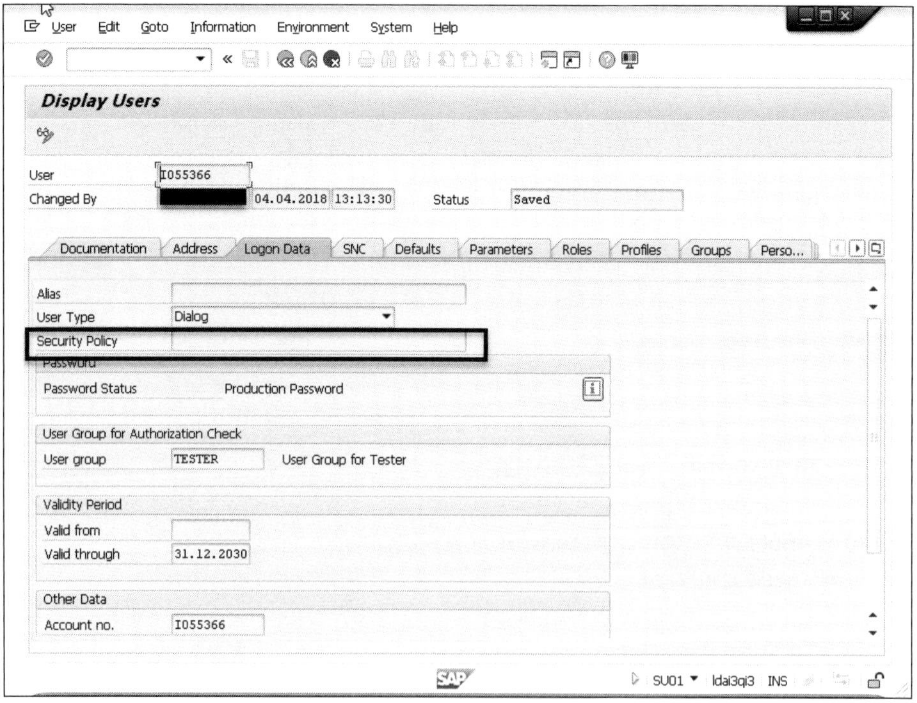

Figure 12.28 Security Policy in a User Master Record

The password profile parameters that can be evaluated with report RSPARAM are only relevant to users who aren't assigned to a security policy.

Authentication, user concept, and password rules are essential and interdependent components of ensuring the integrity of the system; relevant controls are subject to accountability.

Control Requirement 31: Standard Users

SAP criteria for standard users

When SAP NetWeaver AS ABAP is installed, the standard users SAP*, DDIC, EARLYWATCH, TMSADM, and SAPCPIC are automatically created in the client. These must be handled in accordance with SAP recommendations.

SAP (see *http://help.sap.com*, keyword "Standard Users") recommends that you regularly check the following criteria to protect the standard users.

- Maintain an overview of your clients, and ensure that no unknown clients exist.
- Make sure that SAP* exists and has been deactivated in all clients.
- Make sure that the default passwords for SAP*, DDIC, and EARLYWATCH were changed.
- Make sure that these users belong to the supergroup in all clients.
- Lock users SAP*, DDIC, and EARLYWATCH. Unlock them only when absolutely necessary.
- By default, user DDIC is set up to transport the background job (`RDDIMPDP`). SAP recommends that you set up another user for this job so that you can lock DDIC.
- The user requires the authorizations `SAP_ALL` and `S_A.SYSTEM` because the job prompts function modules for several applications that can't be determined for all cases.
- Delete SAPCPIC if you don't need it. At least make sure that you've changed the default password for SAPCPIC.
- Change the default password of TMSADM.

Proof that these requirements have been implemented and that they are subject to regular checks should be included in documentation of the procedure.

Control Requirement 32: User Administration

SAP's security guides are unique in terms of the authorization management that must be observed: authorizations and users in the productive system must not be maintained by one single user. Separation of functions into the three users involved is strongly recommended:

- **Role administrator**
  The role administrator maintains the authorizations in roles but isn't permitted to generate the corresponding profiles or assign the roles to the users.
- **User administrator**
  The user administrator is permitted to maintain the user master records and assign roles but can't change roles or generate the corresponding profiles.
- **Profile administrator**
  The profile administrator is permitted to generate the profiles belonging to the roles but can't change or assign roles.

A minimum dual control principle must be demonstrated. The data protector will document this even if proof has to be provided by auditing activities or administration.

Control Requirement 33: Transparent Authorization Risks

In Control Requirement 7, we described the principle of minimization for assigning authorizations. Transparent authorization risks reach far beyond this. In our opinion, it should always be possible to account for data protection risks that exist effectively in the authorization system. This must be made transparent as soon as authorizations are assigned. The relevant approval procedure and supplementary organizational instructions are also necessary.

Control Requirement 34: Backup and Disaster Recovery

The data protector is to be provided with proof that a well-functioning backup procedure exists. This proof also includes proof that the data can be recovered (disaster recovery).

12.11 Summary

In this chapter, we first developed a framework for controls, which we then checked superficially and by way of example. Only with a few controls, which result explicitly and solely from data protection, have we gone into a little more detail. Nevertheless, remember that the controls outlined are only a small part of the total.

In fact, we expect there to be more than a thousand essential controls. These controls (at least 95% of them) form the "bread and butter" of internal auditing and are subject to good system audits. In some places, however, the directions in which these controls operate change. While from the accounting point of view, an authorization risk exists if there is a conflict over the separation of duties that gives an employee full control over a cash-effective process, the risk in data protection must be related to the purposes of processing. The risk is that someone may have authorization without having an assignment for this purpose. According to Art. 4 (10) GDPR, such an employee would be regarded as a third party to whom data is unlawfully disclosed. System interfaces should also be viewed in a correspondingly different way.

We're of the opinion, however, that, above all, the GDPR changes the necessity of proof. In future, you must be able to prove which protective measures you've taken in terms of data categories and purposes. If you're unable to provide this evidence, you may be fined. We also believe that to manage these controls effectively, they must be integrated into the ICS.

We assume that this is no longer feasible in large companies without introducing appropriate automation. This is, however, possible with the SAP GRC suite, which allows you to automate controls and inspection processes.

Appendix A
Relevant Transactions, Reports, and SAP Notes

A.1 Transactions

Only transactions relevant for data protection are presented in this appendix. The examples of business transactions used in the book, such as creating a purchase order using Transaction ME21N (Create Purchase Order), aren't displayed.

Transaction	Text
AOBJ	Archiving Object Definition
BD64	Maintenance of Distribution Model
BUA3	Display Contact Person
BUP3	Display Business Partner
BUP_REQ_UNBLK	Business Partner Unblock Requests
CVP_DISPLAY_LOG	Disp. Stored Appl Logs for Cust/Vend
CVP_PRE_EOP	Block Customer & Vendor Master Data
CVP_UNBLOCK_MD	Unblock Customer & Vendor Master Data
DB15	Data Archiving: Database Tables
DTINF_ADJUST_MODEL	Adjust Inf. Retr. FW Model
DTINF_PROC_COLL	Process Data Collection Results
DTINF_START_COLL	Start Data Collection
DTINF_TEST_MODEL	Information Ret. FW – Test Model
FILE	Cross-Client File Names/Paths

Transaction	Text
ILMARA	Audit Area Processing
ILM_DESTRUCTION	Data Destruction
ILM_LHM	Legal Hold Management
IRMPOL	ILM Policies
IRMRULE	Business Rule Maintenance
IRMRULE_ACTIVATE	Activate Scheduled Business Rules
IRM_CUST_CSS	IRM: Customer-Specific Settings
PA30	Maintain HR Master Data
PFCG	Role Maintenance
RSAUDIT_SYSTEM_ENV	Client and System Settings
RSUSR200	List of Users per Login Date
RZ11	Profile Parameter Maintenance
SA38	ABAP Reporting
SAIS	AIS – Workplace
SARA	Archive Administration
SARE	Archive Explorer
SARI	Archive Information System
SCASE	Case Management
SCC4	Client Administration
SCU3	Table History
SE06	Set Up Transport Organizer
SE11	ABAP Dictionary Maintenance
SE16	Data Browser
SE16N	General Table Display

Transaction	Text
SE16SL	Field-Based Table and Value Search
SLG1	Application Log: Display Logs
SM19	Security Audit Configuration
SM20	Analysis of Security Audit Log
SM37	Overview of Job Selection
SM54	TXCOM Maintenance
SM59	RFC Destinations (Display/Edit)
SPAM	Support Package Manager
SPRO	Customizing – Edit Project
ST03N	Workload and Performance Statistics
STAD	Statistics Display for All Systems
SU01	User Maintenance
SU21	Maintain Authorization Objects
SU24	Maintain Authorization Defaults
SUIM	User Information System
S_YI3_39000082	Where-Used List for Sec. Policies
TDMS	SAP TDMS Control Center
VL03N	Display Outbound Delivery
VORI	Archiving Control Shipment Costs
WE02	Display IDoc
XD03	Display Customer (Centrally)
XK03	Display vendor (Centrally)

A.2 Reports

Report	Text
RSCRDOMA	Repository Information System: Where-Used List for Domain in Table
RPDINF01	Infotypes and Subtypes
RSPARAM	Display SAP Profile Parameters
RSUSR008_009_NEW	Users or Roles with Combinations of Critical Authorizations
RDDPRCHK	Check Table Logging
CHANGEDOCU_READ	Read Selected Change Documents from Database or Archive
RPUAUD00	Logged Changes in Infotype Data

A.3 SAP Notes

- 1825544 – Simplified Deletion and Blocking of Personal Data in SAP Business Suite
- 1825608 – Simplified Blocking and Deletion of Central Business Partner
- 2007926 – Simplified Blocking and Deletion of Customer/Vendor Master Data
- 2249093 – Simplified Blocking and Deletion of SCM Location
- 548624 – FAQ: Performance Monitors, R/3 Syslog, System Availability
- 2191612 – FAQ | Use of Security Audit Log as of SAP NetWeaver 7.50
- 2467 – Password Rules and Preventing Incorrect Logons
- 12388 – Tables with Obligatory Logging

Appendix B
The Authors

Volker Lehnert has been working for SAP in various compliance and security positions since 2000. In 2018, he joined the application security team as the senior director of data protection. He is responsible for defining the data protection content provided by SAP S/4HANA; in the past, he served a similar role for SAP Business Suite. In his many years of consultancy work, he has driven many projects in the field of authorizations. To meet legislative requirements, Lehnert repeatedly traces security concepts back to the key questions: business management functions, organizational concepts, and legal requirements. Lehnert (together with Anna Otto) is coauthor of the *DSAG Data Protection Guide*, and also (together with Katharina Stelzner) coauthor of the book *Authorizations in SAP Software* from SAP PRESS. He also co-authored the German-language book *Data Protection in SAP Systems* from SAP PRESS together with Anna Otto and Katharina Stelzner. Furthermore, he publishes technical articles on data protection.

Iwona Luther has been working at SAP in the area of data archiving, which has evolved over the years into SAP Information Lifecycle Management (SAP ILM), for the past 20 years. She initially worked as a developer, then as a project manager, coordinator, and in quality assurance. She is responsible for the respective customer courses BIT660, BIT670, and BIT665, and she is Product Standard Owner ILM. Luther is also the contact person for the DSAG and ASUG Working Group "Data Archiving and ILM."

Björn Christoph is a software architect and has been with SAP since 2002. He has been involved with data protection and software security in SAP software for several years. In today's modern world, he believes both issues are of utmost importance, especially in view of the ubiquitous use of the Internet of Things, Big Data, and artificial intelligence. He enjoys developing creative and original solutions to complex problems.

Carsten Pluder has been with SAP since 1999 and works in the areas of support and development. He currently works for SAP SE Application Innovation Services (AIS) as Lead Architect Data Protection for SAP Business Suite and SAP S/4HANA. Supporting SAP customers in archiving data and using SAP ILM has long since been the main focus of his work. He is particularly committed to using the existing functionality to simplify the blocking and deletion of personal data or to optimize it where necessary.

Contributors

Reiko Enghardt has been a technology consultant at SAP for more than 20 years, during which he has accompanied numerous projects and gained experience with various solutions. He has also been working as a consultant for projects related to master data for more than 12 years. Enghardt has developed, implemented, and documented authorization concepts for SAP MDG in various projects.

Christian Geiseler has been in charge of the go-to-market of master data management solutions at SAP since 2012. He provides technical support in the worldwide sale of SAP products and develops solution strategies in close cooperation with those responsible for the products. His primary goal is to demonstrate the importance of a consistently high quality of master data for companies, working groups, and user associations from a technical and regulatory perspective and to support companies in their projects in this area.

Dr. Boris Hoffarth has been working on the complex transformation of system landscapes since 1996. In recent years, he has also been a member of the SAP consulting department System Landscape Optimization (SLO) and was responsible for TDMS. Based on this, he developed the Data Privacy Task Force with corresponding services. Dr. Hoffarth holds a degree in physics and received his doctorate from the University of Heidelberg in 1995.

Translator

Nicole Fernandes has worked as a translator for English, French, and German texts since 2005. Her fields of expertise are software/information technology and medical research/genetics. Her projects have included the translation of specialized ERP systems and industry-specific software solutions for the temporary employment sector (including documentations, user manuals, etc.). She also works as a senior editor for the online dictionary *linguee.com* (English/German) and contributed sample translations from a variety of fields to the translation machine *deepl.com*.

Index

L

M

N

O

P

T

- Configure application, network, and infrastructure security
- Set up identity and access management with user accounts, authorizations, and authentication
- Strengthen the security of SAP NetWeaver systems, including SAP S/4HANA, SAP Business Suite, SAP Fiori, and more

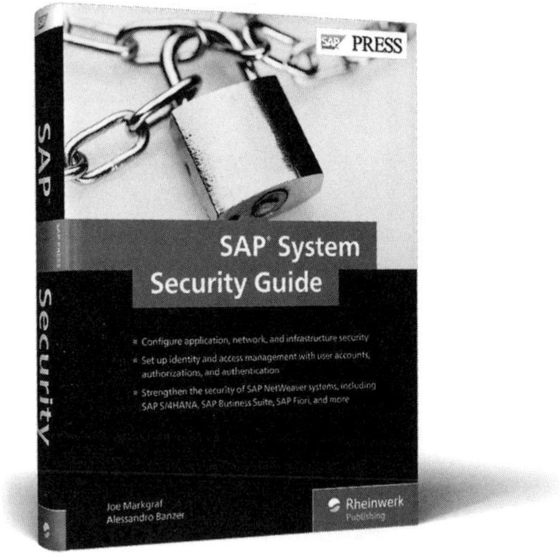

Joe Markgraf, Alessandro Banzer

SAP System Security Guide

If you're a Basis administrator looking to keep your SAP system under lock and key, this is the book for you! Discover information on security-relevant issues, from identity and access management to network and backend security. Get the technical know-how to identify vulnerabilities, defend your system from internal and external threats, and pass audits. Secure your SAP system from the ground up!

574 pages, pub. 07/2018
E-Book: $69.99 | **Print:** $79.95 | **Bundle:** $89.99

www.sap-press.com/4307

Rheinwerk Publishing

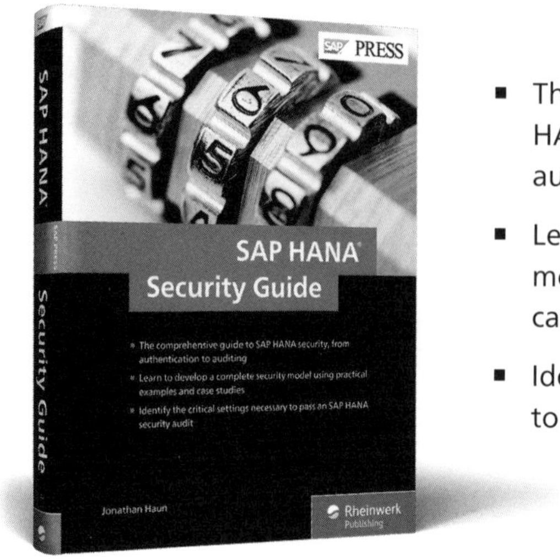

- The comprehensive guide to SAP HANA security, from authentication to auditing
- Learn to develop a complete security model using practical examples and case studies
- Identify the critical settings necessary to pass an SAP HANA security audit

Jonathan Haun

SAP HANA Security Guide

How do you protect and defend your SAP HANA database and application development platform? This comprehensive guide details your options, including privileges, encryption, and more. Learn how to secure database objects, provision and maintain user accounts, and develop and assign roles. Then take an in-depth look at authentication and certificate management before seeing how to enable auditing and security tracing. Up to date for SAP HANA 2.0!

541 pages, pub. 05/2017
E-Book: $69.99 | **Print:** $79.95 | **Bundle:** $89.99

www.sap-press.com/4227

www.sap-press.com

Interested in reading more?

Please visit our website for all new book and e-book releases from SAP PRESS.

www.sap-press.com

SAP PRESS